Tim Page on Music
VIEWS AND REVIEWS

By Tim Page

Foreword by
Anthony Tommasini

AMADEUS PRESS
Portland, Oregon

Thanks to Eve Goodman, my editor at Amadeus Press; Melanie Jackson, my literary agent; William, Robert, and John Page, my children; Vanessa Weeks Page, Dr. Ellis B. Page, Anthony Tommasini, and my colleagues and friends at *The Washington Post* and *Newsday*.

All love and gratitude to Julieta Stack.

Published in 2002 by
Amadeus Press
(an imprint of Timber Press, Inc.)
The Haseltine Building
133 S.W. Second Avenue, Suite 450
Portland, Oregon 97204 U.S.A.

Printed through Colorcraft Ltd., Hong Kong

ISBN 1-57467-076-X

A CIP record for this book is available from the Library of Congress

Tim Page on Music

Credits

In memory of
Elizabeth Thaxton Page, my mother,
and
Katharine Graham, a friend when I needed one most.

Contents

Foreword

by Anthony Tommasini

T HE BIG PROBLEM with music criticism is that it's basically impossible to do. Music resists being written about. It moves us in ways that are powerful, emotional, and intuitive, but nonspecific and nonverbal. Of course, there does exist a precise technical language that specialists use to describe the way a piece of music works. But that language is largely unavailable to nonspecialists, even to many people who love classical music and go to concerts all the time. Making matters worse, the overall level of musical understanding in our culture has never been lower. The typical crowd at Yankee Stadium knows more about baseball—its rules, history, statistics, and strategy—than the typical audience at the New York Philharmonic knows about music.

So the challenge for a classical music critic is to find a way to write about music, to describe the actual way music sounds and the effect of a performance, with commonplace and accessible language. My colleague Tim Page is an exemplar, one of the best ever, of how this can be done.

Make no mistake, Tim brings other invaluable qualities to the job: extensive knowledge of cultural history, especially literature; the instincts and news sense of a sharp beat reporter; the skills of a good storyteller; infectious inquisitiveness; immunity to dogma; and an always-running pomposity detector. But what will keep you reading the pieces collected here—from *Newsday, The New Republic, The New Criterion* and other journals, and especially from *The Washington Post*, where his work won him the 1997 Pulitzer Prize for criticism—is the marvelous way he makes music so vivid you can practically hear it, the way he makes artists so present you feel you are talking with

11

them, and the way he makes issues so lucid you are roused to action, anger, or whatever attitude he is espousing.

He has a gift for the apt phrase, the right image, to convey what music sounds like, as when he writes that the soprano Kathleen Battle, at her incomparable best, sang with "a delighted shiver." His brilliant analytic piece on Sibelius, a composer with whom he is at once perplexed and enthralled, is all the more remarkable because he makes you forget you are reading an analytic piece. Sibelius's music "cannot be codified and it is not easy to explain," he writes, then proceeds to explain it very well indeed: "What would seem meandering and digressive in other composers comes across as either intrepid exploration or sheer strangeness in the best of Sibelius."

A fundamental decency permeates all his evaluations of artists. In his thoughtful article on Mario Lanza he laments the sadly unfulfilled career of this hugely gifted but misdirected tenor and film star, while paying respect to Lanza's singing: "The voice was an extraordinary one—immediately distinctive in its sound throughout all registers, full of sun and ardor, lyrical yet immensely powerful, all combined with what (onstage, at least) was an exuberant and winning personality."

Tim is willing to be a contrarian now and then, and it's fun to read him in this mode. There is his interesting defense of the violinist Nadja Salerno-Sonnenberg, dismissed by many critics for her aggressive virtuosity and attention-grabbing interpretations, whose artistry Tim calls the "musical equivalent of method acting." In debunking Vladimir Horowitz for *The New Republic* Tim allowed himself to be uncharacteristically vehement, knowing that his comments, however smart, would hardly begin to dent the hype that sustains Horowitz's legacy. And you don't have to agree with him about his mixed take on Messiaen (I don't; I think Messiaen was an unqualified genius) to find his essay about the composer's compositions and aesthetic utterly fascinating.

Tim is not afraid to stick it to someone when a barb is called for, as when he describes Paul McCartney's *Liverpool Oratorio* as a "sprawling, mawkish, and to this taste excruciatingly embarrassing 90-minute exercise of the ego." But he also knows when to poke fun and speak the truth with gentle grace, as when he writes: "While I respect Joan Tower enormously, her *Fanfare for the Uncommon Woman* seems fashioned from Copland's rib."

Tim's friends are constantly delighted to find out about the things his latest enthusiasms have led him to—from a neglected Norwegian woman novelist to an amazing used bookstore in downtown Cleveland. A sense of Tim's inquisitiveness comes through here with his pieces on Captain Beefheart; the audiophile and independent record producer Ward Marston, whose specialty is vocal music from the 78s era, clearly a guy in whom Tim, an obsessive collector of old books, recognized a soulmate; or the East Village songwriter Stephin Merritt, whose *The Magnetic Fields: 69 Love Songs*, a three-disc collection of literate, parody-tinged, folk-rockish songs, became practically the theme music for Tim's life in the months after he came upon it.

Here you can read a helpfully demystifying article on Anton Webern, a composer Tim reveres. Yet you will also meet Elizabeth Mensh, the "hat lady" of the National Symphony Orchestra in Washington, who attended the first-ever concert by the orchestra in 1930 when she was 19 and who remained a subscriber every year until she died in 2000. And the poignant, piercing, and totally unsentimental story on the New York composer and pianist Kevin Oldham, who was determined to perform on schedule his piano concerto with his hometown orchestra, the Kansas City Symphony, though he was dying of AIDS, should have won Tim Page a Pulitzer Prize for feature writing.

Tim is a traditional critic in the sense that he uses his post as best he can to influence the field of music, champion the powerless, deflate the puffed-up, and enlighten his readers. But he also understands that criticism is a writer's job. At its best, criticism itself becomes a part of the literary heritage. This is criticism at its best.

Anthony Tommasini is chief classical music critic for The New York Times.

Preface

THIS IS the second collection of my music journalism, a sequel of sorts to *Music from the Road*, which was published in 1992. On the whole, I think it is a better book; a lot of youthful arrogance has burned off and I hope I've purged most of that brash, Robespierrean self-assurance that can be helpful in steering somebody into criticism but is certain to turn poisonous over time. In short, I know much less than I did 10 years ago but I am conscious of much more.

Enlightenment, if it may be so called, has been hard won. In 1999 I left *The Washington Post* and took an administrative position with the Saint Louis Symphony Orchestra. After two decades "on the aisle," during the course of which I attended some 3,000 concerts, I had come to the conclusion that I'd pretty much said most of what I needed to say about music and would now write only freelance pieces when the spirit moved me. "Henceforth," I told my readers in an elaborate farewell column, "it will be time to put theory into practice."

Brave words! Callow ones, too, as it turned out. I limped away from Missouri 10 months later with a few essential lessons under my belt, including a fresh appreciation for the human and logistical miracle that any performing arts organization—even a great one such as the Saint Louis Symphony—must accomplish every time it takes the stage.

I had long been convinced that the sort of barbed, slash-and-run criticism that we find in some film, book, theater, and commercial music reviews had no place in our discipline. With very few exceptions, nobody makes a fast buck in classical music: most composers and performers are acting in good faith, working to the best of their powers, with aspirations to artistic nobility. My experience in the Midwest left me repelled by those reviews of earnest but not terribly inspired concerts that read as if the performer had just thrown the critic's dog from a moving vehicle, rather than simply muff a finale. (I confess that I've written such reviews myself; blood sport seems to be a puberty rite and the better critics outgrow it.) And I am less and less interested in Olympian pronouncements: increasingly, I consider my job one of public rumination rather than the carving of stone tablets.

This is not to advocate a bland, uncritical criticism. Journalists have a duty to tell the truth, and the exposure of ineptitude goes along with the job. Still, the reviewer does not work in a vacuum and negative comments should be chosen with the utmost care. It's all a question of degree—one can say anything one wants but the tone should suit the circumstances.

From the beginning, it was my intention to infuse some of the passion, allusiveness, and occasional irreverence I found in the best writing about jazz and rock into the realm of classical music criticism. Everything has always reminded me of everything else anyway, and I saw no reason why a "high" art was necessarily compelled to be an unrelentingly solemn and straitened one. In fact, my musical education was rounded out in less elevated climes.

Traditional studies at what is now the Tanglewood Music Center were augmented at the Mannes College of Music (in composition) and at Columbia University (in English). But in my teens I helped found a rock band and we traveled throughout eastern Connecticut, performing in soggy dives and high school auditoriums. Then, for a year, I played bad jazz and slightly more skillful cocktail piano at a local restaurant.

These all provided important lessons and I remain convinced that it is beneficial to learn about as many different musics as possible—that a knowledge of jazz, pop, rock, and world genres can only broaden a classical musician. One reviewer of *Music from the Road* was unhappy that I had expressed admiration for the very different talents of Van Morrison and Anton Webern in the same sentence, without any attempt at establishing a ranking order. But such hierarchies seem silly to me—about as profound and meaningful as saying "New Zealand is better than Germany"—and I continue to take good music where I find it.

The critical forbears who mattered most to me were James Gibbons

Huneker, for his effusive, magnificently baroque sentences and high im-pressionism, and Virgil Thomson, because he was everything Huneker was not—straightforward, plain-spoken, endowed with matchless wit. The dry, surgical exactitude of B. H. Haggin's early work was also influential, espe-cially when I was getting started, and I have always admired Harold C. Schon-berg's ability to express complex ideas with the immediacy of journalism. My present position at the *Post* is that of "culture critic"; I'm still in the process of learning exactly what those words mean, which is probably a good sign.

Since 1979 I have made the bulk of my income from writing about music, most of it published in one of four places—*Soho News* (from 1979 to 1982), *The New York Times* (from 1982 to 1987), *New York Newsday* (from 1987 to 1995), and *The Washington Post* (from 1995 to the present). In the same way that I read through most of what I had written up to 1992 to assemble *Music from the Road*, I have now gone over much of what I've written in the last 10 years to create this new collection. Rereading one's own work is always a sobering experience; whatever may be said of the contents of this volume, what I kept is better than what I left out.

Tim Page on Music has the same form as *Music from the Road*. The open-ing (and by far the longest) section, entitled "Views," is devoted to articles about a single artist or organization, arranged in alphabetical order by sub-ject. In "Reviews," shorter pieces, usually written on deadline, have been placed in chronological order, while the final section, "Postscripts," is a catch-all, assembled instinctually. (I have elected to reprint two favorite ar-ticles from *Music from the Road*—one on Van Cliburn, appended with a more recent concert review, and another on Nadja Salerno-Sonnenberg—as they have been unavailable for some time.)

For the most part, I have resisted the temptation to tinker with or update these pieces. In my discussion of Lorin Maazel, for example, which was writ-ten in 1995, there is nothing about his surprise appointment, six years later, as music director of the New York Philharmonic. Marriages that recently have been put asunder here remain intact, and John Corigliano's ancient dog is still limping gently around the composer's apartment. It is my hope that the reader will approach this book as a collection of illumined moments rather than as any sort of fixed and final word.

"The general standard of criticism had sunk so far in New York that almost any change might bring improvement." So wrote Virgil Thomson in 1940 when he agreed to take on the position of chief critic of the *Herald Tribune*. Things are better now—indeed, there are many excellent critics working throughout the country. Still, some of what passes for classical music criticism today is so dispirited, convoluted, poorly informed, and even downright incoherent that I shall conclude this preface with a quick review of what I consider our basic duties.

1. *Get the facts.* While any interesting review will address matters of opinion, it is also necessary to supply your reader with empirical data—when and where the event took place, who the players were, some information about the music, whether or not the program will be repeated. This sounds elementary, but all too often it is forgotten.

2. *Cover the news.* One important newspaper never deigned to notice the Three Tenors phenomenon until almost five years after a recording of the first joint appearance by Plácido Domingo, Luciano Pavarotti, and José Carreras had become far and away the most successful classical album in history (more than 10 million and counting). More recently there was the phenomenon of pianist David Helfgott, a sad spectacle that many of us would have preferred to ignore. In no way am I suggesting that critics should go easy on such events, but the laws of Journalism 101 indicate that they should be acknowledged.

3. *Remember your position, but don't let yourself be seduced by it.* A good critic should be able to keep two opposing ideas in mind at all times. While it would be absurd to pretend that you are only another member of the audience—other listeners do not have the privilege of writing reports that reach thousands of people—you should also avoid becoming puffed up with self-importance. I prefer reviews that come across as one person's plausible, informed opinion, rather than an *ex cathedra* pronouncement delivered from on high. And never feel self-conscious about going out on a limb: a critic without passion and independence is a person in the wrong field. Carefully considered heresy about established masters is well within your rights.

4. *Say it straight.* Complexity is not the same thing as profundity, and the vast majority of musical events can be recorded in direct, stylish, transparent prose. The effect music exerts upon a susceptible listener may be mysterious: your review shouldn't be.

5. *Again—be courteous.* Sharply negative reviews are inevitable, but they should be written with care and tact, in full awareness of the effect they may

have upon a fellow human being. True acerbity should be reserved for the most inept, tawdry, commercialized, and overhyped events; you'll still have plenty of occasions to show off your invective. A few other directives come to mind: return as many of your calls as you can and answer your letters—even the angry ones, so long as they remain within the bounds of civility, comport yourself with dignity, never allow extramusical irritations to affect your tone, and above all, do your best to serve, rather than sever, the art of music.

TIM PAGE
Washington, D.C.

VIEWS

Kathleen Battle: A Lament

The young Kathleen Battle was one of my favorite sopranos. When she was dismissed from the Metropolitan Opera in 1994, my friend Patrick J. Smith, who was then the editor of Opera News, *asked me to write a brief article. I did my best to combine my deep admiration for much of her work with genuine—if saddened—support of the Met management in this particular case. Battle remains a popular concert artist, although her opera appearances have dwindled.*

I REMEMBER the first time I heard Kathleen Battle—a cold night at Tanglewood in the summer of 1980, huddled in blanket and windbreaker under the stars, listening to the Boston Symphony play through a fairly ordinary reading of the Mahler Fourth Symphony. But then, in the finale—the composer's childlike, paradisiacal musical vision of a life after death—the young Kathleen Battle took the stage, began to sing, and the evening chill was temporarily forgotten.

It seemed to me then—and remains in memory—as close to a perfect performance as I can imagine. In those days, Battle projected freshness, innocence, and a certain ecstatic quality that was difficult to define but all but unanimously agreed upon. Pianist Gerald Moore once wrote that Elisabeth Schumann sang with a smile; Battle, at her incomparable best, sang with a delighted shiver.

By the time this issue of *Opera News* reaches its audience, our readers will doubtless have learned all about Battle's dismissal from the Metropolitan

Opera and whatever consequences may have resulted from that action. As I write, in the midst of a February snowstorm, it's hot news—the phones are ringing; the faxes are humming; the BBC, the CBC, National Public Radio, and *People Magazine* are asking what it all means; television shows that haven't run a feature on classical music in years are suddenly planning segments on temperament and the opera diva. A beautiful woman, a spectacular voice, an abrupt departure from a prestigious institution, and presto!—a *story* for hungry journalists. (Would that some of this attention might be directed to a young, struggling composer, or to a plucky opera company defying the odds in a city where the arts budget has been shredded!)

Don't get me wrong. I support the Met's "termination" of Battle's contract for *La Fille du Régiment*. I'd even go so far as to suggest that she probably should have been fired after she walked out of *Der Rosenkavalier* last year, four days before opening night, because of what seem to have been arbitrarily constructed "artistic differences" with the gifted young conductor Christian Thielemann. I've heard all the stories about Battle's "difficult" behavior and I've verified most of them. And I am well aware that an opera company cannot be held hostage to the caprices of a single person, no matter how extraordinary her gift.

Given her recent behavior, Battle had to go, no doubt about it. And yet, as somebody who has loved her art—I've never met her personally—I keep hoping, against what now seem impossible odds, that there will be some sort of happy ending to the saga of Kathleen Battle.

After all, one wonders what it must have been like—growing up in a depressed, gritty Midwestern town; knowing from an early age that you were not only special but *special*, and waiting for somebody else to know it, too; fighting your way to the top in a ferociously competitive business where unique talent can only be a beginning. How does a young artist reconcile the ingrown stasis of an Ohio River city—the humid, mosquito-ridden summer nights, the windswept, barren winters—with the sudden, schizoid shift to a "Lifestyle of the Rich and Famous" that puts one in demand everywhere, with first-class passage on the Concorde, presidential suites in the world's capitals, every whim immediately satisfied? How does one keep one's balance? Think of Patty Hearst, then flip the story around and think of the wildly different ordeal of Kathleen Battle.

I know. I know—we should *all* be so unlucky. And I've never been berated, threatened, snubbed, or dismissed by Battle, so I can't share the righteous ire that will now be welling in those readers who *have* felt her wrath. I've never been told (as a fan was reportedly told in San Francisco) that "one doesn't speak to Miss Battle until one is spoken to." But she must be terribly alone right now—a self-exile, to be sure, but alone is alone is alone. Is there anybody who can sit her down and say, look, this sort of behavior just won't do? Does she have a friend who is still permitted to speak freely?

Whatever her personal failings, Kathleen Battle has been a great artist, one who has brought enormous pleasure to many millions of people. It may be that this really is the end of her Met career—and, by most accounts, she's not especially popular in most of the other major houses. And so perhaps she will spend the rest of her time as a "lite" concert and recording artist—more best-selling discs with Wynton Marsalis and the occasional Madison Square Garden lovefest at $100 per ticket. She'll earn a good living, no doubt about it; pop and "crossover" A&R men wait in the shadows. But those of us who have been exhilarated by Battle's Pamina, Sophie, Susanna, can only hope that this magnificent American soprano will be allowed—will allow *herself*—to realize her full potential.

Opera News
2 April 1994

The Cleveland Orchestra

The New Yorker *commissioned, accepted, and paid for this article, but it was published, instead, in* Fi Magazine, *one of the best of the many music publications that folded at the end of the 20th century. In Cleveland the Austrian conductor Franz Welser-Möst was selected to succeed Maestro Dohnányi at the beginning of the 2002–03 season.*

As soon as one came within a two-block radius of Carnegie Hall the begging began—not the business-as-usual requests for spare change but desperate pleas for extra tickets at any price. Inside the auditorium, always at its most radiant for bonafide events, people who never summer where they winter air-kissed and exchanged pleasantries while hundreds of musicians squeezed their way onto the stage and a few went off to hide in various rafters of the house, to pop up peek-a-boo and play or sing a few phrases later in the evening. Beverly Sills was in the audience, and so were Barbara Walters, and Ellen Taaffe Zwilich, Carnegie Hall's composer-in-residence; and what seemed like half of The New York Times editorial staff flanked the Eastern aisle. Even second-string critics, those who would not be required to write about what they were about to hear, had given up what might have been a precious night off to come and listen—the proverbial "busman's holiday" and the ultimate accolade.

Indeed, not since the last New York appearances of Leonard Bernstein, Herbert von Karajan, and Vladimir Horowitz had the prospect of an evening at Carnegie Hall inspired such widespread excitement, across the board, from the highest of high society to a few lucky music students with borrowed scores under their arms. Gustav Mahler's Symphony No. 8 has been dubbed the "Symphony of a Thousand"—an exaggeration, of course, as most performances struggle by with a cast of a mere 400 or so. But on this clement, smoky spring evening—May 4, 1995—Robert Shaw, in his 80th year and associated with Carnegie Hall for half a century, had assembled 562 choristers from Atlanta, Cincinnati, Oberlin, and Cleveland plus an augmented Cleveland Orchestra for a total of nearly 700 performers (including the soprano Sylvia McNair, who sang, unannounced, with one of the choruses, just for fun) to present this gigantic work.

"It is the grandest thing I have done yet—and so peculiar in content and form that it is really impossible to write anything about it," Mahler explained in a 1906 letter to the Dutch conductor Willem Mengelberg. "Try to imagine the whole universe beginning to ring and resound. These are no longer human voices but planets and suns revolving." And so it seemed at Carnegie, as the organ thundered, the brass boomed from the back of the hall, choruses shouted from stage and balcony, and, late in the piece, the pure, sweet, affirmative declamation of the Mater Gloriosa (sung by Christine Goerke) floated down from what was for many an invisible loft on high.

There were many reasons for the excitement surrounding this concert—the chance to hear a demanding and rarely mounted piece that necessarily makes its strongest impression in live performance; a late opportunity to cheer on the man who, more than any other single figure, put American choral conducting on the map; the sheer, freakish, sonic luxuriance that 700-odd musicians in full thrall can provide. But there was also what might be called the Cleveland factor; after recent (and generally disappointing) visits by the Vienna and Berlin Philharmonics, with the orchestras of Chicago and Boston in decline, and a history of uneven performances by the leading ensembles of New York, Philadelphia, Saint Louis, and Los Angeles, it is to Cleveland that many aficionados now turn for steadily first-class symphonic playing throughout the repertory. Phrases such as "the current champion among American orchestras" (*The Boston Globe*) and "alone at the top" (the *Los Angeles Times*) run like mantras through the group's recent criticism.

"There's been a lot of ranking of orchestras lately and I mistrust that," Donald Rosenberg, music critic for the Cleveland *Plain Dealer*, said recently.

But I think what is special about this particular orchestra is the fact that it doesn't have any identity that is separate from whatever it is playing. You don't think, ah, the Cleveland *sound*, the way you might with Berlin, Vienna, Philadelphia, Chicago. You think you're hearing what is in the score and in the mind of the conductor, period. Whatever the style may be, with perhaps the exception of baroque music, this orchestra can pretty much turn a switch and play it superbly.

John Mack has been principal oboe with the Cleveland Orchestra since its first Golden Age—one of the last remaining players hired by the legendary George Szell himself, who took the helm of a solid, middle-level, provincial ensemble in 1946 and lived to see it recognized as one of the world's great orchestras by the time of his death 24 years later.

"I'll let you in on our secret," Mr. Mack said after a rehearsal at the Blossom Music Center, the Cleveland Orchestra's summer home. It was an oboist's secret, expressed with pardonable pride: "When the orchestra tunes up, I give out a 440 A—exactly 440 cycles per second. We start our performances at 440 and we *finish* them at 440. Other orchestras, the pitch goes up as the players get excited, so they might end up playing at 445 cycles or even higher. We're steady, we work together, and while we've got a lot of incredible virtuosos in this group, nobody craves special notice, nobody tries to steal the show."

One can easily imagine Mr. Mack holding court in a Vienna coffeehouse; he is a genial, talkative man, full of anecdotes, gossip, and good one-liners ("Bernstein? Amazing guy—half genius, half charlatan, but both of them were *real* so what could you do?"). "Szell instilled our steadiness—had us on a choke collar, really, very tight all the time. And then Lorin Maazel, Cleveland's music director from 1972 to 1982, was brilliant—*too* brilliant, I think. Everything was easy for him; he'd get grand ideas about the music and get up in front of the orchestra and recompose it. Like one of those European conductors who really think they've *invented* something, you know, like the boy who stuck in his thumb."

Since 1984 Christoph von Dohnányi has been the music director of the Cleveland Orchestra. He combines Szell's fierce regard for discipline with Maazel's questing spirit. Mr. Mack admires him. "Dohnányi is a gentleman," Mr. Mack said. "He's very polite, very formal most of the time, but he can be a lot of fun, too. He's not so serious as Szell—thank *God*!—but he is exacting.

He wants what he wants—what the composer wants—and we try to give it to him."

Mr. Dohnányi lives in a big house in a neighborhood of big houses on one of the side streets in Shaker Heights, the great, and much-studied, planned suburb of Cleveland. The house is sparsely furnished, meticulously organized, spotlessly clean; the iron-gray, immaculately groomed Mr. Dohnányi could pass for a Hollywood version of a middle-European nobleman. He speaks slowly, softly, and chooses his words carefully, his German accent only slightly disguising his sure, if rather cautious, command of the English language.

"I think the city of Cleveland itself is one of the reasons we have been able to build what we have," Mr. Dohnányi said one recent afternoon.

This is an easy city. If we call a rehearsal, it will take the musicians 10 minutes to get to the hall by car—no train rides, no long commute, no heavy traffic—and then they can play and go back, just as simply, to very comfortable homes. And while some of our musicians teach and others have chamber ensembles, nobody is ringing up every day and asking them to play a studio date, or the score for a film, or in an opera orchestra. There isn't the pressure you find in the larger cities, the competition for attention. Our players can devote their full energies to the Cleveland Orchestra.

"I think the old notion that you can only get the true spirit of European music from Europe is so much nonsense, especially now that the training of music students in the U.S. is so much better than what you find in Europe," he continued.

There's nothing in Europe that can be compared to the Curtis Institute, the Juilliard School, or, for that matter, the Cleveland Institute—these are really great, great institutions. In any event, there's been a European tradition in the United States for quite some time now. Reiner. Toscanini. Stokowski. Koussevitzky. In fact, Bernstein was really the first *American* conductor. And in some ways tradition is better preserved over here than it is in Europe. A C major chord really does sound better when it's played in C major and I believe that it is possible to play just as beautifully, just as soulfully, with an orchestra that is technically on a high standard as with one that is not. In Europe, people talk about some supposed mystical spirit in the music-making but then you sometimes have to tune the orchestra before you can play anything at all.

Mr. Dohnányi, born in 1929, began his own musical studies at the age of five. He came from a cultivated and distinguished family: his grandfather was the Hungarian pianist and composer Ernö von Dohnányi; his father, Hans von Dohnányi, was executed by the Nazis for his complicity in a plot on Hitler's life. (Mr. Dohnányi's uncle, the theologian Dietrich Bonhoeffer, also died in a concentration camp.) After the war, Mr. Dohnányi studied law at the University of Munich but soon decided to pursue a career in music. To this end, he studied composition with his grandfather—who had resettled in Florida and become the grand old man of the Florida State University music department—and conducting at Tanglewood.

In 1952 Mr. Dohnányi accepted a position coaching and conducting at the Frankfurt Opera under Georg Solti; he was subsequently named artistic and music director. He then served as the director of the West German Radio Symphony of Cologne before becoming artistic director and principal conductor of the Hamburg State Opera, where he stayed from 1978 to 1984. In 1984 he was appointed music director in Cleveland for an initial span of four years; the contract has been renewed twice and is now set to run through the year 2000.

"What I want to bring to Cleveland, which maybe it didn't have before, is a sense of breathing, *musical* breathing, like a singer," Mr. Dohnányi said in 1989. "I sometimes think that Szell took one breath before the performance and then another after it. There was always this electric, inner tension in his performances but it was occasionally dangerous to the music-making. Szell was a master, you know, but I think he may not have been so fond of singing. I *am* fond of singing. Once you've conducted a lot of opera, you start to hate bar lines."

Indeed, Mr. Dohnányi has incorporated opera into the repertory of the Cleveland Orchestra. A semi-staged *Magic Flute* at the Blossom Festival in 1985 won national press that was little short of rapturous, and the orchestra is in the midst of recording Wagner's complete *Ring* cycle. (The first opera, *Das Rheingold*, has just been released on London Records.) Last season, Mr.

Dohnányi brought a concert performance of Berg's *Wozzeck* to Carnegie Hall. There, to his everlasting credit, he approached the thorny score as *music*, rather than an excuse to make noisy, pounced-upon dissonances coexist with Frankenstein-ian declamation. Berg's use of *Sprechstimme*—speech-song—was here just that, a musical speech that occasionally blossomed into song. Dohnányi deliberately downplayed the creepy-crawly aspects of *Sprechstimme* and the result was an overwhelmingly convincing argument for the technique.

Mr. Dohnányi is equally persuasive in 19th-century music. In June he conducted the *German Requiem* of Johannes Brahms in Cleveland. This grave, solemn work is caviar for pessimists—it presents a vision of death *without* transfiguration, with no metaphysical revelations of a blissful state to come. Instead, it is an expression of grief, mystery, dignity, resignation, and abiding love for those who have gone before us. "If you want me to weep, you must first weep yourself," the Latin poet Horace instructed writers and actors; Mr. Dohnányi wisely discounted this advice. Indeed, this was as measured, austere, and stoical a performance of the *German Requiem* as I've heard, and all the more moving for it. Mr. Dohnányi kept passion within bounds, the fugue in the third movement was unusually brisk, almost light, and there was no attempt to "milk" anything beyond proper dimensions. The baritone soloist (Andreas Schmidt) seemed less a stolid, reassuring preacher than another in a house of frightened and mystified penitents. To applaud at the end seemed faintly obscene—I found myself wishing we might have obliged the request Sibelius made of audiences for his Fourth Symphony (a request that is never honored) that, when the music is over, the audience would simply get up and leave, in a state of quiet contemplation.

"The requiem is one of the very greatest pieces Brahms ever wrote," Mr. Dohnányi said the day after the final performance,

> but it was written early in his life—he wasn't much more than 35—and it should sound that way. No self-pity, not too meditative, not too romantic. Brahms always looked back to the formal rigor of the older German composers, such as Schütz and Handel—so far as Handel can be considered German. He's not really making much of a point of his own century—he's looking backward and looking toward the future but not really making a statement for or about his time, the way Wag-

ner did so successfully. But he has had enormous influence on the 20th century; Arnold Schoenberg was enormously influenced by Wagner's harmonies, but in his own technique of composition he was more attached to Brahms.

In any conversation with Mr. Dohnányi, talk inevitably shifts from the world of music to the world of ideas, a bracing and welcome change from the more typical conductor's obsession with performing editions, appoggiaturas, and old recordings.

There have been times when it has been necessary to be very radical in order to make a point and this is true in politics as well as art. The early works of Schoenberg and Stravinsky allowed us to discover a lot of new possibilities for expression. The second half of this century has been a different sort of era. People aren't so uncomfortable using the materials of the past because those materials have now been conquered. We've made the jump, we know we can go beyond—but we don't *have* to go beyond, not every time. Composers today are not so rigid about which system they use, and I think that is, on balance, a good development. You just have to write what you want and hope for the best, because as long as you are absolutely stuck in any system, you may be in trouble if the system comes to a dead end.

After the reunification of Germany, people came up to me and said this should have happened much more slowly, that there should have been a period of transition. I would argue differently. You cannot say to a woman—why don't you have your baby in *10* months? It just happens. This is history, this was ripe and mature for happening, and so it happened. Eastern Europe didn't function and it collapsed, a dead end—which doesn't mean the idea of socialism is necessarily *perdu.* I think the idea of socialism is one of the most important ideas of the last 200 years. It doesn't function the way they wanted it to in the Soviet Union, but what idea *does* function when it becomes a faith, an institution? What do you think Jesus would think if he were to see what had been made of his ideas?

Mr. Dohnányi returns to live in Germany when he is not in residence in Cleveland but he does most of his extracurricular work in Austria, where he is a favorite guest conductor with the Vienna Philharmonic and, as such, a regular visitor to the Salzburg Festival. "Germany is much more flexible than Austria these days, I find," Mr. Dohnányi said.

Austria is a country that has consciously traded development for neutrality. People who have to make a choice—who have to choose between right or left—have more possibility of developing and maturing than people like the Austrians who just want to be left in peace, who don't want to deal with the world as it is. They've said "We'll be there for everybody—we'll have our mountains, we'll have the Vienna Philharmonic, we'll have our beautiful country, we'll have our great writers of the past," and so on. Somehow, you miss the train that way. Germans were forced to confront their past, to confront what had happened, and I think the country has grown.

Cleveland, on the other hand, has definitely shrunk. It was once the fifth largest city in the United States but is now counted as the country's fifteenth largest metropolitan area. Yet it fascinates (there must be more books about Cleveland than about any other American city of its size)—a gritty, blue-collar, industrial city that also has first-class libraries and art museums, several universities, handsome and relatively inexpensive housing stock, and a vast parks system that surrounds the area and is known as the "Emerald Necklace." For much of the century, Cleveland has been severely depressed; therein lies both a curse and, for the visitor, a certain charm. Cities such as New York and Los Angeles are rebuilt every generation or two but in Cleveland, because it has been such a long time between booms, many of the factories and skyscrapers, erected in the first years of the century when high-rises were made from red brick and smokestacks stood for progress, are still standing, making for urban landscapes out of Steichen. Then there are the dozen-or-so rusty, elaborately crafted, charismatic bridges across the Cuyahoga River in the center of town; Hart Crane, a native of Cleveland's East Side, entitled his longest poem "The Bridge," and while much of it was directly inspired by his residence in Brooklyn, it is hard to imagine that the author's Cleveland memories played no part in the development of his epic.

Today Cleveland is a polyglot mixture of rich and poor, old and new, desolate clapboard houses and zooty rehabs, thrift shops and excellent restaurants of all kinds. There are more than 600 churches within the city limits.

The magnificent Arcade, a cross between an embryonic shopping mall and a light court, was constructed in 1890 and has been compared to the Galleria Vittorio Emanuele in Milan. At the corner of 25th Street and Lorain Avenue stands the West Side Market, an enclosed shopping area constructed in 1912, featuring a dizzying assortment of fresh cheeses, breads, and meats; here, a careful listener will pick up snatches of Polish, Russian, Ukrainian, Slovak, German, Lithuanian, and the many other languages spoken in an unusually diverse population. The Great Lakes Brewing Company, the last of some 30 breweries that once thrived in Cleveland, makes its beer with only four ingredients—barley, hops, yeast, and water—in accordance, the proprietors proudly assert, with the "Bavarian Purity Law of 1516."

Cleveland has long been a musical city in a musical state (a book entitled *Ohio Musicians and Musical Authors*, published in Columbus in 1942, runs to 238 pages and more than 500 names). Early in the century, the Chicago Symphony played here under Frederick Stock, the Boston Symphony paid a visit under Karl Muck, and Mahler himself led the New York Philharmonic in concert. Annual visits from the Metropolitan Opera were highlights until 1986, when the tours were discontinued (an older generation of Cleveland operaphiles still bitterly resents this termination).

The Cleveland Orchestra itself, however, is younger than any of the other major American ensembles. Mrs. Adela Prentiss Hughes formed the Musical Arts Association (still the orchestra's parent organization) in 1915, and it wasn't until December 11, 1918, that an ensemble of 54 played its first program of works by Liszt, Bizet, Liadov, Tchaikovsky, and Victor Herbert in the old Gray's Armory. In that initial season, the group played 27 concerts in Cleveland, Akron, Oberlin, and Pittsburgh. By 1920 the orchestra had 85 players, and in 1922 it made its first visit to Carnegie Hall. (According to *The New York Times*, as cautious then as it is now, the orchestra players "gave a good account of themselves.")

The conductor in these early years was Nikolai Sokoloff. A genuine *Wunderkind*, he was born in Ukraine in 1886, came to the United States at the age of 12, and won a violin scholarship to the Yale School of Music. At 17 he was playing in the Boston Symphony and he later served as music director for the San Francisco Symphony. He stayed in Cleveland 15 years, until 1933, after which he moved to California and spent his last years conducting in La Jolla, where he died in 1965. "He is remembered by his friends as a sensitive and highly intelligent man who seemed a great person rather than a great conductor," Robert C. Marsh observed gently in his book *The Cleveland Orchestra*. "He had a zeal for work, a flair for pioneering. He was a good choice for the job to be done and he did it well."

It wasn't until 1931 that the orchestra had a permanent home. In that year, Severance Hall, donated by Cleveland businessman John L. Severance in memory of his wife, opened some five miles east of Cleveland's Public Square, in the University Circle area. It is an elegant hall with a curious and eclectic design: the exterior has 11 sides and is of Georgian design, constructed with Ohio sandstone and Indiana limestone, while the interior combines a patrician art deco with a certain silent-movie orientalism. It is a relatively small auditorium—2,000 seats as opposed to the 2,700 at Carnegie or 3,000 at Avery Fisher—and the acoustics, which have been redone twice, are now "live" but somewhat dry (for years, the Cleveland Orchestra made its recordings in a nearby Masonic temple rather than at Severance).

After Sokoloff's departure, the orchestra engaged Artur Rodzinski as his successor. Rodzinski was a skilled orchestra builder who was also music director of the Los Angeles Philharmonic, the Chicago Symphony, and the New York Philharmonic over the course of his long career. The highlight of his tenure was probably the American premiere of Dmitri Shostakovich's *Lady Macbeth of Mtsensk* in the original Russian. Rodzinski was not particularly happy in Cleveland, and after Toscanini asked for his help assembling and training the NBC Symphony, he increasingly divided his time between New York and Ohio. When he finally left for good in 1943, the young Erich Leinsdorf was made music director; four months into his tenure, he was drafted into military service and his duties were assumed by a string of guest conductors. After the war, the Hungarian pianist and conductor George Szell— who had been the most popularly and critically acclaimed of the various Leinsdorf substitutes—was hired as his replacement.

Szell knew what he wanted, and with an efficiency that was usually blunt and sometimes brutal, he went about his business, firing 22 of the orchestra's 94 musicians shortly after his arrival. In 1967 Szell codified his ideal: "My aim in developing the Cleveland Orchestra has been to combine the finest virtues of the great European orchestras of pre–World War II times with the most distinguished qualities of our leading American orchestras. In other words, we put the American orchestra's technical perfection, beauty of sound, and adaptability to the styles of various national schools of composers into the service of warmhearted, spontaneous music-making in the best European tradition."

Szell achieved most of his objectives, although his players might have blanched at the word "warmhearted" in any connection with the prickly maestro. Indeed, Szell was, by most accounts, an exceedingly difficult man. Glenn Gould spoke of Szell's "Dr. Cyclops reputation"; when Rudolf Bing was told that Szell was "his own worst enemy," Bing snapped back "Not while I'm alive." Still, if the Cleveland musicians never grew to love Szell, most of them respected him. "Working with Szell was like being plugged into a 220-volt socket," Mr. Mack recalled. "When you were new in the orchestra, he would hammer you again and again until he was sure he could trust you. Then, finally, if you survived, he'd ease off. But nobody could help but be proud of what we achieved with him."

"[Szell's] approach was classical, for he shared with his idol Toscanini a dedicated respect for the composer's explicit intention, avoiding personalized emotion, showmanship and sentimentality," Philip Hart wrote in the *New Grove Dictionary of American Music*. "When chided for his reserved performance of Mozart, he replied 'I cannot pour chocolate sauce over asparagus.' With his orchestra, Szell was an exacting, often caustic, taskmaster, directing with precision and frequent indications to the players." It was during the Szell years that the orchestra began to record regularly (a few 78-rpm discs had been made as far back as the Sokoloff era) and many of them are still in the catalogue, remastered and transferred to compact disc.

After Szell's sudden death in 1970, Pierre Boulez, who had been appointed principal guest conductor in 1969, served as music advisor until the end of the 1971–72 season. It was during this time that Boulez made his American reputation as a conductor (hitherto, he had been best known as the leading French avant-garde composer of his generation) and it led directly to his appointment as music director of the New York Philharmonic in 1971.

Lorin Maazel was 41 years old when he became music director of the Cleveland Orchestra in 1972. "His appointment provoked initial dissatisfaction among the players, who had in fact voted against his appointment, but critics cheered his first performances and commented that the Orchestra was nevertheless obviously going to cooperate," David Tovey wrote in his book *Symphony Orchestras of the United States*. "While perhaps some of the almost superhuman precision of Szell's tenure faded during the 1970s, it is generally agreed that under Maazel the Orchestra maintained its technical edge with distinction."

Norman Lebrecht, in his engaging book *The Maestro Myth*, was not so charitable and paid Mr. Maazel a double-edged compliment: "Only a highly skilled conductor could have so thoroughly dismantled George Szell's shining instrument." He referred to Maazel's complete CBS Masterworks recording of Beethoven's nine symphonies as a "cycle of such perversity that it became a collector's item."

"As strange as Maazel could be in some of the standard repertory, in the right pieces he was just superb," Mr. Rosenberg remembered. "He loosened the orchestra up quite a bit, brought it into a lot of new repertory, stretched it a bit." But Mr. Maazel was perceived by many as the epitome of the jet-setting, careerist conductor; he was often out of town, fulfilling guest appearances around the globe, and he made no secret of his disdain for living in a small city in the American Midwest. And Cleveland—particularly in the 1970s, a decade during which the Cuyahoga caught fire, a boy-wonder mayor all but bankrupted the city (back in the days before American cities ever went bankrupt), and a host of unfunny "Cleveland jokes" were staples of nightclub humor—was sensitive to any slight and therefore not especially enamored of Mr. Maazel.

Mr. Dohnányi's appointment was something of a surprise, for he had only a modest reputation in the United States and had spent much of his career in opera houses. But he quickly won over the board (through an increase in subscriptions and renewed income from recordings), the critics (with ambitious and creative programming), the city (by taking a house in the area and assuming a role in civic affairs), and the players.

"I would say the musicians like Dohnányi about as well as professional musicians can like their boss," Mr. Rosenberg said. "He can be very difficult in rehearsal. There are times when his compulsion—and that's not the wrong word—goes overboard to the point that he is demanding the impossible. But there is an essential humanity in Dohnányi that absolutely precludes his treating players in a cavalier or disrespectful manner. Unlike Szell or Maazel, if there is a problem between Dohnányi and a player, it is never personal."

Some orchestras—the New York Philharmonic, rightly or wrongly, is notable among them—have reputations for confusing and embarrassing conductors they don't like. According to Mr. Rosenberg, Cleveland presents exactly the opposite problem for a visiting conductor. "The players never behave badly but they concentrate so intently that if the conductor doesn't have ideas of his or her own or is unable to balance the orchestra, it will show. What you hear is pretty close to a pure reflection from the podium."

Thomas W. Morris, the orchestra's executive director since 1987, says that the Musical Arts Association is financially stable. "We're not without financial concerns, of course," he said. "No American orchestra is, but we are not falling backward. Our budget is balanced and our fundraising is fantastically strong."

Mr. Morris is bright-eyed, bearded, quick, and convivial, and has the ability to convey a certain optimism even when he is imparting gloomy prophecy. "I'm sorry to say it but I don't believe every community in America can support an orchestra," he said.

> In healthier financial times, in the '70s and '80s, as with a lot of businesses, a lot of things expanded beyond the capabilities of community support and so there are a lot of overextended orchestras and some of them are folding. The traditional audience for classical music is shrinking and it's going to continue to get smaller. And a symphony orchestra is like a snapshot of a musical time. It's essentially a collection of fine instrumentalists devoted to playing a repertory that is fundamentally European and 19th-century. I'm not making value judgments—we try to play a good deal of contemporary and American music—but that's just a *fact*. Looking 25 years on, I believe the strongest, the very best orchestras will survive and flourish artistically and financially but they will be different and there will be problems.

"Already we're changing our ground rules," he continued.

> When we visit New York now, it's not merely a routine thing—something we do just to visit New York. With all the competition there, there has to be some compelling reason to come to town—some piece that we really want to play and that we have something special to say about. That's why we came with *Wozzeck*, that's why we came with Robert Shaw and the Mahler Eighth.
>
> And with the collapse of musical education in this country's public

schools, I think that organizations such as ours not only should but had *better* take on some of the responsibilities for educating new audiences. But I don't think the way to do that is to bring out video screens and colored lights and rock stars and calculated appeals to a youth audience. Some orchestras need to do that; we don't. It sounds corny but I believe in presenting great concerts of really interesting events.

RCA Victor had recently released an album purporting to be the "Symphonic Rolling Stones," with the London Symphony Orchestra. Mr. Morris broke into delighted laughter when the subject came up. "Oh, God, that's the party record of the year," he said and launched into an impromptu parody of the hapless tenor Jerry Hadley doing a grand opera version of "Sympathy for the Devil":

"Puh-*leese* allow *mee* to intro*dooce* mice-elf." That's a riot. But the record probably sold. Would we work with the Rolling Stones? Let me put it this way: I'd certainly talk with them because the Stones themselves are serious artists in their field. So the question would become, is there a way to create some kind of single event that would take advantage of what each of our groups does best? We could talk that over. But if the answer was to just play symphonic arrangements of Rolling Stones songs behind Mick Jagger—or even Jerry Hadley—I think we'd have to pass. That's not really the sort of thing the Cleveland Orchestra does best.

Fi Magazine
May 1996

Van Cliburn

This is one of only two articles carried over from my earlier collection, Music from the Road *(1992). I remain proud of it, despite Cliburn's spectacular elusiveness. A* Newsday *review of a 1994 Cliburn appearance in New York has been appended and should be self-explanatory. Suffice it to say that it was a concert a critic can never forget, hard as he may try.*

FORT WORTH, Texas

VAN CLIBURN—still the most famous pianist in American history although he hasn't played a note professionally for 11 years—stands in the kitchen of his elaborate Tudor mansion outside Fort Worth, presiding over an informal party.

It is 1 A.M. and the night is young. His mother, Rildia Bee Cliburn, frail but alert at 92, sips soup at the head of the long table. Occasionally, unpredictably, she looks up and smiles a warm, satisfied smile, her dark eyes flashing with cricket vitality. Friends—fellow musicians, Fort Worth civic leaders, acquaintances from church—pass through the halls of the gigantic house, dazzled by its riches but doing their best not to sightsee too blatantly.

There seem to be pianos in every room: big, black, glittering grands. And on the pianos are photographs—Cliburn with former President Ronald Reagan, Cliburn with Mikhail Gorbachev, Cliburn at a party, and again and again, Cliburn with his mother. The walls are covered with citations and posters from throughout his career. "Some life, huh?" one of Cliburn's visitors asks as we meditate, solemnly, on the surroundings.

Some life. Cliburn and his mother moved back to Texas from New York in 1986 and now live in a mansion once owned by Kay Kimbell, the founder of the city's celebrated art museum. The Cliburns reportedly paid well over a million dollars for the estate—a million in depressed Fort Worth, where one can still pick up a handsome house for less than $50,000. And this is only one of the Cliburn homes: there are places in Shreveport and Tucson, a vast storage space in Santa Barbara. In New York, Cliburn lived at the Salisbury Hotel, where his suite ultimately grew to 17 rooms. "Van collects antiques and he needs someplace to put them," Susan Tilley, chairman of the Van Cliburn Foundation, explained.

Reputation to the contrary, Cliburn is no recluse in Texas. Indeed, Fort Worth society clusters to him. The piano competition that bears Cliburn's name brings money, prestige, and the world musical elite to Fort Worth, and the city is proud of him—not only for what he has accomplished but for the way he has remained true to Texas.

"He's one of the great men of the world, yet he came back to live here in Fort Worth," one acquaintance told me. "Did you know he still attends Broadway Baptist Church every week?"

Cliburn is gentle, charming, and likable. He seems an eccentric but genuinely happy man. He is now 54 years old, but the description that comes inevitably to mind is "boyish," and his unaffected use of honorifics like "sir" and "ma'am" only heightens the impression of youth. "Does everybody have everything they want?" he asks in a soft Texas drawl. Assured that they do, he glides on, person to person, group to group, kissing the women on their cheeks, patting the men on their backs, a body in motion, transcendent.

One might say that Cliburn has been in the world but not quite of it for almost a dozen years. He is now almost as well-known for *not* playing as he used to be for playing. He has never completely retired. There have been occasional private performances for friends such as President Reagan and Ferdinand and Imelda Marcos, and there was one benefit appearance for the Bob Hope Cultural Center in Palm Springs.

But next week Cliburn will take the stage for his first public concert since 1978. He will perform the Piano Concerto No. 1 of Peter Ilyich Tchaikovsky—the work that brought him fame—in a program at the Fredric Mann Center in Philadelphia. And the musical world is expected to turn out en masse to hear this legendary pianist of the past play once again.

Some life, indeed. To find a parallel to Van Cliburn, one must look beyond the rarefied world of classical music and search instead the pantheon of solitary American heroes. Then the analogy comes easily: Cliburn is a musical answer to Charles A. Lindbergh.

Both men were tall, loosely knit, determinedly homespun country boys who were transported, literally overnight, to international celebrity. Both were loners who charted their own courses and then followed them through, unerringly, to fruition. Both men carried an extraordinary amount of geopolitical baggage: Lindbergh was credited with uniting the new world with the old, while Cliburn's victory represented one of the few civil moments in the chronicle of Soviet-American relations during the 1950s.

And, finally, the lives of both men are, necessarily, studies in anticlimax. Lindbergh and Cliburn earned their places in the history books with two or three incredible days in their mid-20s. For all that Lindbergh accomplished, for good and ill, after *The Spirit of St. Louis* made its way across the Atlantic Ocean, everything pales when set beside those 33 airborne hours.

And whatever Cliburn may do with the rest of his life, one suspects he will always be remembered as the Texas boy who found his way to Moscow at the height of the Cold War and brought home the gold—first prize in the Soviet Union's most prestigious musical competition, the Tchaikovsky.

Cliburn, who was then 23 years old, had already won several important American competitions, among them the Kosciusko Foundation's Chopin Prize and the Leventritt Award. But his career had begun to falter. By early 1958 he was living back home in Kilgore, Texas, tending house for his parents (Cliburn's father was a purchasing agent for a local oil company). The decision to go to Moscow had the desperate quality of a last chance.

His success was extraordinary, unprecedented, and reported on the front pages of newspapers throughout the world. At a time when there seemed no common ground between the United States and the Soviet Union, Van Cliburn provided one. He was mobbed in Moscow with a fervor of startling intensity. Women wept and fainted at his concerts; Khrushchev himself embraced the young American.

Time Magazine put him on its cover with a banner that read, "The Texan Who Conquered Russia." Fans ripped off the door of his limousine during a visit to Philadelphia. RCA Victor signed him to an exclusive contract and his first recording—the Tchaikovsky Piano Concerto No. 1, of course—quickly became the best-selling classical disc of all time, a position it retained until *Switched-On Bach* was released a decade later. By the time he was 24, he was the subject of a biography, written by the late critic, composer, and pianist Abram Chasins. It was called *The Van Cliburn Legend*. Few young pianists have ever had so many expectations to live up to.

Not surprisingly, Cliburn apparently found it an impossible task. "From the mid-1960s, it seemed that he could not cope with the loss of freshness," Michael Steinberg wrote in the *New Grove Dictionary of Music and Musicians*. "His repertory was restricted; his playing, always guided primarily by intuition, took on affectations and the sound itself became harsher."

In 1978 Cliburn played his last concert and settled down to live quietly with his mother in New York. Nobody knew if he would ever play again.

Like many aerialists, Cliburn seems a little uncomfortable with life on the ground. Sitting him down for a talk—a *serious* talk, beyond flutter and pleasantries—is all but impossible. ("You don't interview Van, you experience him," one friend told me.) Although Cliburn is always terribly polite and never quite says no, he won't give an interview. He would rather change the subject or give a diplomatic, courteous non-answer and breeze on, nothing revealed, no positions taken. Even an innocent social question about whether he misses New York is handily depersonalized: "Well, New York is one of the great cities of the world." And the subject is closed.

But late that evening—or rather, early the next morning—Cliburn reluctantly sat for an interview. The party safely in swing, he closed off the music room (two pianos instead of one) and settled into a comfortable, overstuffed couch to discuss his long absence from the concert stage.

"I can remember when I was about 18 and some friends of mine were going to Europe for the summer and they asked me to come," he said. "And I thought I'd get there to play sometime anyway, so I didn't go. You know how when you're young, you do all this prognosticating which later turns out to be right or wrong. And I told my friends that I would work very hard for the first part of my life, and then I'll take an intermission and then work very hard the last part of my life.

"Well, anyway, I was very busy for a long time," he continued.

And then, in January 1974, my father died. And then less than two months later, Sol Hurok died. I had been supposed to see Mr. Hurok in New York in January, but I canceled because of my father's death. So he said, "Oh, when you come next month we will talk." But I missed having that last lunch with him because he was dead by the time I came back to New York.

And I realized that I was missing lots of little lunches and dinners with my friends, and that too many of those friends seemed to be departing. And I decided I wanted a little bit of time to enjoy my friends because things don't last forever. I want some personal memories, too, as well as the memories of meeting wonderful people in the concert halls and interesting times traveling. So I planned in 1974 to take some time off but never announced it. I just stopped accepting engagements. Because my wonderful memories of concertizing are so vivid, I feel like I've never left. It's like the intermission was a little longer than I thought, but it's all still part of the same concert.

"You know, I love to be able to go to concerts and hear my friends perform," he said.

That really pleases me, and I really wasn't able to do that for—oh, the longest while. I made my orchestral debut with the Houston Symphony when I was 12. And then I was playing lots of recitals throughout what we call the Arklatexas area. And then I made my debut with the New York Philharmonic when I was 19. So from childhood on, it was a lot of work. I've enjoyed my time off immensely. It's been a grand time, and I've had an awful lot of fun.

One cannot escape the suspicion that the "time off" may ultimately prove to be a permanent state of affairs. For Cliburn is vague about every aspect of his return to the stage. "I'm not going to be playing a million concerts again, I can promise you that," is about as definite a statement as he will make.

He says that the reason he is playing in Philadelphia is largely sentimental. "It's a tribute to two very good friends of mine who have died recently— Eugene Ormandy and [patron of the arts] Fred Mann."

When Cliburn is pressed about pieces of music he wants to learn or to perform, nothing comes to mind (he is playing his signature piece, the Tchaikovsky, in Philadelphia). Recordings? "Well, yes, I plan to make some records, but I haven't really gotten into the planning stage yet." A solo recital? "I have some lovely offers, and I may well just take one of them up." Other pianists? "I thought the four that we had here last night were all wonderful." If Cliburn feels an urgent need to make music, he keeps it to himself.

I was reminded of one of Aaron Copland's last interviews, 10 years after he had written his last major piece. "I'm amazed I don't miss composing more than I do," Copland said. "You'd think if you had spent 50 years at it you'd have the feeling that something was missing and I really don't. I must have expressed myself sufficiently." And so, perhaps, has Cliburn.

This is not to suggest that Cliburn cannot perform, only that, from the point of view of a prodigy who was driven hard from the beginning of childhood, it may well be liberating *not* to. One suspects that he will continue to play occasional benefits, visit the White House now and then; there is talk of a return visit to the Soviet Union—all circumstances where the principal interest is extramusical.

The rest of the time, there will be the loving friends, the sparkling parties, the fulfilling church life, the adulation of his native state, the challenge of the Van Cliburn Competition, and the legacy of some fine recordings (now in the process of reissue on RCA Victor compact discs).

Whatever may happen in Philadelphia next week or in the years to come, Van Cliburn knows that his spot in history is assured.

"I remember calling my mother from Russia and telling her I'd won the competition," he said with a grin.

I had no idea that the story had become so big. So I asked her if she'd told Mrs. So-and-So across town that I'd won. And she said yes, she knew all about it. And I asked her if she'd told Mr. So-and-So in the next town over that I'd won. And she said yes, he knew about it, too. And I felt pretty good, because it was all very well to be known in your town, but what *really* mattered was if your reputation had spread to the next town. Then you'd really made it.

He smiled and shook his head, and there was a note of awe in his voice. "I was mighty proud that night," he said.

Newsday
11 June 1989

MUCH OF THE ELECTRIFYING—and often excruciating—drama that coursed through Van Cliburn's comeback concert at the Metropolitan Opera House Tuesday night was extramusical. It would be less than professional to allow the evening's painful circumstances to determine one's critical verdict, but it would be less than human not to take them into account.

Cliburn walked onto the stage a few minutes after 8 P.M. in what can only have been a state of complete sensory overload. Last Thursday his mother, Rildia Bee Cliburn, 97 years old, suffered a severe stroke. Cliburn flew to her bedside, did not play scheduled weekend concerts in Saratoga and the Boston suburbs, and—briefly—called off this New York appearance.

But finally, through some combination of "show must go on" trouper spirit and the recognition that the 100 musicians of the Moscow Philharmonic Orchestra (not to mention the producers and promoters of the current tour, Cliburn's first in 16 years) were dependent on him for their livelihood, he played. And if it was not the out-of-the-ballpark smash that some of us had hoped for, it remained an altogether creditable, occasionally inspired—and sometimes wrenchingly moving—evening of music-making.

It was also a sort of "This Is Your Life, Van Cliburn!" summary of the pianist's whole career. Rildia Cliburn was not only Cliburn's mother, first teacher, and most important mentor, but, by all appearances, she has been his closest and most beloved companion as well; he has lived with her virtually all his life. Moreover, the concert came about as close as is currently possible to duplicating Cliburn's big moment in the history books—those amazing days in 1958 when the lanky, polite, soft-spoken small-town kid from Texas won the Tchaikovsky competition (and world adulation) playing with the Moscow Philharmonic in what was then a belligerent Soviet Union. And once again, Cliburn trotted out his "greatest hit," the Tchaikovsky Piano Concerto No. 1.

How much—and how little—has changed! On Tuesday, Russian and American flags flanked the stage; the Soviet Union is no more; the concert carried no political baggage. And yet Cliburn, now 60, looked remarkably as he did in those grainy old newsreels—and he often played that way too, for better and for worse. Sadly, there is no getting around the fact that this is a supreme case of arrested development. Has Cliburn, who might have been the Great American Pianist after William Kapell, learned a new piece in 25 years? Where are the searching performances of the masterpieces of the piano literature that we might have expected from him by this point? Has even Cliburn's thrice-familiar rendition of the Tchaikovsky deepened with the years?

The concert? A solid, impassioned, idiomatic, and sometimes less than perfectly coordinated Tchaikovsky concerto—some ravishing, dulcet *pianissimos* making up for some stiff and clattering octaves—with earnest, enthusiastic accompaniment by the Moscow Philharmonic under the direction of Vassily Siniasky. Aaron Copland's *Lincoln Portrait* is a loathsome piece: Kansas-in-August popular-front Americana, complete with a recited selection from the words of Abraham Lincoln that might have been distilled by Earl Browder and Gertrude Stein one drunken night. Cliburn read it well, however, in his best Jimmy Stewart Aw-Shucks manner.

The most affecting moment of the evening came after Cliburn spoke longingly of his mother, then read one of his own poems. This sounded rather like a not terribly well-organized outtake from Tennyson's "In Memoriam," and I might have dismissed it as mawkish had I not realized, when it was over, that my eyes were wet. Then Cliburn went to the piano and played a prismatic, furious, almost desperate performance of Szymanowski's Etude, Op. 4, No. 3. One had the extraordinary (if not entirely comfortable) sense that 4,000 people were eavesdropping on an intensely private moment, as Cliburn, oblivious to the world, child and man, conquering hero and bereft son, sat alone on the stage, playing his heart out, triumphant and inconsolable.

Newsday
4 August 1994

John Corigliano

THE CLARINET squealed high and loud, resounding throughout the darkened recesses of New York's Avery Fisher Hall like klezmer gone mad.

Composer John Corigliano, on hand to help rehearse a performance of his 22-year-old Concerto for Clarinet and Orchestra, smiled in wonder. "This fellow is *so* good!" he whispered. "And just listen to that orchestra!"

It was indeed impressive, this early-morning runthrough of Corigliano's challenging score, made only more so by the fact that many, perhaps most, of the players in the Juilliard Symphony Orchestra—including the soloist, clarinetist Alexander Fiterstein—weren't even born when the piece was written. Still, the concerto's first performance was played in this same hall, back in 1977, when Stanley Drucker was the soloist and Leonard Bernstein conducted the New York Philharmonic. And now the work has achieved the status of a modern classic.

Another Leonard, this one named Slatkin, will conduct the National Symphony Orchestra in the premiere of Corigliano's latest work, *A Dylan Thomas Trilogy*, Thursday night at the Kennedy Center, with additional performances on Friday and Saturday. It promises to be a major statement from a distinguished and original lyrical master.

Corigliano, who turned 61 last month, abounds with enthusiasm and confidence these days. Despite his white hair, he looks at least a decade younger than he is—put a laurel wreath on his head and he'd make a plausible pageant Apollo—and he seems to have grown cheerfully into his status as one of America's Grand Old Composers-in-training.

"So many of us just celebrated our 60th birthdays," he marveled. "Joan Tower, John Harbison, William Bolcom, Charles Wuorinen, Steve Reich. Ellen Zwilich is next, I think." He could hardly have named a group of more disparate creators, all of them pursuing their own different musical paths. And yet that is the principal direction in American classical music today; rather than follow any pet theories or hard-and-fast rules, a composer now chooses not only the content of a given work, but its very syntax as well.

In Corigliano's case, those techniques would seem to be just about everything. He handles an orchestra superbly, with a full command of its resources (including an occasional dash of electronic music). Without losing his train of thought, he can turn on a dime from lush romanticism to the most exotic expressionism (let's not forget that one of his biggest early successes was the soundtrack to Ken Russell's film *Altered States*). He has written music for films, for operas, for chamber groups, for solo instruments, and for full orchestra.

The NSO won the most prestigious classical Grammy award, "Best Classical Recording," for its 1996 disc of Corigliano's Symphony No. 1 (1990). The composer called this 50-minute threnody a "personal response to the AIDS crisis" and some lazy critics dismissed it as pure editorial. But it is a score of such consummate skill, furious power, and sheer musical interest that it can stand on its own—and then some.

Even better, in some ways, was the opera *The Ghosts of Versailles* (1991), written with librettist William M. Hoffman, which was the first new work the Metropolitan Opera had commissioned in almost a quarter century and which became a runaway hit after its world premiere in December 1991. It is a wonderful opera—by turns funny, sad, tender, lush, lyrical, sophisticated, and phantasmagorical—fashioned with grateful, elaborate, multi-tiered arias and ensembles that tested, but never quite exceeded, the limitations of the world-class singers the Met assembled.

In keeping with the sustained quasi-hallucination of Hoffman's libretto, Corigliano tried on a lot of different styles—from neo-baroque frippery to the highest of modernisms—and yet such is his fluency, individuality, and seriousness of purpose that he never devolved into self-conscious eclecticism for its own sake.

He makes an important distinction. "Style is like handwriting," he said. "Your compositional style is an unconscious choice, I think—it comes with who you are—but the techniques you adopt are deliberate choices. Will you be a minimalist, a 12-tone composer, a neo-romantic? Or will you mix it up?"

In fact, Corigliano is a highly formal composer who plots his compositions out carefully before he sits down to write, reserving the option, of course, to amend the music as it goes along. Thus, the opening of *The Ghosts of Versailles* was originally plotted on graph paper, with several different colored pencils weaving in and out of one another's orbit. The score would be incomprehensible to anybody but the composer; still, it provided a seed for the music to come.

Thereafter, Corigliano put into words a sketch of what he wanted to happen in this first scene. "Write several chords—nonrelated but building blocks," his notes read. "Cluster 'dissolves' notes one by one to leave chord. . . . This sounds like volume going up from nothing and down again, provides motion." Eventually the eerie scene took shape; Corigliano follows this process with all his later works, and it adds a structural rectitude to his welcome flights of musical fancy.

The Brooklyn household in which Corigliano grew up could hardly have been more musical. For years, he was known as John Corigliano, Jr.; his father, who bore the same name, was the concertmaster of the New York Philharmonic from 1943 to 1966. Young Corigliano was therefore a regular visitor at Carnegie Hall (where the Philharmonic played before moving to Avery Fisher Hall in 1962) and he heard most of the great musicians of his time.

"I grew up with the sound of the orchestra in my head," he said, "but I'm still anxious about my own ability to orchestrate. I have to look everything up. I wrote a band piece not long ago and I really couldn't hear it—I don't know band music that well—so I had to show it to somebody. Fortunately, he said it was all right."

Corigliano is bright, articulate, and welcoming, but obviously deeply sensitive. Although most reviews of *The Ghosts of Versailles* were positive—some of them were downright ecstatic—the composer visibly paled when I mentioned one prominent and decidedly negative article. Indeed, in the past few years, Corigliano has abandoned reading any critiques of his music.

"Really, how much can you tell about a new piece the first time you hear it?" he asked heatedly.

Imagine taking Picasso's *Guernica*, putting it on scrolls of paper, and then unfurling it over a half-hour duration. Probably nothing would stick in your mind—there's a horse, there's a lightbulb, but it would add up to gibberish because you couldn't take it all in. No, I don't place much stock in the critics. When I'm told that a good review has come in, I tell my publicist to use it but not to make me read it. When a bad review comes in, I just don't want to know about it.

Much of this sensitivity dates from Corigliano's childhood, when his father would send him out to buy *The New York Times* and the *New York Herald Tribune* for morning reviews of the Philharmonic. "I remember the misery on his face, the unhappiness he'd feel when he'd read about his supposed faults in the paper. Nobody wants that. If I hadn't been able to shake off some of the bad reviews I've gotten, I wouldn't have been able to continue in this field."

Corigliano's parents were deeply opposed to their son becoming a professional musician. But he had the bug—and nothing else would do. He studied composition at Columbia University with Otto Luening and at the Manhattan School of Music with Vittorio Giannini. After graduation, Corigliano decided to follow a pragmatic, "hands-on" musical path, rather than go into academia. And so he worked in radio and television, arranged rock music, produced recordings for Columbia Masterworks, and generally played the role of all-around musician throughout the 1960s and early '70s.

The piece that earned Corigliano his first fame was his Sonata for Violin and Piano (1963), which won the Spoleto Festival Competition for the Creative Arts. Putting aside whatever private objections he may once have felt, John Corigliano, Sr., went so far as to learn the sonata and record it with the pianist Ralph Votapek. It is a wiry, exuberant, splendidly crafted exercise in a neoclassical genre and has since been played and recorded many times.

Corigliano himself refers to his early style as "a tense, histrionic outgrowth of the 'clean' American sound of Samuel Barber, Aaron Copland, Roy Harris, and William Schuman, rather than a descendent of the highly chromatic, super-romantic German school." In retrospect, it is not surprising that he later turned to opera, for there was always something intensely theatrical about his work; one listened to a new Corigliano piece with a distinct sense of wanting to find out where it was going, rather as one waits for the final pages of a good thriller.

Although *A Dylan Thomas Trilogy* was fashioned especially for the NSO, parts of it date back 40 years, to a long-ago day when a friend gave Corigliano a collection of Thomas's poetry.

"It was a revelation," Corigliano recalled. "Both the sound and structures of Thomas's words were astonishingly musical." The 21-year-old composer decided to set a youthful poem called "Fern Hill" as a tribute to his high-school music teacher, Bella Tillis, who later conducted the world premiere.

As it turned out, "Fern Hill" was only the beginning. In 1969 when Charles Wadsworth, the founding director of the Chamber Music Society of Lincoln Center, commissioned a work for the fledgling troupe's opening season, Corigliano responded with a setting of Thomas's "Poem in October."

"When I set 'Fern Hill,' I had been just the same age as Thomas was when he wrote the poem," he said. "And then he wrote 'Poem in October' to commemorate his 30th birthday. 'Fern Hill' is about childhood, but in this second poem, the central character climbs a high hill and looks back on his past and forward toward his future. Well, I had just turned 30 myself and I found that this poem reflected my own feelings perfectly."

The third part of the trilogy was written for the United States Bicentennial in 1976 at the request of the late Paul Callaway, who was then the director of the Cathedral Choral Society of the National Cathedral. Corigliano was by then approaching the same age Thomas was when he died (in 1953, at 39, after a mammoth drinking session at the White Horse Tavern in Greenwich Village), and he decided to set a brooding late poem entitled "Poem on His Birthday."

"The piece ends as the poet sails out to die," Corigliano observed in his program notes for *A Dylan Thomas Trilogy*. "Yet even at this dire moment, intensity of experience is still its own reward. Even as the poet realizes that he is closer to, rather than farther from, the last of his days, he cannot help but exult that 'the closer I move to death, the louder the sun blooms.'" The *Trilogy* received its premiere at the cathedral on April 24, 1976.

Corigliano thought he was finished with Dylan Thomas. Still, he returned to his creation again and again over the years and found it incomplete. Increasingly, he felt that the two opening sections were not so closely related to the final movement as they might have been.

"This is a very personal piece, one that I've been working over for a very long time," he said. "It's Thomas's life, but, by this point, it's my life too. And if the character I was presenting was supposed to be an adult making sense of his future through his past, then I needed to present 'Fern Hill' and 'Poem in October' not as real-time events but as implied memories, heard from the perspective of the man who wrote 'Poem on His Birthday.'"

Now Corigliano has lived a short lifetime longer than Dylan Thomas himself was permitted. "And I'm happier and more at peace than I've ever been," he explained as we rode to the Upper West Side apartment he shares with his companion of three years, the composer (and former *Washington Post* music critic) Mark Adamo and a hobbling, sweet-tempered 19-year-old dog.

"I thought perhaps there was something new to say from a vantage point that Thomas never reached—that point where you really come to terms with who you are and how you got there, reconciling your youth with maturity." And so, with the invitation of Slatkin and the John and June Hechinger Fund, who commissioned the new version, Corigliano set to work one more time on the *Dylan Thomas Trilogy*.

He made a new setting of the first 51 lines of Thomas's own "Author's Prologue" to his collected poems, which Corigliano calls a "lavish, exultant poem that bellowed and shouted with lust and life." "Fern Hill" now follows it immediately in the playing order, and then the remainder of the "Author's Prologue," a revised "Poem in October," and finally "Poem on His Birthday." The entire work has been rescored, and roughly half an hour is brand new. "Poem on His Birthday" now concludes with what Corigliano calls a reconciliation and "vocal apotheosis"—in short, a "happy ending."

"You know, I keep waiting for that famous repose that you're supposed to feel when you reach a certain age," Corigliano said.

> That hasn't happened yet. But I used to be the most unfashionable guy around—a lot of the avant-garde composers dismissed me out of hand and the public didn't seem to be interested in any contemporary music. Now—I hope—my attempts to communicate with an audience aren't seen as pandering, but rather as an effort to put some things across so that a new audience can get at least one percent of the material on a first hearing.
>
> I guess I'm saying that just because an audience likes something doesn't make it bad. It doesn't necessarily mean it's good, of course—

but it might be. After all, even Beethoven pulls you in right away; it's only later that you discover that there are at least 100 layers underneath.

The Washington Post
7 March 1999

Plácido Domingo

When I interviewed Plácido Domingo his first performance of Tristan und Isolde *was planned for Vienna in 1996, with a Met Tristan a rumored possibility. Ultimately he decided not to sing Tristan at the Met, although he has recorded a good sampling of selections.*

O H, DEAR. You say you want to talk with Plácido?"
The worried person on the other end of the line was Plácido Domingo's press representative, a gentleman usually not at all averse to putting his clients before the public eye. And, yes, I most certainly *did* want to talk with "Plácido." After an extraordinary season at the Metropolitan Opera, during which the 53-year-old tenor—always one of our most serious and penetrating artists—surpassed himself, again and again, so that even long-time Domingo followers could only listen in delighted amazement, it seemed time to sit down and find out something about how this was accomplished.

"I'm sure he'd be happy to see you," Edgar Vincent said finally, after a sigh and a moment's calculation, "It's just that his schedule is *unbelievably* busy right now. Can you possibly come to Europe? It will be much easier to catch up with him there."

Easier, to be sure, but not exactly easy. Plácido Domingo spent the month of May yo-yoing between Austria and England. In Vienna he conducted Bellini's *I Puritani* at the Staatsoper. In London he sang Don José in a rapturously received production of *Carmen* at Covent Garden. Vienna-London,

Bellini-Bizet, conductor-singer—back and forth all month long. Meanwhile, he served as adjudicator for the Plácido Domingo Vocal Competition semi-finals and sang the second act of *Die Fledermaus* in an outdoor, televised, free performance to inaugurate a year-long celebration of the city of Vienna.

But Domingo will reach his largest audience this Saturday night when he joins forces with his colleagues Luciano Pavarotti and José Carreras for what is widely known as "Three Tenors Two" in Los Angeles—part of the World Cup USA festivities, to be telecast live on PBS at 11 P.M. from Dodger Stadium. The first teaming of the Three Tenors, in Italy in 1990, was a smash success. Tickets for "Three Tenors Two" start at $360 and ascend to a dizzying $1,012—a sum that would allow the listener to purchase dozens of recordings by the three men, to enjoy them at home, forever, rather than watching (likely through binoculars) and listening (*definitely* through amplification) as three men try to fill an entire stadium with sound.

Domingo might well have been in Los Angeles this week anyway, even if he hadn't been scheduled to sing. A confirmed sports fanatic, he is full of enthusiasm for games, players, and racing events throughout the world. Even during the midst of his own May marathon, for example, he managed to escape to the San Marino Grand Prix, where he was just in time to witness the blazing car crash that claimed the life of Ayrton Senna.

"Horrible, horrible," Domingo recalled as we sat in the Red Room of the Hotel Sacher in Vienna, his dark, sensitive brown eyes welling slightly at the memory, speaking softly in accented but near-perfect English. "I know many of the drivers, and they are my friends. I am always at home with them. They take *risks*."

So does Domingo. Certainly it was a risk to take on the part of Verdi's *Otello* back in 1975, when he was in his mid-30s. The role is a notorious voice-wrecker, beginning with what may be the single most difficult minute of music for tenor in the repertory: Otello's entrance, the terrifying "Esultate!"—high and loud, majestic and pivotally important to everything that follows, without even a recitative to warm up the voice.

Now, almost 20 years later, Domingo is recognized as the leading Otello of our time. Yet he continues to sing Rodolfo, Cavaradossi, Don José, and the other gentler, more lyrical leads in the repertory; clearly his voice has survived the ordeal. And in Vienna two years from now he will sing his first performance of Wagner's *Tristan und Isolde*, which is at least as strenuous as *Otello* in its own manner; negotiations to bring the interpretation to the Met soon thereafter are reportedly already under way. If Domingo pulls it off—and it seems more than likely that he will—he may prove the sweetest, most musical Tristan since the days of Lauritz Melchior, half a century ago.

The central difficulty with the role of Tristan—and, for that matter, with most of Wagner—is that it demands stentorian power and near-Herculean endurance, and usually the effort shows. Simply getting through the score, singing above the huge Wagnerian orchestra in full throttle and projecting out to that fabled person in the back row, is an accomplishment in itself. Most tenors (even *celebrated* tenors in our most prestigious opera houses) end up strained and shouting; yet such is the paucity of Wagnerian singers that they will be applauded and re-engaged. After all, one doesn't demand the grace of a ballet dancer from a weight lifter.

Still, on the Met's opening night last year Domingo sang the role of Siegmund in Act I of Wagner's *Die Walküre* with just that mixture of power and musicianship we have long despaired of finding in a single man. Within the next two years he is scheduled to record Wagner's entire *Ring* cycle (of which *Die Walküre* is a part), as well as the same composer's *Parsifal*, Gounod's *Roméo et Juliette*, Verdi's *Il Trovatore*, and, in the nonoperatic repertory, Mahler's *Das Lied von der Erde*.

Last—and probably least—there is "Three Tenors Two." Domingo chuckled a bit when the subject was raised. "Oh, well," he said with a mischievous smile. "I take on different projects for different reasons." It was not necessary for him to elaborate; the single night of work—once telecast, recordings, and other manifestations are factored in—will likely earn each tenor well in excess of $1 million.

"But I sing because I love it, not just for the financial rewards," he said, serious again, looking straight into the eyes. "Right now, I'm doing all these performances of *Carmen* and *Puritani*, flying back and forth all over Europe, and sometimes people ask why I push myself so much. I could do just two concerts and earn much more money. But the music is what matters. If I do 80 performances in a year, 65 of them will be in opera."

"And, I must say, I really enjoy working with Luciano and José," he continued. "People talk about this great rivalry, you know, and it's just not there.

On the contrary, we can appreciate one another, because we know just how hard it is to do what we do. And really, we're all very different."

Indeed they are. One cannot imagine Pavarotti or Carreras singing Wagner. Pavarotti's venture into *Otello* in 1991 was generally judged a disaster, and one may hope that the light, lyric Carreras would never dream of taking on such heavy material. If Domingo's voice lacks some of the sunny luster that Pavarotti, at his best, can command; if his interpretations rarely match the sheer, dapper charm and suavity we associate with Carreras, he remains far and away the most versatile of "The Three." There may be some debate over which man is the "world's greatest tenor" (whatever *that* means), but there can be little argument about which tenor is the most able and multi-faceted musician.

"We not only admire each other, but we see each other socially," he continued. "Of course, we don't often find ourselves in the same city. So it will be fun to meet up in Los Angeles."

Domingo grew up a few hundred miles south of Dodger Stadium, in Mexico City. Born in Spain on January 21, 1941, he moved to Mexico when he was nine years old. "My parents sang operetta," he said, "and my sister and I would grab any opportunity we had to do any tiny part we could onstage. We *loved* it. Our parents recognized our interest in music and started us in on the piano. My father always told me that the one thing he *didn't* want me to do was sing, because it was such a difficult career."

The young Domingo dutifully studied piano and conducting.

> But little by little my parents began to realize that I had a voice. Then my piano teacher died so I had to go into the conservatory for my piano lessons, and I started taking singing lessons on the side. And then, when I was in the chorus of *My Fair Lady*—that's right, *My Fair Lady*—a friend of mine told me I ought to sing opera and urged me to take an audition. I auditioned as a baritone, but they told me I wasn't a baritone and that I ought to sing a tenor aria. And I said I didn't know any tenor arias, but I'd read one for them if they wanted me to.

The newly designated tenor impressed his auditors, and shortly thereafter, while still a teenager, he made his professional debut as Alfredo in *La*

Traviata in the Mexican city of Monterrey. "Then I learned they needed a tenor at the Israel National Opera in Tel Aviv. I contracted for six months but ended up staying two and a half years, singing 280 performances of 11 different operas. And you come out of an experience like that either completely destroyed or pretty well built up."

Domingo built himself up. In 1966 he was chosen to sing the title role in the late Argentine composer Alberto Ginastera's *Don Rodrigo*. It was an event of major importance: not only the opera's North American premiere but the very first production mounted by the New York City Opera in its new home at Lincoln Center. The critics were delighted. "It was for all concerned a brilliant triumph," John Ardoin wrote in *Opera* magazine. And in what was to become a refrain throughout Domingo criticism, Ardoin added that the tenor and his leading lady, Jeannine Crader, "proved to have dramatic instincts as sure and distinctive as their fine voices."

By 1968 Domingo was at the Met; his debut performance was in *Adriana Lecouvreur* opposite Renata Tebaldi. Since then he has sung with the company more than 350 times, in 36 different roles. Although this is an impressive record in and of itself, it doesn't begin to give an idea of Domingo's actual versatility: in June he sang his first performance of Gomes's *Il Guarany* at the Bonn Opera—the 107th role in his repertory.

"I'd say I could sing any one of about 25 or 30 roles tonight, with no preparation whatsoever," Domingo estimated. "And then, if you gave me a week or two to get ready, I could probably sing another 50 roles or so. Some of the modern works would take some time to relearn, and there may be a couple pieces which might now be beyond my capacity. Voices change quite a bit in 30 years!

"I'm in no hurry to stop singing, but I think it is very important to respect the public and not to keep going after it's really time to stop. Sometimes you can be in a production and something can go a little wrong, and you are not quite at your best, you know? But when the day arrives when you are *consistently* not at your best, it is time to retire." Domingo has said that he plans to sing opera for another five or 10 years, then move into conducting, with perhaps a very occasional vocal recital on the side.

Judging from Domingo's performance of *I Puritani* in Vienna, he is certainly a much more capable conductor than most of the many superstars who decide to pick up the baton and, more often than not, make complete fools of themselves. After all, Domingo studied with the composer and conductor Igor Markevich in his youth, he is a trained pianist, and he is much more musically sophisticated than most of his peers. Moreover, this is not new for him: he has been conducting publicly since 1973, when he led *La Traviata* at the City Opera. In *Puritani*, he managed to provide a solid instrumental frame for the highly formal (if not especially complicated) music while allowing the singers ample room to breathe within.

"I don't think anybody can really teach you how to be a conductor," Domingo said.

> You can improve your technique, but if you don't have some deep feeling for the music and a certain authority and sense of direction, you're just not going to go very far. You have to *imagine* the sound, hear every line—the violins, the basses, the solo flute—by itself and as it will sound with the other instruments. And once you imagine the sound, that still isn't enough, because you must find your own way of putting it across.

In London a few days later, Domingo was a tenor again, preparing for the role of Don José in *Carmen* at Covent Garden. "I wish we weren't doing the opera with the dialogue," he said. "I always prefer the fully composed version, even if it isn't all Bizet."

The composer, who died in 1875 shortly after the premiere of his masterpiece, left the score in something of a mess. And so there is no definitive version of *Carmen*; it is sometimes performed with musical recitative (most of it written by a third-rater named Ernest Guiraud) between the big numbers, sometimes with spoken dialogue and occasionally in a sort of hybrid.

In England *Carmen* is almost always performed with the dialogue. This may well be more "correct," but it doesn't especially suit Domingo; one was surprised, again and again, to observe how deeply his acting gifts are tied in with his singing. The "Flower Song," the scenes with Micaëla, couldn't have been much more convincing—both musically and dramatically—but in the spoken passages, he was mostly bumptious and ineffectual, easily upstaged by the sinuous, vital, and downright *dangerously* sensual Carmen of Denyce Graves. It was as if somebody switched Domingo into neutral whenever his singing stopped.

The five more-or-less serious local papers—*The Times, The Daily Telegraph, The Observer*, the *Independent*, and *The Evening Standard*—greeted this *Carmen* with the respect it deserved. In Europe, excellence is still news and culture still *matters*, to a degree that will shock many Americans; the collapse of Western civilization seems so much further away. Indeed, any longtime New Yorker who visits London is likely to experience a sort of Jamesian conversion, however temporary. In its milder form, this may manifest itself in a passion for formal afternoon tea, or Victorian pubs, or the sheer satisfaction of reading several literate newspapers in the course of a day; a true fanatic may return to the States wanting to track down his elementary school teachers and chew them out for teaching children that the Redcoats were the bad guys.

And yet, Domingo, who could afford to live anywhere in the world—and who, as of July 1996, will be serving as the artistic director of the Washington Opera—considers New York his home. "The Met is the theater in which I work most often. I haven't missed a season in a quarter century, and so I'm in New York four, sometimes even five months of the year, and I still think it is the most exciting city in the world." He has been married to Marta Ornelas for more than three decades and speaks with pride of his sons, José, Plácido (who, he says, is an "excellent composer"), and Alvaro.

Domingo names Enrico Caruso, Jussi Björling, and Miguel Fleta as the three tenors from the past he admires most. "Fleta is not so well known as Caruso and Björling; he had a shorter career than the others did. But he had this incredible ability to make a real *diminuendo* on a note—to start it off very large and take it down small, small, small. That is very hard on the diaphragm, and I think he wore out his voice before he had to by abusing it too much. But it was magnificent!" A pause. "And then, of course, he was a Spaniard, and I like that." He smiled.

"With Björling I admire the purity and clarity of his voice, the sweetness of the sound. Caruso loved the darkness—the power and the darkness—and you can hear that in his recordings." (Indeed, Caruso, particularly as he is represented on his later discs, produced a deep, rich sound that was, like Domingo's, almost baritonal; Caruso once made a private recording of the bass aria from *La Bohème*.)

"Certainly my own voice has deepened with time," Domingo said. "But I think that is the secret of my longevity. Being a tenor is not only about high notes, about who can hit the high C. I think the deeper range is an important base to build upon. And what you build on it may just last."

Late afternoon in Vienna, lingering over coffee and pastries in the Sacher, a few minutes' walk from the house where Mozart composed *The Marriage of Figaro* and just around the corner from the State Opera. Domingo had the evening off—a few hours of free time before returning to London and yet another Don José. Toward 6 P.M. the Red Room began to fill up, and the tenor was suddenly besieged by well-wishers. He greeted them graciously, signed a menu for the headwaiter, accepted compliments in English, German, and French from admirers young and old.

Fifty feet across the room, a pianist had begun to play rudimentary versions of Offenbach's Barcarolle, Dvořák's Humoresque, and a few other favorites that even readers who think they know nothing about classical music could probably hum in their sleep. It was actually pretty awful. Somehow, in this most musical of cities, the Hotel Sacher had found a pianist who really couldn't play the piano very well.

Yet, as we prepared to leave, Domingo walked across the long room and gave the pianist a generous tip and a few words of encouragement. The hapless man beamed, then blushed, and the room burst into applause. One last autograph and Domingo was back in the lobby of the Sacher.

"A fellow musician," he said without prompting, just as another group of admirers began to slowly, inexorably, cluster toward him. "We must help one another."

Newsday
10 July 1994

Leon Fleisher

THE SAGA of America's first generation of famous classical pianists is an unhappy one. William Kapell—the oldest and, in some ways, the most brilliant of the group—was killed in a freakish plane crash at the age of 31 in 1953. Van Cliburn now seems content to play little more than his signature piece, the Tchaikovsky Piano Concerto No. 1, and that only on rare occasions. Meanwhile, Byron Janis, Gary Graffman, and Leon Fleisher were all forced to curtail their performing by mysterious hand problems at what should have been the peak of their careers.

Fleisher's story is especially poignant, for some recordings he made in the 1950s and early '60s suggest that he had it all: a technique that knew no difficulties, a bejeweled and expressive tone, a sure intellectual command of musical form, and acute sensitivity to whatever he played. Fleisher made his formal debut in 1944 at Carnegie Hall with the New York Philharmonic, won the prestigious Queen Elisabeth International Music Competition of Belgium in 1952, played in the leading concert halls throughout the world, and was generally accepted as one of the world's best young pianists.

And then, in 1966, at the age of 37, damaged, miserable, and no longer able to control his right hand, he canceled all future engagements and withdrew from performing.

Now for some good news. Last Saturday, the 67-year-old Fleisher returned to Carnegie Hall for his first two-handed concert there in more than 37 years (he has made a number of appearances playing with left hand alone). And this weekend in Washington, he will accompany soprano Phyllis Bryn-Julson in Robert Schumann's song cycle *Frauenliebe und Leben* and participate in a performance of Brahms's Piano Quartet in G Minor, Op. 25.

Fleisher's gradual (and by no means wholehearted) return to two-hand performance has been carefully planned. He played Mozart's Piano Concerto in A, K. 414—the same piece just performed at Carnegie Hall—with the Theater Chamber Players last April at the Terrace Theater, but, at Fleisher's insistence, there was an absolute minimum of publicity. Similar performances in Cleveland and at Tanglewood have been equally discreet.

"This is all part of an ongoing process," Fleisher said in an interview two days before the Carnegie concert. "I'm gaining strength and flexibility every week, but I don't know just how far I can go with it. For the moment, I'm just grateful to be able to play whatever I can, whenever I can."

What happened to Leon Fleisher? Why did he have to give up performing for so long? "Well, my right arm basically turned to stone," he said. "In the early 1960s I was practicing seven or eight hours a day already, and when I noticed some weakness in my right arm, I only practiced harder. It was all wrong. I never allowed my muscles to decontract, and as a result I essentially ruined my arm."

Fleisher was an early victim of what is now known as repetitive strain injury—a sort of "stripping of the gears" that can affect people who overuse certain muscles in the same pattern for hours on end. Fleisher now refers to his youthful manner of practicing as "pumping ivory."

"Back then, we knew nothing about repetitive stress," Fleisher said. "I saw doctors, I saw hypnotists, and nothing worked. There was no explanation. No answer at all. I just couldn't play anymore. Can you imagine what that was like?"

At the time he was afflicted, Fleisher had been preparing to leave on an ambitious State Department–sponsored tour of Western Europe and the Soviet Union with George Szell and the Cleveland Orchestra. Depressed and desperate, he dropped out of the tour and concentrated his efforts on teaching (he had been appointed to the Andrew W. Mellon Chair at Baltimore's Peabody Conservatory in 1959).

During the next 17 years, he underwent a series of muscle-function and nerve-conduction tests, several different therapies, and, finally, neurosurgery at Massachusetts General Hospital in Boston. In the fall of 1982, by force of will, he played César Franck's Symphonic Variations with the Baltimore Symphony for the opening of the new Meyerhoff Concert Hall. Although the reviews were respectful—and the audience response was overwhelming—Fleisher realized that he could use his right hand for only a short time, that it was simply too painful for him to endure long practice and performing sessions.

And so he resigned himself to a curtailed musical life—teaching at Peabody and performing piano music for the left hand alone. (There is a surprising amount of material, by the way. The Austrian pianist Paul Wittgenstein lost his right arm during World War I; Maurice Ravel, Serge Prokofiev, Benjamin Britten, and Franz Schmidt are only a few of the composers who wrote works to accommodate his disability.)

In 1968 in tandem with composer and pianist Dina Koston, Fleisher founded the Theater Chamber Players in Washington. Since then, he has pursued a new career as a conductor (he has made guest appearances with the Boston Symphony, the Cleveland Orchestra, and the San Francisco Symphony, and in the 1988–89 season, he conducted Mozart's *Marriage of Figaro* for the Baltimore Opera). In 1986 he was appointed artistic director of the Tanglewood Music Center in Lenox, Massachusetts.

It has been, by any standards, a rich musical life. Still, those who love the piano and its repertory have dreamed of a full recovery for Fleisher. His old recordings—a transcendent performance of the Schubert B-flat Sonata, D. 960, collaborations with Szell and Cleveland on the concertos of Beethoven and Brahms—have long been highly sought-after collector's items. (Some of these have been reissued on compact disc and cassette on the Sony Classical label.)

Fleisher credits an increasingly popular technique called Rolfing—a form of tissue manipulation discovered in 1940 by a biochemist named Ida Rolf—for his partial recovery. He compares it to a "massage in slow motion." "The therapist searches out points of contraction in the muscle and then applies pressure in such a way as to stretch out the fibers. If the muscle is healthy, there should be no pain; if there is pain, something is wrong. When you resist, you tighten up, but once you give in, the pain will likely resolve itself and disappear."

It was an excited and somewhat apprehensive audience, filled with music lovers of all stripes, that greeted Fleisher at Carnegie Hall Saturday for his appearance with the Orchestra of St. Luke's, under the direction of André Previn. Before the show, Fleisher had acknowledged some anxiety about the visibility of this particular platform: "From the wings to the piano at Carnegie Hall is the longest walk in the world," he said.

Still, 52 years after his Carnegie debut and almost four decades since he last played there unimpaired, Fleisher made the "long walk" briskly, acknowledged the applause with professional calm, and took his place at the house Steinway. He sat with his back to the audience, concentrating intently as Previn lifted his baton and began the concerto. And then, after one of those lithe, immaculate Mozartean orchestral introductions that are, paradoxically, both propulsive and serene, Fleisher began to play.

The listener was immediately impressed by the pearly beauty of Fleisher's sound—as gentle as it was firm, ruminative and intensely poetic yet without any smearing of the melodic line. I would like to be able to report that the legendary right hand is just as good as new. It isn't, but such is the skill with which Fleisher uses it that one was perfectly willing to suspend disbelief. Indeed, I would rather listen to Fleisher, even in his current, delicate shape, than to most other pianists now before the public.

What Fleisher seems to have done is to find a way of working *around* his disability. He has not necessarily conquered; rather, he has adapted. He now uses his right shoulder more than is customary; there is some residual stiffness in his right arm; and he leans deeply into the keyboard as he plays, raising his wrist in a manner that would shock some orthodox piano teachers. Then again, it might be argued that orthodox training got Fleisher into this mess in the first place; the old joke about the kid asking a policeman how to get to Carnegie Hall (answer: practice, practice, practice) takes on a bitter irony in this case.

The Mozart Piano Concerto in A does not make the physical demands that, say, a concerto by Rachmaninoff does; the pianist does not have to produce any sheer quantity of piano tone. And yet the economy of means, the clarity and deceptive simplicity of Mozart's writing, presents difficulties of its own. If Fleisher experienced some technical challenges on Saturday, he met Mozart's musical challenges splendidly. And those, finally, are the great test.

"I could have wished the performance to have been better than it was," Fleisher said yesterday. "The pressures of the occasion were a little rough on me. But I went to the piano the next day and I wasn't harmed by the concert. Indeed, I played better than I had the night before. And since then, I've had my first rehearsal of the Brahms quartet and it went very well. Everything is definitely on an upward curve."

Fleisher says he hopes to achieve a "gradual, progressive increase in my repertory." "I plan to play the Brahms D Minor Concerto with Michael Tilson Thomas and the San Francisco Symphony in September and then the Brahms B-flat Major Concerto with Daniel Barenboim in 1997," he said. "There's been some discussion of a Beethoven G Major Concerto with Claudio Abbado and Berlin. We'll see how it goes."

In the meantime, Fleisher will continue his teaching, continue playing the left-handed repertory, continue conducting—and practice carefully and sparingly.

"We all wanted to be so strong, and it was all a terrible mistake. We all wanted to be like Vladimir Horowitz, to have the killer technique. And we harmed ourselves enormously in the process. I think Gary [Graffman] suffered from repetitive stress. Byron [Janis] had some shoulder complications, as I understand it, but it wouldn't surprise me if there was an element of repetitive stress there."

The late Canadian pianist Glenn Gould was often criticized as eccentric for his insistence upon running his arms under hot and cold water immediately after practicing and before concerts. "Glenn Gould was utterly *brilliant* in that regard," Fleisher said. "He figured it all out. That's exactly what we should have all been doing—anything to bring that circulation back, anything to loosen the tension. But who knew?"

The Washington Post
19 January 1996

Glenn Gould in Retrospect

I have written so much about Glenn Gould that I fear the work is becoming redundant. Thus I accepted this assignment from Fi Magazine *in 1995 with considerable apprehension. Yet I was surprised by what was for me a fresh understanding that only became apparent once I revisited and then sat down to write.*

We are scattered now, the friends of the late Mr. Oliver Offord; but whenever we chance to meet I think we are conscious of a certain esoteric respect for each other. "Yes, you too have been in Arcadia," we seem not too grumpily to allow.

So BEGINS "Brooksmith," one of Henry James's most tender stories, and these lines always come to mind when I run into any of the several people I know who were also acquainted with Glenn Gould. Even while Gould was alive, we knew we were a charmed circle, that we were enormously lucky to be associated with this gentle, funny, brilliant man. Our hours with him seem only the more precious (and curiously mythic) as the years wear on. And we know that, no matter what we do with the rest of our lives, young scholars will always be searching us out with the hope of summoning just one more unpublished anecdote, one more insight into Glenn Gould. Not that we mind such visits. On the contrary, an occasional conversation about Gould brings him fitfully back to life—particularly when the interrogator is sportive, animated, and truly prepared—and we only wish we had more to offer.

Last year, an earnest, well-meaning, but excruciatingly artsy-craftsy movie *cum* meditation entitled *32 Short Films About Glenn Gould* won its subject a new group of admirers. Almost everyone I've spoken to likes this film—everybody, that is, but the people who actually knew Gould. For us, the film was so damnably solemn and reverential, so nuanced and portentous, that it was impossible to escape an occasional, flashing memory of Gould's delighted, childlike, self-deprecating laughter—the laughter with which I suspect he would have greeted all latter-day attempts to portray him as Saint Glenn. On a personal level, Glenn Gould was, above everything, an awful lot of fun; if there were some way to cross the *32 Short Films* with something silly and inspired such as one of the *Airplane!* movies, we might be getting someplace.

Indeed, with the exception of his recordings, more of which are available now than ever before, Gould has not been particularly well served by his chroniclers. He has been the subject of a weird novel by Thomas Bernhard; his meticulously structured film work has been diced up like hash for reissue on videotape; and there has yet to be a satisfactory biography.

It doesn't matter; Gould remains among the most influential musicians of the 20th century and one may wonder why he continues to exert such a fascination. There are a few possible answers. First and foremost, at the risk of belaboring the obvious, it is because he was a very great musician. By "great," I mean that Gould was able to find new depths—and sometimes entirely new *surfaces*—in thrice-familiar masterworks. He knew no technical difficulties (has anybody ever possessed 10 fingers with 10 such independent lives of their own?) but more important was his ability to make a profound connection with the people who listen to him or—after 1964, when he retired from concert playing—to his various electronic manifestations. Whether one "liked" everything Gould did was ultimately a matter of small importance. He was simply *there*, impossible to ignore—even though, paradoxically, he spent so much time carefully hidden from the public eye.

Secondly, Gould was, in a word, entertaining. I don't necessarily mean funny—although, as mentioned above, he was capable of tremendous humor. But he was entertaining on a deeper, more substantial, level. There has been much recent discussion of the division between art and entertainment and I, for one, don't buy the distinction, for any art that does not entertain us on some level is bound for the scrap heap. Samuel Johnson, that greatest of all critics, once said that the first duty of a book was to make us want to read it through, and the statement, appropriately amended, applies to all the arts. If something does not, on some level, seduce us—*entertain* us—it will not hold our attention for very long.

Gould entertained, and on many different levels. He was an ecstatic showman—indeed, Leonard Bernstein is the only other musician I can think of who so reflected what he was actually *feeling* about the work he was performing, in a manner that sometimes approached choreography. And yet divorced from the visual ballet, the best performances of Gould and Bernstein both *sound*. They can stand alone without a visual complement.

Finally, Gould was somebody who made his own world—the truly civilized, educated man who put together his own unconventional manner of living with the means available to him—a hero for an age that is, rightly, suspicious of heroes. It took time, but Gould came to terms with his genius, with the demands it made upon him, and adapted. As Geoffrey Payzant, whose book *Glenn Gould: Music and Mind* remains the finest single volume on Glenn, put it: "Glenn Gould is an exceedingly superior person, friendly and considerate. He is not really an eccentric, nor is he egocentric. Glenn Gould is a person who has found out how he wants to live his life and is doing precisely that."

But Gould was not one of these modernists who are compelled to deliberately break all the rules (therefore remaining forever and inextricably bound to them, if only through reaction). Rather, he was smart enough to adapt the rules to suit his purposes—either that, or to simply ignore the zeitgeist altogether. In one of our last interviews he said something that has always struck me as indicative of his whole philosophy:

> One of the things I find most moving about the final Contrapunctus in *The Art of Fugue* is that Bach was writing this music against every possible tendency of the time. He had renounced the kinds of modulatory patterns he himself had used successfully six or seven years earlier in the "Goldberg" Variations and in Book II of *The Well-Tempered Clavier* and was writing in a lighter, less clearly defined early baroque–late Renaissance manner. It was as though he was saying to the world, I don't care anymore. There are no more "Italian" Concertos in me. This is what I'm about.

And yet it will not do to present Gould as somebody cut off from his time. His love for technology ensured that. I think he would have greatly enjoyed many of the "gadgets" that have become part of our culture in the years since his death. The compact disc he knew, very slightly, and he was delighted with it; he had a number of VCRs in his studio at Toronto's Inn on the Park. I think Glenn would have loved the fax machine, the home computer, even the process of musical sampling—although I don't think he'd be very impressed by what has been done with it so far.

Too much has been made of Glenn's eccentricity. One classic example was the way the press picked up on the idea that Gould would soak his hands in hot and cold water before playing. Every early magazine profile refers to this "quirk" as just one more example of the thin line between genius and madness, or something like that. But now remember what happened to not one but several important pianists who came of age during the 1950s—they eventually lost the use of one or both of their hands through what now sounds suspiciously like overwork. Many newspapers have now had outbreaks of RSI—repetitive strain injury, of which Carpal Tunnel Syndrome is one manifestation—from overuse of the computer keyboard; in some newsrooms, people wander around in splints. And what is one of the very best ways to fend off RSI? You guessed it—soaking the hands in hot and cold running water.

What are the best Gould recordings? The Bach discs, of course—both of the commercial "Goldberg" Variations (1955 and 1981) and, for the obsessed, the 1954 and 1958 live performances, too. The *Overture in the French Style*. The concertos. *The Well-Tempered Clavier*, even though it was recorded during Gould's most willful and, if you like, eccentric period.

Some less obvious choices: the recording of the Brahms intermezzos from 1960, proof that Gould could play romantic music idiomatically and with extraordinary feeling. The disc devoted to works by William Byrd and Orlando Gibbons (Gould often said Gibbons was the composer to whom he felt the closest). The Mozart Concerto in C Minor (K. 491) with Walter Susskind—far and away his finest Mozart performance. An early album of the Beethoven Second Piano Concerto—Gould's favorite of the five—with Leonard Bernstein. His sole venture into recorded conducting—Wagner's *Siegfried Idyll*, probably the slowest performance in history and a reading of melting and surpassing tenderness.

On private recordings, one may find the famous Brahms D Minor Concerto with the New York Philharmonic at Carnegie Hall, complete with Bernstein's bemused disclaimer before the performance. (Bernstein's later recording with Krystian Zimerman is actually several minutes *longer* than the interpretation he disputed in 1962.) And there is an almost shockingly intense performance of the Bach Cantata No. 54, *Widerstehe doch der Sünde*, that he led from the keyboard with the countertenor Russell Oberlin that is currently available among the videotapes but deserves a compact disc of its own.

The Sony release of Gould's videotapes is problematic, to say the least. Why couldn't we have had Gould's own programs, on which he labored with such care, instead of the flashy mash, with soppy connective narration, presented here? To give just one example, I would have much preferred to have Gould's complete 1966 conversations with Humphrey Burton, probably his best films, in one piece instead of the tantalizing soundbites Sony scattered across several videotapes. I suppose we will have to wait for a scholarly edition.

Finally, to the printed word. I have collected Gould's own writings in *The Glenn Gould Reader* (1984). The Payzant book, by far the best book *about* Gould, is not a biography but rather a study of his thought. John McGreevy's coffeetable volume, *Glenn Gould: Variations*, has some good pictures and some articles that are not collected elsewhere but it is finally pretty insubstantial. That leaves two biographical portraits—Otto Friedrich's ambitious *Glenn Gould: A Life and Variations* and Andrew Kazdin's vengeful *Glenn Gould at Work: Creative Lying*.

Friedrich, who was a staff writer for *Time* Magazine, never knew Gould—his biography was assembled from documents and interviews and it is all strangely remote. In Kazdin's book, on the other hand, we have the clear sense of one man telling us about another. We may disagree with Kazdin's conclusions (I certainly do) but there is never any doubt that he knows of whom he speaks.

Kazdin became Gould's record producer in 1964; some 15 years later, Gould unceremoniously dropped him, as both friend and colleague. Still, once one has discounted for a good deal of bitterness, this is the better book. The Gould who emerges from Kazdin's assessment is driven, neurotic, laden with quirks and contradictions. But he is also, for the first time in the Gould literature, a fully developed human being and hence much more interesting than his sanctified legend.

Someday, one hopes, there will be a sympathetic biography that captures Gould in all of his complications. I do not envy that biographer: Gould was paradoxical in the extreme and almost any statement you make about him can be contradicted with an equally valid statement. He was an obsessed perfectionist who took an almost Cagean laissez-faire attitude toward inter-pretation (I'm thinking now of the disembodied "what if?" approach he took toward recording some of the Mozart sonatas). He made some of the best recordings of our time and few of the worst. He lived a life of monklike aus-terity, yet he was one of the jolliest and most spontaneous telephone com-panions imaginable and extraordinarily courteous in person. He was a pro-found individualist who prized rectitude and puritanical moral values, yet he considered himself a socialist and was, in my experience, rather skeptical of religious dogma. He lived in Canada all his life, and loved it, but he despised Canadian nationalism. He loathed ostentatious romantic effusion, yet his favorite 20th-century composer was Richard Strauss. He was reclusive and retiring, yet he wanted to be heard, be seen, be felt everywhere. He is dead al-most 14 years, and yet he is, somehow, with us today, more vital to our musi-cal life than he was when he was alive. We'll be a long time figuring him out; in the meantime, we can listen—and be grateful.

Fi Magazine
November 1995

Jascha Heifetz

SOME 10 YEARS ago, I set out to write the first full biography of Jascha Heifetz. The violinist was then still living—in a grand, gated mansion, toward the top of Beverly Hills—but despite intercession on my behalf from several mutual acquaintances, Heifetz refused to cooperate in any way. He had never much cared for publicity; in 1939 he summed up his life for Deems Taylor: "Born in Russia, first lessons at three, debut in Russia at seven, debut in America in 1917. That's all there is to say, really. About two lines."

Over the next months, however, I conducted almost 20 hours of taped interviews with those who had known Heifetz throughout his life. Mistaking quantity for quality, I thought I was making progress until the evening I played through part of my archive. And then I realized that I had absolutely nothing on which to build a book—only a vague portrait of a rigidly formal, exceedingly isolated, and not especially pleasant man who happened to play the violin with a technique that knew no difficulties and an idiosyncratic and affecting warmth that transcended the patrician authority of his approach.

Apparently, there were few *events* in the Heifetz story: he came, he played, he conquered, again and again—and then he went home. Friendships were uncommon and circumscribed, brought to an end, more often than not, by petty quarrels; there were two marriages, followed by two divorces. One is tempted to say that Heifetz ended up a lonely man, but since there is no evidence that he knew, believed, or even suspected this was the case, all one can do is affirm that most of us would have been very lonely under similar circumstances.

To date, there has not been a reliable life of Heifetz. And so *The Heifetz*

Collection, a vast trove of 65 compact discs (arranged into 46 self-sufficient volumes) issued earlier this year by BMG Classics, may prove the best "biography" of the violinist for many years to come. Certainly it captures everything that was most interesting and attractive about Jascha Heifetz. He had one of the longest recording careers in history—more than 60 years, a span rivaled only by Mischa Elman, Vladimir Horowitz, Yehudi Menuhin, Claudio Arrau, Leopold Stokowski, and the Australian baritone Peter Dawson (some other musicians will be joining this club very soon). And now, with one small but significant omission, the entire discography is available to us, in digitally remastered sound, with program notes that are engaging as well as specific.

String players and aficionados with the means (approximately $600) will doubtless have purchased the entire set by this point. It is by any standard a worthwhile investment—the listener will be rewarded by close to 100 hours of superlative violin playing—but it is also curiously *static*. There is a natural human temptation to funnel facts into tidy narrative, to chart "growth" in our artists over time, but Heifetz was not a markedly better violinist in 1972 than he was in 1917. He seems to have sprung to life fully formed—male-child Minerva with a fiddle—and, if anything, in some of the later Heifetz albums, one has the sense of a perfection that is rapidly tiring of itself.

Still, it is this very technical perfection that made Heifetz so important. One may question his interpretations—indeed, one may actively dislike them—but on a purely objective level, it doesn't matter very much. We live in a century that has placed enormous value on the ability to "prove" merit—remember those 12-tone compositions that were inseparable from their analyses? the art works that came ready-made with theoretical justification?—and Heifetz can be *proven*. Whether or not we like what he does with his violin, there can be no denying that he elevated performance standards to a new level of exactitude. After Heifetz, a slurred phrase was no longer accepted as a soulful indulgence; it was only a slurred phrase. He showed just what could be done with a violin; if Heifetz is partially to blame for the mechanical, metronomic violinists of today—those aging *Wunderkinder* who skate flawlessly and meaninglessly through everything that is put in front of them—the fact remains that he was a genuine Olympian, however austere.

Almost all of Heifetz's recordings were made for what was initially the Victor Talking Machine Company, was then RCA Victor, then RCA Red Seal, and has now been transmogrified into a division of BMG Classics. The exceptions are some fine performances for EMI in the 1930s, a handful of charming smaller pieces for Decca in 1945, and the live recording of Heifetz's 1972 farewell recital in Los Angeles that was issued on Columbia Masterworks. All these have been incorporated into *The Heifetz Collection*; the only known omission among Heifetz's published recordings is a remarkable Russian 1911 disc that turned up in the mid-1980s and for which BMG was unable to secure the rights. (A London-based magazine called *The Strad* issued portions of this precious souvenir on a plastic disc inserted in the pages of its February 1986 issue; suffice it to say that Heifetz was already recognizably Heifetz before he reached puberty.)

Those who don't care for Heifetz's work sometimes dismiss him as a great encore player. Such an estimation is unfairly reductive, but he really *was* an absolute master of the violin miniature. And because the one-sided 78-rpm record could only contain roughly four and a half minutes of music, most of Heifetz's first recordings were devoted to encore pieces.

How well our grandparents knew the music Heifetz recorded between 1917 and 1925, in his teens and early 20s, at the old Victor studios in Camden, New Jersey! Here they are—transcriptions of Schubert's "Ave Maria," Schumann's "Widmung," Mendelssohn's "On Wings of Song," and Chopin nocturnes, fragments from concertos by Tchaikovsky and Mendelssohn, showpieces by Paganini, Wieniawski, Sarasate, and others. The playing is gripping, original, and fully mature. Perhaps Heifetz lacked the intellectual probity of Szigeti, the glowing and gigantic (if sometimes rather glutinous) tone of Elman, and the sheer "olde world" charm of Kreisler. But he made up for these liabilities with performances of unparalleled technical accuracy (no tape splicing in those days), a sure sense of structure (each recording has its own Platonic perfection, with carefully delineated beginning, middle, and end), and what can only be described as the genesis of a modernist aesthetic. There is sentiment in abundance but little sentimentality; while Heifetz does not banish *portamento* altogether, he uses it sparingly and he will not descend to histrionic manipulation. "When [Bruno] Walter comes to something beautiful, he melts," Toscanini once said, in a moment of exasperation. Heifetz never melts, but I can't imagine many 1990s listeners finding these records chilly. The passion is subtle, the artistic personality unusually self-effacing for its era. But both are present.

Throughout much of this century, we have placed an emphasis on what might be called all-purpose musicians; just recently has it become acceptable—indeed, outright fashionable—to specialize (note the careers of such current performers as John Eliot Gardiner and the Kronos Quartet). Heifetz, in common with other early "superstars" such as Toscanini and Horowitz, was not only expected to play *everything* but to play everything equally well —the baroque and classical repertories, the romantic sonatas and concertos, a cautious smattering of contemporary music. In retrospect, through recordings, strengths and weaknesses have become apparent. It used to be heresy to suggest that Toscanini was generally a more convincing interpreter of Rossini and Verdi than he was of Beethoven and Brahms, but for many of us, when we judge from the recorded evidence, such is our conclusion. Likewise, I can affirm that the scores in which Heifetz is the most consistently reliable are those by what Virgil Thomson used to call "cold-climate composers," including music from Heifetz's native Russia.

For example, Heifetz recorded the Tchaikovsky concerto three separate times—in 1937 with the London Philharmonic under Barbirolli, in 1950 with the Philharmonia under Walter Susskind, and finally in 1957 with the Chicago Symphony under Reiner. All of these performances have their excellences; the last boasts vivid recorded sound and the most virtuosic combination of orchestra and conductor (although I continue to find Heifetz's earliest reading of the solo part more dazzling and intrinsically poetic). Still, you can't go wrong with any of them; this is rich, haunting, melodic music, imbued with a gypsy warmth made all the more potent by Heifetz's refusal to milk it beyond its proper boundaries.

The Heifetz Collection contains two chimerical renditions of the Glazunov Violin Concerto in A Minor; only Michael Rabin, on EMI, is more moving, infusing the pyrotechnics with an ethereal sweetness (the disintegration and premature death of this violinist was nothing less than an artistic calamity). Heifetz's first recording of the Sibelius concerto, with Sir Thomas Beecham and the London Philharmonic Orchestra—appropriately cool and sometimes stern, yet always deeply felt and even seductive—has long been the standard by which other performances were judged and found wanting. (I would place Heifetz's 1959 interpretation, with the Chicago Orchestra and Walter Hendl, among the preterite.) There are two recordings of Prokofiev's Violin Concerto No. 2, both with the Boston Symphony (Koussevitzky's conducting is rather more idiomatic than Munch's, although the sound is pallid by comparison). And there are numerous encore pieces—vignettes by Shostakovich, Khachaturian, Rachmaninoff, Glazunov, and Tchaikovsky, exciting and nostalgic by turn, inevitably given their full due.

Heifetz is also consistently top-drawer in what might be described as capital-V "Violin Music"—the works of Wieniawski, Vieuxtemps, Sarasate, Kreisler, and Paganini. Not all these pieces are necessarily capital-A Art, but they provide heroic challenges for a violinist. Heifetz's command of his instrument is virtually flawless, of course, but he is not satisfied with mere athleticism. He never forgets that this is *music*, after all, and he plays it with neither undue grandiloquence nor flashy "Look at Me!" condescension. Pity the listener with heart so hard that the Bruch violin concertos and "Scottish Fantasy" no longer stir a misty tenderness.

Heifetz's Bach was controversial, even before the early music movement had established its strictures. The 1946 recording of the Concerto for Two Violins is a stunt—Heifetz plays both solo parts—and not a very successful one; the piece profits from two distinct personalities weaving around each other, in surprise and symbiosis. (A later reading, with Erick Friedman, one of Heifetz's rare students, is also less than persuasive.) Heifetz recorded all the solo sonatas and partitas in 1952; the performances are fast, strenuous, bristling with nervous energy, and to this taste, rather brutal. He places an emphasis on attacks and contrasts, to the detriment of line and continuity.

Some Bach performances from 1935 are more musical. Indeed, as a rule of thumb, when one has a choice between two competing Heifetz recordings of a given work, it is likely that the first version will be preferable. A case in point is the Mozart Concerto No. 5 in A (K. 219). Heifetz recorded this three times; in 1935, 1951, and 1963. The later performances have their strengths (and some of the weaknesses we find in the 1952 Bach solo pieces) but the 1935 recording (with Barbirolli) is sublime, from the unaccompanied, triadic entrance of the violin, so pure and serene that it seems to emanate from another plane of understanding—"above the battle," in Romain Rolland's phrase—through the cheerfully industrious reiterations of the concluding rondo. The central movement is particularly beautiful—long-breathed and exquisitely nuanced, with a grace and gentle stillness strangely enhanced by the burnished antiquity of the recorded sound.

It is unfortunate that Heifetz's only recording of Mozart's Divertimento in E-flat (K. 563) should have been made with the constrictions of the 78-rpm disc so obviously in mind. The performance—by Heifetz, William Primrose, and Emanuel Feuermann—is artful and lively (even though the tempos will sound stressed to latter-day listeners) but this is music that takes time to unfold, and the neglect of Mozart's indicated repeats diminishes it. Put another way, we need more than 33 minutes for this particular piece.

Heifetz was an uneven collaborator. The late series of Heifetz-Piatigorsky chamber concerts (with admirable musicians such as Primrose, Jacob Lateiner, and Leonard Pennario) are some of his worst records. A sense of hurry prevails, the Heifetz tone all too often takes on a wiry astringency, and on some occasions the playing is downright sloppy (a ghastly violin-cello arrangement of the Stravinsky *Suite Italienne* should never have been released). The 1961 performance of the Schubert Cello Quintet (D. 956) sounds uncomfortably like a disappointed violin concerto, as does a Mendelssohn octet dating from the same year. Heifetz's influence on his fellow musicians was sometimes baleful; Primrose made a spacious, elegant, and altogether cherishable recording of the Mozart Sinfonia Concertante (K. 364) with the American violinist Albert Spalding, but when he came to record this work with Heifetz, his playing was distinctly *agitato* (as was Heifetz's own) and the result might be described as "Dueling Fiddles."

Yet there are some marvelous collaborations in the Heifetz discography. I am especially fond of the Brahms Sonata in D Minor (Op. 108) that he recorded with the brilliant young American pianist William Kapell—two fiery temperaments in full force, relentlessly goading each other on, yet somehow maintaining a unified lyricism. (Heifetz and Kapell had planned to record all three Brahms sonatas; after Kapell was killed in a 1953 plane crash, the violinist lost interest in the project, and so Heifetz's way with Op. 78 and Op. 100 can only be imagined.) The piano-violin-cello trio recordings with Arthur Rubinstein and Emanuel Feuermann (and, after Feuermann's death, with Gregor Piatigorsky)—Beethoven, Brahms, Ravel, Mendelssohn, Tchaikovsky—are empathic, honey-toned, and justly famous. If some of these "Million Dollar Trio" recordings are now period pieces—and they are definitely of their time and place—that period now seems a golden age, one that we may only look back upon with affection and wonder.

In general, Heifetz's recordings of Beethoven's 10 sonatas for violin and piano are fleet, furious, charged with dramatic tension—"shot from guns" as the old advertising slogan might have had it. This manner is most effective in the later sonatas, with their inherent *Sturm und Drang*; I prefer a more genial, expansive, playful approach to early Beethoven, whose sense of humor has long been undervalued. Mention should be made of Heifetz's two principal accompanists, Emanuel Bay and the long-suffering Brooks Smith; the latter was a superb partner—necessarily deferential (throughout their 20-year association Heifetz never permitted Smith to call him by his first name) but always musical, always precisely *there.*

In this century, very few of our most celebrated performers have done much for the music of their time; the obvious exceptions—Koussevitzky, Stokowski, Rostropovich, Pollini—merely prove the rule. It was left to a young unknown named Louis Krasner to bring us the violin concertos of Alban Berg and Arnold Schoenberg, to Albert Spalding to commission (but not play) the Roger Sessions concerto and to play the first performance of the Samuel Barber concerto.

Still, several concertos were fashioned for, then played and recorded by, Heifetz—pieces by Mario Castelnuovo-Tedesco, Louis Gruenberg, Erich Wolfgang Korngold, Miklós Rózsa, and William Walton. The last of these is probably the best of the bunch (and it is the only one to have entered the repertory), although the Korngold and the Rózsa have a sumptuous "Hapsburg in Hollywood" majesty, and Heifetz's recording of the Gruenberg is rightly prized as an extraordinary example of violin velocity. Heifetz never recorded anything by Berg, Schoenberg, Webern, or Bartók; he played only minor works by Shostakovich, Milhaud, and Stravinsky; he may have been entirely unaware of the music of a newer generation of modernists. He did well by Ernest Bloch, however—wailing, rhapsodic performances of the two violin-piano sonatas—and he made one album of sonatas by Howard Ferguson and Karen Khachaturian (Aram's nephew) with his University of Southern California colleague Lillian Steuber.

The 46th and final box in *The Heifetz Collection* deserves some special attention, for it was not only the violinist's last recording but his last public performance anywhere (October 23, 1972). The entire recital, a benefit for USC, was preserved, something that would have been unthinkable in 1917. Aside from that, the program—both its planning and its execution—was not markedly different from one Heifetz might have offered decades before.

From the beginning of the Franck sonata—rapt, centered, directly linear in its phrasing, immaculately aristocratic in its bearing—there can be no mistaking the artist. The Richard Strauss sonata, a product of the composer's 16th year, follows immediately, and Heifetz brings pride and surging power to this brash youthful declaration of genius. Alfred Frankenstein, who was covering the concert for *The New York Times*, thought three movements of the Bach E Major Partita were "absolutely perfect"—and so they were, from Heifetz's subjective standpoint; certainly he does exactly what he wants to do with them, and purists be damned. And, finally, there are the encores, including Debussy's "La plus que lente" (which Heifetz had first recorded back in 1925), some Bloch, Kreisler, Rachmaninoff, Ravel.

The same old stuff? Perhaps. But there is something noble about Heifetz's constancy. He knew what he wanted and he spoke his piece; if it was essentially the same piece at 72 that it was at 17, so be it. Few performing artists have exercised such meticulous control over their creative lives, in such a tumultuous era. (One wonders, sadly, whether a "new" Jascha Heifetz would be recognized by the record companies—would he be deemed hip enough? would he have the right hairdo? would he have "attitude"?) In any event, eight years after his death, Heifetz's life story can still be told in something like the "two lines" he gave to Deems Taylor. But *The Heifetz Collection* speaks volumes.

The New Criterion
September 1995

Philippe Herreweghe

T HE EARLY MUSIC movement has finally produced a choral conductor whose best interpretations can stand with the complex and majestic statements of such men as Willem Mengelberg, Otto Klemperer, and Karl Richter.

This conductor is named Philippe Herreweghe, and he has been slowly amassing a library of recordings on the Harmonia Mundi label—the *German Requiem* by Johannes Brahms, the respective requiems of Mozart and Gabriel Fauré, Bach's Mass in B Minor and *Saint Matthew Passion*, Beethoven's *Missa Solemnis*, much of the choral music of Felix Mendelssohn and others. All of these may be recommended; some of them are revelatory.

Let's start with Herreweghe's recording of the *German Requiem*. This is one of those works that affect listeners strongly, either one way or another. The playwright and sometime music critic George Bernard Shaw was a famous detractor; he deigned to acknowledge Brahms's craftsmanship, only to insist that the piece must have come from the workshop of a "first-class undertaker." Many other listeners have agreed with Shaw—for them, the *German Requiem* is too heavy, too reiterative, too unrelievedly gloomy.

I happen to love the piece. Indeed, the *German Requiem* seems to me a highly appropriate response to the death of a dear one. Solemn, stoical, and unflinchingly to the point, it concentrates on our wrenching grief and loss, yet allows for an occasional nostalgic sweetness (especially in the fourth and fifth movements) to remind us that there were some happy times, too.

The *German Requiem* is customarily presented with a huge orchestra and chorus; such performances impress with their sheer mass and density. Yet

Herreweghe has somehow managed to realize a *German Requiem* with qualities of a different sort—textural clarity, contrapuntal singing that harkens back to the simple perfection of chant, and a welling tenderness in every phrase.

This is partially the result of the relatively small ensemble Herreweghe employs—only about 60 orchestral players and a chorus of 48. Yet the climactic passages never seem vitiated and the performance is exciting throughout. And if Herreweghe's tempos are mostly more-or-less standard ones, there is not a measure in his performance that seems perfunctory or received. Moreover, he had the wisdom to choose two young, fresh singers—soprano Christiane Oelze and baritone Gerald Finley—for the solo passages.

Yet it is Herreweghe himself, with his fathomless understanding of the score, who persuades. Somehow, he manages to combine Brahms's Teutonic grandeur with the grace and intimacy more usually associated with a composer like Fauré. "My origins were in choral music, in early music, which is almost exclusively religious," he once told an interviewer. "The music I love most is music that confronts the soul with the reality of the world." For those listeners who think they don't like the *German Requiem*, this is the recording that may change their minds. The rest of us will simply marvel at the new dimensions Herreweghe has uncovered.

Born in Belgium in 1947, Herreweghe attended the Ghent Conservatory as a boy, where he studied piano and developed an early fascination with Renaissance and baroque music. In 1970 he founded his first vocal ensemble, the Collegium Vocale, with which he still records. By 1977 Herreweghe was based in Paris, where he founded La Chapelle Royale, a small chorus and orchestra devoted mostly to baroque music; in 1991 he formed the Orchestre des Champs-Élysées, a somewhat larger group with which he has moved increasingly into the romantic and early modern repertory. And with other organizations he has now recorded works by Bruckner, Mahler, Schoenberg, even Kurt Weill.

Herreweghe's first discs—all devoted to early music—have some of the didactic wispiness that characterized so many recordings from the formative years of the early music revival. And so, fine as it often is, the conductor's mid-1980s performance of Bach's *Saint Matthew Passion* (three discs) impresses this listener as rather too careful. Tempos are generally quick and strict and Herreweghe seems positively determined to avoid romantic "sentimentality" at any cost. The soloists include soprano Barbara Schlick, the splendid baritone Hans-Peter Blochwitz, and the alto René Jacobs, who has since turned into a distinguished early music conductor himself, but who always struck me as a prim and mannered vocalist. Ultimately, one too often feels that Herreweghe has set out to prove a theory about what baroque music should sound like, in drastic flight from traditional conceptions of the score—an odd sort of reactionary radicalism.

In Herreweghe's later performances, what once seemed scholarly wispiness has turned into a profound and appreciative gentility. A new performance of the Mass in B Minor (two discs) with the Collegium Vocale Chorus and Orchestra, pays appropriate attention to baroque style and dance rhythms, yet seems downright improvisatory compared to the *Saint Matthew Passion* of a dozen years back. Herreweghe is now confident enough to permit a much greater degree of interpretive emotion—or, to borrow a phrase from the bebop era, he now knows how to "wing it." The soloists—Johannette Zomer, Veronique Gens, Andreas Scholl, Christoph Pregardien, Peter Kooy, and Hanno Müller-Brachmann—are uncommonly well-matched, and the performance skillfully combines lightness and gravity. If I still prefer the exultant old Richter recording on Archiv, well, perhaps that is, as they say, a generational thing. But Herreweghe's Mass in B Minor has a great deal in its favor.

Even better is Beethoven's *Missa Solemnis* from 1995. This is wild and mercurial music to begin with (does anybody really understand what Beethoven was doing here—and does anybody doubt that what seems willful strangeness is in fact a sublimity that still eludes our full understanding?). Herreweghe's tempos are quite broad—he takes the opening Kyrie at an especially slow pace—but the performance is charged with a dramatic unity that is rarely sustained through this particular piece.

Once again, the soloists seem unusually well-mated—soprano Rosa Mannion, alto Birgit Remmert, tenor James Taylor, and bass Cornelius Hauptmann—even in a score that demands them to sing both high and loud for most of the time. Yet how clean and temperate Alessando Maccia's violin solo in the Benedictus sounds; how thrilling the fervent shouts of "Gloria!" And if Herreweghe brings a different sort of otherworldliness to the *Missa* than, say, Toscanini and Klemperer did, it is otherworldly all the same.

Felix Mendelssohn was the most serene and temperate of the early romantic composers, and Herreweghe is exceedingly well attuned to his creative aesthetic. He has recorded both of the large oratorios, *Elijah* and *Paulus*, teaming together all three of his ensembles—Collegium Vocale, La Chapelle Royale, and the Orchestre des Champs-Élysées. Both recordings are sympathetic and highly musical; this is romanticism with a decided classical mien, always proportionate.

But Herreweghe's best Mendelssohn recording to date may be the one devoted to the choral Psalms and the "Ave Maria." The music is calm and lovely, and the performances are imbued with a glowing inner radiance. How maligned Mendelssohn has been—all those comments about how he was "born a genius and died a talent"—simply because he dared to look backward in his music, rather than forward to the subjective brave new world of the romantics.

Indeed, such is Herreweghe's sense of classical form that he even managed to convince me that F. X. Süssmayr's "completion" of the last movements of Mozart's Requiem has a certain musical integrity. I've always disliked these movements and have been heartened by recent recordings and performances that ignore them altogether. And yet, through a quick tempo and steady, understated dynamic range, Herreweghe even manages to make the embryonic Sanctus (far and away the weakest of the Mozart-Süssmayr movements) fairly convincing. The rest of the recording is likewise excellent—a little reserved but all the more moving for it.

After hearing Herreweghe's recording of the Brahms Requiem, I yearned immediately to hear what he might do with Fauré's gentle masterpiece in the same vein. Not surprisingly, his rendition is thoughtful, introspective, and deeply touching, created with the Chorus of the Chapelle Royale, the Children's Choir of Saint-Louis, the Ensemble Musique Oblique, and soloists Agnes Mellon and Peter Kooy.

Once again, the orchestra is a small one but the range of tone and feeling Herreweghe illuminates on the small canvas is astonishingly rich. The timpani sound like distant thunder, much too far away to do anybody harm; the solo violin in the Sanctus is sweetly citric; the boys' choir is little short of seraphic. With the possible exception of the classic rendition by Nadia Boulanger (who was, in addition to her other accomplishments, a Fauré student), I don't think I've ever heard a performance so in keeping with the muted, graceful sadness of this music.

Herreweghe is now 50, only beginning to reach toward his full maturity. One will observe his progress with intense interest, but he has already given us some of the most haunting and effective choral recordings of our time.

The Washington Post
19 April 1998

Michael Hersch

As this book is published, Michael Hersch is barely 30 years old. He is a composer of spectacular gifts, and it is heartening to see him continue to receive the acclaim he deserves.

MICHAEL HERSCH seems excruciatingly shy as he fumbles a cassette of one of his latest compositions into the player, after which he stands still as a statue, with his back to his listeners, watching the tape spin around for the entire 15-minute duration of the piece. But if this 27-year-old composer is reticent, his music is anything but.

In the past few years, Hersch, who was born in Washington and raised in Reston, Virginia, has inspired remarkable—and sometimes ecstatic—excitement in the world of classical music. "There is no doubt in my mind that this extraordinary creator, who already has his own special voice, will be a major force," composer John Corigliano wrote recently. Another esteemed composer, George Rochberg, has called Hersch a "rare and unique talent," gifted with an innate understanding of the "dark places of the human heart."

Ricardo Cyncynates, the assistant concertmaster of the National Symphony Orchestra, nominates Hersch as "by far the most impressive composer that I have had the opportunity of meeting" (the reader should bear in mind that orchestral musicians meet a lot of composers). And John Henry Carton, the chairman of the music faculty at Baltimore's Peabody Conservatory, declared Hersch's work simply "brilliant." "Creation of music such as this would be astonishing for one of any age," he said. "Never before have I had the notion that a young Beethoven was showing me his future."

This is all pretty heady stuff for a young composer, particularly one who had never taken a music lesson until eight years ago. But the excitement is genuine, and Hersch continues to inspire more.

Hersch—tall, lean, and poetic-looking, with dark brown eyes that very scrupulously avoid excessive contact—is a natural musician, one of the few such artists who never played an instrument. Indeed, he was already 19 years old when he started to study music.

"Before that, I'd listen to the radio now and then," Hersch said one afternoon during an interview on Manhattan's Upper West Side. "I remember that when I was five, my pet bird died and I went to the radio, hoping that a song would come on that could sum up my feelings. I kept listening and listening."

Such memories aside, the young Michael Hersch would seem to have shown little interest in music. Instead, as he remembers it, he was pretty much like the other kids in his neighborhood, albeit one laden with a rather melancholy soul. He did his homework, he read books (mostly when they were assigned), and he liked to play sports. One of the few things that set him apart was a natural, if limited, ability with the visual arts. "I've been drawing since I was about two or three years old, and can reproduce anything," he said. "But I don't have a single, genuinely creative instinct in the visual arts. All I can do is copy."

By the time he was in his late teens, Hersch had worked in construction, on ranches, and in suburban pizza parlors. "My father, Jay Hersch, is a businessman and my mother, Patricia, is a writer," Hersch noted, "and so I was raised with a pretty strong work ethic. I tried out a number of jobs, but becoming a musician really never crossed my mind. That was something my brother did."

As it happens, Jamie Hersch, two years younger than Michael, is a gifted brass player and is now the assistant principal hornist in the Singapore Symphony. "It was my brother who got me interested in music," Michael Hersch remembers. "He gave me a videotape of Georg Solti conducting Beethoven's Fifth Symphony." And everything changed.

"It was like someone had opened up a hydrant valve full force inside me, and everything in my whole life came gushing forth," Hersch said. "I didn't know what to make of it. I just kept watching and listening to the tape over and over, hundreds of times." Jamie then gave his brother a theory book; within two weeks, Michael was writing music day and night. By now he has composed some 50–60 hours of music, with the promise of much more to come.

"I guess I'd call my 1993 Piano Fantasy my first real work," he said. "I'd only really been exposed to Bach and Beethoven and a few other composers, so there is a sameness to it. It's grandiloquent and immature, but I recognize my voice. I guess I knew from the beginning what I wanted to say."

After that, music began to fall from Hersch as fruit from an unusually generous tree. By his own estimation, he hit his stride in 1994, when, over the course of a single year, Hersch composed a 50-minute cello sonata, the 45-minute Symphony Concertante for Trumpet and String Orchestra, a 35–40-minute set of piano preludes, a 20-minute set of variations for organ, an unaccompanied violin sonata, and his first orchestral piece, a prelude and fugue.

By then he was studying at Peabody, where his principal teacher was Morris Cotel; he has also worked with Corigliano, Rochberg, and Christopher Rouse. In 1997 he took his master's degree in Baltimore, then won a Guggenheim Fellowship and admission to the prestigious Tanglewood Music Center. The same year, his music began to be performed regularly: Marin Alsop led the Concordia Orchestra at Lincoln Center in the premiere of Elegy in February 1997, and three months later Movement for Orchestra received its world premiere at Carnegie Hall.

Since then have come performances by the Colorado Symphony, the New York Chamber Symphony, and the Chamber Music Society of Lincoln Center, among other ensembles. Hersch has been commissioned to write works for the Brooklyn Philharmonic, the Orchestra of St. Luke's, and the Pittsburgh Symphony. Most notably, a full-length symphony has been commissioned by the Dallas Symphony Orchestra for a premiere in November.

One of the more extraordinary things about Hersch has been his isolation. By his own admission, until recently he has known very little about what contemporary composers were doing. "All my music used to come from inside me, and I somehow knew the last note of a piece by the time I had written the first," he said. "It was all very internal. But now I'm really interested in what is going on around me—all that fantastic work being done in Europe, for example, and a lot of what is being written at home, too."

Hersch credits his wife, Jennifer Tibbetts, a 24-year-old singer he married last October, with bringing a new stability to his life. "She's beautiful and self-confident and has really pulled me out of being a loner. So much of my music was always so pained, so introverted, with an overlying cloak of sadness. These days, my music is sometimes actually pretty funny!"

To call Hersch's music deeply felt would be to understate the matter considerably; at times, it seems pure feeling—a stream of musical consciousness that wells naturally and inevitably. Hersch has been described as a neoromantic, which is a fair assessment so far as it goes, in that his music is highly personal and intensely expressive. Yet he is not to be confused with the tidy, retrogressive composers who have adapted the term "neo-romantic" as a bright label to convince potential audiences that their music won't contain any of those nasty dissonances—or, for that matter, anything else that might demand close attention.

Watching Hersch play one of his earlier works, his own piano transcription of an orchestral work called *Recollections of Fear, Hope, and Discontent*, is instructive. Although the 20-minute composition is only a year old, that is a significant amount of time when one considers how quickly things have moved for its creator. Because it is a transcription, it is impossible to imagine the orchestral colors that would illuminate it in a full performance. But it grabs and maintains one's interest.

Throughout the piece, one hears elements of composers who have long since been accepted into Hersch's own pantheon—Mahler, Shostakovich, Prokofiev, Liszt, and some earlier masters. There are plenty of pregnant pauses, sudden flurries of notes, personal appropriations of familiar gestures that seem renewed in Hersch's gifted hands. Above all there is a sense of line; despite some digressions, some rhetorical shifts, and some long silences, the listener senses that this is a work with a structure and that everything is somehow joined together.

Hersch has been a natural artist; now he is deep into the process of becoming a conscious one. He combines a mixture of urgency and facility that is dazzling; one suspects that he could improvise literally all day and keep a listener's attention. But now he is learning to live with his music before putting it out there in the world—to compose a little less, perhaps, but to compose more completely.

"Until recently, once I copied something out, I thought that it was automatically the very best way I could say it—that whatever came naturally was the best," he said. "But now I'm learning that all my pieces can be improved and they will be improved if I sit with them for a while and let them settle. It used to be that I just wrote, and that was that. Now I'm learning to tinker, to go over other possibilities in my head, to force myself into fresh discoveries.

"You know, the possibilities really are endless," Hersch reiterated with a smile.

The Washington Post
6 June 1999

The High Llamas

More than any other musician of the present day, pop or classical, the High Llamas' Sean O'Hagan seems to have perfected a genuine postmodernism —a style that manages to encompass and expand upon a multitude of different traditions—without descending into either self-conscious imitation or parody.

I N THE LATE 1960s Brian Wilson, who had been fashioning hit record after hit record for the Beach Boys, suddenly turned inward. Instead of churning out more of the luminous, catchy three-minute paeans to surfing, cars, girls, and the "California dream" that had made his fortune, Wilson withdrew from the commercial world and began to produce fractured, elaborately ornamented musical clockworks, distinguished by their brevity, their vaporous, all-but-intangible beauties, and their sheer sonic splendor.

For a variety of reasons, Wilson soon abandoned this path and never explored its promises. Still, it is tempting to describe the best albums by the wonderfully inventive English pop band the High Llamas as a vast set of "Variations on the Ideas of Brian Wilson," so closely are these discs derived from those legendary 30-year-old experiments.

But that would not be fair to Sean O'Hagan, 39, who founded the High Llamas in 1992 and who continues to write, arrange, and produce its songs today. To be sure, O'Hagan has absorbed Wilson's late-'60s aesthetic (as well as what sometimes seems the entire history of American popular music), but he has then gone on to build something original on the foundation. And if we sense, now and again, the influence of Old Master Wilson on the High Llamas, O'Hagan is already a master himself. Moreover, with any luck, he is just getting started.

The High Llamas, who have a cult following in Europe but only a handful of ecstatic admirers in the United States (to date, only one of their records has cracked the 10,000 mark on this side of the Atlantic), are sometimes described as a "retro" group. I disagree: the word "retro" implies a conscious attempt to re-create the work of other times and places (Liverpool in 1964, for example, or San Francisco a few years later). The High Llamas are very definitely a '90s band, but they make no attempt to exclude the past. On the contrary, they glory in what has come before them, while continuing to push forward in their own inevitable direction.

Still, as creative artists so often do, O'Hagan has chosen a roster of pet figures from the past and then proceeded to reinterpret and expand their work in his own manner. A diverse heritage indeed: O'Hagan has obviously listened closely to the later Beatles, but also to such much-derided '70s FM favorites as Steely Dan, America, and the Eagles. The austere minimalism of Steve Reich has been influential, but so has the deliciously airy fluff of Herb Alpert and Burt Bacharach. Electronic beeps and groans pervade these discs, but the seductive, string-kissed, folk melancholy of Nick Drake is in there, too.

What is extraordinary about O'Hagan is that he has managed to incorporate all of these different musics into something that is his own—organic, unpretentious, and absolutely fresh, with none of the sniggering, above-it-all irony that so often typifies such "crossover" efforts. Listening to the three best High Llamas albums—*Gideon Gaye* (1994), *Hawaii* (1996), and *Cold and Bouncy* (1997)—one is struck repeatedly by musical juxtapositions that, on paper, may seem preposterous but in practice sound just about perfect. Who could have imagined that Stephen Foster, the German electronic composer Karlheinz Stockhausen, the 1920s band leader Paul Whiteman, the acid visionary Van Dyke Parks, and the mordant Kurt Weill (in his *Three-Penny Opera* period) might share paternity of a 1996 rock album? Put on the High Llamas' *Hawaii* and marvel.

But try *Hawaii* only once you're acclimated to the High Llamas, for it is in many ways a dense and difficult album. I recommend either *Gideon Gaye* or *Cold and Bouncy* as a starting point. *Gideon Gaye* is O'Hagan's first great work—a sumptuous, surrealist dream of a record. After an eerie opening passage for strings and electronics that sounds as if it were borrowed equally from Wilson's "fire" music and George Crumb's ferociously modernist string quartet *Black Angels*, a sturdy old barroom piano strikes up a sad song and O'Hagan's reedy, tremulous voice enters.

Gideon Gaye is suffused throughout with a gentle wistfulness that is never quite made explicit. One skeptical critic has dismissed this as "an album about a collie and a goat," but O'Hagan's spare, elliptical lyrics, which allude to much but describe very little, suggest a deeper resonance. The collie and the goat are principal characters, to be sure, but for a reason: they represent benign, bewildered witnesses to the urgent follies of late-20th-century human beings—the collie "by the bar stool, patiently sat," listening to eternal confessionals at the local pub; the goat looking on as a new supermarket is erected on a virgin English hill ("construction workers dressed in green"). Meanwhile, bored executives make their way to the airport, tickets wait, more roads are paved, and the quirky charms (and financial health) of small towns disappear into the new international economy. Everything is disconnected, uprooted, and O'Hagan is understandably concerned. As he sings on another record, "Let's rebuild the past, because the future won't last."

If there is protest here, it is protest in the muted, bucolic English manner —a truly conservative (that is, not "radical right") reverence for tradition, a suspicion of modernization for its own sake, a love for land and landmarks. Throughout the disc, one has the sense that O'Hagan knows the hour is late—too late—but there is still time to commemorate and memorialize what is so rapidly being lost.

Gideon Gaye is also intriguing on a purely formal level. The album's elaborate centerpiece is "The Goat Looks On," yet the entire disc might be described as a study of the creation of a song called "The Goat Looks On." We hear our first hints of the melody scored for strings and an electronic instrument not much more complicated than a metronome. A few minutes later, we have the entire seven-minute song, with its soaring Wilsonlike harmonies and an ethereal xylophone descant over the melody. Immediately thereafter, part of the song is played backward on tape. (Yes, the Beatles did something like this in 1966, but effective techniques are ageless—are we to give up the C major chord merely because it's "been done"?) Finally, at the end of the album, as if in distant memory, the whole cut is repeated, start to finish, but now the lead vocal is missing and we are lost in a lambent miasma of voices and mallet instruments.

"Track Goes By," the longest song on *Gideon Gaye*, is also its strangest. For the first four minutes or so, it might be taken for the best song Steely Dan never recorded—terse, suggestive lyrics, jazz-tinged harmonies, an irresistibly rocking chorus, a charging but never overwhelming beat. But in the midst of this pleasant nostalgia, the song itself goes off the track. A starkly simple riff is repeated more than a hundred times with unrelenting intensity, rattling on for a full 10 minutes, until many listeners will be either half-hypnotized or ready to throw the CD player through the nearest window. Steve Reich himself never wrote anything so magnificently insistent. Above this riot of reiteration, a flute whirls and trills, the percussion flutters, guitars whine and dance, bass lines drop in and out. Finally, somewhere in the far background, a child shouts exultantly and the song fades away—a glorious madness indeed.

By the time *Gideon Gaye* was recorded, O'Hagan had been part of the British rock scene for more than a decade. Born and raised in Ireland, he moved to London in the early 1980s as one of two founders of Microdisney. This zippy, animated New Wave group was notable for its mixture of catchy tunes and unusually hostile lyrics (one early single was titled "We Hate You White South African Bastards").

Microdisney broke up in 1988, and O'Hagan supported himself for a time as a rock journalist. In 1990 he put out an unremarkable album that was called, rather confusingly, *The High Llamas* (the name was inspired by a magazine picture of a Victorian hot-air balloon). A more rewarding musical endeavor, however, was O'Hagan's association with the dark and fascinating London band Stereolab, which continues to this day.

The essence of Stereolab, another group with a curious but obviously carefully chosen pedigree, might be likened to the earliest and wildest tracks by the Velvet Underground, roaring and feeding back at full tilt, with fierce electronic dissonances that threaten to enclose the listener. Yet their melodies and harmonies are equally likely to call to mind the French "girl groups" of the late 1960s, or American funk bands of the 1970s and 1980s, or silly, ephemeral top-40 hits (one single was based entirely on the Archies' 1969 smash "Sugar, Sugar").

The influence of early Philip Glass is very strong (particularly his 1977 album of miniatures, *North Star*). All sorts of auditory games are played, including those old speaker-to-speaker Ping-Pong sound effects we remember from early stereo demonstration discs. Finally, the group dresses its discs in covers that are virtually indecipherable, gives its songs bizarre titles that seem to have nothing to do with their content, and sings its lyrics in a manner that is generally inaudible. (The words seem a mixture of giddy nonsense and contemporary French philosophy—which are not always the same thing.)

Stereolab's heterodoxy had a profound effect on O'Hagan, and in 1992 he founded the High Llamas with Marcus Holdaway, Jon Fell, and Rob Allum. Too poor to make an album, they made an initial short disc of only seven songs—*Apricots*—which was clearly influenced by Paul McCartney (and, it must be said, infinitely more lively and attractive than most of what McCartney has done since the Beatles broke up). Shortly thereafter, a record company in France enticed them to record two more tracks and a full-length CD was issued in the United States as *Santa Barbara*. Most of it is fairly traditional, straight-ahead pop, albeit beautifully arranged, but there are some moments that are decidedly unusual.

For instance, the final track, "Apricots," is a hung-over (physically and spiritually) meditation on a beach from somebody who realizes his youth has suddenly vanished. In the background, half-submerged by electronic sound, we hear a mother arguing with a recalcitrant child. "Get in the car!" she screams. "No! No! I'm not going," the child shouts back. This "dialogue" continues, inconclusively, until the song fades away—an oddly touching fragment of tape music that seems both universal and ongoing.

Gideon Gaye, recorded in the winter of 1993–94 for only a few thousand dollars (the exact amount varies from report to report), was originally issued on the Brighton-based Target label and has since been reissued twice (it is now with the rest of the High Llamas catalogue on the V2 label in the United States). This won the band a fervent cult following and inspired generous funding for *Hawaii*, the massive, symphonic-length suite that would follow.

Hawaii—a full 77 minutes, released with a 30-minute disc of outtakes and obscure singles—is one of the most complicated albums of popular music ever made. If so much of early American classical music was a new gloss on European manners, this is a decidedly European take on American popular music (with some British touches here and there, such as the unexpected reference to the James Bond soundtracks that we hear in the second track).

Here, in no particular order, we find flashes of Wilson, Henry Mancini, harpsichord flourishes, "Ramona"-style Mexican-American music (complete with mariachi pulses and firefly strings), melodies that would sound just right around a campfire, swooning Hawaiian guitars, long trumpet solos that would have done Bunny Berigan proud, and just about everything else— layer upon layer, all pulsing with ideas and intelligence.

With *Hawaii*, O'Hagan has transcended rock-and-roll. It might almost be described as an "easy listening" album, although it really isn't. While nothing in a first encounter will offend the ear, the album's form is likely to perplex. In the first place, *Hawaii* is startlingly long (longer than all but one of the Mahler symphonies, to choose a far-fetched comparison) and its very length is an integral part of the musical experience. Second, the separate songs—29 of them—are generally either quite extended or extremely short. O'Hagan often subverts our traditional expectations of a pop song by letting the accompaniment repeat itself for a minute or two after the melody has been put to bed (a minimalist device he understands perfectly). Other tracks will last a mere few seconds (some of them little more than an electronic whoosh) and the album will be off in another direction.

Hawaii is dazzlingly sophisticated and accomplished. In some ways, O'Hagan reminds me of the novelist Thomas Pynchon, with the same ability to combine the highest poetry cheek by jowl with the silliest vernacular, playing across history with ease and grace, seemingly effortlessly.

The latest High Llamas album is *Cold and Bouncy*. This is in some ways the group's easiest record since *Santa Barbara*, despite the fact that it contains more electronic music than any of the others. After an ephemeral synthesized prelude, here and gone, the opening track is a cheerful toe-tapper called "The Sun Beats Down" that initially sounds like Burt Bacharach at his happiest, until a simple thread of melody darkens the song like a cloud, and the cheer becomes façade. "Over the River" is a mantric refrain for banjo and muted wah-wah trumpet, "Three Point Scrabble" sounds like some deliciously choreographed collaboration between a samba band and Steve Reich, while "Evergreen Vampo" calls to mind nothing so much as riding through an automated car wash (one listens, as if in darkness, to the distant melody, as countless little mops squish and squirm in the far background). There are myriad details to explore and admire.

All in all, *Cold and Bouncy* might well be described as a sort of punch-drunk Muzak—soothing and gently evocative sounds, almost New Age, that are punctuated with drips, bloops, and blurps that arrest one's attention just as the lull becomes pervasive. (Here, too, one thinks of Pynchon's habit of changing subjects in the middle of a long paragraph, to the befuddlement of the careless reader.) Every time you think you have your finger on what the High Llamas are doing, they throw in a twist. "Bouncy," yes, but hardly cold. I can't wait to find out where they bounce next.

The Washington Post
10 January 1999

Vladimir Horowitz: A Dissent

This was, to put it mildly, a revisionist assessment of Vladimir Horowitz's musical contributions, and it was quite controversial in its time (to the extent of inspiring a long denunciation in The New York Times *Arts and Leisure section). My distaste for much of Horowitz's work continues, but I hope the reader will bear with my attempts to justify and elaborate upon this heretical position.*

ONE SLOW Sunday afternoon in 1986 I finished filing a long article scheduled to run in the next morning's *New York Times.* My editor read the story, approved it, and sent me home. But then, as I waited for the elevator, she urgently called me back and, visibly frustrated, told me that she had received "orders from on high"—my piece had lost its prominent place on the culture page and would have to be cut to 100 words if it were to run at all. Knowing the exigencies of daily journalism, I accepted her verdict, but wondered just what had happened to push the piece—a major discovery? a looming strike? a genius dead? Nothing of the sort, she muttered disgustedly: "Vladimir Horowitz burped in Moscow."

The dispatch wasn't quite *that* trivial, as I recall, but everything Horowitz did was reported as news and this was only the latest in a seemingly endless string of articles we'd run about the pianist's return to his native land. His decision to make the trip had made the front page—and not just at the *Times*—and there had been follow-up items about the negotiations for the tour, about the transportation of his own special Steinway, and, of course, thorough coverage of his first concert at the Moscow Conservatory, which was also telecast throughout the world.

But let Harold C. Schonberg, who starts his new biography *Horowitz: His Life and Music* with the occasion, tell the tale:

> On April 20, 1986, the wheel came full circle for Vladimir Horowitz with an audible click, and he recognized it as such. His life, as he later said, was "now completely rounded out." The man generally considered the world's greatest pianist, the archetype of Romanticism, the most electrifying pianist of his time, the last great direct descendant of the old Russian school of piano playing, the virtuoso supreme, on that date appeared on a Russian stage after an absence of 61 years.

I can heartily recommend Schonberg's book to any reader who agrees with this assessment of the pianist, and there are ample pleasures here for the rest of us as well. Schonberg, the chief classical music critic for *The New York Times* from 1960 to 1980 and "gray eminence" ever since, is a lively and engaging writer who deftly combines judicial authority with the common touch. After a lifetime of listening to and writing about music, he is still passionate about the art; he particularly loves the piano and writes lyrically about its practitioners. Moreover, he has a flair for drama (Schonberg accords Horowitz's several retirements from the stage with roughly the same importance Ingmar Bergman accords the silence of God).

And so this book is vintage Schonberg—informed, informal, inviting, and digressive, full of anecdotes, asides, and enthusiasm. But there's something rather sad about it all—a pervasive sense that, while a debased form of life may continue, the Golden Age is gone for good, nothing can ever take its place, and only a few old-timers know enough to care. Schonberg writes with the nostalgic tone of a baseball fan still mourning the day the Dodgers left Brooklyn.

The sports analogy is apt, for Schonberg has a clear penchant for musical athletes, as anybody who has read his recently updated *The Great Pianists* (Fireside Books, paperback) already knows. That entertaining volume has a Jovian mien, a stern sense of laying down absolute standards, but is in fact a deeply subjective and, indeed, rather eccentric book. (A much more appropriate title would have been something along the lines of "My Favorite Pianists" or "Pianists I Like.") Technical command is crucially important to Schonberg—above all else, or so it sometimes seems. He admires thundering oc-taves, cascading scales, demonic furies, larger-than-life personalities. He paeans competition winners, keyboard superstars, with something that ap-proaches hero worship in the manner of Thomas Carlyle.

Schonberg's aesthetic might be described as a 19th-century pianistic machismo (how fast can you play *La Campanella*, kid?). The extraordinarily tender pianist Mieczyslaw Horszowski, who was still recording and concer-tizing at the age of 99, is dismissed with a quick pleasantry, almost in passing, as are such patrician artists as Edwin Fischer, Wilhelm Kempff, and Yves Nat. Chapters on reserved, thoughtful pianists such as Artur Schnabel and Mauri-zio Pollini have a detached, dutiful quality; one senses that Schonberg can hardly wait to get back to some bug-eyed, monk-robed, golden-maned 19th-century "titan" gazing heavenward and playing Liszt.

And Horowitz, it will be immediately clear to the reader of this biography, was, for Schonberg, a titan among titans. The critic was far from alone in his estimation. Indeed, for several generations of music lovers, Horowitz was *the* pianist, in the same way that Jascha Heifetz was *the* violinist, Arturo Toscanini (and later Leonard Bernstein), *the* conductor, and Enrico Caruso (and later Luciano Pavarotti), *the* tenor. Horowitz became a secular icon (*The Last Roman-tic* and *Horowitz the Poet* were the titles of two typical late recordings); he was paid more than any other classical artist of his time and attracted many thousands of people who had no interest in concert music but were fascinated by the dapper little man in the bow tie with the impeccable control of dynam-ics and articulation that ranged from an ethereal *pianissimo* to a veritable Niagara of sound. During the last 35 years of his life, despite ticket prices that eventually climbed to $75 a head, Horowitz never played to an unsold seat.

"All artists pursue a Grail, that all-but-impossible quest for those rare mo-ments when the light of the music transfigures them to the point where per-former, composer and audience are one," Schonberg writes. "Vladimir Horo-witz consistently achieved that goal, and that is why he was the dominant figure in piano playing for the last half of the 20th century."

Schonberg's advocacy has inspired me to dig out some of my old Horowitz recordings and to investigate several others I had passed up. And now I have emerged, dismayed and astonished, from an orgy of pianism on vinyl and compact disc, wondering, in good faith, what on earth all the fuss was about.

Let's start with a rule of thumb: in general, the cheaper the music Horowitz took on, the better the performance. I cannot imagine that anybody soon will give us a more visceral, muscular, glittering, and exciting piano transcription of "Stars and Stripes Forever," and Horowitz's version of his own *Carmen* Fantasy is, of course, definitive. Nobody, to my knowledge, has ever brought such superbly controlled fury, such all-but-superhuman velocity, to the sonatas of Prokofiev and Kabalevsky. And Horowitz's performances of some ambitious pieces by Scriabin and Liszt are characterized by a prismatic sense of color, combined with a "Hound of Heaven" urgency, that suits their fuzzy, "daemonic" metaphysics perfectly.

But is this really what we want from a pianist? Maybe it is—for Schonberg, anyway. He decries what he calls "a cultural snobbism that swept the international musical life."

> One heard such comments about any musician as, "Oh, yes, it's all very well that he plays Rachmaninoff, Liszt, and Scriabin. But how can we tell how good a musician he is until we hear him play Mozart and Schubert?" Anybody who timidly suggested the reverse—"Oh, yes, he plays Mozart and Schubert very well, but how good a musician can we tell he is until we hear him play Rachmaninoff, Liszt, and Scriabin?"—would have been branded a musical yahoo.

This strikes me as absurd, especially coming as it does from the man who held the most august and elevated position in music criticism for 20 years; who was the last *Times* chief critic to have any really significant impact on American musical life; and who regularly said such things in his Sunday column. Nobody would brand Harold Schonberg a yahoo and yet it is obvious to me that there are vast qualitative differences between Mozart and Schubert on the one hand and Rachmaninoff, Liszt, and Scriabin on the other. ("Oh, yes, he plays Hamlet very well but how good an actor can we tell he is until he does some *magic tricks*?")

For the sake of expediency, however, let's agree that Horowitz played Rachmaninoff, Liszt, and Scriabin very well; Mozart and Schubert quite a bit less well (although Schonberg mounts a spirited defense of the mannered, mincing Mozart recordings the pianist made for Deutsche Grammophon a year or two before his death), and move on to the center of the repertory—the works of Beethoven, Chopin, and Schumann.

And how does Horowitz fare here? Well, to this taste, pretty poorly. In general, his performances of the standard romantic repertory impress me as flashy, brittle, and arbitrary, an idiosyncratic mixture of fussy, impedimental detail and an aggressive charge toward the goal line. The compositions, all too often, turn into mere "vehicles"—the musical equivalent of weights to lift or hurdles to leap. Horowitz is intent on proving, first and foremost, that he can do anything with a piano; he usually succeeds in this quest but we're occasionally left unsure whether he will ever be able to yoke his acrobatics into a linear statement.

For example, Horowitz recorded the first Ballade of Chopin commercially four times; I've heard three of these, and each version is radically different. (Schonberg approvingly notes that Horowitz never played a piece the same way twice.) But there *are* similarities: they all contain, moment for moment, some spectacular pianism and they are all, judged as a totality, essentially incoherent.

One suspects, finally, that Horowitz had no sense of proportion. He bangs his way through the beginning of such works as Chopin's B-flat Minor Sonata and the B Minor Scherzo with the same steely tone and get-out-of-my-way manner he employs for Prokofiev. The result is clatter. It is sometimes *magnificent* clatter—you and I couldn't do it, even if we practiced for 100 years— but it is clatter all the same. Conversely, when Horowitz conjures up a "pretty" sound, it is often ravishing—floating, resonant, bell-like. And yet it seems so studied, such a conscious turning-on of the charm (with the impersonal self-assurance of a gorgeous starlet showing her teeth) that, for me at least, the ultimate effect is repellent.

Another of Horowitz's favorite tricks (and it usually *sounds* like a trick) was to play very loudly and then immediately taper to near-inaudibility while retaining full, immaculate clarity. These sudden *diminuendos*—the musical equivalent of stopping on a dime—are sometimes brilliantly effective but when they are not precious, they are pure Chico Marx.

Horowitz is probably at his most convincing in sets of miniatures, where he can hit and miss, lose listeners with a maladroit conception of one piece, win them back with a bejeweled tone or a torrent of octaves in the next. When a big masterpiece falls into his hands—the more complicated Beethoven sonatas, the greater Chopin, the Schumann Fantasy—he is, interpretively speaking, absolutely at sea. He simply cannot turn these works into anything more than a succession of highs, a motley of singular "events."

According to the press, he "deepened" in the years between the beginning of his sabbatical in 1953 and his return to the stage in 1965. I don't hear it. He recorded the Schubert B-flat Sonata twice—in 1953 and in 1986—and both renditions are remarkable mainly for their emphasis on all the wrong details. Time and again, our attention is drawn not to the music but to what the pianist does *to* the music (meaningless *accelerandos*, swooning resolutions). In both performances of this sonata, Horowitz goes right to the toenail, rather than the heart, of the matter.

The best recordings? There are some good ones: Samuel Barber's piano sonata, written for Horowitz, was dashed off with a glittering, glassy grandeur that has never been equaled. Some wonderfully epical performances of Scarlatti (for those who don't mind hearing baroque harpsichord pieces played on the dread, decidedly "inauthentick" modern Steinway). Horowitz's early rendition of the Liszt Sonata in B Minor and (if you can stomach some of the emptiest, yet most pretentious, music ever written) the same composer's *Funerailles*. The charming Clementi album, recorded at Horowitz's Manhattan home in the mid-1950s: the pianist accepted the fundamental modesty of this music and belabored it not at all, playing instead with both love and affinity. And, of course, the encores and showpieces, with which Horowitz dazzled audiences for 60 years.

The best book on Horowitz? This one, I think. Glenn Plaskin's dishy 1983 biography contains a great deal of information but does not command the authority that rings through every page of Schonberg's volume. And David Dubal's *Evenings With Horowitz: A Personal Portrait* is a malicious "bread-and-butter note" from a member of the Horowitz inner circle who, after the pianist was safely buried, betrayed his trust by publishing dinner chatter, while casting himself as the book's beleaguered, Byronic hero. Reading Dubal, one is reminded of a pampered, quivering lap dog who yaps and snaps the moment the petting stops.

Schonberg, on the other hand, has studied Horowitz's work for more than half a century and even if one does not happen to share his admiration, this is an important summing up from a distinguished critic. And Schonberg acknowledges different points of view from his own, even though he implies, in crankier moments, that they are part of some kind of whippersnapper "plot."

In fact, there were dissenting voices all along. B. H. Haggin (who was for a time the music critic of *The New Republic*) long ago deplored what he called the pianist's "fussing with tone and phrase-color with no regard for the character and requirements of the music." Composer and critic Virgil Thomson described Horowitz as a "master of distortion and exaggeration" and added that he was "out to wow the public, and wow it he does. He makes a false accent or phrasing anywhere he thinks it will attract attention." And Michael Steinberg, in one of the few passages of censure in the entire *New Grove Dictionary of Music and Musicians*, concluded that "Horowitz illustrates that an astounding instrumental gift carries no guarantee about musical understanding."

Myself, I like what Sergei Rachmaninoff wrote to the young Horowitz after hearing him play the Tchaikovsky Piano Concerto No. 1 in 1928. "Mr. Horowitz," the letter began, "you have won the octaves race. Nobody has ever played them like you. But I will not congratulate you because it was not musical."

The New Republic
30 November 1992

Lang Lang

THIS IS A CITY of hiding places. Wander away from the narrow, clotted avenues of Center City and within seconds you can find yourself in a small-scale, sweetly antiquated urban maze—neighborhood within neighborhood, block within block, cobblestone alleys that lead to ancient stables, hushed gardens, and tiny houses bedecked in flags and history.

Lang Lang lives in such an area, on the second floor of an old row house, not far from the Curtis Institute of Music, where he is still a student. And yet this 18-year-old pianist is also already a seasoned master, hailed as one of the most extraordinary piano prodigies to come along since Evgeny Kissin astonished his first audiences in the 1980s.

This Friday and Saturday, Lang Lang will play the Grieg piano concerto with the Baltimore Symphony Orchestra under the direction of Yuri Temirkanov. Immediately thereafter, pianist, conductor, and orchestra will embark on a six-city East Coast tour, the highlight of which will be a performance at New York's Carnegie Hall.

"Carnegie Hall!" Lang Lang repeats the syllables with obvious delight. "It is a magical place. I played there once—an audition when the house was empty. But never a real concert! It will be incredible!"

A reporter is tempted to place exclamation points at the end of most of Lang Lang's sentences, for he is an eager and animated conversationalist whose enthusiasms are explosive. Indeed, the sense of urgency with which this friendly, boyish young man is conquering the world is so openhearted and unabashedly cheerful that his master plans come across as disarmingly endearing rather than aggressively ambitious. He wants you to share his joy;

106

he clearly loves music, loves people, loves life and what seems its boundless prospects.

And his enthusiasm is reciprocated—by critics, musicians, and audiences. "This is an innately musical performer, technically adept but never merely dazzling," Sarah Bryan Miller wrote in the *Saint Louis Post-Dispatch* after a recent performance. "His playing is deeply felt and astonishing in its profundity."

"He is the biggest, most exciting young keyboard talent I have encountered in many a year of attending piano recitals," John von Rhein wrote in the *Chicago Tribune*. "It was not simply his colossal technique that impressed but the deep and instinctive musicality behind it."

Temirkanov is one of the young pianist's fans. "Lang Lang can play anything," the conductor said at the groundbreaking ceremony for the Strathmore Hall Arts Center on Wednesday. "I want to work with him often. You can't compare him to anybody. If you could compare him to anybody, he wouldn't be unique."

To date, Lang Lang—he always uses both names—has appeared with the National Symphony Orchestra, the Cleveland Orchestra, the Saint Louis Symphony Orchestra, the Los Angeles Philharmonic, and the Chicago Symphony, among other distinguished ensembles. Engagements with the leading orchestras in Philadelphia, St. Petersburg, Hamburg, and Helsinki are scheduled for next year—as is a Washington recital debut at the Kennedy Center Terrace Theater. A recording for the Telarc label, with music by Brahms, Haydn, Rachmaninoff, and Balakirev, is out and selling briskly, and Lang Lang is already the subject of a full-length biography in his native China.

He was born in Manchuria in 1982. Due in part to China's strict population laws, he was an only child; his parents now live with him in Philadelphia. Guo-Ren Lang, Lang Lang's father, was a professional musician, a master of the erhu, a two-stringed Chinese instrument that is bowed like a cello and produces a haunting, plaintive sound. Lang Lang began to pick out melodies on the piano before he was three. When the boy was nine, the family journeyed to Beijing to further his studies at the China Central Music Conservatory.

"I still remember the time I played a grand piano for the first time," Lang Lang said. "For so many years, I had only played on upright pianos. The grand piano was like a new world. A whole new world of sound!"

At the age of 13, Lang Lang won the Tchaikovsky Young Musicians Competition. Through video and audio recordings, he came to the notice of Gary Graffman, the president of the Curtis Institute, who had been both a prodigy and then a distinguished professional pianist himself.

"He's a very major talent," Graffman said. "We don't accept students at Curtis on the basis of recordings—all auditions have to be in person, for any number of reasons—and I was a little bit reluctant to encourage somebody so young to come from so far away. But I was amazed at the maturity he displayed in the Chopin F minor concerto, so I asked for some more tapes. And so he sent me all of Chopin's 24 etudes—just incredibly difficult music!"

Indeed, the etudes are so demanding that Arthur Rubinstein, whose name was all but synonymous with elegant Chopin performances for more than half a century, never played most of them.

"By that point, I thought it was pretty obvious that Lang Lang would be accepted," Graffman continued, with a laugh. "He can learn anything within a couple of weeks. He just swallows the music whole. His technique is incredible, but he makes music with it. When he plays these very hard pieces, he plays the music, not just the notes."

Every successful musician, no matter how talented, needs a "break"—and Lang Lang's came with a gala concert with the Chicago Symphony in August 1999. Pianist André Watts had been forced to cancel at the last minute, due to a fever, and Lang Lang, then 17 years old, took the stage to play the Tchaikovsky Piano Concerto No. 1. It was, by all accounts, a magnificent performance, and a capacity audience of 12,000 gave him a lengthy standing ovation. Word travels fast in musical circles, and Lang Lang soon found himself booked to capacity through the 2002–2003 season.

He currently practices the piano for four or five hours a day. "Sometimes I play less," he says with a trace of apology. "I'm traveling so much these days—I play up to 80 events a year—and I don't always have the time to sit down and practice. But when I was a boy in China, I practiced six or seven hours every day."

It is a lot of work, and such a busy schedule leaves time for few distractions. The thought of an afternoon at the movies brings out the kid in Lang Lang. "*Crouching Tiger*! Oh, what a film! So thrilling! All those people fighting in the trees! And my friend Tan Dun just won the Academy Award for the music!"

Lang Lang calls himself a sports fan, although the only game he plays is ping-pong. "I like watching the NBA, but it wouldn't be good for my hands to play basketball," he explains. He has "a lot" of friends but no romantic interests—"not yet!"

He is particularly excited about an upcoming tour of the Far East with the Philadelphia Orchestra with its outgoing music director, Wolfgang Sawallisch. "The Chinese love the Russian composers so much," he says. "But I am going to play Mendelssohn—first concerto. They will love that, too. Maybe I can make it sound Russian!"

He names Rubinstein, Vladimir Horowitz, and Rudolf Serkin as some of his favorite pianists, although he was born too late to have heard any of them in person. Among living pianists, he admires Watts, Richard Goode, Mitsuko Uchida, and Murray Perahia. "And Christoph Eschenbach—who is both a conductor and a pianist. He has so many ideas!"

The walls of Lang Lang's apartment are covered with dozens of photographs of his celebrated friends and mentors—Isaac Stern, Lorin Maazel, Midori, and many others. Now he wants to meet Yo-Yo Ma. "He is both a great musician and a great person," Lang Lang explains. "If you can be either one of those things, that is fantastic, but if you can be both of them at once . . ." He trails off in wonderment, and the smile says it all.

Indeed, it sometimes seems Lang Lang stops smiling only when he plays the piano, at which point a mask of fiercest concentration settles upon his face. What sets his playing apart—aside from his stupendous technical command—is its distinctive mixture of cool logic and impassioned fancy. Moment by moment, his interpretations are richly detailed, full of invention and a quasi-orchestral density of sound. And yet it is Lang Lang's attention to the most basic elements of music—melody and form in purest distillation—that win one over. At no point does the listener ever feel lost; everything has a formal beginning, middle, and end, and there is never any doubt where Lang Lang is at any point.

"Lorin Maazel told me something very important," he said. "He reminded me that every time I play, there will be people in the audience who will never have heard the piece before. And so I must find a way to make them understand—the very first time!" Lang Lang has clearly taken these words to heart.

Nobody can predict the course of a career in music; too much is subject to chance. Yet Lang Lang seems unusually well equipped to face the future, what with his enormous talent, sunny nature, and powerful advocates. But this pianist is much more than just another cute kid, somebody the classical music industry will find profitable to market at age 18 and expedient to throw away at age 25. Many, perhaps most, prodigies are interesting only because they are extremely advanced for their years, but Lang Lang's best performances would do credit to an artist of any age.

Right now, Lang Lang is content to concentrate on immediate challenges. He wants to learn some more of Beethoven's piano sonatas. He is looking forward to recording Rachmaninoff's Piano Concerto No. 3 with Temirkanov and the St. Petersburg Philharmonic. He wants to add some more concertos to what is already a formidable roster of 32 in his active repertory. And he wants to find a bigger apartment, although he has established amicable relations with his neighbors.

"The lady downstairs used to complain when I played," he said. "You know—does it have to be so loud? But now everything is fine. I think maybe she is beginning to enjoy it."

The Washington Post
15 April 2001

Mario Lanza

A new biography of Mario Lanza provided the impetus for this meditation on the tenor's lasting fame.

636 CHRISTIAN STREET is only a 15-minute stroll from the corner of Broad and Market Streets, the intersection that is sometimes considered the very center of Center City, Philadelphia. But to take that walk is to venture into a different land—into a miraculously preserved ethnic enclave in the midst of what has become a vast international city.

From the vantage point of Christian Street, the skyscrapers of central Philadelphia loom like glittering steel sentries, as distant and unreal as the Emerald City must have seemed to Dorothy from her poppy field. South Philadelphia is a world unto itself—where the houses are modestly scaled yet meticulously maintained, where Ralph's Restaurant still serves the heaping, flavorful plates of spaghetti that have been its specialty for nearly a century, where neighbors hail one another from across the street (and regard outsiders with polite but decided reticence), where the accent is overwhelmingly Italian.

It was in an upstairs bedroom at 636 Christian Street that Alfredo Arnold Cocozza bellowed his first on January 31, 1921. If you are lucky—or merely tenacious enough in your inquiries—you may still find somebody in South Philly who knew the Cocozza family, who may have shopped in the tiny grocery they operated below their cramped apartment, who joined in the neigh-

111

borhood celebrations on those uproarious occasions when young Alfredo returned home in triumph, after he had become world famous as Mario Lanza.

Some four decades after Lanza's death, the tenor's name is still celebrated—and not just in Philadelphia. There have been half a dozen biographies by now, the most recent (and most authoritative) by Roland L. Bessette
published earlier this year by Amadeus Press. Lanza's recordings continue
to generate more than $100,000 every year for his estate, a staggering sum
for a classical or semiclassical musician who has been gone so long. And
Lanza's films—particularly the ones he made for MGM, such as *That Midnight Kiss, The Toast of New Orleans*, and *The Great Caruso*—are still staples
on late-night television and easily found in the better video stores.

Tenor and Washington Opera artistic director Plácido Domingo has acknowledged that *The Great Caruso*, in particular, exerted a great influence
on his career. So has Luciano Pavarotti, who, according to biographer Bessette, "pinpointed his early aspirations to a sense of awe at hearing 'Be My
Love,'" Lanza's greatest hit, as a teenager in Italy. "Third Tenor" José Carreras
has gone even further: "[Lanza's] wonderful voice and the charismatic appeal of his personality had a profound effect on my life, and I decided there
and then that I too would one day sing the great operatic roles." And last summer in Chicago's Grant Park, some 12,000 people showed up to hear tenor
Richard Leech narrate and sing a tribute to Mario Lanza.

Obviously, a lot of people are still out there listening. Yet Lanza is rarely
taken seriously by classical musicians. You will search in vain for his name in
most of the critical histories of recorded opera, despite the fact that he
recorded many of the best-known arias in the repertory. He is often dismissed as a vulgar bawler or, at best, as a calculated creation of big money
and bigger hype, like Andrea Bocelli.

Still, conductor Arturo Toscanini is said to have called Lanza's "the greatest natural voice of the 20th century." The attribution is a little shaky—it was
first published two years after the maestro's death—but there can be no
doubt that other unquestionably important musicians held Lanza's gift in
esteem, among them the conductors Serge Koussevitzky and Julius Rudel,
the baritone (and one-time director of the Kennedy Center) George London,
and the soprano Licia Albanese, who recorded with Toscanini, as well as such
legendary tenors as Beniamino Gigli, who once said that Lanza had "a greater
voice than Caruso."

Lanza himself had no doubts that Albanese's assessment was correct. "Caruso?" he once said, "You study that ridiculous legend? That guy could not even whistle properly."

This last quote may provide a clue to the reason Lanza's star imploded at just the moment it should have been forever established in the firmament. For there is no getting around the fact: despite his abundant talent, Lanza could be a lazy, strutting, arrogant, and undisciplined jerk. He had an insatiable appetite for food, liquor, and women, all of which he abused with shocking insensibility. He could barely read music and refused to learn how, preferring to mimic the recorded performances of other people. He was known to balloon up to 250 pounds in the middle of making a motion picture, sometimes delaying production by months. Even Bessette, in what is generally a warm and sympathetic biography, acknowledges that Lanza is "a strong contender for the title of the most truculent, morose, demanding star in the history of Hollywood."

He had the endearing habit of urinating whenever and wherever he felt like it—sometimes in front of his leading ladies and, on one memorable occasion, out the window of Philadelphia's toney Bellevue Stratford Hotel in full view of some astonished reporters. He was a foul-mouthed and belligerent colleague who regularly addressed women in the vilest of terms. Despite the fact that he was one of the top-grossing stars at MGM, he was summarily fired by studio boss Dore Schary.

Later, at a time when he was hundreds of thousands of dollars in debt, Lanza drank his way through an extended Las Vegas engagement that might have quickly restored his solvency but resulted instead in a devastating lawsuit. On October 7, 1958, at the age of 38, he died in Rome from what was diagnosed as a heart attack. As in the case of the extraordinary jazz musician Bix Beiderbecke, it might be better said that Lanza really died from "too much of everything."

It is naive and idealistic to expect our great artists to be great human beings as well. Some are, some aren't; the actress who transcends all our pretenses and frailties, touching our soul with her art, may be frostier than February when she is offstage, and the wittiest and most companionable of storytellers are often revealed to have been dour, disdainful, and bitter men.

It doesn't matter: in the long run, the shortcomings of Mario Lanza the person will be forgotten. But what of Mario Lanza the artist, as immortalized in his films and recordings?

Such early films as *That Midnight Kiss* (1949) and *The Toast of New Orleans* (1950) present us with a spirited, affable, and charismatic young man who seems born to sing. These are light romantic comedies, ingratiating rather than laugh-out-loud funny, both of them based loosely on Lanza's own life—the poor but plucky boy with a terrific voice who rises to the top of society and gets the girl. Fifty years later, we can still understand Lanza's immediate appeal. The postwar era was one of rapid and profound democratization, and Lanza seemed a normal guy (albeit an unusually handsome and gifted one) with none of the supposed elitism Joe Sixpack generally associated with the world of opera.

The Great Caruso (1951) was more problematic—and not merely because this cinematic biography had virtually nothing to do with the facts of the Neapolitan tenor's life. Here Lanza was actually setting himself against Caruso, in some of the most celebrated arias in the repertory, and here the young man's shortcomings began to show.

For Lanza had never received either the training or the seasoning that might have placed him among the important opera singers. He was offered the training—he worked with a number of vocal instructors throughout his career, most of whom ultimately threw up their hands at his lack of discipline and unwillingness to practice. But he had no time to grow; he appeared only a few times in operatic roles, for the simple reason that he became a star so terribly quickly, through his concerts and radio appearances. After Hollywood had enfolded him, he elected to lose himself in the ready-made Satyricon available to handsome celebrities rather than in the service of a noble art.

And so what we hear, throughout Lanza's films and recordings, is magnificent and tragically unfulfilled promise. The voice *was* an extraordinary one —immediately distinctive in its sound throughout all registers, full of sun and ardor, lyrical yet immensely powerful, all combined with what (onstage, at least) was an exuberant and winning personality. Lanza always seemed to sing directly from the heart, from one person directly to another, and this is something that has eluded many better-trained artists.

But he often displayed a tendency to sob and shout—as if to overwhelm the listener even when nothing of the sort was called for. Somebody once said that Caruso always sang as if he were about to burst a vessel; the same can be said, with much greater acuity, for Lanza. He brought a desperate urgency to such masterpieces of bel canto as "Una furtiva lagrima," which ought to spin out naturally, as if an inward reverie.

Moreover, Lanza's phrasing, for all of its occasional charm, was too often sloppy and unreflected. The very spontaneity that was one of his principal gifts also worked against him; we have the sense that he is merely singing the way he feels at the time, rather than making a conscious decision about the course he wants to pursue in the delivery of a song or aria. (Indeed, there are times when it is difficult to believe he knew what the words he was singing really meant.) Here, Lanza could have taken lessons not only from professional opera singers but from his contemporary Frank Sinatra, the brainiest of all pop phrasers.

The soprano Frances Yeend, who worked closely with Lanza throughout his early career, once said that the tenor "provided a great treat for the ear, but nothing for the mind." This is not quite fair, for there can be little doubt that Lanza still "owns" such popular hits as "Be My Love," with that explosion into a luscious and unforgettable radiance on the word "love." Moreover, he brings an enormous and idiomatic charm to songs like "I'll Never Love You," "The Loveliest Night of the Year," and "Ciribiribin." Even if one believes, with Yeend, that the tenor provides "nothing for the mind" in these songs, certainly he provides something for the heart.

There is no way to assess Lanza's career as anything but a tragedy. He was yet one more victim of the ferocious struggle between talent and self-destruction that has so often plagued American music, from Stephen Foster through Jimi Hendrix and beyond. If his artistry had kept pace with the sheer abundance of his gifts, Mario Lanza might now be remembered as America's leading tenor. But it was not to be.

Still, out of the chaos and disrepair of his life, Lanza left us a number of recordings and motion pictures that are still listened to with appreciation and affection throughout the world. All things considered, that's not a bad legacy.

The Washington Post
6 June 1999

Otto Luening: In Memoriam

I CAN SEE him now—walking cautiously but deliberately down Riverside Drive, clad in a dark coat and hat that seemed almost Muscovite, resolutely facing the winter wind. In the days before I knew Otto Luening, before I had joined the many other New Yorkers fortunate enough to call him friend and mentor, I used to marvel at the sheer fact of his continuing presence. This was the late 1970s, after all—a confused and unbridled time when the most heated aesthetic arguments seemed to be about the relative merits of punk rock and disco—and I could scarcely believe that there was somebody still living in my neighborhood who had helped bring electronic music into the world, who had studied with Ferruccio Busoni and collaborated with James Joyce, and had then played an active role in American music for more than half a century.

The call came in the summer of 1980. I was listed, he was listed, and he rang me up to offer some commentary on a review of his autobiography that I had fashioned for the long-defunct *Soho News*. And so I walked down to an enormous apartment overlooking the Hudson River and we sat in over-stuffed armchairs and sipped brandy as the sun turned orange and then disappeared.

Was there another figure in music who had such a wide circle of people who loved him? How many other composers have maintained into their 90s such a deep, urgent, and generous interest in what their younger colleagues were up to? Otto wore his historical importance lightly; strangers might approach the living legend with appropriate awe, but they usually left his presence with the exhilarating sense of having acquired a new friend.

116

Of Otto's historical importance, there can be no doubt. He wrote his first composition at the age of five—it was what he later called, with that characteristic twinkle in his eye, a "very modern" waltz. He was still composing 90 years later; his legacy includes symphonic and chamber music, film scores, numerous songs, and one opera, *Evangeline*. And his autobiography, *The Odyssey of an American Composer*, was as hearty and engaging as the man himself.

Otto Luening was born on June 15, 1900, in Milwaukee, Wisconsin. His mother, Emma Jacobs Luening, was an amateur singer and was said to have had a beautiful voice; his father, Eugene Luening, had numbered Richard Wagner among his acquaintances and had studied with Ignaz Moscheles and Carl Reinecke in Leipzig. The elder Luening taught music for many years at the University of Wisconsin and served as an early conductor of what was then known as the Milwaukee Musical Society and later became the Milwaukee Symphony.

The family moved back to Europe in 1912 and settled in Munich. At the outbreak of the "Great War," the Luenings, classified as enemy aliens, took refuge in Zurich. It was there that Luening studied composition with Philipp Jarnach and Volkmar Andreae, played flute in the Tonhalle Orchestra (under the batons of, among others, Richard Strauss and Arthur Nikisch), and in his "spare time" worked as an actor and stage manager in the productions of Joyce's English Players.

But the most important influence on the young Luening was undoubtedly Ferruccio Busoni, among the greatest piano virtuosos in history and a composer of highly cerebral, markedly original music. (His unfinished opera *Doktor Faust* is generally regarded as the most intellectually engaging of the many settings of the old tale.) Busoni encouraged Luening's budding modernism, and he particularly admired the Sextet (1918) and the String Quartet No. 1 (1920).

Luening moved to Chicago in 1920, where he earned a living playing music for silent films. In 1922 he led the first performance of the Chicago-based composer Charles Wakefield Cadman's opera *Shanewis*, the first of many American operas to benefit from his steady hand and unusual ability to coordinate stage action with whatever was going on in the orchestra pit. In later life, he would conduct world premiere performances of Gian Carlo Menotti's highly dramatic *The Medium* (1946), the second of the Virgil Thomson–Gertrude Stein collaborations, *The Mother of Us All* (1947), and his own *Evangeline* in 1948.

By this point, Luening was the Joline Professor and chairman of the music department at Barnard College and also the music director of the Brander Matthews Theater at Columbia University. In 1949 he joined the faculty of Columbia University as a full professor; he would remain with Columbia until 1970, and continue to live in the neighborhood—actively interested in anything going on "up the hill"—until his death.

In 1959 Luening, Vladimir Ussachevsky, Milton Babbitt, and Roger Sessions became the first codirectors of the Columbia-Princeton Electronic Music Center, which would prove vastly influential in the decades to come and is in fact a direct predecessor of such modern musical think tanks as Pierre Boulez's IRCAM in Paris. Seven years before that, Luening and Ussachevsky had participated in a historic concert of tape music at the Museum of Modern Art. Such deliberately "Brave New World" Luening works as *Fantasy in Space, Low Speed,* and *Invention in Twelve Notes* now seem enormously charming, rather than eerie, but they must have made listeners sit up in their seats half a century ago.

Yet Luening never devoted too much time to electronic music. The concept fascinated him, and he was proud of his significant contribution to an emerging idiom, yet he knew that his own predilections, for the most part, lay elsewhere. Most of his work is for traditional forces: orchestral pieces, a good amount of chamber music, many songs and choruses (set with an admirable attention not only to the words of their texts but to the phonemes as well), and some vigorous and idiomatic music for piano.

He seemed to be interested in everything. He was absolutely without dogmatism: during his tenure with Columbia University, he taught composers of radically different stylistic orientations—John Corigliano, Charles Dodge, Charles Wuorinen, Mario Davidovsky, Wendy Carlos, and John Kander (*Cabaret*)—a diverse group of creators indeed. And he admired musicians whose work was very different from his own, attending the New York premiere of Philip Glass's *Satyagraha* in 1981, for example, and then proceeding directly backstage to embrace the composer, whom he had never met.

"I never tried to make a maestro thing out of teaching," he told John Rockwell in 1980. "I used my knowledge of psychiatry and psychology to size up the *potential* of every one of those people and then to encourage them as much as I could to be what they *were* to be themselves."

"I've always tried to be in touch with people who wanted to free this great creative force we have in this country," he continued. "In American music today there's a terrific amount of differentiation, a variety of styles and approaches. And that's the American story: this enormous, broad thing."

Otto remained in remarkably good health through his middle 90s. He was to be seen at contemporary music concerts throughout Manhattan and was still open to young visitors almost up to the end. One of his favored crusades in later life was against the ubiquity of noise pollution, particularly in New York City. "There's just too much sound, all around us," he would say with unusual irritation. "It's ruining our ears and it won't let us think."

Otto Luening died on September 2, 1996, a day of mourning for the music world. An especially touching response came from the scholar and author Jacques Barzun, a friend since the early 1930s, who sent a warm note of consolation to Catherine Luening, Otto's wife since 1959.

"Your only frequent comfort can be the thought of his magnificent life, one not only of great achievements, a host of admirers and many warm friends, but also one marked by the most honorable conduct at all times," Barzun wrote. "His artistic ambitions were fulfilled, but never at the cost of mean behavior, as is often true of otherwise admirable artists."

"I was never interested in sharpening my talents to become a star," Otto told *The New York Times* when his book was published in 1980. "I wanted to be a loyal servant of the art of music. My line is 'Don't whimper and don't complain. Figure out how you can make the system work and still stay yourself; figure out how you can compose with enthusiasm and romance.' I've been treated decently by practically everybody I've met for 80 years. I've had a good life and I've got nothing to complain of."

That "good life" lasted another 16 years and Otto never changed his sentiments. As deeply as we miss him, as sorry as we are that we will never see him again, I suspect that most of us who knew Otto can only look back on him with a smile and a full heart.

Notes for a memorial concert
Privately printed, 1996

Ward Marston

"**W**AIT A MINUTE! You've *got* to hear this!"

Ward Marston bobs and weaves gracefully through his spacious suburban home outside Philadelphia, feeling his way toward an 80-year-old recording that he believes represents the late American soprano Geraldine Farrar (1882–1967) at her very best.

By all rights, this should take a while. Marston shares his living quarters with at least 25,000 78-rpm records, more than 500 early cylinders (wax and otherwise), some 5,000 LPs, and a proportionate number of compact discs. Moreover, the 46-year-old Marston has been blind since birth and must rely upon a mixture of memory, intuition, and some old braille-stamped bindings to find just what he wants. And yet, within moments, the recording is cued up and its owner is beaming. "Listen to that energy, that control!" he urges his visitors as the long-dead voice fills the room once more.

Marston wants to bring out a compact disc devoted to Farrar's singing. He also intends to put together a 25-CD set that would trace the history of classical singing in France from the dawn of the recording era to the present. And then there is his plan to collect the voices of some celebrated figures from the Victorian era—Alfred, Lord Tennyson, Robert Browning, Florence Nightingale, and Sir Arthur Sullivan, all of whom made cylinder recordings in the late 19th century—that Marston wants to remaster and re-release for 21st-century listeners.

It all sounds quixotic in an era when an "oldie" often means something by the Beatles or Elvis Presley. Yet Marston has supervised more than 400 historic reissue projects within the last 15 years—for labels such as BMG Clas-

120

sics, EMI, CBS Masterworks, Romophone, Pearl, Biddulph, and VAI. And more recently he has launched his own record label with his partner, Scott Kessler, a label that is entitled—appropriately enough—Marston.

To date, Marston's company has re-released more than a dozen projects. These include the first complete version of Massenet's *Manon* (a tremendous rarity originally issued in 1923 on 24 bulky, fragile, and heavy 78-rpm discs, now distilled to two CDs); a number of vocal recitals, including the complete recorded legacies of 19th-century legends Adelina Patti and Victor Maurel; and individual sets featuring pianists Josef Hofmann, Ernst Levy, and Emil von Sauer, the last of these a pupil of Franz Liszt.

The Marston discs are splendidly packaged, with authoritative liner notes and illuminating photographs. One particularly impressive recording is the two-CD set dedicated to the art of the Hungarian-American soprano Alma Gluck (1884–1938). She is probably most commonly remembered today for her performance of James G. Bland's "Carry Me Back to Old Virginny" (which became the first disc to sell a million copies) and she recorded a good deal of other popular material, not all of it of the first order. Marston, sensing a historical injustice to her memory, has issued more than two hours of Gluck's best recordings—49 selections in all—that do justice to her bright, silvery tone, her innate command of baroque and classical style, and her limpid interpretive gifts.

Another important soprano, Rosa Raisa (1893–1963), spent most of her American career in Chicago, where she became a local favorite. Unfortunately, then as now, the center of the American opera world was located in New York and, for whatever reason, Raisa was never invited to sing at the Metropolitan Opera. Nor did she record for either of the two largest American record labels, Victor or Columbia. Thus she has been unjustly forgotten. *Washington Post* music critic emeritus Paul Hume was certainly not alone in his belief that Raisa's voice was the greatest he had ever heard; we hear in her complete recordings, now issued on three Marston CDs, the sound of a magnificent dramatic soprano, full of emotional intensity and desperate passion, yet imbued with a certain arresting regal quality.

Marston presses his discs in editions of 2,000; more can be made quickly on the off-chance that one of them will sell out, but as might be imagined, this is hardly a commercially driven endeavor. His biggest "hits" so far include the recordings devoted to Hofmann and Gluck. "This isn't a profession, nor is it an avocation," Marston says. "This is my life. I love good friends, good food, good wine, but preserving these historical documents—." He breaks off. "I can't even begin to say what that means to me. It sounds corny, but this is a true labor of love."

And, as Marston says this, his large, expressive, sightless eyes trained vaguely on his guest, it doesn't sound corny at all.

Marston was born in 1952. When he was five years old, he came across an old record player and a stack of 78s in a relative's basement. He still doesn't know what it was about this chance encounter that moved him so deeply. "They put on an old Caruso recording for me—it was called 'Hosanna' and it was by a forgotten composer named Granier—and I asked them to play it over and over again. I was fascinated by the tune, by the singing, the sheer sense of history I felt when I was listening to the record."

When Marston was eight, his parents took him to the Met to hear Leopold Stokowski conduct Puccini's *Turandot*. After that, the boy was hooked. He began studying piano and became a solid jazz musician by the time he was in his teens. (He still performs today, mostly at private parties, some of them in the Washington area.) He also spent his spare time combing through the backrooms of Philadelphia record stores, where discontinued 78 recordings might be found. By the time he entered Williams College, Marston had already built a substantial library.

While at Williams, he became involved with the college radio station. "I wanted to play some of the great performances I had collected on the air," he once told *The Boston Globe*.

In the early 1970s, there weren't a lot of good transfers on LP, particularly of instrumental and orchestral material. I wanted to play the [Fritz] Kreisler performance of the Mendelssohn Violin Concerto conducted by Leo Blech and the only transfer was way off pitch. So I taught myself how to join the four-minute sides of 78-rpm recordings together and my method worked much better than what other people were doing at the time. Most people simply spliced together the sides, which to my ears sounded abrupt. It hurt my sense of musicianship to hear that jolt, so I worked at overlapping the sides.

In 1976 Columbia Masterworks (now Sony Classical) engaged Marston to prepare an edition of some old Budapest String Quartet recordings. (Back issue releases are usually rather profitable for record companies, since all recording costs and royalties have usually been paid long ago.) Other offers followed, and before too long, the name Ward Marston became synonymous with careful reissues of the great performances of the past.

Marston calls his work "audio conservation" rather than "restoration." "When I start on a new project, I try first to get every single bit of sound I can off an old record and transfer it into a digital format," he explains.

> Then I take out most of the clicks and pops—either one at a time or through a computer program. In the old days, when you removed the clicks and pops, you were also removing tiny bits of the music as well. Nowadays there are some computer programs that allow removal of the clicks without removing the music. Still, if you are overly zealous, you can do more harm than good. You simply have to expect a certain amount of surface noise from an old recording.

The sound on Marston's discs is remarkably clean, however, even on the earliest and most primitive recordings he "conserves." Throughout his house one finds a wide variety of different record players—old Victrolas, old Gramophones, machines that play the early Edison and Bettini wax cylinders, as well as modern turntables, DAT machines, and tape recorders. Some early stereo recordings were made in 1932 by Bell Laboratories with the Philadelphia Orchestra. In these discs, the sonic information, rather than being buried within the grooves of the record, actually lies on the protruding groove itself. For a project such as this one, Marston has had to actually invent his own record player, featuring a sort of two pronged, saddlelike needle that rides the groove as if it were a horse.

Choosing the proper equipment on which to play an old recording is only the beginning of the battle, however. Although we refer to most early disc recordings generically as "78s," the pioneer companies actually made their records at anywhere between about 65 and 90 revolutions per minute. For example, one tenor who recorded at an unusually slow speed was Fernando De Lucia; when his discs, originally made at about 69 to 72 rpm, were played (and then reissued) at the 78 speed, they gave his voice an inhuman, bleating sound that did not reflect the glorious voice referred to by his contemporaries. As a result, only recently have authentic, appropriately pitched De Lucia recordings become the rule. Marston has a turntable that allows him to speed up or slow down the playing speed and therefore significantly change the pitch of any recording on which he is working.

In addition to his efforts for his own label, Marston continues to work for other companies, including the splendid Romophone, which has issued most of the recordings of Rosa Ponselle, Elisabeth Schumann, Amelita Galli-Curci, and Pol Plançon, among other distinguished singers.

Most recently, Marston has completed a 10-CD collection in celebration of the 200th anniversary of "The President's Own" United States Marine Band. Beginning with a startlingly vivid "Farewell to Dresden" recorded informally in 1891 on a Columbia cylinder, continuing through the glory days of John Philip Sousa and on through the tenures of such band maestros as John R. Bourgeois and Timothy W. Foley (who leads the group today), it is a veritable treasure-trove of 109 years of American music. Unfortunately, this limited edition is not available commercially, but it may be found in better libraries.

Although Marston probably knows as much about recording equipment as anybody working today, he claims that his ear is the final arbiter. "I have been involved in music all my life, and I have a good idea in my head of what a violin, a piano, a singer sounds like," he once explained. "A lot of transfers of old recordings simply make them sound like old records. What I try to do is to make them sound as much as they can the way they would sound if they were live performances."

What next? Down the line, Marston wants to do another complete Caruso collection; he is no longer satisfied with the early 1980s edition he created for Pearl Records. He is in the midst of a commemorative project for the Philadelphia Orchestra centennial next year. On the day of my visit, he was hurriedly preparing a transfer of the Hungarian composer Zoltán Kodály conducting his own music in the 1940s; Philadelphia Orchestra music director Wolfgang Sawallisch wanted to hear it right away and a messenger was already on the way.

And he has some personal crusades he wants to realize. Marston considers the late contralto Dame Clara Butt (1873–1936)—known to Anglophiles of a certain age for her deep, booming renditions of "Rule Britannia!" and "Land of Hope and Glory"—a "much-maligned artist." "I love her work and want to do something wonderful with her," Marston says eagerly. "I can't think of any singer with better diction. And she had a great pitch sense, a gorgeous trill, and a surprising expertise in coloratura singing."

He leans back in his chair and grins again. "And finally, her records touch the heart. And that's what it's all about. You know?"

The Washington Post
21 February 1999

Bobby McFerrin

CONDUCTING is the most mysterious of musical talents. Who hasn't wondered what that person was really *doing* up there anyway, making those funny faces, testing out idiosyncratic sign language before a stage full of professional musicians? What are the rules of communication? What is proper decorum? If Leonard Bernstein—who seemed caught in the midst of an unusually wrenching orgasm throughout his performances—was a great conductor, what does that say for Pierre Boulez, who leads an orchestra with the brisk, dispassionate air of a bank teller making change?

An ideal conductor combines the best virtues of shaman, sports coach, psychologist, and traffic cop. In Bobby McFerrin's case, add the skills of an extraordinarily inventive and ever-so-slightly daft stand-up comedian—Robin Williams has nothing on this guy.

One recent morning, McFerrin stood on the stage of Symphony Hall in Newark, leading the New Jersey Symphony Orchestra through a rehearsal of music by Copland, Bizet, and Vivaldi. Dressed in a purple T-shirt and blue jeans, his baton stored for the moment within the deep thicket of his dreadlocks (rather the way one might keep a pencil behind the ear), McFerrin bobbed and wove to the music, listening to his players and feeding back to them, stopping every now and then to correct a note, suggest a phrasing, pay a compliment.

It sounded good. *Really* good. And McFerrin, who will be conducting the New York Philharmonic in Central Park tomorrow night, was unquestionably the focal point, the fount of inspiration; this was not merely an orchestra playing by itself. Unlike those privileged folk who attain eminence in one field, then take up the baton to enhance their prestige (or at least their egos— movie stars, heads of multinational corporations, and at least one university president), McFerrin actually knows what he is doing, proving once again that conducting may be mysterious but there are some people who do figure it out. His comments are concise and specific ("Try that again; the oboe should have a B-flat there, not a B-natural"), and they make a difference in performance. He knows when to cue the horns, when to allow the strings to surge forward, when to clarify a possible smudge, when to stand back and let it all be.

At the end of the rehearsal, the orchestral players—toughest of all audiences—broke into spontaneous applause. A delighted McFerrin beamed, clasped his hands together, closed his eyes blissfully, bowed low, and walked off the podium, singing something in a bright, clear falsetto. The melody sounded familiar—yes, that was it! The New Jersey Symphony's guest conductor was singing "My Baby Does the Hanky Panky."

Definitely *not* your typical maestro. McFerrin—best known as the man with the prismatic, multi-octaved, miracle voice whose "Don't Worry, Be Happy" was an enormous international hit in 1988—took up conducting about seven years ago.

"My 40th birthday was approaching, and I thought it would be neat to give myself a present," he explained.

It was the summer of Leonard Bernstein's 70th birthday, and I went up to Tanglewood to participate in the celebration, sing a couple of numbers. After it was over, I wrote him a letter and asked him if I might have a lesson. And he said, yeah, sure, come on out next year, and we'll get together. So I spent three weeks in the summer of 1993 at Tanglewood, hanging out with the student conductors, attending the master classes, and finally having my private lesson with Bernstein.

There we were, looking at the score of Beethoven's Seventh Symphony together, and I'm trying to find my way into this new discipline. I read music and all, but singers only have to follow one note at a time, and my piano-playing was done by ear, so looking at this score, with all these instructions for different instruments playing different melodies at the same time was really *formidable*. And Bernstein sensed my discomfort and said, "Bobby, it's all jazz, it's all just *jazz*, you know." And for some reason that clicked with me. He was teaching me that music was music, and it made me feel better about where I was coming from as a musician, about my background. He was giving me permission to look at those compositions from my own viewpoint.

"Of course, on some level Beethoven *was* my music," he continued.

My parents were both classical musicians—singers at the Metropolitan Opera, no less—and I grew up listening to everything that sounded. Mainly classical music and jazz at home, but back in the late '60s, early '70s, if you tuned into a top-40 station, Herb Alpert would be followed by James Brown, who might be followed by Eric Clapton or Stevie Wonder or the Beatles. You'd hear movie soundtracks, even occasional pop versions of the classics. It was a real education. Now the stations are so specialized that you hear only one kind of music—people tune in specifically to hear that kind of music, and anything else would be a shock. There's no adventure anymore. I'd like to mix it up again, there's a lot of wonderful music and it should belong to all of us.

McFerrin was born in New York in 1950. He grew up in Southern California, where he worked as an usher at the Dorothy Chandler Pavilion (then, as now, home of the Los Angeles Philharmonic), played in jazz and rock bands, even had a gig backing up the Ice Follies. "Then," he says,

when I was 27, after I decided I was a singer, I started doing piano bars and then singing with John Hendricks here in New York in 1980. Bill Cosby heard me, liked me, told people he liked me, and things started to happen. I made records, did some touring and then, by the time "Don't Worry, Be Happy" came out in 1988, I was getting a little tired of the road. I wanted to be with my family more often [McFerrin is married and the father of three children] and I was getting a little lonely up there by myself onstage. So I took some time off, and it was then that I started to think about conducting.

In addition to his work with Bernstein, McFerrin studied with conductors Benjamin Zander and Gustav Meier.

All in all, I know about 45, 50 pieces now, I guess, some much better than others. I made my debut in 1990 with the San Francisco Symphony, conducting the Beethoven Seventh. And I did *okay*, you know, but not much more than okay. I was very intimidated, very nervous, and I was happy once the concert was over.

Still, the word got around that I'd conducted in San Francisco, and I started to get offers for gigs. At first they were mostly pension-fund benefits—you know, send in the celebrity and make some money—but then I started to get more and more calls, and I decided to take it seriously, build a rep list. I like Beethoven a lot; Stravinsky—it'd be great to do *Rite of Spring* someday; just did Dvořák's "New World" Symphony, and I really, really loved that. Not much contemporary music—not yet, anyway. I sort of like the classical top-40, you know?

It was a "classical top-40" concert with a difference that McFerrin offered Newark. The program included the scherzo from Mendelssohn's *Midsummer Night's Dream*, Bizet's *L'Arlésienne* Suite No. 1, and the overture to Mozart's *Marriage of Figaro*. But the most moving moment came when McFerrin joined the orchestra's concertmaster, Christopher Collins Lee, for a performance of an Andante from Vivaldi's Violin Concerto in G (RV 532).

This is an unassuming little piece: a simple melody with conventional chordal accompaniment, originally scored for two mandolins following and imitating—even teasing—one another. McFerrin had transcribed it for violin and voice and the resultant performance was radiantly beautiful—full of nuance, detail, and loving appreciation for the modest melody that has somehow survived two chaotic centuries to beguile us today. Lee and McFerrin worked together in pure symbiosis, the violin sweet and suave, the voice now crooning, now echoing ecstatically.

After that, McFerrin's playful side came out. He divided the audience in two, gave us some notes to sing, conducted us by hopping from one part of the stage to another, led us in a rousing, omni-dynamic chorus of "John Jacob Jingleheimer Schmidt." On the spur of the moment, with no rehearsal and no scores on the music stands, he told the orchestra to play the opening 90 seconds of Richard Strauss's *Also Sprach Zarathustra* (oh, all right, the *2001* music) and, from memory, the musicians did a credible job, the timpanist bouncing back and forth between tonic and dominant like King Kong on amphetamines. McFerrin then started an informal orchestral jam session, scat-singing with the basses, calling in the clarinet, and before long he was twittering and sputtering like Mel Blanc's celebrated impression of an old Maxwell car breaking apart.

Before intermission, McFerrin gave us a demonstration of his solo work. "Blackbird," one of Paul McCartney's best songs, was a genuine show-stopper: He sang it a cappella, with no electronic enhancement whatsoever; and yet, so fast can McFerrin leap from one register to another, there was nothing missing from the harmonic setting. He approximated a rich contra-puntal stew complete with gentle cooing, uncanny impressions of melodic fragments trapped within an echo chamber, and at one point the unmistak-able sound of wings flapping off "into the light of a dark black night."

What now for McFerrin? Anyone who spends any time with him cannot but be impressed by the range of his talent; indeed, he is perhaps the most nat-urally and irrepressibly musical person I've met since Bernstein. He seems a living embodiment of the art of music—a genius, if you like, but one of those geniuses who has not yet given us a masterpiece. His vocal recordings are spectacular—he has helped invent a new glossary for the voice—but only for a little while, after which the mind wanders. And though he has the charisma and musicianship to become a fine conductor, perhaps a great one, it is hard to imagine this wild, bristling energy channeled into the sort of im-mersion and study that make for truly personal, idiomatic, and revelatory renditions of the very greatest works.

Perhaps McFerrin has an even higher calling. I think his greatest gift may be his ability to convey the wonder and magic of music—all it can mean, all it can be—with simple language, simple gestures, putting it across to the widest possible audience, young and old. Should there ever be another series of televised *Young People's Concerts*, McFerrin is just the man to lead them. And with the continuing decline in music education in our schools, we need something like the *Young People's Concerts*—which galvanized an entire gen-eration with the love of music—more than ever.

McFerrin now is the "creative conductor" for the St. Paul Chamber Or-chestra in Minnesota. Not content to be a jet-set star conductor (with the traditional penthouse in New York or London and the occasional visits to his "job"), McFerrin has moved his family to Minneapolis. "Much as I loved San Francisco, I was a little bit concerned about the environment that my kids were growing up in," he says. "I wanted them to have a sense of freedom, to be able to get on their bikes and just *go*, walk to the corner store in safety. When we first moved to Minneapolis, it was downright spooky. I couldn't believe that we were five minutes from downtown and five minutes from uptown, and fifteen minutes to the airport. We're on a lake and it's quiet and green and luscious and there are mosquitoes. Great public schools. We're happy."

In the late 1980s McFerrin was the target of some flak for "Don't Worry, Be Happy," which some critics interpreted as a mindless, feel-good affirmation at a time when, in their opinion, there was not much to cheer about. He sighs when the subject is brought up yet again.

"I don't mind talking about this, but"—he fishes for the right words—

> but the press tends to be so cynical about these things. I've always had a very deep faith in God, and I've always felt that when Jesus tells us not to worry about our lives, it's because worry and faith don't go together. But it really is going to be *all right*, you know. I believe in having a very positive outlook on a daily basis. Regardless of what's happening around you, you are personally responsible for the way you react to life. In that song, I wasn't saying to ignore all the problems—we're all aware of them and we do what we can—but instead of being weighted down, depressed, and angry all the time, we can be available and compassionate to the next person we meet. Look at the prayer of St. Francis of Assisi—"Lord, make me an instrument of your peace." That's what the song was about.

J. S. Bach used to say that all art was for the greater glory of God. McFerrin nods agreement. "If you are entrusted with a talent, it is your duty to use it to serve God and your fellow man," he says, fixing the interviewer with his eyes.

"That sounds so serious—and I am very serious about my faith—but there are many kinds of service," he continued.

> You mentioned Bach. He was a great improviser, and if I were running the music schools, I'd make sure that every one of them had a course in

improvisation so that our connection with these masters isn't cut off. Improvisation is a wonderful way to free your voice and maybe your spirit, too—to spend some time with yourself, try things that you normally wouldn't. You don't have to ask permission when you improvise. It gives you a chance to be your own person. Experiment. Have fun. Be foolish. Go a little crazy. Take risks. Challenge your fears.

About 30 Newark youngsters, a few with curious parents in tow, pack an upstairs conference room of Symphony Hall to meet with McFerrin. In private conversation he is quiet and intense; with a group like this, he is just as uninhibited as he seems onstage. He repeats any questions he is asked and then answers them—fully, often funnily, always without condescension.

Did I grow my hair long to be fashionable? Nope, my head was just screaming out for long hair for some reason, and I gave in. Do I like to practice? Sure. I know it scares people because it involves discipline. But discipline is very important—someday you'll be parents and the most important thing you can do is to discipline your kids. And, anyway, you can make practicing interesting. I like to do it standing in line at the grocery store, at the bank, walking down the street. How do I take care of my voice? Well, I'm very careful with what I eat before a performance. No milk, no cheese, no bananas, no meat, nothing mucus-forming. What do I listen to? Everything. Everything positive. You eat good food to nourish your body; if you listen to good stuff, you'll nourish your mind.

Michael Jackson had recently been accused of anti-Semitism in the lyrics to one of the songs on his *HIStory* album. A young man ventures that he has no problem with what "the brother" was saying and asks McFerrin what he thinks. Suddenly, the easy manner dissipates.

"Michael Jackson has a tremendous responsibility," McFerrin says quietly.

Forty million people buy his records. Now some people think that freedom means you can do anything you want. But freedom does not give you license to hurt or to defame. More people are wounded by words than by bullets—it's true, think about it. In a case like this, it's better to deny your own freedom than to put anybody else down. I really mean that. If it's worth saying, there must be some way of saying it without hurting anyone. Change the lyrics.

McFerrin fields some more questions from the kids. "Wait a second, folks, I've got to rest up for the show tonight, so I can only stay a little longer. But, listen, the orchestra has my address, and you can write me a letter. Do I take the time to read my mail? I most certainly do. And if you write me, include your phone number, because I've been known to call people from the road."

"What's my favorite song? My *favorite*? In the whole *world*? Okay. Wait, I'll try to sing it for you."

He launches into a catchy, haunting song, beautiful and strange, almost mantric, punctuated by sound effects, lip smacks, and knee slaps. "That's my favorite," he says when it is over. "And you know why? Because I just made it up, and now I'll never sing it again."

Newsday
30 July 1995

The Loyal Listener: Elizabeth Mensh

When I became the music critic of The Washington Post in 1995, I received an unhappy letter from a reader named Elizabeth Mensh who felt that my reviews had been unnecessarily hard on the National Symphony Orchestra. Shortly thereafter, I learned of her long association with the orchestra, and, to my gratitude, she agreed to sit for an interview. We subsequently became fast friends, and until her death in 2000 she continued to attend most first-night NSO performances at the Kennedy Center. All orchestras should have such fans.

S HE'S IN her seat at the Kennedy Center every Thursday night—cheerful, interested, immaculately dressed, and wearing one of her dozens of hats. Indeed, players in the National Symphony Orchestra have come to refer to Elizabeth Mensh as the "hat lady," and she is a beloved figure in Washington musical life.

Almost 67 years ago—on January 31, 1930—a new and shaky ensemble known tentatively as The National Symphony Orchestra of Washington, D.C., played its first concert. Elizabeth Mensh was there, listening from the balcony of Constitution Hall. When the orchestra began its first full season the following year under the leadership of its initial music director, Hans Kindler, Mensh became a charter subscriber. She was 19 years old.

Since then, hundreds of players and conductors have come and gone, but Mensh has remained fiercely faithful to her cherished orchestra. Until the end of the 1990–91 season, she was a subscriber and she would undoubtedly still be one today, had not the NSO presented her with a special ticket, one that would be good "forever" for the opening concert of every program.

Mensh is a convivial and wide-ranging conversationalist. Like many music lovers who never took advanced lessons, she knows and understands the art better than she thinks she does, and her opinions are usually generous and wise. And she has unquestionably "heard 'em all."

Sergei Rachmaninoff? "Oh, my God! This little shy man, completely wrapped up in himself—I don't know whether he knew English or not, he seemed so uncomfortable. But such a performance and such music!"

Vladimir Horowitz? "Never missed him. There was an intensity, a magnetism about him that I never found in any other pianist, not even Rubinstein."

Kirsten Flagstad? "What a soprano! She sang a 'Liebestod' [from Wagner's *Tristan und Isolde*] that had me loving it for the rest of my life."

That life has been spent entirely in Washington. Her parents, Louis and Hannah Rebecca Mensh, moved here at the turn of the century from the province of Galicia, which was then part of the Austro-Hungarian empire and has now been incorporated into Poland. Louis Mensh ran a grocery store at the corner of Ontario and Kalorama roads NW, and the family lived upstairs. "The building is still there, but it's now an annex for a black Baptist church," Mensh said.

> Along with most of my brothers and sisters, I was born upstairs, delivered by a midwife. There were 10 people living in a house with one bathroom. If that doesn't teach you to get along, nothing will!
>
> When World War I broke out, Papa went to register and he was asked about his family. He said that he had eight children, and the lovely old lady who was in charge said, "You go home now, Louis Mensh, you've got an army already."

The neighborhood in which Mensh grew up is now known as Adams-Morgan, and even then it was integrated, at least by the standards of the day. "Black and white, it made no difference to us," she recalled. "There was no difference. These were nice people. You could leave the doors and windows open all night. There was nothing to be afraid of."

The Mensh family store extended credit to neighbors and made quick deliveries both to area homes and to the embassies that then lined 16th Street.

We all worked putting inserts in the newspapers that were to be delivered. In fact, it was work that saved two of my brothers' lives when the roof of the Knickerbocker Theater collapsed in 1922 after a blizzard. We lived only three and a half blocks from the Knickerbocker—it was at the corner of 18th and Columbia, where the Crestar Bank is now—but the papers were late that day and so my brothers couldn't do their inserts in time to get to the theater. And that's what saved them. One of the kids down the block didn't get saved. Oh, that was a horrible tragedy—so many dead. I remember they got baskets at Papa's store to carry out the bodies.

Elizabeth Mensh graduated from business high school at the age of 16.

I was two years younger than everybody else in the class and I was given a scholarship to law school, which I did not take—that was stupid on my part. But I got a job at Shannon & Luchs real estate, which at that time was one of the biggest such organizations in the city. It was supposed to be a temporary job but when my boss dictated 45 letters in the morning and I had them all written and mailed by 5:30, they asked me to come back the next day. That would have been 1928. In 1929, when the crash came, we went from 157 employees to only 19. I replaced 10 people in the insurance department and the stenographic department.

Shortly after the outbreak of World War II, Mensh became an agent for the Massachusetts Indemnity Insurance Co. "This was an era when women hadn't really gone into business as they have now," she said. "There weren't many women lawyers, many women doctors. And men simply didn't want a woman telling them about insurance and death and wills and all that sort of stuff." She shook her head. "That's all changed now, but it was pretty tough for us back then."

For five years, Mensh wrote a regular column for what is now *Washington Jewish Week.* "Do you know what a mensch is? It means a person of character. And so I called my column 'Among Us Mensches' and then wrote about anything that I wanted to write about. I interviewed everybody—I don't think anybody ever turned me down, not even Jascha Heifetz."

Throughout it all, Mensh kept up her subscription with the National Symphony. "It's important to have a subscription," she insists, "because it helps the orchestra know the bills will be paid, and it gives the listener an opportunity to find out about new things." She has vivid memories of all the music directors. Kindler, who led the orchestra from 1931 to 1949, was an "enormous presence," she says. "He had wonderful hands, some of the most expressive hands I ever saw, outside of [Leopold] Stokowski. Nobody had hands like Stokowski."

Mensh was personally acquainted with Howard Mitchell, who took over the orchestra in 1949 and conducted it until 1969. "He was a charming man with a lovely wife and several children. Our cantor at Adas Israel, Robert Barkin, was very friendly with the Mitchells and used to ask me to come along when they socialized. Poor Howard Mitchell got panned a lot by the press, but he worked hard and did quite a bit for the symphony."

Still, the music director she admired most was Antal Dorati, who led the orchestra from 1970 to 1977. "As far as I'm concerned, with my meager musical background, Dorati was responsible for changing the orchestra forever. A huge change—just night and day. And I don't understand to this day why they let him go. He was attractive, dignified, professional, a complete musician."

Mensh has mixed feelings about Mstislav Rostropovich, music director from 1977 to 1994. "He was one of the greatest cellists I ever heard and quite a celebrity," she said. "But I always had the sense he didn't know the music the way he might have. He was always looking at the score. A wonderful woman who sat next to me summed him up perfectly—instead of the music being in his head, his head was always in the music!"

She seems both intrigued by and slightly afraid of the agenda set down by the current music director, Leonard Slatkin. "After all the Shostakovich and Prokofiev and Russian stuff with Rostropovich, Slatkin is going to emphasize American music and turn this into a real national symphony," she said.

> I think that's wonderful in a lot of ways. But what Slatkin is doing is surgery, and he's giving us a lot of things that are very difficult for me to listen to because I don't find them beautiful to my ears. So much of it is a reflection of the ugliness in our society—in some pieces, I feel like I can hear the traffic going by—and I don't always leave the concert hall uplifted and feeling beautiful the way I used to. But he is a great musi-

cian, and very personable, and I want to support my orchestra and I want to become one of his fans.

Mensh knows many of the musicians in the orchestra. "Some of the older players used to come to Papa's store," she said.

John Martin, who just retired and played cello in the NSO for about 50 years, lived just up the street from me. I used to call him up every now and then. I've been friends with the man who beats those things—you know, the timpani—for years, Fred Begun. Some of the people there may not know who I am, but I know most of them by name. I love the way [associate concertmaster] Elizabeth Adkins plays; I think she's wonderful.

Once, Mensh almost stopped going to concerts. "I gave up my subscriptions to both the Boston and the Philadelphia orchestras because I was scared to come out by myself after dark," she said simply. "Much as I love the place, it's hard to get to the Kennedy Center—I still wish that they'd built it at 15th and Pennsylvania, where it would have been convenient to everything, with a Metro stop right there. In any event, I didn't know anybody who could give me a ride home. I used to take a bus in and out, but I started to get nervous late at nights waiting to go home."

Her problem was solved one evening when two neighbors, Robert and Sheilah Pinsker, saw her waiting for a bus after a concert.

They stopped and said, "Don't you live on Connecticut Avenue?" And I said that I did, and they said, "Come on in, we do too, and we'll take you home." And these two wonderful people have been taking me home now for about 10 years and they won't let me do anything for them in return, not even pay for parking. But I've just won a raffle for a dinner at a little French restaurant on Connecticut Avenue, and maybe I can coerce them into coming along with me.

"It saddens me to be afraid to go out at night, after having lived a long and full life in Washington," she continued. "This used to be such a wonderful city. The trees were taken care of, the streets were swept, even the gutters were cleaned out every day—I know, because when we were kids we'd lose a tennis ball or something down there, and we'd wait for the man to come clean it out and give us our ball back."

Mensh is equally concerned about the high cost of concertgoing.

> My sister sent me something that she'd cut out from an old NSO program book dating from the 1941–42 season. Back then, the orchestra used to play seven concerts a year at the Lyric Theater in Baltimore. And an entire subscription, all seven concerts, with great soloists like Joseph Szigeti and Rudolf Serkin, cost only between $9.99 and $13.53, including federal and state tax. Today, it's hard to find a single seat for $13.53! You might have to settle for an obstructed view.

One might expect such a devoted music lover to have many recordings. In fact, Mensh has neither a cassette machine nor a compact disc player—indeed, she doesn't even have an old turntable. "Isn't that terrible? I have absolutely no mechanical aptitude whatsoever and the thought of having to go out and buy something and having to set it up and fool around with it—" she gives a faint shudder. "I'm still living in another world, I guess. I still have most of Mama's old appliances, although I did have to replace the Toastmaster and the vacuum cleaner."

Although she has a radio and television, she is not pleased with much of what she finds on their stations. "So much garbage is coming to the American people," she said.

> It's all so lowbrow. We have to find a way to get the National Symphony Orchestra on television—interviews with the conductor and musicians, performances. We have to let people know that this great music is out there and that everybody is welcome to partake of it. I've been responsible for introducing my nieces and nephews to music, and some of them have become concertgoers. I love literature and reading, but there is something about music for my soul that makes life worth living.

Now in her mid-80s, Mensh remains active in community affairs. "I go every Monday to a retirement home on Connecticut Avenue and make a presentation of local, national, and international news, with some personality stories and some humor to sweeten it up," she said. "And then I stay and have lunch. I'm older than a lot of the people who live there, but one of my best friends in the home just had her 101st birthday. It's only recently that she's gone a little off—such a shame!"

On Wednesdays, Mensh participates in a book club at the Cleveland Park Library. Thursdays, she can be found at the greetings office of the White House. "Every day, there are 30 to 40 volunteers opening up mail for the president and first lady," she said. "Everybody wants to invite them for weddings, bar mitzvahs, graduations all over the country. If they're over 80, they might want a card saying 'Happy Birthday.' Millions of pieces of mail must come into that office. This has been going on since Eisenhower."

And then, of course, on Thursday night Mensh will be back in her seat at the Kennedy Center Concert Hall, continuing a tradition that has enhanced and enriched her life for almost seven decades, and wearing her hat. "Listen, at my age, if they don't know me for anything else, at least they call me the 'hat lady.' It's a fun thing. I love hats."

Mensh doesn't know just how many hats she has. "I put them in boxes the way they do at a millinery shop, one inside of the other," she said. "And I've got a lot of those boxes. I rarely, if ever, throw out a hat, but I sometimes give them to people I like." Her favorite is one her sister brought her "all the way from Europe on the *Normandie* ocean liner. It has some beautiful rose red velvet in front," she added. "I don't have the nerve to wear it today, I don't think, but I'll keep it forever, out of sheer sentiment."

Whatever she wears, Mensh looks grand and proud as she walks down the aisle of the Kennedy Center—a vital, vivid reminder of a more elegant era in the nation's capital. "Can you believe it?" she asked, her expression growing suddenly wistful. "Nowadays, most of the time I'm the only person in the house who even wears a hat."

The Washington Post
29 December 1996

Stephin Merritt and the Magnetic Fields

THERE IS a distinct whiff of Disney to the Lower East Side these days. Tidied and fattened by the Manhattan real estate boom, the area would seem to be well on its way to becoming a sort of "Bohemialand," and its legendary scruffiness has recently been embraced by New Yorkers who want some residual trappings of anarchy along with easy access to Wall Street.

This transformation rather revolts longtime residents, who have always taken pride in the neighborhood's mixture of inexpensive housing and laissez-faire individualism. Today the town house on St. Mark's Place where both Leon Trotsky and W. H. Auden once lived is a gleaming, upscale Italian restaurant with a chrome facade—a metamorphosis that could be fodder for one of the smart, mordant pop records of a present-day East Villager, songwriter Stephin Merritt.

"I haven't seen *Rent*, but I did review the original cast album," Merritt recalled with a grimace one recent afternoon. "And my sense was that it was a description of the East Village as it might have existed 20 years ago but that it had absolutely nothing to do with contemporary reality. It's impossible to get a studio apartment here for under about $1,000 a month these days—$1,400 would be more likely. I just got back from England, and I was shocked to learn that New York is now more expensive than London. Everything has changed."

Yet we were sitting in the garden of a welcoming and unpretentious East Village tavern, where nobody seemed to care that only Merritt had bothered to order anything from the menu—and an inexpensive pot of tea, at that. Moreover, Merritt's pet Chihuahua (named Irving, for Berlin) was not only

141

accepted but also greeted warmly by the staff, as if it were a tiny, tremulous old friend. Such hospitality is not easy to find amid the sharply vertiginous sensory ride that is New York 2000. Perhaps that is why Merritt has adopted this place (which he has requested be left unidentified) as his hangout, de facto office, and workplace.

It was here—only a few minutes from the terraced bloom and bustle that is the renovated Tompkins Square Park—that Merritt, sipping tea or stronger libations, jotted down many of the melodies and lyrics that would eventually find their way into *69 Love Songs,* an encyclopedic, flabbergastingly ambitious, opera-length set of three compact discs. In fact, Merritt is the latest in a long line of songwriters, ranging from Stephen Foster to Irving Berlin and on to the early Lou Reed, who have called this neighborhood home.

69 Love Songs was issued last September by an independent label called Merge, which has been bringing out Merritt's discs for the better part of a decade. Merritt has supervised and participated in recorded performances of his songs with at least four of his own bands under different names, but this adventure was credited to his main group, an informal gathering of friends called the Magnetic Fields. A limited edition of 2,500 sets was planned, but at least five times that many are now in circulation.

And small wonder, considering the reviews *69 Love Songs* has received. "Pop hasn't seen a lyricist of Merritt's kind and caliber since Cole Porter," Douglas Wolk wrote in *Spin* magazine. "Bittersweet, sometimes just bitter, often goofy and sentimental at once, he's never met a love-song cliché he couldn't twist inside-out or make legitimately touching." *Magnet* magazine compared *69 Love Songs* to the work of John Dos Passos and Thornton Wilder. And the album made the "10 best of 1999" lists in *Rolling Stone, Spin,* and *The Village Voice.*

This epic begins with the breathless, loopy, deliciously befuddled "Absolutely Cuckoo"—a musical house of mirrors in which Merritt sings a duet with himself over a simple, reiterative pattern that would sound just great on a calliope. Almost three hours later, the offhanded, Kurt Weill-flavored "Zebra" brings everything to a close, with a quavering final chord that hovers unsteadily in midair, as if it didn't quite believe that the album could really be over. Throughout, *69 Love Songs* is a dazzling exercise in songwriting craft— songs exultant and despairing, hilarious and bleak, coolly dismissive and achingly confessional, icily sophisticated and on-the-knees pleading.

Merritt has filled *69 Love Songs* with tunes that would stand out in the most urbane cabarets ("Nothing Matters When We're Dancing," "Blue You," "Busby Berkeley Dreams") and in the raunchiest of roadhouses ("I Don't Believe in the Sun," "A Chicken With Its Head Cut Off"). There are at least half a dozen songs so catchy that they will, with justice, become pop standards, among them "I Don't Want to Get Over You," "I Think I Need a New Heart," "The Sun Goes Down and the World Goes Dancing."

And more—"It's a Crime," which Merritt describes as "Swedish reggae" and actually sounds like it. "Love Is Like Jazz" is a meandering series of disconnected plucks and groans that concludes with the observation that both love and jazz are "divine . . . asinine . . . depressing . . . and almost entirely window dressing."

Parody and cliché are taken to that giddy and exhilarating point where they become fresh once again. "Punk Rock Love," a hysterical succession of pants and shrieks, evokes an entire subgenre in a cut-and-paste minute, complete with awkward tape splices, while "For We Are the King of the Boudoir" is purest Gilbert and Sullivan. "Papa Was a Rodeo" is a country-music depiction of a barroom encounter with a world-weary macho man who, by his own admission, "never stuck around long enough for a one-night stand." It sounds like a gay/absurdist love song that might have been written by Jean Genet and Eugene Ionesco for Johnny Cash.

Some of the best tracks on *69 Love Songs* create and perfect their own forms. "Asleep and Dreaming" is haunting in its tenderness, a folkish expression of rapture and affection sung over the simple, steady breathing of an old accordion. And the desolate "I Shatter" is an etude for two notes at the very bottom of Merritt's vocal register, croaked in an appropriately sepulchral manner while cellist Sam Davol saws and scratches his way through what sounds like a furiously whirling dance from Philip Glass's *Einstein on the Beach*. What an astonishing amount of music Merritt has absorbed and made his own.

"The Death of Ferdinand de Saussure" is the song that has likely received the most critical attention, due to its arcane and unusually brainy subject material. Merritt's musical collaborator and manager, Claudia Gonson, has summed it up succinctly: "Mild-mannered pop songwriter Stephin Merritt encounters the great father of linguistics who annoyingly deconstructs love to death, so Stephin pulls out a gun and kills him in the name of the great Motown songwriting troupe Holland-Dozier-Holland."

Merritt, who will not give his exact age but is in his mid-30s, speaks softly and slowly, in a husky voice that betrays his chain-smoking. He chooses his words carefully, sometimes pausing at such length that, believing an answer to be finished, I found myself interrupting him inadvertently. Writers have described Merritt as "surly" and "difficult"; during our visit, he seemed quite the opposite—a thoughtful, gracious, and rather shy individual, fascinated by all manner of music, literature, and ideas. He is well aware of his own powers—false modesty would be out of keeping with Merritt's matter-of-fact approach to his art—and attempts to address questions completely. Yet he remains vaguely distracted, as if he were always "on duty," always making songs.

Norman Mailer titled one of his books *Advertisements for Myself.* According to Merritt, *69 Love Songs* might be described in a similar manner. "I was sitting at a bar one night, listening to a pianist play through a Stephen Sondheim song, and I was thinking I really ought to get into theater," he recalled.

And I thought, what can I do? And then I thought, well, maybe I could write a revue—a musical without a story line, like *Jacques Brel Is Alive and Well and Living in Paris* or *An Evening with Tom Lehrer*, my favorite theater piece ever. Sondheim once said, jokingly, that anybody who wanted to break into theater should start with the poster. So I came up with the idea of a Warholian poster that said "100 Stephin Merritt Love Songs," but quickly decided that would be too many, so I cut it down to 69. And then I realized I'd have to write and record the songs before they could be put into a revue.

I wanted to say, This is what I can do. Here I am, and I made 69 songs, and I think they're all good even though they're all built on the same general theme. I like the fact that *69 Love Songs* insists that there is a genre called "love songs" that has nothing to do with instrumentation, nothing to do with conventions, nothing really to do with lyrics or melodies. The only thing that holds this collection together is something extramusical—which is love.

Merritt is interested in the eclectic professional songwriters of old—Berlin, Porter, Noel Coward—and also in those contemporary pop musicians who seem to be at home working in a wide variety of different traditions. I've been writing record reviews for *Time Out New York*, and so I get dozens of discs every month," he said.

And it seems to me that this is a fantastic time for reissues and an incredibly horrible time for new releases. I'm astonished by how awful most recent music is. There's been nothing new in disco music since 1973 and "Rock Your Baby." Rock has been around since 1955, and rap hasn't changed much since 1979. Who's buying this stuff? I blame it in part on radio formatting—almost every station plays only one kind of music these days, so there's no cross-fertilization anymore.

He names as his favorite contemporary groups such hybrid ensembles as Stereolab and the brilliant High Llamas. He also expresses continuing reverence for the multilayered pop records of the Beatles, the Beach Boys, Fleetwood Mac, the Bee Gees, and his particular favorite: the Scandinavian quartet Abba.

"I learned to write songs almost entirely by listening to Abba," Merritt said. The hyper-Nordic Swedish group produced a string of elaborately orchestrated pop hits in the 1970s, hits that seemed to fly in the face of all that was considered respectable by the "serious" rock intelligentsia of the time, but have enjoyed a small-scale though passionate revival in the past 10 years. "I remember discovering a punk rock magazine in Provincetown about 1976 or 1977, with an article about how terrible Abba was, how it was something your little sister would listen to, and so on. So I instantly realized that Abba was something my big brother probably wouldn't like, but I didn't have any big brother so I didn't worry about that."

Merritt was raised by his mother, whom he describes as "an itinerant Tibetan Buddhist hippie teacher," and grew up in a series of houses and communes in places ranging from Maui to Boston. "I was an obnoxious, precocious little brat with hair down to my knuckles, who had been spoon fed Shakespeare and was very interested in mythology. I got my first synthesizer at 14 but had already started writing songs before that. It was something to do. I didn't have any friends when I was little." Today, the Merritt canon includes more than 200 songs.

Merritt met his closest musical associate, Gonson, while they were both attending Harvard University in the mid-1980s. They began to work together as the Magnetic Fields—in addition to her managerial duties, Gonson sings in an affectlessly pure soprano and plays piano and drums—and put out a first disc, *The Wayward Bus*, in 1992. Since then, there have been five Magnetic Fields recordings (before *69 Love Songs*) as well as discs by Merritt's "other" bands—The 6ths, the Gothic Archies, and Future Bible Heroes—which in fact are often made up of many of the same players.

It may seem counterproductive to put out albums under different names, but these discs do, in fact, explore different aspects of Merritt's talent. The 6ths' recording, *Wasps' Next*, features musicians from other groups (such as Yo La Tengo, Luna, and Superchunk) singing Merritt songs; the Future Bible Heroes sound is gorgeous, baroquely orchestrated pop fluff that Merritt created with a Boston friend, Christopher Ewen; and the Gothic Archies emphasize a dark strain of techno-experimentation.

Merritt plays most of the instruments on his records. He has been working with electronic instruments for more than 20 years, plays guitar, piano, and "found" instruments (everything from Slinkys to old bicycle bells), and sings in a manner that is by turns witty and narrative, morose and deadpan—and sometimes all of those at once. It is not a "beautiful" voice by any means, and yet it is perfectly suited to his songs.

Still, there are many songs here that beg for cover versions by other artists, something Merritt warmly encourages. Indeed, he holds the concept of the confessional singer-songwriter in disdain and goes so far as to swear that there is not "a single autobiographical song" in the set. "I have been in some of the situations that I describe in those songs, but so has everyone else over the age of 18. I suppose I could have written 69 songs about my life, but that would be incredibly boring most of the time."

Mac McCaughan, one of the founders of Merge Records, has noted "something bizarrely traditional about Stephin."

"I think he'd like to put himself in the tradition of people like the Gershwins and Cole Porter," he said in a recent interview, "and I think he belongs in that tradition. Stephin isn't doing anything radical within the form of the song. He's content to work within certain parameters, and then within those parameters make amazing music."

When the late Paul Hindemith, as pragmatic a composer as the 20th century has produced, was asked where he got his inspiration, he held up his pencil.

"That's it," Merritt said. "I agree. One of the funny things about *69 Love Songs* is that it's such a denial of inspiration and confession and autobiography and sincerity. I simply set to work."

Perhaps, but *69 Love Songs* is filled with a plethora of human experience—from leaping joys to harrowing sorrows—and such knowledge cannot have been easily won. Whether or not there is autobiography in *69 Love Songs* doesn't really matter in the end, but the personal insights into glory and suffering are Merritt's own.

Right now, Merritt is recovering from the year-long process of recording *69 Love Songs* instrumental track by instrumental track, vocal by vocal, in his own apartment. He confessed that he was glad the disc was finished, but was already wondering what to do next.

His facility does not seem likely to desert him. As a sort of hypothetical test, I asked him if, over the course of the next few hours, he could write a song about anything—say, about sitting in an East Village restaurant on a spring afternoon and giving an interview, about a day when the stock market seemed about to collapse and worried patrons clustered around the television set, about the fire extinguisher hanging on the plaster wall and a ketchup bottle on our table.

Merritt sat quietly, mulling this over. "Sure," he finally said. Long pause. "I might want to take out the ketchup bottle, though."

The Washington Post
7 May 2000

Olivier Messiaen: In Memoriam

Accorning to legend, when the young Alfred Tennyson learned that Lord Byron had died, he went into the woods and carved "Byron is dead" on a stone.

I don't know exactly what this private gesture meant to Tennyson but I understand the impulse. The anecdote came to mind last April, when I was told that Olivier Messiaen had died at the age of 83. A world without Messiaen was obviously a very different thing than a world *with* him, and why shouldn't the nature he extolled and exalted reflect his passing?

For more than 80 years, Messiaen really *mattered*—both within the music world and, increasingly, to the general public as well. Messiaen inspired no little controversy during this time, but there was one point on which both his admirers and detractors could agree: there was nobody like him, and now that he is gone, there is nobody who can take his place.

A mystic Catholic who sought inspiration from birdsong and claimed to see colors when he composed, Messiaen was a complex, original thinker who, from the beginning, went his own way. His music combined angular melodies, intricate rhythm, and dense formal schemata in a manner that was subjective, passionate, extravagantly colorful, and often swooningly romantic.

The most celebrated French composer since Ravel, Messiaen was probably best known for his *Quatuor pour la Fin du Temps*—"Quartet for the End of Time"—a 50-minute composition for piano, violin, cello, and clarinet written while he was a prisoner of war in 1941. He chose these four instruments because they were the only ones available to him; the piano was missing some notes, a fact Messiaen took into account while fashioning his piece.

The *Quatuor* was first performed in Stalag VIIIa, a Silesian camp, for what was a genuinely captive audience of 5,000 prisoners, and it has since entered the repertory.

Other important works include *L'Ascension* (1933), a set of four "symphonic meditations"; *Vingt Regards sur l'Enfant Jésus* (1944), a two-hour cycle for solo piano, and the *Turangalîla* Symphony (1948), a massive creation for piano, large orchestra, and an electronic instrument called the ondes martenot. And at the time of his death, Messiaen had completed a 150th Anniversary commission for the New York Philharmonic, the 90-minute *Éclairs sur l'Au-delà...* .

Like Bach, Messiaen thought all music should be written to the greater glory of God. "I have not written liturgical music but rather meditative music on the mysteries of faith," he said in the early 1970s. "These works can be played in church, or in concert, or in the open air. I want to write music that is an act of faith, a music that is about everything without ceasing to be about God."

Messiaen was born in Avignon on December 10, 1908. At the age of 10, he discovered the music of Debussy and resolved to become a composer. He entered the Paris Conservatory the following year, where he studied improvisation and organ with Marcel Dupré and composition with Paul Dukas. Immediately after finishing his studies, he became principal organist at La Trinité in Paris. He joined the French army in World War II and was imprisoned in Silesia; upon his release in 1941, he joined the faculty of the Paris Conservatory.

There, he proved a tremendously influential teacher, who numbered Pierre Boulez, Karlheinz Stockhausen, and the young British composer George Benjamin among his most successful students. One of his principal technical innovations was a device he called "nonretrogradable rhythm"— that is, a sort of rhythmical palindrome that was the same coming and going. He taught at the conservatory for many years, as well as in Budapest, in Darmstadt, and at the Tanglewood Music Center (where this writer audited his lectures in 1975). His classes, like his personality, were unconventional, and embraced not only the masterpieces of traditional Western music but also Greek meters, Hindu rhythm, and birdsong.

This rapturous, retiring, devout, and conservative Catholic was not a natural candidate for leadership in the postwar avant-garde. In an era that made a fetish of concision, Messiaen was not afraid to be expansive: one piano work, *Catalogue d'Oiseaux* (1958) was 175 pages long and required almost three hours for performance. *Saint François d'Assise* (1983), his only opera, lasts nearly six hours.

Moreover, he wrote about his music in what was, on occasion, literally purple prose. Like Rimsky-Korsakov and Alexander Scriabin before him, Messiaen felt that music had a strong visual aspect. "When I hear music I see colors," he said, "not through my eyes but through my intellect. When I compose, I see the colors as I hear the sounds." He described one of his harmonic sequences as going "from blue striped with green to black spotted with red and gold, by way of diamond, emerald, purplish blue, with a dominant pool of orange studded with milky white." Once, while watching a ballet, he got a stomach ache because the violet hue of the lighting clashed with his conception of the color of G major.

Messiaen was particularly drawn to the works of Mozart, Berlioz, and Debussy. He had respect, rather than affinity, for the music of Arnold Schoenberg and his disciples; admired Stravinsky's *Le Sacre du Printemps* and wrote a celebrated analysis of its rhythms; acknowledged a tempered liking for Bartók; thought Varèse important; and considered Boulez the "greatest musician of his generation, and perhaps of his half-century."

He experimented with electronic music, utilized a variety of unusual percussion instruments, and wrote two microtonal works which he later dismissed as of scant value. Of aleatoric, or chance, music, he remarked: "As a good Catholic I do not believe in the elements of chance. Living under the conditions we do, I do not entertain or visualize any use of chance. But the great serialist composer is a master of chance, only he sets out his chances ahead of time."

Messaien's last work, *Éclairs sur l'Au-delà...* (Illuminations of the Beyond) received its premiere from the New York Philharmonic only a few months after the composer's death. Among other things, the score called for gongs, wind machine, and whips—and utilizes no fewer than 49 distinct bird-calls, including that of the Superb Lyrebird, the Chestnut-Crowned Laughing Thrush, the Large Wren-Babbler, the Helmeted Friarbird, the White-Bellied

Cuckoo Thrush, and the Tawny-Breasted Honey Eater, so that portions of the work sound like an aviary gone mad.

Whether or not one *liked* a given piece by Messiaen—and, to this taste, he wrote some of the best and some of the worst music of our century—it was always the expression of a unique sensibility. For better and for worse, there was never any doubt as to the composer's identity. Along with such divergent creators as Stravinsky, Copland, Harry Partch, Meredith Monk, Cecil Taylor, Brian Wilson, and Philip Glass, Messiaen made the listener aware, within a few measures, of a distinct voice, both personal and specific, which one might then take or leave.

This doesn't necessarily make the music good, of course (the famously horrible rock band The Shaggs is also immediately identifiable). But give the man credit: from the beginning, Messiaen spoke his piece, through six of the most eventful decades in music history. The flaws and virtues in *Éclairs sur l'Au-delà...* are very much those found in *From the Canyons to the Stars* (1974), the *Turangalîla* Symphony (1949), or even something so early as *L'Ascension* (1933). Here, Messiaen combines epical grandeur; thick, complicated harmonies (their modernism sweetened by a waft of incense from the organ lofts of Widor and Vierne); an acute sensitivity to musical color and timbral shadings; idiosyncratic, repetitive rhythmic mottos; and a stark, stiff, almost neo-Primitivist, sense of form. (At times, one cannot avoid the thought that Messiaen made his works with cosmic building blocks—or, perhaps, seraphic Lego.)

Reclusive by nature, Messiaen spent his summers in a small house in the Alps, where he could compose in solitude and listen to the morning cries of the birds. "I'm probably wrong to be this way," he said in 1967. "As a Christian, I should interest myself in everything and love my neighbor. But I must say that my current neighbors' principal preoccupations seem bizarre to me. Absurd, and completely different from my own state of mind."

It may have been just this alienation—this sense of being *in* the world but not quite *of* it—that made Messiaen such a hero to successive generations; this, and the way he combined a specific, unmistakably personal voice with a multiplicity of musical meanings. Formalists studied his technical innovations; minimalists were fascinated by his idiosyncratic use of repetition; mystics carried his scores around like holy writ; neo-romantics embraced his effusion and panoramic scope; postmodernists applauded the incorporation of non-European elements into his work. And it is certainly possible that some aching young composer slipped into the woods last April 28, in search of an appropriate stone.

Stagebill
1992

Midori at 21

By LATE MORNING on this first Friday in August, the "No Vacancy" signs were on and blinking most of the way down Route 7 to the Connecticut border. Lenox, the center of summer activity in the Berkshires, was clotted with automobiles, and despite the traffic cops' best efforts, there were the usual near-collisions at the irregular intersection where Walker Street meets Lenox-Pittsfield Road. The better restaurants were booked till Sunday, and merchants had extended their hours with the hope that the brief, bustling season would pay the bills through the cloistered winter just ahead.

It was, in fact, the very peak of the Tanglewood season—cool and clement, the perfect weekend for a Berkshires jaunt. Friday night, the legendary Italian pianist Maria Tipo would be playing Beethoven. On Sunday afternoon, Seiji Ozawa was scheduled to conduct the Boston Symphony Orchestra in Mahler's gigantic Third Symphony. But the popular attraction—the weekend's "star," as it were—was unquestionably Midori, the spectacular prodigy who began playing the violin at age four, entered Juilliard six years later, appeared at the White House before she was a teenager, and is now, at 21, among the most famous, highly paid, and critically acclaimed classical musicians in the world.

She stood on the Tanglewood stage, tiny even in her high heels, weighing less than 90 pounds, made up like a movie actress, her skirt and blouse aglow with the bright artificial coloring of lime and cherry Popsicles. David Zinman, the guest conductor, had just led the orchestra through the "Fingal's Cave" Overture and the "Italian" Symphony, in preparation for the following night's all-Mendelssohn program, stopping a dozen times along the way to correct little details. But Midori played right through Mendelssohn's violin concerto uninterrupted. A few pleasantries at the end, an admonition from Zinman to the orchestra to play more delicately in one passage that Midori takes especially softly, and the rehearsal was over. There was nothing more to do.

Theoretically at least, Friday morning rehearsals are open only to students of the Tanglewood Music Center. And there they sat—a privileged merciless audience made up of musicians in their teens and 20s, most of whom believe they can do anything and hunger fiercely for the opportunity to prove it.

The more caustic among them must have found this morning's performance frustrating. To begin with, Midori is not some wizened, superannuated "old master" but a *contemporary*—younger, in fact, than most of her select audience. More important, perhaps, there was virtually nothing to criticize; if Midori rarely surprises, she never disappoints. Her tone is always full, lustrous, and variegated; she inevitably hits every note exactly in its center, and she is a smart and sensitive musician.

Midori's interpretations might fairly be described as "middle of the road" —her playing is startlingly devoid of any tics or mannerisms—but her traditionalism is much more than learned mimicry; every note sings, every phrase bears the force of conviction. There are certainly more "interesting" violinists around, but it is hard to think of one who pleases so consistently. Midori does not provide an emotional high-wire act *à la* Nadja Salerno-Sonnenberg, nor cerebral, quasi-structural modernism in the manner of Gidon Kremer; there are rarely any "events" on which a critic may seize. Rather, she presents carefully planned, immaculately executed, glistening, and highly virtuosic standard performances of the standard repertory.

Her Stradivarius safely packed away, Midori walked toward the dressing room, followed by a pulsing, appreciative mob of admirers. Somebody's mother wanted to pass on best wishes from an old schoolmate (Midori was glad to hear he was well); one woman asked when Midori would next be playing in Texas (this fall, she thought, but wasn't sure just when); there were hugs to receive, compliments to acknowledge. She politely refused to autograph one admirer's score of the Mendelssohn concerto ("You don't sign your name on the Bible," she explained later). A friend from Juilliard, Boston Symphony cellist Owen Young, was invited into the dressing room and the two talked music for a few minutes—gigs, festivals, gossip, life on the road. "I got heat stroke while playing in Turkey," Midori told him, rolling her eyes. "I went to Israel next, and the whole time I was there, I lay on my bed like a dead duck."

Midori is a study in contrasts. At 21, she seems a mixture of very little girl and very old soul. There are Snoopy images inside her violin case and on her watch; her body language—when she isn't playing the violin—is that of a child, one well aware of its Lilliputian charm. She is unfailingly gracious to fans and to interviewers—indeed, in any one-to-one conversation—yet she does not meld easily into group discussions and often will withdraw into an impassive silence. She is obviously both bright and curious, but her knowledge is deep and narrow rather than integrated and wide-ranging. After a detailed, learned discussion of Willa Cather's novels, one that would do credit to a doctoral student in English—*My Antonia* is a favorite; *Death Comes for the Archbishop* was set in Santa Fe; *Song of the Lark* was based on the career of diva Olive Fremstad—Midori added that Cather was an early friend and supporter of the violinist Yehudi Menuhin. That's right, the reply came, and of Truman Capote, as well. At this, her face took on a look of gentle bewilderment.

"Who's Truman Capote?" she asked.

Of course, that Midori knows anything beyond the violin is in itself remarkable; many prodigies far less driven than she have no outside interests whatsoever. And Midori *is* driven. She cannot remember a time when she didn't play the violin; she apologizes for the fact that she now practices "only" four or five hours a day (pianist Arthur Rubinstein used to say that anything beyond two hours was superfluous); and she has a stubborn streak and a penchant for exactitude that occasionally smacks of the schoolmarm. (Alice Miller's classic psychological study, *The Drama of the Gifted Child*, comes up during a lunch conversation. "That's not what it's called," she said, reprovingly. "It's called *The Drama of Being a Child*. You'd better go back and check that again." I did; it's *The Drama of the Gifted Child*.)

"I look back on my childhood with great fondness," Midori said over a dessert of pistachio ice cream and chocolate cake in a Lenox restaurant. "Of course, I never had another childhood to compare it to. But I'm glad it was the way it was."

Midori Goto was born in Japan in 1971; she changed her name to Mi Dori in 1983—the year her parents were divorced—and later condensed it to the single word Midori. She began her violin studies in 1975; her mother, Sietsu Goto, was her first teacher. In 1980 a tape of her playing was sent to Dorothy DeLay, the celebrated (if controversial) Juilliard violin instructor who also taught Salerno-Sonnenberg, Shlomo Mintz, Cho-Liang Lin, and Nigel Kennedy, among others. Calling the playing "absolutely extraordinary," De-Lay accepted Midori as a scholarship student at the Aspen Music Festival. There, Pinchas Zukerman heard her play a Bartók concerto.

"Out comes this tiny little thing, not even 10 at the time," Zukerman later told the critic K. Robert Schwarz. "I was sitting on a chair and I was as tall as she was standing. She tuned, she bowed to the audience, she bowed to me, she bowed to the pianist. . . . She had a tiny little half-size violin, but the sound that came out—it was ridiculous. I was absolutely stunned. I turned to the audience and said, 'Ladies and gentlemen, I don't know about you, but I've just witnessed a miracle.'"

By 1982 Midori was studying at the Juilliard School with DeLay; she later abruptly severed all ties with her. DeLay, for one, has always insisted that Midori's mother was responsible for what seems to have been a fairly nasty rupture, but Midori insists it was her own idea. "It was the first time I made a really big decision," she said in 1990. "My mother, in fact, forced me to go back to one more lesson, but I couldn't take it anymore." Today, Midori avoids the subject; what *really* happened between the young violinist and her teacher has inspired much rumor and speculation in the restaurants and bars around 57th Street and Lincoln Center. As usual, however, those who talk most likely don't know and those who know definitely don't talk.

In any event, by the time she dropped DeLay in 1987, Midori already was a celebrity. She had made her reputation the summer before at Tanglewood, at the age of 14, with a display of professional grace under pressure that landed her on the front page of *The New York Times*. Toward the end of a performance of Leonard Bernstein's Serenade for Violin and String Orchestra, under the composer's direction, Midori broke a string. Unfazed, she borrowed the concertmaster's violin and continued playing. Another string broke; she borrowed the acting associate concertmaster's violin and kept on. "When it was over, audience, orchestra, and conductor-composer joined in giving her a cheering, stomping, whistling ovation," John Rockwell wrote in the *Times*.

"What could I do?" she wondered aloud two days later. "My strings broke and I didn't want to stop the music."

"She is diminutive, unpretentious, with a shy smile," I reported at the time. "She has thin arms and delicate fingers; her handshake is neither guarded nor effusive. Questions are answered succinctly but politely; she seems genuinely perplexed by all the fuss."

Seven years later, one senses that Midori may still be a little perplexed, but that she has gotten quite used to the fuss, which has grown exponentially. And yet, although she must make close to a million dollars a year, she continues to live with her mother in a modest apartment in an unfashionable corner of the Upper West Side. She does not drive (the Boston Symphony put a car and driver at her disposal in Lenox), has no romantic involvement ("How would she have time?" a friend asked when the subject came up), and her personality, like her art, is curiously removed from the untidiness of everyday life.

By any standard, it is an unusual existence, and Midori occasionally calls to mind some sort of benign, exquisite, alien visitor. Although she recently cut back a killing schedule that had her playing 95 concerts annually, Midori estimates she is home seven or eight weeks a year. The rest of the time she is on the road (she named New England, New Mexico, and Israel as her favorite places). "I like the feeling of waking up in the middle of the night and not knowing where I am," she said. "I sleep in total darkness, with sunglasses on. It's very mysterious." Indeed it is, a listener is tempted to add—in more ways than one.

Midori is fast approaching the crucible all prodigies must face: the moment when they become ex-prodigies. Throughout her professional life, much of her popular appeal has been based not only on her first-class musicianship but on the fact that she is also a genuinely *cute kid*. Now she no longer is the youngest violinist on the lot; that distinction belongs to Sarah Chang, in her early teens, who is getting a promotional buildup not unlike the one once accorded to Midori.

The transition into adulthood is a cruel one and not all prodigies survive it: Michael Rabin, perhaps the most naturally gifted violinist of all, lost himself in drugs and depression during his 20s and died at age 35. Another prodigy, Josef Hassid, made eight superlative recordings in his teen years that have ensured his reputation for almost half a century, then went mad and died in a mental hospital.

These are extreme cases. More often, the artist simply stops growing (one might argue that Yehudi Menuhin's finest records are those he made as a child). Midori, on the other hand, seems to have deepened. "I was always very disciplined," she said, "but now I'm learning how to work more spontaneity into my playing. I needed the discipline in the same way a building needs columns. But as I experience things and grow, the music will change so long as I'm honest with the music and myself.

"Of course, I felt things pretty intensely as a child," she continued. "A child can have important events in its life that may not seem so important to an adult. When I was six years old, my dog died, and it was a very profound experience for me, and it certainly affected my playing. Adults don't give children a chance to express their emotions, which can be just as deep but different from the emotions one feels as an adult."

Last year, Midori established a foundation (entitled, appropriately The Midori Foundation) with the expressed intention of bringing "the performing arts closer to the everyday lives of children." The foundation, with offices in New York, California, and Tokyo (and a board of honorary trustees consisting of Wynton Marsalis, Zubin Mehta—and Charles M. Schulz), presents free lecture-demonstrations by Midori and other artists in schools and other places.

"The programs will be designed to allow children to understand firsthand that involvement in music is not limited to a career for those with the requisite talent and ambition, but can produce an expanded sense of self-awareness, and bring them enjoyment for the rest of their lives," according to the foundation's statement of purpose. "Exposure to leading performers will also allow children to realize that major artists are human, and share many of their own thoughts and dreams." Midori played more than 40 foundation concerts worldwide last year; in all cases, she donated her services, and on several occasions she paid for the students' transportation to and from the events.

"I'd love to teach someday," she said. "I learn a lot when I conduct master classes. The fact that there are now younger violinists embarking on careers is not frightening for me, nor would I call it liberating. But I'd call it a good feeling. I see these young people performing and I sense a connection between my world and theirs. I'm sharing something with them, and as they grow up and mature the connection will only grow stronger."

What advice would she give to the young—or, rather, *younger*—Midori from her present vantage point? The answer came quickly. "Don't focus so much on one thing," she said with a sudden somberness. "I loved to play the violin and that's all I did. I learned so much after I left Juilliard when I was 15. I went to concerts, to the ballet, to the opera—*Turandot, Katya Kabanova,* and *The Ghosts of Versailles* were three of my favorites. I'd never had the time to enjoy music before. When I was 14, I loved the violin. Now I love music."

Newsday
19 September 1993

The National Symphony Orchestra in Europe

It's always exciting and illuminating to accompany an orchestra on tour, especially when that involves a couple of weeks in Europe. After years of uneven playing, the National Symphony Orchestra came into its own under Leonard Slatkin, and it has continued to surpass itself.

CENTRAL EUROPE has a deep significance for all who love classical music—this was the land of J. S. Bach, G. F. Handel, W. A. Mozart, Ludwig van Beethoven, Johannes Brahms, Richard Wagner, Anton Bruckner, and Anton Webern, among many others.

However, Leonard Slatkin and the National Symphony Orchestra decided to steer clear of all these composers but Beethoven on the troupe's 1997 European tour. Instead, the NSO played music by Americans: Arthur Foote and William Bolcom, Joseph Schwantner and Walter Piston, Charles Ives and Aaron Copland.

"One American orchestra came to Europe recently with a program that consisted of the Bruckner Fourth and the Schumann piano concerto," Slatkin said an hour before curtain time at the Musikhalle in Hamburg, Germany. "Moreover, its music director made a point of telling the press that he didn't want his group to be thought of as just an American orchestra. Well, I don't want to be just an American orchestra either, but we are an American orchestra and I want the audiences here to know something about the music of our country. I want people to remember not just how we played but what we played.

"When the European critics ask me about my selection of American music for this tour, I always want to reply, Well, how come your orchestras always bring us so much Bruckner and Brahms?" Slatkin continued. "First and foremost, you want to play good music, of course—that's above and beyond any nationalistic concerns. But, after that, I think it's important to take along something of our own."

In fact, American music is everywhere in Europe. The taxi driver who took me to the Rudolf-Oetker-Halle in Bielefeld, Germany, the first engagement on the tour, was a rock fan and his radio played throughout the ride—Madonna, Tom Petty, Bruce Springsteen, and others. He spoke no English but knew every word in every song and sang along without a trace of a German accent. (Later that night, I would hear some Bielefeld punkers—purple hair, nose rings, black leather, the works—bantering with one another in what can only be described as Teutonic Cockney.)

There is American jazz in the nightclubs and a sort of California-meets-MIT New Age concoction—pan flute and synthesizer whoosh—dribbling from the speakers during televised weather reports.

However, American symphonic and concert music has never really caught on, either in Europe or, until recently, at home. It is true that a few works have entered the standard repertory—Barber's Adagio for Strings, the tuneful orchestral confections of Gershwin, Bernstein's *Candide* Overture and Symphonic Dances From *West Side Story*, an occasional symphony from Ives or Copland. But the impression persists that much American music in this genre is either secondhand or second-class. Slatkin and the NSO are trying to set the record straight.

This was the orchestra's first venture abroad since 1994, and the first international tour of any kind since Slatkin became music director in 1996. The chartered Lufthansa took off from Dulles International Airport a little after 7:45 P.M. September 29, carrying some 140 people associated with the NSO—not only musicians but stage managers, technicians, operations directors, and the tour physician—all intent on ensuring that the leading orchestra from America's capital city would give the best possible account of itself Over There.

By the end of the 20-day tour last Sunday afternoon, the NSO had played 14 programs in 12 cities, including Vienna, Amsterdam, Paris, and London. There had been concerts in vast, elaborately ornamented 19th-century music palaces, and in dry, functional '60s-modern lecture halls. There were nights that culminated in standing ovations and others when the applause was so reserved that the NSO hardly had a chance to play its encores. Yet the rigor of traveling was easily made up for; the sheer differentness of everything, from the language spoken around you to the urgent, startling whoops of the European telephones, served to stimulate a peculiarly content and cheerful sense of alienation.

"Within certain bounds, we have allowed each city to choose its own program," Slatkin explained. "After all, our presenters know their audience and they have to sell the house and try to make a profit, while we collect the same fee no matter how many people show up." But it was one of Slatkin's prerequisites that every program include American music, and in addition to Verdi's overture to *La Forza del Destino* and Beethoven's "Emperor" Concerto (two of only four European works the NSO brought along), Bielefeld had opted for Aaron Copland's Symphony No. 3.

This is a modern, interested city and the audience responded warmly to the concert. "It's fascinating to gauge a European audience's reaction to something like the Copland Third," Slatkin said. "They don't usually know the piece, and I don't think they're really sure whether or not they like it until it's over. And then it seems to sink in that they've just heard something very good and the applause becomes more and more enthusiastic as it goes on."

The Copland would become one of the tour's highlights. It is both long-breathed and syncopated (a combination rarely found in European music) and the extended slow movement does not seem searching and mystical so much as still and open, without affect, almost motionless—as full of space as a prairie vista.

After the show, some members of the NSO turned in for the night, while others made for the hotel bar. Musicians are a social lot and the conversation went on late into the evening. There was general satisfaction with the Bielefeld performance, along with a certainty that better concerts were to come. Contrabassoonist Lewis Lipnick was eagerly anticipating the visit to Stuttgart the following day. Like the oboe, the English horn, and the standard bassoon, the contrabassoon is a double-reed instrument, and one of the world's best reedmakers just happened to live in the Stuttgart area. "I plan to take home pretty close to a hundred reeds," he said. "That ought to hold me for a while."

First oboist Rudolph Vrbsky makes his reeds. It is a point of pride with many players, rather as rolling one's own cigarettes used to be in a less health-conscious generation. "I wake up, I carve a reed, I play on it for a while, then touch it up some more before the concert." Every morning? "Every morning. I always say—a reed a day keeps the psychiatrist away."

In other corners of the bar, the talk was more intimate. There were candid discussions about the state of the orchestra and its various sections. NSO veterans swapped tales of previous tours—the trip to the Soviet Union with Mstislav Rostropovich, say, or the Asian jaunt three years ago and the all-but-incurable jet lag it brought on. Finally, it was time to make our way upstairs— to find our rooms, cover ourselves with the thick down pillows the Germans prefer to blankets, and listen to the northern rain batter against the window.

By the time we arrived in Stuttgart the following afternoon, the city was garrulous pandemonium. It was Reunification Day, a bank holiday, and most of Germany took a vacation. The trains were overflowing with families, and in the parks and plazas throughout the city, young people listened to rock bands, watched jugglers and light shows, and swigged pilsner and Rhine wine. Charles Baudelaire once wrote about the inexplicable joy of "taking a bath in crowds" and that's what a walk through Stuttgart felt like on this fine Friday in early October. The mood was exuberant—indeed, positively over the top but inevitably polite—and a visitor was welcome to join in the celebration.

And why not? Who among us, raised during the Cold War, could have imagined the events of 1989–91—that the Berlin Wall would be torn down, that Eastern Europe would free itself from 45 years of subjugation, that the whole Soviet Union would simply implode? For a younger generation, this series of interrelated developments made up the historical event of a lifetime.

Indeed, throughout our 11 days in Germany, the greetings were unmistakably friendly, and particularly in the larger cities, some English was usually spoken. When a German doesn't know any English at all, he or she will likely beam and find some mysterious way of conveying the memory of that marvelous time in Florida one winter. Having no gift whatsoever for foreign languages, I briefly acquired the absurd habit of trying to make myself understood by pronouncing American words with a German accent ("Steak mit on-YONS, ja?"), but gave it up for fear of sounding like a dialect comedian.

Europe is a different world, no doubt about it. The intelligence and general cultivation of the people comes as a salutary shock; the collapse of Western civilization may not be quite so imminent as we think. Even a railway newsstand in a provincial city like Bielefeld will have more substantial books —more books in English —than all but a few major American airports. Much of the harebrained movie star coverage is gone from the European editions of the American newsmagazines, replaced by thoughtful, searching articles about actual events (including at least two wars I'd never heard of). Even CNN International is several steps ahead of what is telecast back home, and if you change the channel, you may run across a production of Shakespeare or Glenn Gould playing Bach.

Although the Beethovenhalle in Stuttgart proved one of the poorest halls on the trip, it was here that Slatkin unveiled perhaps the strongest of the American works on the itinerary, Walter Piston's Symphony No. 2. It was written for the NSO in 1943, and it is beautiful—grave, brooding, mostly consonant but never deliberately nostalgic, meticulously wrought yet brimming with feeling. Another American beauty was Arthur Foote's Suite for Strings—mellow, welling, richly sentimental but always remaining within formal bounds, like the late music of Richard Strauss.

Even the performances of standard repertory had a distinctly American edge. For example, Slatkin and pianist Emanuel Ax deliberately played down the pomp in the "Emperor" Concerto. Instead, in the outer movements, we heard bright, lean melodies presented with an unfettered thrust and exuberance, while the Andante was spun lovingly, with a Chopin-like dewiness in the pianism. Ax's modesty, friendliness, and collegial spirit made him a great favorite with the NSO players, who accorded him that coveted tribute from musician to musician—the stomping of onstage feet—at the end of his performances.

Another morning, another airport. As we prepared to depart for Vienna, Slatkin was presented with a magazine article that called him the "*Wundermann aus Washington*." "Better than *Uebermensch*, I guess," he said, a little embarrassed. In fact, Slatkin was not feeling at all wonderful; a 24-hour cold was circulating within the NSO, and his number had come up. After working on some crossword puzzles during the short flight and making small talk during the ride from the airport to downtown Vienna, Slatkin grabbed a snack in the cafe of the Hotel Imperial, went up to his suite, and fell asleep for the afternoon.

No matter how often one stays in Vienna, it always feels like a final exam. Just how "civilized" are you anyway? How shiny are your shoes? How oversized your calling card? How authoritative the dressing-down that is expected of you when the waiter brings you coffee and you have ordered tea? This is a proud and curiously involuted city, both haunted and infatuated by its past. The Lipizzaner stallions are trained to dance to Mozart minuets and the cafes are filled with dowagers feeding chocolates to sweatered dachshunds, but indoor laughter from a child, no matter how soft and sweet it may sound to American ears, is taken as an affront to the general peace.

And yet the visitor is always surprised by sudden—and genuine—displays of generosity and sentiment; the heart still beats, if not necessarily in the waltz time for which the city is famous. Vienna has an unparalleled musical heritage; even though most important decisions in the international music business are now made by management offices and record companies in New York, London, Hamburg, and Tokyo, the residents of Vienna know their chosen music more intimately and care about it more passionately than does any other audience in the world.

A tough sell then, Vienna—particularly for Americans playing American —and the response to the first concert, at the Konzerthaus, was tepid. This was due in part to native reserve, in part to the hall's acoustics (the musicians claimed they could not hear one another), and in part to some weak scores (a meretricious piano concerto from William Bolcom and William Schuman's workmanlike but uninspired Symphony No. 5). At the conclusion of this disappointing program, I found myself wishing the NSO had packed a show-stopper—an American work of especial power and virtuosity. John Corigliano's Symphony No. 1, which this orchestra plays as nobody else does, would have fit the bill; if past performances were any indication, it would have left even the coolest Old World audience shaken and spent.

But, as it happened, just such a show-stopper was deployed the following night when Evelyn Glennie played the first Viennese performance of Joseph Schwantner's Percussion Concerto at the legendary Musikverein, where symphonies by Brahms, Bruckner, and Mahler received their world premieres. Over the concerto's 25-minute duration, Glennie leapt from one instrument to another with the efficiency and exactitude of an Olympic gymnast, drawing out wave upon wave of sound—now ferocious thunder from the bass drum, now rapid-fire quasi-minimalist patterns for marimba, now a bright, glassy explosion of chimes. For all her stamina, strength, and dexterity, however, it was Glennie's musicianship that won the night—the conviction she radiated, the subtle gradations of tone and color she brought to every phrase.

The percussion concerto—and Glennie—exhilarated the Musikverein audience and inspired a whistling, stomping ovation that went on for more than 10 minutes, something highly unusual in Vienna. Oboist Vrbsky thought it was one of the peak moments of the tour: "I loved to see the Viennese swinging and swaying with Schwantner."

What a difference a concert hall can make! In the Musikverein—where the acoustics are considered among the best in the world—Schwantner's sounds washed over us like an aural tide. Two nights later, in Hoechst, a close suburb of Frankfurt, the auditorium seemed better suited to a science class or a minor political debate. The music sounded terribly far away; there was no immediacy whatsoever (we watched and listened as through a telescope, backward). Still, Glennie brought the crowd to its feet here, too—and the NSO sold 75 copies of its new RCA Victor CD of the Schwantner in the lobby.

Frankfurt is sometimes disparaged by Germans, who consider it a gigantic depot without any national character (it contains both the largest airport and busiest train station in the country). In fact, the inner city was charming and antiquated, and the skyscrapers were mostly relegated to the outskirts. From Frankfurt onward, a good amount of time was spent on Germany's Bundesbahn railroad. The trip north through the Rhineland permitted views of 13th-century castles above the river, and the commodious stations where we boarded our trains—crowded, animated, filled with chocolate shops and groceries and bars amid the October light pouring down through the glass and dust—were hives of activity. High-pressure American advertisement is a rarity on the platforms here, although there were ads in every station for Meredith Brooks, billed as the "*neue* U.S.A. superstar," and her new album, *Blurring the Edges* (why do so many of these pseudo-tantalizing gender references sound like a problem for an oculist?).

The city of Cologne (where the orchestra played in an unusually fine modern hall) is dominated by the spires of its ancient cathedral, almost 1,000 years in the construction. The general atmosphere there was that of an affluent, just-bathed Bohemia—galleries, performance spaces, and some of the best restaurants in Germany. The next night we were off to Dusseldorf, 25 miles away, which couldn't have been more different. This is one of the wealthiest cities in Germany and one had the sense that somebody had blown up a pretentious suburban American shopping mall and then settled all the stores—H. Stern, Bally, Versace, and the rest—right along the main street.

The NSO moved into Hamburg along with the first cold front of the year. There can be few things more intrinsically poetic than an autumn walk through a northern city—the leaves aflame, the sky a spectrum of grays, horse chestnuts decorating the bleached grass like littered dollops of mahogany. As it was a Sunday morning, bells began to chime—austere, heavy tolling from downtown, gentler ringing from the suburb of Altona, different tones from near and far, this neighborhood and that, steeped in history and fresh as the day, a tintinnabulation that overwhelmed the visitor with the sensation that Hamburg itself had been turned into music.

The Hamburg Musikhalle was sumptuous and the orchestra played a strong concert (the highlight was a sweeping, expansive, minutely detailed Sibelius Second Symphony). And then it was off to Amsterdam and the last great hall of the tour—the Concertgebouw.

Because Amsterdam itself is below sea level, the Concertgebouw was actually found to be settling into the canals a few years ago (reinforcements were immediately put into place). This is a warm, lush, superbly maintained, and wonderfully old-fashioned building (one can easily imagine it in gaslight), less ornate than the Musikverein but equally beautiful in its patrician manner. The boxes and balconies were inscribed with the names of composers past, some of them likely known only to Dutch musicologists. The welcome was probably the warmest of the tour; the patrons looked like happy characters in a Bergman movie. One watched their faces intently, as they listened, gently glowing, to the beloved music. There was a full-hearted and immediate standing ovation after the Beethoven Piano Concerto No. 3, after which Ax performed a solo encore and the applause redoubled. It was obvious that the audience would have listened all night.

Ax was pleased to reach Paris, the day after the triumph in Amsterdam. "This is my favorite city, but I never get to see it because I have to practice," he said with a mixture of contentment and regret. He was less than pleased with the unresponsive piano in the Théâtre des Champs-Élysées. Nor did Slatkin much like the hall: "Dry and distant, a little bit like a very tall version of the Eisenhower Theater," he said. "But Paris is Paris—what a city!"

Throughout the tour, the press was respectful—and often enthusiastic—although rarely especially searching or precise, at least on the Continent. The

Frankfurter Rundschau called Slatkin "the old master of the baton" (an odd compliment for a man who passed his 50th birthday only two years ago) but complimented the "thrillingly live, virtuoso performance" of the Copland symphony. The critic for the *Stuttgarter Nachrichten* was unimpressed by the American music (the Schuman was academic and "decidedly retrospective," while the Piston had "the same pious, powerful effect as many other American works of the '30s and '40s") but praised Ax and the "Emperor" Concerto. The critic for the Vienna *Kurier* inexplicably found elements of jazz and ragtime in the Piston symphony and thought the NSO rhythms too smooth for Gershwin's *American in Paris*.

The last two concerts took place at London's Royal Festival Hall, on the south bank of the Thames, and then in Birmingham, perhaps the leading musical center in the English Midlands. Tim Ashley in *The Guardian* thought the Copland a "showpiece for the Washington sound—big and beefy, with glorious brass," and Barry Millington in *The Times* praised the "high octane" performance of the Schwantner.

Relaxing backstage in Paris with one of the American root beers that follow him everywhere, Slatkin declared himself "very satisfied" with the progress of the tour. "The Europeans know now who we are and what we're all about," he said. "And we've been able to hear ourselves in some of the best halls in the world—as well as a few poorer ones, of course. It's a little like playing the same record on a lot of different stereo systems; there really is a difference. And, after this tour, I'm convinced that the new Kennedy Center Concert Hall will probably rank with the best."

At that moment, there were only eight days left before the grand opening back in Washington. Reminded of that fact, Slatkin laughed and shook his head. "Wow," he said. "Believe it or not, most of the time when orchestras get back from a tour, they get to take it easy for a while."

The Washington Post
26 October 1997

The Ordeal of Kevin Oldham

This may be the most agonizingly difficult article I ever wrote, and it re-mains the one of which I am most proud. Kevin Oldham was dying fast when I set to work, and as the reader will soon discover, there were no assurances that he would fulfill his duties with the Kansas City Symphony. And so I fed the article, paragraph by paragraph, to my waiting editors at Newsday, *as Kevin suffered and endured. The story ends on what turned out to be a note of false hope: Kevin felt fine on the morning we last spoke, but later in the day he was back in the hospital, and he never came out. I remember him as a gifted, courageous, and gallant young man, and I re-main grateful for—and amazed by—his candor under enormously trying circumstances.*

KEVIN OLDHAM, weary and gaunt, lay on his bed, propped by pillows, surrounded by medications, speaking softly into the telephone. It was January 7, some four and a half weeks after the diarrhea had begun in earnest, and exactly 10 days before he was due to play his piano concerto with the Kansas City Symphony.

"I'm just trying to hold myself together," he told his caller. "I think I can handle the physical stuff if I rest a lot, pace myself—yeah, we're trying out another new treatment. What worries me is the psychological stress. Ever since the hospital, I'm just really *scared* all the time."

It has been five years since Oldham, now 32, tested positive for the HIV virus, and a little more than two years since he developed full-blown AIDS.

Since then, pneumocystis pneumonia has come and gone, Oldham's weight has dropped to 135, his T-cells have fallen below 100, and he has become all too familiar with the workings of AZT, Bactrim, pentamidine, and the rest of our inadequate medical arsenal. One month ago, he was in the Lenox Hill Hospital AIDS ward, 8 East, fighting for his life. He survived that battle and returned home to prepare for yet another—the first professional performance of his largest work, set to take place in the city where he grew up.

"Local boy makes good," Oldham reflected with a sad smile as he hung up the phone. "I just wish the circumstances were more cheerful." He lay back and shut his eyes for a moment. Soon Stephen Rotondaro, a costume designer and his lover of three years, would be home from work. ("He gets tested regularly and consistently comes back HIV-negative," Oldham said with what seemed a wistful pride.) Then the two of them would share a small supper—if Oldham felt up to eating, by no means a foregone conclusion in the last few weeks. Outside in the hall, Oldham's cat, a handsome, exotic-looking Oriental Shorthair named Jeffrey, mewed for admittance while, across the Hudson from Oldham's high-rise West Side apartment, the lights of New Jersey sparkled in a cold dusk.

For every Rudolf Nureyev, Michael Bennett, or Rock Hudson, for every celebrity who dies from AIDS at or near the pinnacle of his profession, there are a thousand writers, dancers, musicians, actors, and other artists who didn't have time to fulfill their potential. We will never know whether Kevin Oldham might have turned into a great composer; he has written only a few lively and touching songs, some spectacularly virtuosic piano music, a handful of choral works, and this piano concerto, by far his most ambitious creation. The rest is silence—and the memory of promise. The closest analogy to what has happened to the arts in the past decade would be that slaughtered generation of young Englishmen—a much more authentic "lost generation" than anything associated with Ernest Hemingway—who blithely marched off to war in 1914, leaving behind fragments of novels, some chamber music, short books of poems, and a profoundly diminished national culture.

"I set goals for myself to keep going," Oldham said as he sipped from a cup of water on the nightstand. "You know, if you're going to hang glide from one peak to another, if they're not too far apart, you know you can do it. But if you see one that's way off in the distance, you start to worry. You start to say, whoa! I'm really not sure I can make it. I've known the Kansas City Symphony wanted to do my concerto for almost a year. And for me, in my condition, that's a long time to glide."

"But I'm almost there."

Two days later, Karen Kushner was distraught. Just back from holiday vacation with her family, Kushner, a close friend for 15 years, a fellow Midwesterner, and a fine, sensitive pianist herself, had paid her first visit to Oldham since he left the hospital, and she was visibly alarmed by his condition.

"He's so frail," she said over wine in a Lincoln Center restaurant. "He wanted to play through the concerto for me, and he kept forgetting where he was. He'd get very angry—slam his hands down and say, 'Damn it, I *know* my own piece.' And I'd say, 'Of course you do, Kevin. But who *wouldn't* have some memory slips with all you're going through, with all the drugs you're on?'

"Kevin was a couple years behind me at Northwestern," Kushner recalled. "Talk of his pianistic abilities spread quickly throughout the music school, and I was most curious to meet him. When I did, I was impressed with his technical mastery and his natural musical talent, but I must admit that I was unprepared for his warmth, his humor, his charisma, and his charm. I was instantly won over, and I grew to love him deeply."

Her brown eyes moistened. "This concert means so much to Kevin. I only wish I were more confident that he was going to make it."

Oldham flew out to Kansas City on Sunday afternoon January 10, several days before the first rehearsal, to rest up and visit with his parents, whom he described as "two of my dearest, closest friends." "They have been extremely supportive throughout my illness, very open, and my mom has gotten a lot of the most recent books about AIDS to read up on the subject and understand what's going on with me."

Rotondaro remained at home in New York, with reservations to fly out the day before the concert. "Kevin told me he was HIV positive shortly after we met," he said, "and, quite frankly, it was really hard for me to decide whether I wanted to continue seeing him. But he was so musical, so funny, so warm and good that I knew he was already terribly important to me, and we've been together ever since."

"Will he make it through the concert? Well, here's a little story. The way I knew Kevin was really sick the night before he went into the hospital was because he wasn't playing the piano. He loves music and he loves performing; Old-Ham is not a bad last name for him. If there is any way he *can* play, he *will* play. That's for sure."

Kevin Oldham was born in Kansas City on August 30, 1960. His father, William Oldham, directed choruses in local high schools and churches; his mother, Barbara Oldham, a soprano, occasionally appeared as a soloist. "I started piano when I was five," he said.

> And then when I was about nine I got the theater bug, because my dad was directing summer shows in the park—you know, *Mame*, *The Music Man*, that kind of stuff—and I would audition for the children's roles and usually get them, not because of my father but because I was a pretty good boy soprano. And then my voice changed, and I went back to the piano, played in some local competitions, and lost one of them. I think that's the first time I was ever really depressed, and I made up my mind that it wasn't ever going to happen again.

And so Oldham, determined to become a concert pianist, began practicing eight hours a day. "My favorite composers were Ravel and Debussy; I also loved Scarlatti." He entered Northwestern University on a piano scholarship and won several competitions in the Chicago area. "But I always had this feeling that I should be in New York, that my life wouldn't be complete unless I was in the big leagues."

He moved to New York in the summer of 1981 and entered the Juilliard School, where he studied with Sascha Gorodnitzki and Herbert Stessin. The same year, he began his first serious love affair, with a man he now identifies only as Tom. "We were introduced by some friends and that was *it*, you know—my jaw just sort of hit the pavement. He had recently broken up with his lover and had moved his stuff out and I remember that he was particularly glad to lose the upright piano because it took up too much space. Little did he know that I'd soon be moving in with a seven-foot grand!"

Oldham and Tom lived together for seven years. In the fall of 1988, although he felt completely healthy, Oldham had himself tested for the HIV virus, almost out of curiosity. He was stunned when the test results were positive. "Tom was furious with me for finding it out. He said it dashed all of his hopes. And I said to him, 'Look, if it's there, you might as well find out and start doing something about it.' But that wasn't his belief."

The two separated shortly thereafter but remained friends.

Life went along fairly smoothly until the fall of 1990 when Tom tested positive and at the same time found out he had tuberculosis. He started treatment and got better, then he came back, abandoned all of the conventional medical drugs and started this wild alternative therapy called uropathy—drinking a cup of your own urine every day. It was just ludicrous.

Well, you don't mess around with TB. Two months later Tom looked like a Dachau refugee and was in the hospital. I notified his parents, which really angered him, and he wouldn't speak to me for a while; he had just told them things like "I'm sorta sick," you know? They brought him back to Omaha and nursed him for a while; then he came back to New York, caught pneumonia, and died within two weeks.

I'll send these words out on the wind
You'll feel their warmth; it's in the breeze
The thought is clear; My heart is breaking
You're oh so far away . . .
—"Not Even If I Try," a song by Kevin Oldham

"I had written 'Not Even If I Try' for another friend, a guy named Doug Sayers," Oldham said.

God, it's been almost five years now. I hadn't talked to him for a couple of months and then I called him up and his phone had been disconnected and changed to another number with a different area code. And I called there, and it turned out Doug had found out he had HIV, driven to New Jersey, and killed himself with carbon monoxide.

But now that song has come to have very close associations with Tom. I sang it on June LeBell's show, *The Listening Room*, on WQXR shortly after he died, and I cracked a few notes—my heart *was* breaking—but we got a strong response. And after we did the broadcast June recommended me to the conductor of a summer festival out in New Jersey, and he asked me if I could write a piano concerto for them. And I said, Sure, sure, a piece of cake. A whole piano concerto in six months? No *problem*. Needless to say, it was a hell of a lot harder than I thought.

Oldham set to work immediately, but progress was slow.

And then in mid-April I got sort of sick. And June LeBell had been asking, you know, how's it going? And I said it was going okay, but I was going to have a hard time with the orchestration. Throughout this time, I had kept my job in the public relations department of Jim Henson Productions, and it was a real high-pressure thing, trying to do my work and compose on the side, all the while fighting to maintain my health. But, unbeknownst to me, June had written about 40 or 50 letters to people in our chorus—we sang together in the Marble Collegiate Church Choir—asking them to donate part or all of their fee for singing one Sunday into a seed fund to get me some help. And so I was able to finish a two-piano version and hire an orchestrator [Steve Cohen]— with a lot of my own suggestions about which instruments I wanted where—and we finished it up in time for the concert.

The premiere of Oldham's piano concerto took place in 1991; he played the solo part with the Festival of the Atlantic in Point Pleasant, New Jersey. "It was a decent performance, but it was a summer orchestra, we had only about an hour to rehearse a half-hour piece, and it was played outside, so the acoustics were all wrong. But when it was over we got a screaming, roaring standing ovation from several thousand people. And I felt pretty good; I could stand having one of those every night."

Oldham sent copies of the tape to various orchestras, recording companies, and foundations. The response was limited—orchestras and recording companies are drowning in unsolicited tapes. Still, in January 1992 he received a call from the Kansas City Symphony asking him to play the concerto the following year on a program devoted to composers from the area (of whom the late Virgil Thomson was only the most illustrious).

"We had been aware of Kevin for a long time." Susan Franano, the general manager of the Kansas City Symphony, said.

> He played for William McGlaughlin and me several years back, and we decided then to look for an opportunity to use him as a piano soloist in one of our concerts. When we heard his concerto, we decided to build our program around him, to bring a local composer home in triumph from New York to play in Kansas City. And then he told us he had AIDS. We were saddened, of course, but it made no difference to our programming; we really liked his piece, and we really wanted him to play it, AIDS or no AIDS. It was a musical decision: we didn't put the concerto on our program because Kevin had AIDS, and we certainly weren't going to take it off for that reason. And Kevin was generally still feeling well when we first talked about it.

By the middle of 1992, however, it was obvious that Oldham's health had begun to fail, and by the end of the year, he was no longer able to take care of himself.

> I'd planned to practice the concerto all through December. But then I started getting very sick and on December 3, I checked myself into Lenox Hill. I was there three weeks, and they were the worst weeks of my life. The doctors just couldn't figure out what was wrong, despite all the invasive tests—liver biopsy, bone biopsy, lung biopsy, colonoscopy —man, I'd rather have somebody push an 18-inch television screen up into me than go through a colonoscopy again! All these tests I swore I'd never submit to—I'd made a list and I just checked them off as I had them, one by one.
>
> But I continued to get worse, and nobody knew why. And finally my doctor—who really meant well, really cared a lot—sat down, and we had a very blunt 20-minute talk. And he said, "You've gotten worse since you've been in here. We may never find a cure for what you have or even figure out exactly *what* you have. We keep looking and looking and nothing turns up. You're already on some oxygen and if your breathing gets worse, do you want to be on a respirator?"
>
> And I said, "No, no—I have a living will, and there's no *way* I'm going on a respirator." So then my doctor left, and I was just numbed; it takes

me a while to assimilate information. Stephen, who has been so good, so patient with me, showed up about 10 minutes later, and it was just like a bad scene from *Terms of Endearment*. The hospital was having its Christmas party, and we were both sitting on the bed, crying in each other's arms while they were singing "We Wish You a Merry Christmas" out in the hall.

So that night I got angry about it all and started thinking about my own body. And I really didn't feel I had a foot in the grave. I decided that part of what was making me sick was the mental stress of being in the hospital—although the staff couldn't have been much more wonderful, I must say, and under the most trying circumstances. Still, I'd seen three people die in the ward since I'd been there—a lady down the hall, one guy who just coughed so much his body couldn't take it any more, another who had pancreatitis and was moaning all the time. My poor roommate, bless his heart, was incontinent the whole time; he couldn't make it to the bathroom, so it all ended up on the floor between our beds and stayed there most of the night until housekeeping came in. He died two days after I left.

Anyway, I just decided I'd had enough and that it was time to get myself out of there.

Although nobody wanted to admit it (or even to *think* it) at the time, the first rehearsal of Kevin's piano concerto, at the Lyric Theater in Kansas City on Friday, January 15, was something of a disaster. Playing the piano—especially playing the sort of charged, strenuous, exultantly virtuosic music Kevin writes—takes a great deal of physical stamina and on this particular afternoon he simply couldn't summon enough of it to do the job. Time and again, although conductor McGlaughlin did his best to subdue his forces, Kevin was virtually drowned out by the orchestra.

Kushner had arrived from the airport, and after greeting Barbara Oldham with a hug, she listened apprehensively from a middle row at the Lyric Theater. There was some cause for hope: the second movement, a nostalgic, bittersweet Andante tranquillo, was eloquently phrased by both pianist and orchestra. And although it would have been immediately apparent to anyone that Kevin was sick, he looked much better than he had the week before.

"Kevin's put on four pounds since he's been home," Barbara Oldham, a kind-faced, sad-eyed woman, said with maternal pride. "If he has to excuse himself at dinner, we make sure there's some more food on his plate when he comes back. And he'll say, 'Hey, I thought I finished that Jell-O,' and we'll all laugh." She grew pensive. "If I could just keep him here for a while, I'm sure I could fatten him up."

From the journal of Kevin Oldham:

I'm beginning to panic and get stressed out. My hands shake, legs shake, and I have a 100.8 fever. I was a mess after practicing tonight. I can barely hold anything to write. Depressed. . . . Had first rehearsal today. Bill McGlaughlin is great to work with and it gets me all choked up when I hear them play my music. Thank God for adrenaline. I made stupid mistakes. I really do think I have an eye problem and memory blackouts. . . . Am very nervous and that may be part of the memory problem.

Stephen arrives today. Yay!

"He's shaking like a leaf," Kushner whispered as Oldham took the stage late Saturday morning for the second rehearsal. It was true; his arms and hands trembled feverishly, uncontrollably, as if he were suffering from a nervous palsy. And yet, through force of will, very little of this physical discomfort found its way into the actual sound of the playing. There were a few memory slips, a few approximated passages, and even a few "clinkers"; certainly, it was not the fire-breathing, slam-bang performance Oldham could have de-livered even a few months before. But it was in every way respectable, and when it was over McGlaughlin and the orchestra applauded and Oldham broke into a big smile that seemed to take years off his age.

"Every time I get to that one section, I think damn it! Why'd I make the piano part so hard?" Oldham said.

"Don't worry about it," the unfailingly cheerful and supportive McGlaugh-lin replied. "It's sounding fine, and we're with you all the way." Indeed, by this point, it was obvious from the players' faces—from the way members of the orchestra visibly tensed when Kevin approached a difficult passage and then just as visibly relaxed when he had conquered it—that they were deeply involved, to a degree that far exceeded mere professionalism, with the human drama unfolding upon their stage.

"This is the sort of piece nobody else is writing just now—a real piano concerto in the grand manner," McGlaughlin said during a break. "It is full of beautiful melodies, and there are some wonderful display passages for the soloist. The third movement is so brash, so Broadway, so full of pizzazz—it sounds like what Jerome Robbins might have written if he'd composed a piano concerto."

After the rest of the musicians had packed their instruments and left, Oldham and Kushner sat together on the empty stage, sharing confidences and talking piano, the way they had at Northwestern, back when none of this could have been foreseen.

Stephen Rotondaro answered the phone at the Oldham residence late Sunday morning, three hours before showtime. "Kevin didn't sleep at all last night," he said. "He was just too tense. He went down for a rest after breakfast, and I hope he's fallen asleep now."

He hadn't. Five minutes later, Oldham returned the call, and at least some of his fatigue seemed to have mutated into serenity. "I'm completely worn out, but I'm getting used to that by now," he said. "And I'm pretty well prepared. We'll see how it goes. My pride catches me up sometimes—I really feel I should be capable of playing all the right notes in my own piece, and I get so frustrated when I can't."

The *Kansas City Star* ran an article and a picture on the front page of its Sunday arts section. "A Pianist Grows into a Composer," the headline proclaimed. In smaller type it added "KC native Kevin Oldham doesn't have the luxury of time. He has AIDS." It was the first mention of his condition in the local press, and it no doubt inspired the woman who dropped off an encouraging, compassionate, anonymous letter, infused with Catholic theology and complete with a rosary, at the Lyric Theater shortly before Oldham took the stage.

Some 750 people came downtown this cold, clear afternoon to hear the program McGlaughlin dubbed, appropriately, "Goin' to Kansas City." Mc-

Glaughlin conducted an array of different works—fragments from Virgil Thomson's *Symphony on a Hymn Tune*, a Charlie Parker medley, a hastily scheduled memorial tribute to the late Dizzy Gillespie, and several works by local composers—before introducing Oldham. Immaculately groomed in a dark suit (Rotondaro and Kushner had spent the first half of the concert keeping him company and helping him dress), Oldham walked from the wings, bowed smartly, sat down at the keyboard, then took a deep breath and rolled his eyes nervously toward McGlaughlin as if to say "I'm as ready as I'll ever be," and waited for the downbeat.

The concerto may be faulted for a number of technical shortcomings: Oldham never took formal composition lessons, and he has yet to fully transcend his influences. Moreover, one learns through experience, and this concerto is Oldham's first full-fledged orchestral piece. But these imperfections in no way preclude appreciation of a genuine and bounteous talent and the rhapsodic, mercurial—and sometimes achingly beautiful—work it has produced. And although there is considerable humor in Oldham's concerto (particularly in the last movement), one is especially impressed by its seriousness of purpose. It was not written for an academic degree; it was not written for money; it was not written for career advancement. It was written as a testament.

And Oldham played it that way, with ferocious concentration and all the strength he could muster. It was as if he were determined to tell the world that there was once a man named Kevin Oldham and *this* was the way he felt about life and *this* was the way he wrote music and *this* was the way he could play the piano—a conscious culmination of the years of practice, the long hours of meditation, the genetic predisposition and family relations, the friendships, love affairs, joys, and sufferings that sometimes, mysteriously, combine to create an artist. It should have been Oldham's first great triumph; it may well have been his last. Under no illusions, he blinked out across the footlights and savored the standing ovation—laughing, crying, exhausted, grateful, overwhelmed.

Monday morning; the day after. Oldham, sounding stronger and more relaxed than he had in weeks, was pleased with Scott Cantrell's favorable critique in the *Kansas City Star*, under the headline "Ailing Composer's Concerto Draws Ovation."

"I think he summed it up pretty well—the good and the bad," Oldham said.

> You know, when it was all over, at first I was very upset with myself. I made some obvious mistakes—at least, they were obvious to me. But when I think back to my time in Lenox Hill, only three and a half weeks ago, when it didn't seem that I had much of a chance to leave the hospital, let alone play this concert, everything turned out pretty well. It was the best I could do and I have to accept that.

His voice brightened. "Anyway, Bill McGlaughlin told me he wants to program the concerto again, and I'm going to try to raise funding for a recording, maybe later on this spring."

Hang gliding to yet another peak? Kevin laughed gently. "I guess so," he said. "I guess so. And you know what? Maybe I can make it."

Samuel Ramey

FROM AN AIRPLANE, the farms and flatlands of western Kansas look like nothing so much as a vast linoleum floor, countless squares and rectangles framed by black borders that, upon closer inspection, turn out to be highways. The town of Colby, the final exit on Route 70 before the Colorado border, is within the darkest, coldest, and least settled part of the state. The terrain has a stark, simple beauty: the roads seem to lead everywhere and nowhere—straight lines into the horizon that can almost persuade a visitor of the "flat earth" theory.

Samuel Ramey was born and raised in Colby, and it was from here that he boarded a Greyhound bus in the summer of 1969, a degree from Wichita State University, a few addresses and phone numbers, and most of what he owned in tow. He was bound for New York and determined to become an opera singer.

Late last month, Ramey returned to Kansas to sing "A Date with the Devil," an evening-length program of arias for operatic demons and villains, extracted from Gounod's *Faust*, Boito's *Mefistofele*, Berlioz's *Damnation de Faust*, Offenbach's *Tales of Hoffmann*, and Meyerbeer's *Robert le Diable*, among others. He will bring a similar program to Washington Wednesday night at the Kennedy Center Opera House, under the auspices of the Washington Opera. Then, on Saturday, he will present a second recital, this time a lighter program of operatic, musical comedy, and popular song selections.

Both concerts are sold out, of course. Ramey is now perhaps the most celebrated bass before the public and a particular favorite in Washington, where he was most recently heard in Boito's *Mefistofele* in 1996. He is also a favorite in New York, London, Milan, San Francisco, and the other operatic capitals, and with countless listeners who know him only through his television appearances and recordings (Ramey is believed to have made more discs than any other bass, past or present).

There are several reasons for Ramey's eminence. His voice is toffee-smooth, steady in all registers, and spectacularly versatile. He is capable of singing a florid, richly embellished Handel opera one night and a dramatic, declamatory Verdi thriller the next. Moreover, Ramey is a tall, trim, handsome, and athletic man, gifted with genuine stage presence, a latter-day operatic answer to Errol Flynn or Douglas Fairbanks.

And so, as Ramey leaves the last rehearsal before his January 29 concert at the Lied Center in Lawrence, Kansas, he is politely mobbed by his Midwestern well-wishers.

"Kansas is so proud of you," one woman with a beige coat and a wool hat enthused, as she clutched her newspaper against the gusting wind.

"And I'm sure proud to be back in Kansas," Ramey replied with a grin.

"I heard you back in the late '80s, when you last came through Lawrence," a 60-ish gentleman with a woolen tie said. "We had a whole different auditorium back then."

"I know. I'm looking forward to working in the Lied Center—although I enjoyed singing in your other hall, too."

One woman had waited patiently until the crowd began to dissipate. Seizing her moment, she approached gingerly. "Oh, Mr. Ramey," she said, flushing a deep scarlet, "I was kissed on the cheek by somebody who kissed *your* cheek!"

Upon which Ramey himself began to blush.

Pavarotti would have kissed her. But Samuel Ramey is an affable, courteous, yet rather shy man—and, one senses, still very much a Midwesterner despite the cosmopolitan life he now leads. Barely a week earlier, he had been in St. Petersburg, Russia, for a concert with the Kirov Opera, under the direction of Valery Gergiev. After that, he stayed over for a night in London, then flew to New York, where he participated in a photo session for the cover of a new duet recording with baritone Thomas Hampson. And then it was time to come to Lawrence, a college town some 400 miles east of Colby, in the far suburbs of Kansas City.

As it happened, January 29 was a local holiday, "Kansas Day," the anniversary of the date Kansas became a state in 1861, and therefore an appropriate time for the return of a local hero. Ramey was named Native Kansan of the Year in 1996 and he has many friends—"and thousands of cousins"—throughout the area.

The son of a Colby meat cutter who later became a deputy sheriff, Ramey was born on March 28, 1942. His first musical experience was singing in the Methodist church choir as a child—"I was a pretty good boy soprano," he recalled. "And then, in high school, I was in a little pop group, singing at school dances and that sort of thing. I fancied myself another Pat Boone. But my real dream was to be a professional baseball player. I never knew anything about opera until my first year of college. As a matter of fact, I thought I disliked everything about it."

That all changed when a music teacher at Wichita State assigned him to learn an aria from Mozart's *Don Giovanni*. "My teacher thought I should listen to a recording and find out how it's done by an expert. So I went to a record store and came across an album by Ezio Pinza."

Pinza (1892–1957) was considered the outstanding Italian bass of his era —a fluent and magnificent singer, an elegant and dynamic presence, and a natural actor who enjoyed a long post-operatic career as a star in film and musical theater (*South Pacific*). According to the English critic J. B. Steane, whose book *The Grand Tradition* remains the most searching study of the vocal art, Pinza was the "richest bass" on record. "His sonority was round and full, yet could be diminished to a finely supported *pianissimo*," Steane wrote, and added that Pinza "commanded wonderful evenness in scale-work over a big range, and he had a . . . sensuous and flexible way with the voice."

The record changed Ramey's life. "It was all very mysterious, but something about Pinza's voice just sort of struck me and I started going to the library and listening to more opera—as much opera as I could, really. And then I started collecting records seriously. Pinza and Cesare Siepi [another great bass who made many celebrated recordings in the 1950s and 1960s] are still my favorite singers in my vocal range."

He began to take regular lessons with the baritone Arthur Newman, an early member of the New York City Opera, and spent summers as an apprentice with the Central City Opera in Colorado and the Santa Fe Opera. Following a tour through the South with the Raleigh-based Grass Roots Opera, Ramey decided it was time to move to New York and begin to pursue a musical career.

"The bus trip took four days and I was grubby and tired when I got to town," Ramey said. "I stayed with friends downtown, near Little Italy—the Festival of San Gennaro street fair was going on right outside my front door, so it was loud and lively and very different from Colby. I took a job writing advertising copy for a book company, sang in churches and synagogues on the weekends, and studied voice with Armen Boyajian."

Boyajian, a distinguished coach and teacher, worked intensively with the brilliant but unseasoned young artist and has remained one of his most important advisors. In 1972 Ramey was a finalist in the Metropolitan Opera National Council Auditions, a program designed to identify and support promising young artists. He had also begun to storm the New York City Opera, the company where Beverly Sills and Plácido Domingo had won fame.

"I went through the City Opera's standard cattle call," he remembered.

> The first audition is usually downstairs, in a chorus room. So I went down there, and I sang, and I never heard anything back from them. And then, a few months later, they called me and said they'd like to hear me on a stage. And so I went and sang and still didn't hear anything. And then they called one morning and asked me if I could come in and do a stage audition this afternoon at one. And I said, yeah, sure —fortunately the boss at my publishing house was very understanding. And I'm sure that this last audition was responsible for my debut, in the role of Zuniga in Bizet's *Carmen*.

Zuniga is only a tiny part, but suddenly Ramey was in the door. Soon he was singing Mephistopheles in *Faust*, Henry VIII in Donizetti's *Anna Bolena*, Seneca in Monteverdi's *Coronation of Poppea*, and the title role in Mozart's *Don Giovanni*. "Finally, [City Opera artistic director] Julius Rudel came up to me after a performance and asked me whether I'd ever thought of singing Boito's *Mefistofele*. And I said, 'Well, of course I have.' And Julius said, 'Well, we'd like to bring it back and we want you to do it. It may be in two or three years but we want to bring it back for you.'"

Mefistofele had been a big hit for the City Opera once before, in the late 1960s, when bass Norman Treigle had sung the title role. But Treigle was now dead, and the production—considered highly innovative in its day—had been put into storage.

It is a quirky opera, almost entirely dependent on a strong central figure, and those who have seen Ramey only in the arch, mannered production offered by the Washington Opera two seasons ago have no idea how exciting his interpretation can be. Prancing around the stage in an unusually fancy Halloween devil suit (complete with tail and little red horns), singing, whistling, hissing, and tumbling with unbridled ferocity, Samuel Ramey's *Mefistofele* was the sensation of the opera world in 1977. Offers from Vienna, London, and La Scala poured in.

Only the Metropolitan Opera was silent. This largest and most prestigious of American companies has always been strangely reluctant to take on artists from the City Opera, no matter how excellent they were (even Beverly Sills never sang there until late in her career). "It's not as if they never offered me anything," Ramey said. "One time, they called and I was already booked up; another time, I was offered what was just too uninteresting a role for something so important as a Met debut. I figured it was better to take my time."

The strategy paid off. In 1984 Ramey made his initial appearance at the Met in Handel's *Rinaldo*, the first baroque opera ever presented by the troupe. He played the villain, Argante, and came from the wings in a baroque chariot hitched to wild-eyed demons. "Samuel Ramey's brilliant voice—secure, agile, truly large, complete in technique—handled every moment of Argante's music with breathtaking command and quality, showing he has emerged as the world's preeminent bass," Robert Jacobson wrote in *Opera News*. The magazine's editor, Patrick J. Smith, still calls the evening "unquestionably one of the most exciting debuts I've ever witnessed."

By this point, Ramey had become a copious and versatile recording artist. To date, he has recorded more than 30 operas, including two versions apiece of Mozart's *Don Giovanni* and *Le Nozze di Figaro*, in which he sang different bass-baritone roles in each performance. On the lighter side, there are recordings of *Carousel, Kismet, Man of La Mancha, On the Town*, and an album entitled, simply, *Sam Ramey on Broadway*.

"I'd like very much to do one of the great Broadway shows onstage sometime—*Man of La Mancha* or *South Pacific*," Ramey explained. "Actually, a couple of years ago, some producers were planning a revival of *Kiss Me Kate*, and they asked me to do it. But I was all booked up. A good limited run of one of the old shows would be fine. It might even keep me in town for a while!"

Ramey lives with his wife of 27 years, Carrie Tanate Ramey, in a building on Manhattan's Central Park West that is also the East Coast home of Barbra Streisand. "One inevitable day, the elevator door opened and there she was with a mutual acquaintance, who introduced her to Sam," Barry Paris wrote in a recent profile. "As they shook hands, the world-renowned dramatic bass reverted to starstruck Kansas boy with an immortal line: 'Hi, nice to meet you, uh—I'm a singer, too.'" Streisand smiled politely and moved on. "It was one of those moments when even as the words were coming out of your mouth, you wished you could reel them back in," Ramey later observed.

He is, in fact, about as far from a grandstanding egotist as any superstar around. During a preconcert interview at a radio station in Lawrence, the host repeatedly referred to him as "Thomas Hampson." The first time, he spoke up gently—"Um, excuse me, but my name is Samuel Ramey." There were profuse on-air apologies, but then it happened again, upon which he simply let it pass. (He did, however, admit to having been somewhat per-turbed when PBS television host Charlie Rose referred to him throughout an entire program as Samuel *Raney*, "Somebody in his position really should get the facts right," he said with a shake of his head.)

Friends credit Ramey's Kansas upbringing and longstanding marriage with keeping him steady within the tumultuous and sometimes corrosive world of international opera. Still, when he took the stage at the Lied Center to sing "Date with the Devil" that evening, Ramey seemed charged with a lithe, forbidding, and appropriately sinister malevolence. Accompanied by the Kansas City Symphony under the direction of William McGlaughlin, he was at home in all of the material—the odd and deeply personal classicism of Berlioz, the ranting spells of Boito, the grand, sweeping gestures of Meyer-beer. The standing ovation was immediate and impassioned, and Ramey obliged with three encores—the decidedly un-devilish "Night and Day," "The Impossible Dream," and "Ol' Man River." It was obvious that Lawrence would have listened to him all night.

Ramey now sings 65 to 75 performances a year—"too many," he insisted.

> I'm starting to taper off a bit because I had something of a scare, a bad
> sickness in my lung last season. I decided that there was probably noth-
> ing wrong with me physically, just a bit of burnout. And so I canceled
> the whole summer and studied *Boris Godunov* [a new role which he
> sang at the Met in late 1997], worked out at the gym, and got some things
> done in my apartment that I'd been meaning to do for a long time. It
> was great—the longest unbroken period I'd been at home in years.

In fact, Ramey has established occasional, temporary "homes" in most of
the cities where he appears regularly: Chicago, London, Milan, Vienna, and
Paris. "But it gets a little strange when I'm on a concert tour," he said. "You
know, there are times when I wake up in the middle of the night and really
don't know where I am for a minute or two."

Ramey is now 55, at an age when many singers begin to tire of nomadic life
and settle down into a less stressful schedule. Although his vocal capacities
are undiminished, some of Ramey's friends have suggested that he would
make a terrific teacher.

He disagrees. "I just don't think I'd ever be comfortable in a teaching situation," he said. "I've tried doing master classes a couple of times but never felt
very happy about it. Right now I don't think I really have a right to try and tell
somebody else how to sing. I'm still learning myself."

The Washington Post
15 February 1998

Arthur Rubinstein

ARTHUR RUBINSTEIN made his United States debut at the Philadelphia Academy of Music on January 8, 1906. Seventy years later, at the age of 89, his vision so clouded he could barely see the keyboard in front of him, the pianist played his final American concert in April 1976.

It is not quite the longest performing career in history—that title likely belongs to another Polish-born pianist, a gentle Methuselah named Mieczyslaw Horszowski, who made his first professional appearance in 1901 and was still spinning soft miracles nine decades later. But Horszowski's following was mostly confined to his fellow musicians, while Rubinstein was a genuine popular hero for much of his life. A vast number of people considered him *the* pianist of his era, and the release of a glorious and extravagant 94–compact disc set—*The Rubinstein Collection* (BMG Classics)—only serves to support such a conclusion.

Ninety-four CDs. 106 hours of music. One central artist. Is this overkill? We have clearly entered the age of massive retrospective packages from our record companies (BMG alone has produced similarly gargantuan releases devoted to recordings by violinist Jascha Heifetz and conductor Arturo Toscanini, among others). It is not a new phenomenon: 100 years ago, Victorian publishers issued mammoth uniform editions of Ruskin, Thackeray, Longfellow, and Bulwer-Lytton, and they may still be found in secondhand bookstores, their leaves pristinely uncut.

While a healthy suspicion of the recording industry's incessant ancestor worship is justified, this is not the right time to argue such a case. For the *Rubinstein Collection* is not only terrific aural history but a profoundly satisfying trove of musical art, with magnificently restored sound and splendid and authoritative documentation. It is not exactly a casual investment—the price hovers around $1,400. In June, however, 29 of these discs will be released separately, with another 20 of them slated to follow in the fall. After two years, virtually the entire set will be available in 81 reasonably priced modules. And for that we may be glad, because the best of Rubinstein's recordings are little short of revelatory.

His ascent was hardly preordained. He was born in the dreary industrial city of Lodz, Poland, on January 28, 1887, the seventh child of Isaac Rubinstein, a factory worker, and his wife, Felicia. His talent was apparent in his early youth: after studies in Warsaw and Berlin (one of his early mentors was Joseph Joachim, to whom Johannes Brahms dedicated his violin concerto), he made his professional debut in 1899 and presented his first tour of the United States in 1906, while still in his teens.

He was not an unqualified success. Richard Aldrich of *The New York Times* called the playing "imposing" (whatever that may have meant) but found "no thought of any deeper significance that lay behind the notes." "There is little warmth or beauty in Rubinstein's tone and little variety in his effects," Aldrich continued. Several other critics thought the playing glittering but insubstantial.

It is curious that Rubinstein should have been dismissed as a mere virtuoso when he arrived on the scene, for the pianist himself later acknowledged that his technical command was not at all what it should have been. (One can yet hear an abundance of glitches in his initial recordings, made 22 years later.) The young Rubinstein devoted all too much of his time to the pursuit of pleasure—his two autobiographies, written in the 1970s, grow rather tiresome with their litanies of celebrity walk-ons and dashing seductions. It was not until the summer of 1934 that he decided to take himself seriously.

"I didn't want my kids to grow up thinking of their father as either a second-string pianist or a has-been," he recalled later. "So I bundled my wife and baby into a small Citroen and we drove up to Saint-Nicolas-de-Veroce, a tiny village. I rented the only piano in the community—an old upright—and moved it into an empty, windowless garage just below our room. That became my studio. It had no electric light, so I put a candle on top of the piano and then I buckled down to work—six hours, eight hours, nine hours a day. And a strange thing happened. By the time we returned to Paris, I'd begun to discover new meanings, new qualities, new possibilities in music that I'd been playing regularly for more than 30 years."

Rubinstein made his first recording in 1928; two decades later, he had become far and away the best-selling classical pianist in history, on disc and in recital. In 1948 he earned the staggering sum of $110,000 in record royalties alone—this at a time when the average American income was less than one fortieth that amount. He lived well and guiltlessly, comfortable with his riches.

But he never stopped working. In 1937 he took on the incredible task of touring Europe, South America, Australia, South Africa, and the United States in a single year; 14 years later, he played 20 concerts in 23 days during a visit to Israel. In 1961 it was a set of 10 concerts at Carnegie Hall, from which the proceeds went to charity. His playing, increasingly informed by a steady practice regimen, a patrician disdain for aural effects, and an acutely sensitive comprehension of life's joys and sorrows, grew ever more wonderful as he matured.

Or didn't mature, as the case may be, for the famously "gregarious" Rubinstein could be quite petty in his dealings with the people closest to him. Harvey Sachs's authoritative biography sometimes seems a chronicle of theatrical breaks and reconciliations. Although Rubinstein married the former Aniela Mlynnarska in 1932, he carried on numerous affairs throughout their union and finally dropped her altogether in the mid-1970s, when he was almost 90, after which he took up with a much younger woman, Annabelle Whitestone.

According to Sachs, Rubinstein's four children (the last of whom was born when he was over 60) remember him with a mixture of love, awe, anger, and disappointment. His daughter Eva put it succinctly: "He was a man who never should have had children. Perhaps he should have had his wife and a merry old time all over the world, but once there are children it's not so easy. He saw himself as the paterfamilias and Jewish patriarch, but he didn't know what that involved."

Throughout the 1940s Rubinstein was part of an active musical community on the West Coast that included the violinist Jascha Heifetz and the cellist Gregor Piatigorsky. (When you add into the mix writers such as Thomas Mann, Aldous Huxley, and Christopher Isherwood, as well as composers Arnold Schoenberg and Igor Stravinsky, all of whom were California residents during this time, it seems a safe assertion that Los Angeles has never before or since played such a prominent role in the life of the mind.)

By 1954 Rubinstein had moved to New York City and he spent his last years mostly in Paris and Switzerland, where he died, from cancer, in Geneva, on December 20, 1982. Because he had become a prominent and outspoken supporter of Israeli causes, it was in Jerusalem that his ashes were buried, after a restrained and appropriately intimate private service. Rubinstein's passing was front page news throughout the world and many people felt as if they had lost not only a great artist but a cherished friend.

A rule of thumb for those who would approach the daunting, delicious plentitude of the *Rubinstein Collection*—in general, the later the pianist's recording of any given piece, the wiser, more musical, and altogether better played it is likely to be. (There are many exceptions, of course, and in the last few years of recording—after 1971, say—the listener will encounter some distinct signs of physical deterioration.) Still, as a general maxim, this is a pretty reliable one. Rubinstein continued to grow in artistic stature until he was well into his 80s, and his most consistent single decade was undoubtedly the 1960s.

This may prove a helpful tip, for many works are duplicated throughout the *Rubinstein Collection* (which contains not only all the pianist's approved and previously released performances but also a few short pieces never before published). There are three complete sets of the Beethoven piano concertos, recorded in 1956, 1967, and 1975. Chopin's Piano Concerto No. 2 was recorded four times—in 1931, 1946, 1958, and 1968—while the same composer's Barcarolle (Op. 60) is represented in five different versions, dating from 1928 to 1964.

What was it that made Rubinstein so outstanding? Certainly, he never developed the sort of "How in the world did he do that?" technique that became the stock-in-trade of his supposed rival, Vladimir Horowitz. But Horowitz excelled in a sort of ostentatious, arbitrary brilliance that was alien to Rubinstein's organic and deeply rooted musicianship. The best of Horowitz is to be found in recordings of display pieces—his own set of variations on themes from *Carmen*, for example, or a Niagara-like burst through a transcription of *The Stars and Stripes Forever*. (Some unaccountably restrained performances of Scarlatti and Clementi are also quite fine.) But most of Horowitz's Chopin twitches frightfully, and there is an emphasis on momentary flash rather than structural continuity. One has the dismaying feeling that the forest has been sacrificed for the trees, and the trees have been sacrificed for a few of the lichen on their bark.

In Rubinstein's Chopin performances, there is always a sense of pulse and place. It is not surprising that he loved the composer's 51 mazurkas so much; he infuses these small, sturdy Polish dances with Homeric poetry, but never forgets that they are, after all, dances, and not untethered meditations. Every piece, no matter how tiny, has its beginning, middle, and end, and Rubinstein always knows infallibly where he is. This was the very essence of his art. In many ways, he was a distinctly modern player: earlier pianists had often treated Chopin's works as showpieces, tuneful opportunities for pearly lines and pretty smears that pleased audiences but did a tremendous disservice to the 19th century's most pristine and concentrated miniaturist.

Most of Chopin's major works are here, sometimes in two or three interpretations, and as good as Rubinstein's early performances of many of these pieces are, they rarely compare to the ones he made in fullest maturity. The set of nocturnes he recorded in 1965 is unmatched: a miraculous balance of singing line, tonal luster, poetic nuance, romantic fancy, and classical form. Indeed, one finds an uncanny essentialism in Rubinstein's late recordings. The tempos, as if informed by some golden mean, are neither propulsive nor lingering, only perfect. The musicianship is imbued with a familiarity and simplicity that is anything but easily won, and the noble lines from T. S. Eliot's "Little Gidding" come to mind:

> We shall not cease from exploration
> And the end of all our exploring
> Will be to arrive where we started
> And know the place for the first time.

Unfortunately, there are some important omissions in Rubinstein's Chopin catalogue. Although he recorded the ballades, the scherzos, the polonaises, the impromptus, and many other works, he never felt comfortable with the technical challenges in the two sets of etudes, Op. 10 and Op. 25, and recorded only selected numbers from both of them. (The posthumously published, ethereally beautiful *Trois Nouvelles Études* are of an altogether different character, and exist in two heartbreakingly lovely renditions.) And he recorded the complete set of preludes (Op. 28) only once, much too early in his career. These 1946 performances are tense, harsh, erratic, and bizarrely offhanded. Rubinstein himself knew it; "My Preludes aren't good enough," he wrote to a friend in 1974. What a shame he never returned to them.

Rubinstein was especially at home in music of the 19th century—not only with Chopin, Schumann, and Brahms, all of whom he recorded extensively, but also with César Franck, Edvard Grieg, and Franz Liszt. It was often claimed that he played Mozart in a manner that was effusively romantic, but the five late concertos included here are exemplary, shot through with the tragic intensity and urgent drama that most performers of Rubinstein's era chose to ignore in these scores. (The legend of Mozart as a dainty, peri-wigged, perpetually sunny *Wunderkind* took a long time to die out.)

Although Rubinstein's performances of Beethoven's concertos were widely admired, he only recorded seven of the 32 sonatas and few listeners are likely to count them among his stronger discs. The pianist seems to have put Beethoven on a pedestal; the magnanimous wit, grace, and ease that typ-ify most of Rubinstein's interpretations are rarely to be found. Is it possible that Rubinstein agreed with his colleague Claudio Arrau's flabbergastingly wrongheaded observation that Beethoven—Beethoven!—had no humor?

If one considers Rubinstein an artist of the post–World War II generation —and he did indeed play for a full 30 years after V-J Day—it may seem that he did little or nothing for contemporary music. But the pianist's sheer longevity skews our perspective. Let us not forget that Brahms, Fauré, Dvořák, Tchai-kovsky, and Saint-Saëns were all alive and working when Rubinstein was born, that Claude Debussy was still only in his mid-20s and unknown, that Rachmaninoff was a teenager, and that Stravinsky had yet to celebrate his fifth birthday.

Rubinstein played music by all these men (a pity that he detested Stravin-sky's *Piano Rag Music*, which had been dedicated to him, although he regu-larly included transcriptions from *Petrouchka* as encore pieces). He recorded a good deal of unfamiliar work by composers from Spain and Latin Amer-ica, among them Heitor Villa-Lobos, Manuel de Falla, Isaac Albéniz, and En-rique Granados. He was devoted to the music of Karol Szymanowski, a fellow Pole and near-contemporary who has yet to receive his full due. He champi-oned the compositions of younger men such as Serge Prokofiev, Darius Mil-haud, Francis Poulenc, and even went so far as to record the Second Prelude for Piano by George Gershwin.

Most of Rubinstein's recordings were for solo piano. Yet he was a sensitive and collegial partner in chamber music performances, whether with established legends such as Heifetz and Piatigorsky or with the young Guarneri String Quartet. The austere and reclusive Glenn Gould, who was in so many respects Rubinstein's temperamental opposite, once called the Rubinstein-Guarneri recording of the Brahms quintet "the greatest chamber music performance with piano that I've heard in my life." ("I'm drunk on it," Gould continued. "My notion of what Brahms represents has been changed by your recording.") As for Rubinstein's recordings with orchestra, there are collaborations with conductors ranging from Eugene Ormandy, John Barbirolli, and Fritz Reiner through Zubin Mehta and Daniel Barenboim. The most convincing set of the Beethoven concertos is the one featuring the Boston Symphony Orchestra conducted by Erich Leinsdorf (1967), although the 1956 version with Josef Krips and the Symphony of the Air (formerly Toscanini's NBC Symphony) is charged with a certain brisk majesty. Plodding tempos and palpable frailty exclude the final version with Barenboim and the London Philharmonic (1975) from consideration.

By then, Rubinstein was growing tired. There would only be a few more concerts, a few more recordings—a Brahms concerto with the Israel Philharmonic under Mehta, Schumann's *Fantasiestücke*, and finally Beethoven's Sonata in E-flat (Op. 31, No. 3), a sweet, playful valediction. The final disc in the collection—number 92—contains three illuminating interviews with Rubinstein, recorded in the early 1960s, when he was still at the height of his powers and positively exuding *joie de vivre*. A handsome hardcover book, with texts in German, French, and English, completes the set.

When we listen to Rubinstein at his finest, we come into contact with that rarest of rarities—a healthy, sanguine, affirmative genius. On disc, as it was in person, the playing is full-hearted and honest, without distortion or neurotic excess. Melodies, textures, and ideas well over from the piano and flow from heart to heart. At such moments, we can only echo the words of pianist Eunice Podis, who once told Harvey Sachs that the listener walked away from a Rubinstein concert "in an altered state of being."

"It was more than a satisfying musical experience," she continued. "It was on a different level from most performances. You thought the world was a better place and you were a better person."

The Washington Post
5 March 2000

Nadja Salerno-Sonnenberg

WILLIAM McKINLEY, the 25th president of the United States, shot to death in 1901 by Leon Czolgosz, lives on in Canton, Ohio. This small city, located some 70 miles south of Cleveland, seems a veritable shrine to McKinley, who won his first election here as the prosecuting attorney of Stark County more than a century ago. His impassive face stares from local billboards, his name graces streets and parks, and with the possible exception of the Professional Football Hall of Fame, his memorial is the area's most celebrated tourist attraction.

One Saturday night, in the basement of Canton's McKinley Senior High School, Nadja Salerno-Sonnenberg was pacing furiously around a narrow dressing room. Upstairs, the Canton Symphony Orchestra was playing a new work by William Bolcom, under the direction of Gerhardt Zimmermann, to a packed house. Immediately thereafter, Salerno-Sonnenberg was scheduled to take the stage to play Shostakovich's Concerto for Violin and Orchestra No. 1 in A Minor.

The Shostakovich—sardonic, astringent, and something of a masterpiece —is not a natural crowd-pleaser, and it is probable that many in the audience would rather have heard Salerno-Sonnenberg in Tchaikovsky or Mendelssohn. But she had proven herself in Canton before, and this time around she wanted to choose her concerto. In any event, one week earlier, when she had played the Shostakovich in Winston-Salem, North Carolina, no sooner had the last note died away than the audience rose, as if by command, to give her a wild, roaring ovation. And now it was Canton's turn. "I probably need more rouge, huh?" she asked, straightening out her jacket with an irritated tug, puffing on another cigarette. In fact, she looked striking—olive-skinned, neither tall nor short, her body trim and athletic, her Mediterranean face surrounded by a thick aureole of auburn hair. But one could sense that she wanted to burst the confines of the dressing room, with its lumpy, institutional white walls that seemed to have been fashioned from cottage cheese.

"The glamorous life of a performing artist," she said with an ironic grin, as she looked over her surroundings. Salerno-Sonnenberg's voice is husky and tobacco-tempered; she speaks bluntly, with a street-smart accent she picked up as a child in Philadelphia. "Actually, this is a damned good orchestra," she continued. "Canton is right up there with Pasadena on my list of the best community groups. I'm doing two concerts here, and the Saturday crowd is the more reserved one—the audience that's tougher to please. So if it goes well tonight, we'll really knock them out tomorrow."

She has been "knocking them out" around the country for some time now, in auditoriums and on talk shows, with ensembles great and small, infusing classical music with her own do-or-die urgency. Such is her draw that the name "Salerno-Sonnenberg" on a roster will help sell out an orchestra's season, and she rarely fiddles to an empty seat.

Detractors call her playing flamboyant and theatrical. For others, she is one of the most exciting young musicians to come along in many years. The guitarist Sharon Isbin calls Salerno-Sonnenberg the "Edith Piaf of the violin." Conductor Michael Tilson Thomas phrases his approval even more succinctly. "She *is* the music," he said.

She's doing well, too: her annual income is in the high six figures, and she has recently purchased an elegant three-bedroom apartment on the West Side of Manhattan. But she doesn't get to spend very much time there, for she plays almost 100 concerts a year. And then there are rehearsals, recordings, television appearances . . .

Salerno-Sonnenberg picked up her violin, nervously played through a passage from the Shostakovich, then put down the instrument and glanced once more into the mirror. She was dressed in the same moderately high heels that she always wears onstage, tight dark pants, and a strapless blouse, which she covered with a smartly tailored jacket. She made a face, goofing on the cultivated image with a tomboy's sarcasm. "That'll have to do, I guess."

Nobody came to fetch Salerno-Sonnenberg; when she heard the applause at the conclusion of the Bolcom work, she made her own way through the labyrinthine basement of McKinley High, cluttered with discarded sets from school plays gone by, and joined conductor Zimmermann in the wings. The two are old friends, and they indulged in some joking banter in the minute before they walked onstage. ("Laughter is a great release," Salerno-Sonnenberg explained later. "Even if you've played something a thousand times, you're still worried about playing it again. Ever seen Itzhak Perlman before a show? Just like Robin Williams. Hilarious!")

When Salerno-Sonnenberg took the stage, however, all was coiled intensity and she exploded into the Shostakovich. Not for her the tidy, tapered, empty proficiency that too often passes for elegance in our concert halls. She is an expressionist, and every piece she plays seems a personal battle to be won (in this sense, she is very much like one of her avowed idols, Maria Callas). Her performances may thrill or they may fizzle, but they always force one to listen anew. And, in Canton, the house came down.

"Nadja never plays it safe," her teacher, Dorothy DeLay, said recently. "She very often puts herself in danger, playing as fast as she can move, taking a phrase to a really high point. Or in a slow passage, as she draws the bow across the string, the note gets softer and softer as she sustains the tone longer and longer. You'd think it wouldn't be possible. It's breathtaking—the kind of thing you hear opera singers do."

Yet Salerno-Sonnenberg has not wanted for detractors. A good deal—probably too much—has been made of her onstage behavior. I remember a 1985 concert, in which she played Mozart's Concerto No. 3 in G (K. 216) at the 92nd Street Y, under the direction of Maxim Shostakovich, the composer's son.

She fidgeted constantly, rolled her eyes, made myriad faces, whispered loudly to the conductor during the opening tutti, tugged on her dress with the impatience of an eight-year-old in first finery, and raced offstage immediately at the conclusion of the work. She seemed frenzied, practically oblivious to the audience, as if she were wrestling with a hundred phantasms that all but had her pinned.

But those who dismiss Salerno-Sonnenberg as a high-class circus act are not listening closely. Her playing is the musical equivalent of method acting. It teases, twitches, mumbles, and soars. She breaks the melodic line into twisting shards of sound, which somehow maintain their organic consistency.

Hers is not the gift of simplicity—she has a tendency to charge folkish, uncomplicated music with more import than it will bear—and the lack of discipline one finds in her stage manner occasionally spills over into her playing. But it is vital, alive, and genuinely creative music-making, rather than one more dutiful bow to tradition. It is possible to dispute what Salerno-Sonnenberg does, even to dislike it. But when she succeeds, a listener is reminded of just how powerful and affecting music can be, how deeply it can penetrate, how much it can all mean.

"I don't really mind if a critic hates my playing," Salerno-Sonnenberg said over lunch at a Canton restaurant—a meal interrupted several times by well-wishers and admirers, greeted cordially.

> Anyone is welcome to dislike my work, but I get angry when they call me a fake. What irritates me is the implication that I sat around with my publicity agent and decided to play the way I do to attract attention. *Do they think this is a joke?* Twirling my violin onstage is a *horrible* habit, one that I'd like to break, but I can't do it. And I've tried to play the violin without any facial expressions. I did a concert last year— I won't tell you which one it was—and I spent the whole time concentrating on keeping my face straight. And I heard a tape of the concert afterward, and it sounded as if I'd gone to sleep. *Boring!*

Although she remains decidedly controversial, with few critics and musicians entirely abstaining from the fray, Salerno-Sonnenberg has achieved an unusual popular success in the past few years. She has signed an extensive contract with EMI Angel, and her first recording for the label, Mendelssohn's violin concerto and two encore pieces, has been issued. Recordings of concertos by Tchaikovsky, Shostakovich, Brahms, and Bruch are planned. And she is preparing to record an album of sonatas with her old friend, the pianist Cecile Licad.

"Cecile and I go back to the Curtis Institute together," Salerno-Sonnenberg said. "I've known her since I was 12, and I taught her a lot of bad things— all the secret nooks and crannies at Curtis, hideouts galore. Now we're all grown up, and we live close to one another in Manhattan, and I'm godmother to her child. Times change."

Salerno-Sonnenberg was born in Rome 27 years ago. After her family was abandoned twice—by her father, then by her stepfather—her mother took the advice of young Nadja's violin teachers and moved to the United States, so that the girl could study with the best. At the age of eight, Salerno-Sonnenberg enrolled in the Curtis Institute, one of the youngest students in the conservatory's 60-year history.

"I had started playing when I was five," she said. "It was not my idea. Everybody else in my family played an instrument, and my mom was afraid I would get a complex or something unless I joined in. I kind of liked playing from the beginning, but never wanted to practice. I wasn't really committed to being the best violinist I could be until I was 19 years old and already pretty good.

"Curtis was wonderful," she continued. "I think that I had a very happy childhood." When she was 14, she entered the Juilliard School, where she earned a reputation for an unpredictable, potentially explosive, combination of talent and irreverence.

But by the time Salerno-Sonnenberg was in her late teens, problems had developed. "It was by far the worst time of my life," she recalled, solemnly. "I had adopted a very destructive lifestyle, and I was abusing myself terribly. My grandmother had died. A love affair had broken up. I was living in this rat hole on West 72nd Street and I was snappy to everybody—my teachers, my friends. I wasn't even speaking to my family.

"I had ridden so long on my talent," she continued.

I had played with the Philadelphia Orchestra, and I'd gotten to be a pretty damned good violinist, by most standards. But I'd never really worked for anything. I had been bucking Dorothy DeLay, my teacher, for so long about changing my position that I suddenly realized that everybody else at Juilliard was playing better than I did. It was like, "Whatever happened to Nadja?" That sort of thing. And I was just letting myself go to hell. I didn't have the courage to put 100 percent effort into anything, to give it my all, because then I could really *fail*, and I thought it was a lot better to just be lazy and fade away than to try and then fail.

So, anyway, I'm flunking everything at Juilliard. But I kept coming in to Miss DeLay every week, just to talk with her, you know, without my violin. She indulged me for a while, but then one week she sat me down outside her class and pointed out that it had been 12 or 13 weeks since I had played anything for her. I said I knew that. And she spoke very quietly and said she wanted me to prepare the entire Prokofiev violin concerto the next week. And I said that I couldn't possibly do that, because I'd never even played through it. And Miss DeLay said "Yes, you can do it. You can buy the music today and start practicing tonight." And she said she wanted the whole concerto by the next week or she was kicking me out of her class.

Now this is my surrogate mother talking! I was incredibly shaken. I called Cecile and just cried and cried. Cecile doesn't talk much, but what she said to me then really turned me around. She told me, in so many words, that I was throwing my life away and she begged me to get to work, to do something with my talent. And I listened—for once. It's hard to believe, but 15 words from these two people changed the course of my life.

So Salerno-Sonnenberg threw herself into her music, practicing upward of 10 hours a day. As she recovered and then surpassed her former mastery, she decided to enter the Walter W. Naumburg International Violin Competition. "I knew I didn't have a chance of winning," she said, "but I thought that if I worked really hard, I might place. And so I practiced and practiced—literally 13 hours a day—until the week of the competition, when I was so keyed up and freaked out that I couldn't even touch the violin.

I almost got evicted from my apartment the day of the semifinals. I was frying some sausages and the place caught on fire. I grabbed my violin and my cat and ran. The super told me to get the hell out. I begged him to let me have just a few more days, and he finally did, but only those few days. I would have had to have left anyway, because I didn't have the next month's rent.

So I got a call that night telling me I'd placed into the semifinals. And the next night they called and told me I'd placed into the finals. The finals! God! All those conflicting feelings I felt. On the one hand, I wanted to drop out; I was so frazzled that I didn't think I could ever play again—couldn't ever face a jury, an audience, anybody. But I also wanted to win.

The next morning, Salerno-Sonnenberg played music by Tchaikovsky and Ravel at Carnegie Hall, just before luncheon.

> It was over. I was so glad that I tore off my gown—literally tore it off; it couldn't be repaired—and went out for lunch with some friends. And over the course of the luncheon I had four beers. And then I suddenly thought, what if there are recalls! What if they want to hear me again! I'm entered in this great competition—I'm a *finalist* in this great competition—and I'm *drunk*.
>
> Anyway, I went back to Carnegie and Robert Mann [the founder and first violinist of the Juilliard Quartet] came onstage and gave the usual speech—the judges were impressed, very difficult decision, and so on. Then he said that they had decided not to award a second or third prize that year. And I was sure that it was all over and I felt really low. I had finally allowed myself to believe I might have a shot for second or third place, but this killed it. Then he said that I had taken first prize, and I couldn't believe it. Total shock. My goal the week before had been to make the semifinals—to get back into the race, and start to tread water again. Instead, I won it all.

She had indeed won it all, by the unanimous decision of the judges. Salerno-Sonnenberg was the youngest first-prize winner in the history of the Naumburg competitions. "I ran to this other guy in the competition who had become a good friend of mine, and I threw my arms around him and hugged him and said 'I'm sorry, I'm sorry.' It was weird. I didn't so much feel happy for myself as I felt sorry for him. And he was great; he just smiled at me and said, 'Don't be sorry. I'm proud of you.' God, what a day!"

Since winning the Naumburg in 1981, Salerno-Sonnenberg has added several other honors to her résumé, most notably the Avery Fisher Career Grant, which she received in 1983. Fiercely articulate, with a colorful and engaging personality, she has also been the subject of several television profiles—unusual for a classical musician—and she has become one of Johnny Carson's favorite guests on *The Tonight Show*.

She has taken considerable flak for the television appearances. "Occasionally I've had orchestra managers say. 'We don't want to play with her;

she's not a serious musician.' I don't get it. Should I apologize for the fact that I can talk? For the fact that I can be a comedian for 20 minutes? Millions of people see those shows, and I hope that I can provide an introduction—maybe not the ideal introduction, but an introduction all the same—to music for some of those viewers."

With celebrity have come some new difficulties, however. "I get a lot of letters these days, and some of them are pretty weird," she said.

> I moved recently and I don't give out my address, so the letters are filtered through my management and my public relations people. And a lot of them are wonderful, and most of the rest of them are pretty innocent—"I think you and I could make a pretty good team" and that sort of stuff—but I've also been getting notes from some guy who writes really sick, violent stuff on torn up bits of paper. And there was another person who followed me from city to city, leaving a single black rose in my dressing room before every show. I feel vulnerable and I don't like it.
>
> I'm also tired of this schedule. I wake up sometimes and I don't know what city I'm in. It used to be that I'd arrive in a new town and spend the afternoon walking around, getting to know the place. Now I get off the plane and go to the hotel room. I take care of business and try not to tire myself out before rehearsals and the concert. There are times when I get depressed, angry, for no real reason. Today, for example, I have to spend the day at the hotel in Canton, doing nothing, just resting and waiting to play. I mean, it's a *nice* hotel and all, but . . .

Salerno-Sonnenberg is now booked two years in advance. But she has arranged for a sabbatical in June 1989.

> There are some technical problems about playing the violin that I never paid attention to when I was younger, and they're starting to bother me now. My technique isn't really all there, and I have to work very hard to play some passages that other violinists just breeze right through. I have seen the writing on the wall: I really want to still be playing when I'm 40. I don't even want to turn 30 and still have to worry about these things. I want to have full control of the violin so I can just concentrate on making music.

So I called my manager [Lawrence Tucker of Columbia Artists] and said that I wanted some time off. And he said, sure, how long? I said five months, and he didn't even blink. I was so grateful: I really consider him a friend. But now I've got to wait more than a year before my vacation. I've been warned about the dangers of leaving the scene. But I think I'm at the point where I can do it now, and five months sounds like such a luxury—almost half a year to sit around my apartment, practice, see my friends, cook, and have a *life* again.

She will not talk about her personal relationships. "Just write that Miss Salerno-Sonnenberg politely declined to discuss her romantic involvements," she said with a grin. "Johnny Carson always asks about that stuff, and you can't really say 'no way' on national television, so once I made up a story that I was deeply involved and terribly happy, but usually I just say something along the lines of 'I'm too busy to find the right person, Johnny.' And that's basically the truth, although I still politely decline to discuss my romantic involvements. It's nobody's business, anyway."

She is only slightly less reluctant to discuss her influences. "I never really had many heroes, you know," she said.

I looked up to David Oistrakh when I was growing up, although my playing is not like his at all. At all! But I admire him; you can put on a record and hear his soul. Heifetz had a phenomenal technique, but I never liked the way he played Mozart or Bach very much. For me, he was not a complete musician, although nobody ever played the Bruch "Scottish Fantasy" like he did. I think Callas was phenomenal—as an artist and as a woman. Such fire and intelligence. I have a videotape of some of her performances and you can't take your eyes off her.

Leonard Bernstein is the artist she most wants to work with. "I've played under him in a student orchestra, but never with him, as a soloist," she said. "I have dreams about doing the Brahms concerto with Bernstein in Carnegie Hall; I've had the same dream since I was a very little girl. He really epitomizes music for me.

"The Brahms concerto is one of my favorite pieces," she continued. "Everything is in it, from A to Z. But it's a funny piece in some ways. In that gorgeous second movement, the violin never gets the melody. First the oboe gets the theme, then the strings, but the violinist never gets it at all. It's frustrating, like having somebody you love who refuses to look at you."

Another favorite is Serge Prokofiev's first Sonata for Violin and Piano, which she has recorded and played several times in New York recitals. "It's rilly deep, man, rilly deep," she said, affecting a spacey accent. Then, serious again, "I don't know what caused Prokofiev to write such a somber piece—I really *should* know, I guess—but I've made up my own story about what is happening in the music, and it's never failed me yet.

"And I'm never more comfortable than when I'm playing Mozart," she said. "I can't really talk about music very well; it's too personal. But when I play Mozart, I think about how many years it's been since the music was written, and how many other violinists have played it since then. And I feel so honored to be part of that continuum."

The continuum is real, and Salerno-Sonnenberg has added her own distinctive contribution to it. She works hard, lives hard. In her best performances, there is always a sense that she is testing boundaries, flirting with the edge. Her persona is closer to that of a rock-and-roller than to the cool, calm, collected classical musician of legend (in Winston-Salem, her arrival onstage was greeted with enthusiastic war whoops from the audience).

One hopes that she will never trade impulse for routine and settle into a fastidious sameness. "If I ever bland out, it will be because of my health and nothing else," she said. "It's exhausting to play the way I do, to give your all, and I'm not so strong as I used to be. I had to cancel some dates last month, and I was not at all happy with two of my last New York appearances because I was simply worn out. I've had tendonitis, and I had bronchitis all through my Mendelssohn recording sessions—we called them the 'Chloraseptic sessions.'"

Salerno-Sonnenberg settled back into the booth and lit another cigarette.

But I could never really play without feeling it deeply. Look, this is Canton, Ohio. This performance won't make or break my career. Chances are that a lot of the people in the audience don't know the piece. I don't need to be afraid of the local critic. I could be very smug about the whole thing.

But how can you play a work like this and not be involved—involved with 100 percent of your body and soul? It's still Shostakovich, wherever you play it, whomever you play it for. It's great music and I owe it everything I have. And throughout this crazy business, I can take solace in the music. Whatever the critic thinks, whether or not the audience likes the piece, whether or not I'm invited back next year, I have done my best for the music I played. And that makes it all worthwhile.

Newsday
12 June 1988

Esa-Pekka Salonen

The appointment of Esa-Pekka Salonen, barely in his 30s, to the music direc-torship of the Los Angeles Philharmonic took many by surprise. His tenure, now 10 years old, has been remarkable for its originality and integrity.

E SA-PEKKA SALONEN, the 31-year-old music director designate of the Los Angeles Philharmonic Orchestra, was practicing his trade in colder climes earlier this month.

One recent afternoon in Cleveland, Ohio, Salonen sat on the stage of Severance Hall, leading members of the Cleveland Orchestra through a rehearsal of Olivier Messiaen's vast, ambitious *Turangalîla* Symphony. The symphony—80 minutes long, scored for huge orchestra, a riot of sound that is alternately gaseous and silly, profound and exalting—is a favorite of Salonen's and this affection came through in his leadership, which was detailed, meticulous, animated, and unfailingly musical.

Cleveland is a great orchestra and the musicians had done their homework, so a relaxed Salonen ended the rehearsal 15 minutes early. The following night's performance was greeted by an unusually fervent ovation, and the conductor was called back repeatedly to take his bows. To many in the audience it must have seemed remarkable that a man of Salonen's apparent youth could control a work of such enormous complexity.

In fact, the *Turangalîla* Symphony presents few problems for a conductor of Salonen's skills. Mastering the Los Angeles Philharmonic may be another matter.

When I first came, someone said to me—it was one of the
principal players—Philadelphia is famous for the strings,
Chicago for the brass, and Cleveland for the cleanliness.
We're well known for the management.
—André Previn, former director of the
Los Angeles Philharmonic

The L.A. Philharmonic management *is* legendary, as Previn found out to his
cost. Previn, the orchestra's music director since 1985, abruptly stepped
down last April. The departure was said to result from a rift between the conductor and Philharmonic general manager Ernest Fleischmann. "Ernest
wants to be music director," one musician who is familiar with Previn,
Fleischmann, and the orchestra said at the time. "That's it, plain and simple."

Fleischmann, the orchestra's brilliant and abrasive general manager for
more than 20 years, has always taken an active role in musical as well as administrative affairs. Reports of a developing feud between Fleischmann and
Previn began almost as soon as the conductor was hired. Matters came to a
head when Fleischmann negotiated a contract promising Salonen a tour
with the orchestra—without consulting Previn.

"It turned out at the time that all official tours were the music director's
prerogative," Martin Bernheimer observed in a postmortem for the *Los Angeles Times*. Of course, "Previn objected to being bypassed on his own turf.
This, no doubt, was an example of the managerial interference that he cited
as the reason for his resignation. Understandably miffed, Salonen pulled out
of his commitment to serve as principal guest conductor here. It was feared
that he might hold a grudge and choose permanently to take his business
elsewhere.

"Instead, he has opted for the last laugh," Bernheimer continued. "It
should be a beneficial laugh."

When Salonen was named music director in August, he became unquestionably the youngest leader of a major orchestra in the country, perhaps the
youngest in the world. After the announcement of his appointment, he immediately went into seclusion in his native Finland, then led some performances in London, where he now lives. And then, in late November, he

returned to Los Angeles where he led performances of Stravinsky's *Oedipus Rex*. Significantly, the photograph that the *Los Angeles Times* ran on page F1 was not the standard glossy pose of the conductor-as-hero but rather a snapshot of Salonen *and* Fleischmann, falling into a bear hug.

For all the conductor's unquestioned talent—and it is immense—certain lessons in musical politics must be learned through experience. Salonen is aware that there is some cynicism in musical circles about his appointment; the Philharmonic is reportedly split between admirers and those who consider him little more than "Ernest's man."

"This whole story has gotten out of hand," Salonen said backstage in Cleveland, immediately after rehearsal, in accented but accomplished English. "I anticipate smooth sailing. I wouldn't have accepted this offer had I believed there would be a great deal of trouble"—he flashed an ironic grin—"*sharing* the power."

Salonen is movie-star handsome, compactly built, confident and serious in his conversation. His demeanor alternates between youthful enthusiasm and the grand manner of an established maestro. "The meetings we've had have been pleasant and productive," he continued. "And the main point is what we can accomplish as an orchestra." But can he stand his ground? A moment's silence, as Salonen formulates an answer. "So far, there have been no problems whatsoever. What happens in the future one cannot know, but I foresee no immediate problems."

Indeed, thus far Salonen has encountered few problems in what can only be described as a meteoric career. "I started my musical studies late," he said. "Oh, my mother tried to make me play the piano when I was four or five but I refused because I thought it was silly, sissy, and simply uninteresting. She was wise enough to let it go. But then, when I was about nine, I suddenly got interested. My first instrument was the French horn and then I took up the piano. And then I started to compose, although I really didn't know how, from any technical standard."

It was as a composition student that Salonen entered the Sibelius Academy, Finland's most prestigious conservatory. After graduation, he studied in Italy with Franco Donatoni and Niccolò Castiglioni. "But you can't make a living as a composer—at least I couldn't, so I started to conduct," he said. "I became a guest conductor at the Finnish National Opera in 1981, mostly conducting *Giselle*. Good training, I guess, although I hated it."

Salonen's international career may be said to date from 1983, when he replaced an ailing Michael Tilson Thomas in a performance of the Mahler Third Symphony with the Philharmonic Orchestra in London. He learned the 90-minute work in five days and later, with characteristic jauntiness, declared it "pretty simple for someone of my generation."

CBS Masterworks promptly signed Salonen to a contract; to date, he has recorded Nielsen's Symphonies 1, 4, and 5 (part of a complete cycle of the Danish composer's symphonies) as well as works by Grieg, Sibelius, Lutoslawski, Messiaen, and Prokofiev. One of his finest discs is devoted to Richard Strauss's forlorn and moving elegy to 19th-century Germany, *Metamorphosen*. This is a late work, composed when Strauss was in his 80s, and it is too often played in a feeble, enervated fashion that is mistakenly deemed appropriate for the music of an octogenarian. In Salonen's reading, Strauss's pain and anger are given free rein, and the results are deeply affecting.

Salonen names Wilhelm Furtwängler and Erich Kleiber as the conductors of the past he most admires. He will not talk about living conductors: "If I mention anybody, I'll be leaving somebody else out." He continues to compose but does not like to lead his own music; too nervous, he says. Among American composers, he respects the music of Elliott Carter, dislikes the music of Philip Glass, and believes that John Adams, who combines the minimalist aesthetic with a strong traditionalism, has evolved "a syntax that makes sense."

The Los Angeles Philharmonic is generally ranked a step below the so-called "big five" American orchestras (Boston, Chicago, Cleveland, New York, and Philadelphia) but it is overdue for an upgrade. The community is rich—financially, musically, and otherwise—and a great deal of attention will likely be paid to Salonen's progress.

"I don't want to create a 'Los Angeles sound' or anything like that," Salonen said. "I want to create a sound that is appropriate for each composer—a Beethoven sound, a Brahms sound, a Debussy sound, a Stockhausen sound."

So far, the press in Los Angeles has been encouraging but mixed. "I read my reviews," Salonen said.

Everybody does, actually, but I'll admit to it. Criticism is something you can't control: sometimes you think you did something wonderfully and you get a terrible review and vice versa. You have to learn not to be devastated by bad reviews; they're part of life. I used to write reviews myself, when I was just starting out, and I know how bloody difficult it is. So when I read a nasty but intelligent review about my work, I can take it, because I was such a smartass myself.

Newsday
24 December 1989

Robert Shaw: The Last Interview

It took me most of the summer of 1998 to arrange an interview with Robert Shaw. Known to be wary of journalists, he was clearly in no hurry to partici-pate. When we finally sat down, however, he couldn't have been more accom-modating and expansive. Unfortunately, this turned out to be Shaw's last long interview, as he died on January 25, 1999, just four months after our talk.

B Y THIS POINT, Robert Shaw is living history—a musician who worked with Arturo Toscanini, Serge Koussevitzky, George Szell, and Igor Stra-vinsky, among hundreds of others. And at the age of 82, the man who more than anyone put American choral conducting on the map is still at the peak of his powers as an exhausted century comes to a close.

This week, Shaw will be at the Kennedy Center to conduct a complete per-formance of the *Missa Solemnis*, a grand start for the National Symphony Orchestra's Beethoven Festival and, indeed, a fit and ennobling beginning for the 1998–99 classical music season in Washington.

One afternoon last week, in his suite at the Watergate, Shaw talked about his long association with the *Missa*.

"The first thing that any vocalist or instrumentalist has to remember about Beethoven's *Missa Solemnis* is that it was composed by a deaf pianist," Shaw said.

"This is very great music indeed," he elaborated. "But it is enormously dif-ficult—physically, philosophically, intellectually. Moreover, it was written by a man whose principal instrument was the piano and who was also completely deaf by the time he started to work on it. And so *of course* there are some awkward spacings, *of course* some of the writing for voice is all but impossible to sing. But at its finest, the *Missa* attains a depth of meditative speculation that is comparable only to Beethoven's last quartets."

Shaw is a gracious host—welcoming, informal, good-humored, yet somehow conveying a tender vulnerability that is rarely found in a conductor. He prefers exact questions, but once he is comfortable with a visitor, he is likely to lose himself in some vastly amusing anecdote. After six decades making music throughout the world, he knows a lot of them.

Robert Lawson Shaw was the son of minister Shirley Richard Shaw and his wife, Nelle Mae Lawson Shaw, who was usually the leading vocalist in his church choirs. Imbued with an evangelical spirit, Shirley Shaw changed pulpits so often that every one of his five children was born in a different California town. Robert, who entered the world in Red Bluff on April 30, 1916, was the oldest son and regularly helped his father with his musical duties. Before he was in his teens, Robert Shaw was already an experienced choral conductor.

Still, it was the late songwriter and band leader Fred Waring who led the young man into professional music. "I was at Pomona College and part of the glee club there," Shaw recalled.

> Fred came to town with a variety show and we were invited to participate. Afterward, we asked if we might sing some of his own arrangements. Well, he gave them to us and we used them in our home concert. Then he asked me if I wanted a job. Well, I said no—I was studying comparative religion and English literature and I planned to go into the ministry. But about a year later, I changed my mind, moved to New York, and put together the Fred Waring Glee Club.

Shaw remembers Waring as a "fine natural musician."

"He had a clear sense of what he wanted," he continued, "and it was excellent training. It was 1938 when I began working with Fred—pretty tough times, economically, and we didn't have a lot of money to throw around. But I put together a glee club of 24 voices from a pool of 600 applicants. I wonder if there's ever been a group of voices to equal it, dime for dollar."

However, the Waring singers were positively wealthy compared with the singers in Shaw's own ensemble, the Collegiate Chorale, which he founded in 1941. This was an amateur chorus with 200 singers, in which every member paid annual dues of $10. Profits from their concerts were funneled back to defray expenses, and all important decisions were reached by majority vote. The group made its debut at Carnegie Hall in 1942, under the direction of Leon Barzin.

Shortly thereafter, Shaw met Toscanini for the first time. "There were all sorts of stories about Toscanini's temperament," Shaw recalled, "but I always found him very kind and very modest. We met to prepare a performance of Beethoven's Ninth Symphony, and he seemed gloomy about the prospects. 'Oh, Maestro,' he said—here I am in my early 20s and Toscanini is calling me Maestro!—'Oh, Maestro, I've never heard a good performance of this work. The soloists are always wrong, the chorus is never quite precise, something always goes wrong.' He was terribly worried about being humble before the composer.

"Well, after our performance, he came back and told me that he had never heard the piece really *sung* before," he continued. "After that, our association was easy." Shaw prepared the chorus for two of Toscanini's most famous recorded interpretations, the Beethoven Ninth and the *Missa Solemnis*, both issued by RCA Victor and still available all these years later. Some of Shaw's other early performances were recorded with his own Robert Shaw Chorale, which could deliver nuanced and exciting performances of everything from Masses by Poulenc and Mozart through Broadway show tunes, Christmas carols, and, of course, the hymns with which the young conductor grew up.

Shaw was always a great proselytizer for choral music; over the years he must have led more than a million voices in song. As it happens, one of those voices belonged to this writer's father, Ellis B. Page, now a professor of educational psychology at Duke University.

"In the early 1940s we belonged to the University Christian Church in San Diego, where Shirley Shaw was then the minister," Page said in an interview. "Robert Shaw was already successful in New York and known to the rest of the country from his work on radio, but he came back one year and led his father's chorus. He started off by telling us we were going to be singing notes we never knew we could sing—and it was absolutely true. He gave us all sorts of exercises—singing high, singing low, singing loud. He expanded our limits, opened us up. It was inspirational."

By the early 1950s Shaw was without a doubt the most famous of American choral conductors. He appeared regularly on radio and television and brought some of his father's evangelism to the propagation of choral music throughout the country. But he was increasingly interested in symphonic conducting as well, and held posts with the San Diego Symphony and the Cleveland Orchestra (where he served as associate conductor under George Szell). Ultimately he became the music director of the Atlanta Symphony, where he led the orchestra from 1967 to 1988, and is widely credited with building the group into a first-rate ensemble.

The period in Cleveland was crucial for Shaw. "In my first year I conducted some 50 different programs," he said. "And Szell was famously demanding, with the saving grace that he was at least as demanding on himself. I remember coming offstage after one of my first programs in Cleveland, which seemed to have impressed the members of the audience, some of whom were on their feet. In any event, Szell was waiting for me and he said, 'Bob, you have no right to have such a successful concert after the miserable rehearsals you conducted this week.'"

Shaw now believes that rehearsal methods make up the essential difference between choral and orchestral conducting. "By the time of actual performance, there should be no difference in the two jobs whatsoever," he said.

> You come out and conduct; most of the real work has been done earlier. But when you are conducting a professional orchestra, you are dealing with a group of highly schooled musicians. Imagine how much time and effort it takes before you're even ready to audition for an orchestra! String players can play 12 notes a second. And so most orchestral players can say, with some justification, look, we don't need to know about the spirit, we don't need your philosophy, just tell us how loud and how fast and we'll be all right.
>
> You know, the professional level among our musicians now is probably higher than it's ever been. Our schools are so demanding—Indiana University in Bloomington has three different orchestras!
>
> But when you are conducting a chorus, you need some metaphor, some turn of phrase, some humorous saying to put across the correct *idea* to your singers. Certain exercises will help out, too. When we work on the *Missa*, we will start off singing very quietly, and I will allow the

sopranos to take the music down an octave at first if that will help them. Then I introduce some metric counting—one and two and three and four—until the rhythm is understood. I never try to do everything at once. Rather, I bring in text, rhythm, dynamics, and intonation one element at a time. We might sing the text on a monotone until it's fully learned. And we will rehearse at a speed where it is all but impossible for anybody to make a mistake. That way, nobody can memorize errors. If you prepare this way, you will ultimately end up with a steady, unified, assured, and beautiful sound.

The *Missa* is particularly dear to Shaw's heart. "It's almost as if Beethoven were reinventing Christianity," he said. "There are all sorts of contemporary early-19th-century elements in the work—the romantic revolution, the Enlightenment, the idea of a brotherhood of man. Here, I sometimes think Beethoven created God in the image of man, instead of the other way around. In the *Missa Solemnis*, you have the sense that God, too, is suffering."

"I suppose that the most striking first impression of the *Missa Solemnis* is that of unqualified seriousness, solemnity, and majesty," Shaw wrote in a 26-page letter that he passes out to his prospective choristers before the preparation of any performance. "When the chorus enters with three *fortissimo* cries so dramatically and humanly stifled, it surely must be inescapable to the serious listener that there will be no easy questions and glib answers."

Shaw calls the long, rapt, and serene passage that links the Sanctus and Benedictus movements "Beethoven's greatest violin concerto." "These are immensely moving measures," Shaw wrote. "The 'Benedictus' is the vast, timeless repose toward which the 'Gloria' and the 'Credo' have been rushing. One hopes it will go on forever."

Many feel the same way about Robert Shaw's influence on American culture. As the American composer Bernard Rogers once wrote: "Shaw is the friend of all that is good in music. His service to music of all schools cannot be measured. It is unique, passionate, and selfless. Our debt to him is very deep."

The Washington Post
6 September 1998

The Resurrection of Sibelius

MUSICAL REPUTATIONS come and go. A hundred years ago, Mozart was regularly dismissed as an exquisite lightweight while J. S. Bach occupied a respectable but somewhat forbidding place on the fringes of the repertory. Back then, neither of them was considered in the same league as, say, the revered opera composer Giacomo Meyerbeer, who created such massive spectacles as *Les Huguenots* and *Le Prophète*, now seldom performed and generally judged beyond resuscitation on those rare occasions when they do find a stage.

However, it is hard to think of any composer who has risen so high, fallen so low, and then climbed so high again as Jean Sibelius. For most of his 91 years—he lived from 1865 to 1957—Sibelius was accepted as the natural heir to the symphonic legacy of Beethoven and Brahms, not only admired by fellow musicians but enormously popular with the public. His native Finland issued a postage stamp to commemorate his 80th birthday; closer to home, when the Soviet Union invaded Finland at the beginning of World War II, a relief campaign in the United States fashioned an effective fund-raising poster. It bore the image of Sibelius and four simple words—"I need your help."

Even then, however, a strong reaction against Sibelius had begun in musical circles, one that intensified during the 1950s and '60s and began to relent only in the late 1970s. With the exception of a few pieces (*Finlandia*, above all, but also *The Swan of Tuonela*, the *Karelia* Suite, the violin concerto, and, to some extent, the Second and Fifth Symphonies), his music fell from grace. Proper modernists dismissed him as an outright reactionary for the consonant harmonies and romantic sweep of his most familiar music. The

216

composer Virgil Thomson, who was chief critic for the *New York Herald Tribune* from 1940 to 1954, took every opportunity to cut him down. "I realize that there are sincere Sibelius-lovers in the world," Thomson sniffed in 1940, "though I must say I've never met one among educated professional musicians." The French composer and conductor René Leibowitz went so far as to write an intemperate pamphlet called *Sibelius: The Worst Composer in the World.* (And what, one cannot resist asking, has René Leibowitz done for us lately?)

In any event, as the century comes to a close, Sibelius has been triumphantly rehabilitated. He is once again a hero to many composers, ranging from the onetime British avant-gardist Peter Maxwell Davies to such post-minimalist Americans as John Adams and Ingram Marshall. Moreover, his work is available on an enormous number of good recordings with new releases coming along every month—the ultimate "cold-climate" composer is positively *hot.*

Jean Christian Sibelius was born in Finland on December 8, 1865. He played the violin from an early age and, like many composers, was writing music before he formally "knew how." A rather stern-looking young man, he only grew more austere in appearance as his hairline receded. He studied in Berlin and Vienna before returning to Finland, where he immersed himself in the movement for Finnish independence from czarist Russia. (Finland has, at different times, been forced to fight not only the Russians but also the Swedes and the Danes to hold on to its national identity.) Nordic legends and episodes from the great Finnish epic *The Kalevala* figure in much of the composer's music, and he became a proud nationalist. Indeed, *Baker's Biographical Dictionary of Musicians* has called Sibelius the "last representative of 19th century nationalistic Romanticism," but he is much more than that, which is why he fascinates and perplexes us today.

There are two things to be said straightaway about Sibelius. First, he is terribly uneven (much of his chamber music, a lot of his songs, and most of his piano music might have been churned out by a second-rate salon composer on an off afternoon). Second, at his very best, he is often very weird.

For example, the Symphony No. 6 (1923) is one of the century's most curious masterpieces—serene, beatific, almost Mozartean in its clarity and grace, suffused with warm winter light. It is rarely played, has little to do with anything else Sibelius ever composed (what to make of the second movement, that long series of musical question marks?), and its interpreters have a habit of trying to turn it into Tchaikovsky or the more traditionally "romantic" Sibelius Symphony No. 5, or something else that they might recognize—trying, in other words, to make it fit into a pattern. And it *doesn't* fit—which is not at all to say it doesn't work.

Because Sibelius was such a quirky and intensely personal creator, he has had remarkably few disciples. The other great composers who worked through the first quarter of the 20th century—Richard Strauss, Arnold Schoenberg, Igor Stravinsky—are easier to imitate because their music has immediately identifiable traits and generally obeys certain laws (the composers' own, more often than not). And so a whole school of French music was able to spring directly out of Stravinsky, while every American university had a mini-Schoenberg or two in residence throughout the 1960s and 1970s.

But how does one write imitation Sibelius? Even Sibelius himself couldn't do it, and he left no new "laws." None of his last five symphonies has much in common with any of its neighbors; philosophically speaking, they all start pretty much from scratch. His music cannot be codified and it is not easy to explain—what would seem meandering and digressive in other composers comes across as either intrepid exploration or sheer strangeness in the best of Sibelius. There is nothing academic in his nature; he did not invent a compositional system (as did Schoenberg), nor did he attempt to perfect any specific style (such as the neoclassicism of middle-period Stravinsky). Indeed, for the most part, his musical syntax was not particularly unusual; rather, he used a common language to say uncommon things.

A great Sibelius performance will likely be as contradictory and surprising as the scores themselves—simultaneously wild and dramatic, Spartan and dignified, "passionate but anti-sensuous," as the late Glenn Gould once described them. And despite the large symphonic forces for which his best music was written, silence has a disproportionate importance in the work of this most sonorous of composers. If silence can be defined as an absence of sound, it may be helpful for the novice, when coming to Sibelius, to consider his music a temporary respite from quietude. The image of Sibelius as a brooding poet of the spare, near-motionless, unpeopled North is fairly hackneyed by now, but it is no less true for all that.

Among the many Sibelius recordings available today, one stands out as a spectacular bargain: the complete symphonies, set down in the late 1970s, featuring Sir Colin Davis and the Boston Symphony Orchestra on the Philips label. Not only does this provide listeners with most of the essential Sibelius (in addition to excellent and idiomatic performances of the symphonies, it includes the violin concerto with Salvatore Accardo and the tone poems *Finlandia*, *The Swan of Tuonela*, and *Tapiola*), but it does so on four specially priced compact discs that most retailers sell for less than a full-priced two-CD set.

Other editions that ought to be considered include the vibrantly emotive cycle conducted by Leonard Bernstein with the New York Philharmonic (Sony Classical—avoid his late, turgid renditions with the Vienna Philharmonic on Deutsche Grammophon), Paavo Berglund with the Helsinki Philharmonic (EMI Classics), and a startlingly persuasive recent set with Jukka-Pekka Saraste with the Finnish Radio Symphony Orchestra, issued last year on Finlandia.

Those listeners in search of individual symphonies have a spectacular range of recordings from which to choose (there are at least 50 renditions of the Symphony No. 2 alone). If you are at all fond of Sibelius, it is also advisable to pick up his early symphony-*cum*-oratorio *Kullervo*, a panoramic treatment of Finnish lore for large orchestra and chorus that dates from 1892 and was suppressed by its composer during his lifetime. Indeed, I find it more interesting than the much later Symphony No. 1, which is a lot like Tchaikovsky but not so personal and assured. *Kullervo*, in the original Finnish, is available in a bang-up performance by the Los Angeles Philharmonic, under Esa-Pekka Salonen on Sony Classical.

I have no special recommendation for the Symphony No. 1; Vladimir Ashkenazy on London, Bernstein on Sony, and Herbert von Karajan on EMI Classics are all more than acceptable. My favorite recording of the Symphony No. 2 is a thrilling old Pierre Monteux disc with the London Symphony Orchestra, once available on RCA Victor, later on London, and probably set for CD release in the not-so-distant future. The insistently repeated theme in the last movement can either be beguiling or terrifying; most conductors opt for charm, but I prefer the suggestion of fierce northern wind (Toscanini, on

RCA, does a suitably unrelenting job here but the sound is dated). Bernstein with the New York Philharmonic is a little too lilting in the finale for some tastes, but he does bring an eerie ferocity to the second movement as well as his usual bristling excitement throughout. One might also consider the new James Levine performance with the Berlin Philharmonic on DG and the recording Herbert Blomstedt made with the San Francisco Symphony on London.

After the Symphony No. 2, we find a new Sibelius in place with each new symphony. The No. 3 is sweet tempered, folkish, and not immediately arresting (it is probably the least played of the symphonies). Yet it inspires affection among many who know it well, and it is very beautifully rendered by the London Symphony Orchestra, under Davis on RCA Red Seal, with a strong, solid version of the Symphony No. 5 as its disc-mate; when this new cycle is complete, it may be the edition of choice—the first installments in the series have been even more authoritative than the versions Davis made with Boston.

The Symphony No. 4 is as baffling and forbidding as any work in the 20th-century repertory. I've loved this piece for almost 20 years, play it incessantly, and still don't think I understand it fully. Bleak, spare, nothing if not mysterious, the symphony has been likened to a sort of musical cubism, and as such analogies go, that's a pretty good one (the first movement, in particular, is built block by sonic block, with an absolute minimum of padding). Oddly enough, the smooth, creamy textures that von Karajan elicited from the Berlin Philharmonic suit it perfectly; they complement the work's strangeness rather than dulling or drowning it. I prefer von Karajan's mid-'70s recording on EMI Classics to both his later (and earlier) readings on DG. Saraste and Blomstedt are also particularly fine in this symphony.

The No. 5 marks a partial return to form. "God opens his door for a moment and His orchestra plays the fifth symphony," Sibelius wrote in his diary during the process of composition. This is noble, affirmative, heaven-storming high romanticism, without any self-consciousness (and certainly without any trace of the modernist fragmentation we found in the No. 4). Here, again, von Karajan is excellent (any of his several recordings) but Bernstein is also riveting, as is Simon Rattle on EMI Classics. Indeed, for whatever reason, there seem to be more satisfactory recordings of the Symphony No. 5 than any of the others. For a different take on this piece, pick up Osmo

Vanska's recent album for Bis Classics with the Lahti Symphony Orchestra—an early, four-movement version that was quickly (and wisely) rejected but makes for a fascinating comparison.

We have already discussed the Symphony No. 6; my favorite recording is the first one made of it, dating from 1934 with Georg Schneevoight and the Helsinki Philharmonic. Tranquil and radiant, somehow conveying a humble and profound gratitude for the experience of life and living, it is now available on the Finlandia label (distributed by Warner) on a disc called *Historical Sibelius Recordings*. Among more modern recordings, Davis and the London Symphony on RCA can be recommended.

To this taste, the Symphony No. 7 marks a falling-off after its three predecessors—it seems an elaborate jaunt around the periphery of a prepared catharsis that never quite occurs. But many will disagree (the British critic Cecil Gray thought the Sibelius Seventh the most perfect symphony ever written). In any event, Bernstein and the New York Philharmonic do it up proud—gorgeous, caloric string textures and lowing, majestic trombone chorales.

Setting aside the symphonies and the best of the tone poems, the other essential large Sibelius work is the violin concerto (which dates from roughly the same period that produced the Symphony No. 4 and the eerily fascinating *Luonnatar* for soprano and orchestra and shares some of their luminous darkness). Two historic performances of the violin concerto have been recognized as classics all along—the first recording by Jascha Heifetz and the somewhat less dramatic but more expansive and graceful recording by the short-lived French violinist Ginette Neveu. Both of these are available on EMI Classics. Among recent recordings, the Russian emigré Viktoria Mullova's disc with Seiji Ozawa and the Boston Symphony Orchestra on Philips is terrific—and it shares a disc with an equally valuable performance of the Tchaikovsky violin concerto.

Sibelius left four string quartets of which only one is a fully mature composition. *Voces Intimae* (Intimate Voices) is a sort of sustained study of various shades of musical gray, quite beautiful in its measured way. The readings by the Guarneri and Juilliard quartets (on Philips and Sony, respectively) are too unwontedly dramatic for this very static music; I suggest one of the Finnish quartets, such as the Sibelius Academy Quartet on Finlandia or the Voces Intimae Quartet on Bis.

Among the smaller works is bass-baritone Tom Krause's carefully chosen selection of the songs on Finlandia. And Glenn Gould's album of the otherwise unremarkable sonatinas for piano has a fascinating quirk that should make it irresistible to anybody interested in Gould and his philosophy. He recorded the music with several microphones, to capture the same performance from different vantage points, and then used the tapes in the same way a movie director might coordinate a roomful of cameras. And so one phrase might be in "close-up"—recorded only a few inches from the sounding board of the piano—and the next phrase might be far away, a "long shot," with the piano in the sonorous distance. Whatever else this recording may be, it's unique; Gould never tried this experiment again.

Sibelius basically stopped composing around 1930, more than a quarter-century before he died (his last major work is the ruminative *Tapiola*). For years, there were rumors of an in-progress Eighth Symphony, but nothing turned up after the composer's death; there is some evidence to suggest that the symphony was written and then destroyed. Whatever the case, this "silent period" has been the subject of much speculation. Did Sibelius lose his gift? Was he debilitated by alcohol, of which he was very fond? Was he inhibited by his enormous reputation or, perhaps, by the innovations of young composers? Had he simply said his piece?

Another Sibelian mystery—as compelling as the enigmas we find in his music.

The Washington Post
29 September 1996

Frank Sinatra

H E CALLED HIMSELF a mere "saloon singer" from Hoboken, New Jersey. But Frank Sinatra, who died late Thursday at the age of 82, was much more than that.

With his bourbon-smooth baritone voice; his suave, intimate singing style that was both tough and tender; and an uncanny ability to embody public fantasy that made him an idol of millions, Sinatra attained a position of power and influence without equal in the entertainment industry.

"Frank Sinatra is by any reasonable criterion the greatest singer in the history of American popular music," critic John Rockwell wrote in his 1984 book *Sinatra: An American Classic.* As a performer, Sinatra was a consummate stylist who changed the course of popular singing. He eschewed the crooning manner of his most obvious predecessors, Rudy Vallee and Bing Crosby, in favor of emotional ballads with provocative lyrics that were delivered with feeling (indeed, sometimes an excruciating vulnerability) and superb phrasing. Crosby once declared that he wasn't really a singer in the traditional sense but rather a phraser. The same could be said, with even more justification, for Sinatra.

He recorded hundreds of songs, some of them several times. (Cole Porter's "Night and Day" exists in almost a dozen versions, including an ill-advised disco rendition from the late 1970s.) His first hit was "I'll Never Smile Again" in 1942. Half a century later, when Sinatra was 78, he was still on top—his first *Duets* album was released and immediately went platinum. This disc, which the critic Will Freedwald has called Sinatra's "economic zenith, technological masterpiece and artistic nadir," featured him singing (mostly through studio overdubbing) with such disparate performers as Carly Simon, Barbra Streisand, Bono (lead singer in the band U-2), Gloria Estefan, Julio Iglesias, and Kenny G, and brought him yet another new audience.

In his prime, standing close to the microphone with a snap-brim hat and a sports jacket slung over one shoulder, Sinatra achieved a complete, symbiotic identification with whatever he was singing. Yeats mused poetically on just how to tell the dancer from the dance; when Sinatra was at his best, it was difficult to separate the singer from the song.

Much of his material could have been autobiographical (one thinks immediately of "My Way," written for Sinatra by Paul Anka, "September of My Years," and "It Was a Very Good Year," among others). He specialized in the intimate love ballad, evocative and sensuous, either wooing with visions of moonlight dancing, champagne, rising cigarette smoke, and promises of a night on the town, or playing the lonely man sitting on a bar stool at closing time. His voice grew deeper and less versatile with time but took on an additional poignancy that only made his singing more affecting.

Still, singing was only part of the Sinatra appeal. He made more than 50 films and won an Academy Award for best supporting actor in 1953 for his portrayal of the doomed GI in *From Here to Eternity*. He had television shows in the '50s on two networks. Thereafter, he appeared regularly on television specials into the 1970s.

In short, Sinatra was ubiquitous. You heard his records on the jukebox, in the taxicab, in the barroom and steakhouse. Several radio stations presented regular "all-Sinatra" programs; one New York station converted briefly to an all-Sinatra format. Grandparents, who had danced and shrieked to Sinatra when they were young, lived to see their descendants run out and buy his records again. Somehow, he was always there.

"His life has touched on innumerable facets of our culture over the last half-century," Rockwell observed,

> the struggle of ethnic subgroups within American society; the stylistic revolutions of popular music; the rise of electronic technology and its impact on the business of music; the connections between music and films, entertainment and the underworld, and entertainment in politics, left and right. His career has been shaped by the tangled links between classical music, jazz, pop and rock; by the ambivalent bonds

between ethics and art; by the mass sexual hysteria of youth; by the pain of romantic love and the dry desperation of aging bachelorhood; by the personal distortions that celebrity status inflicts upon those who so eagerly desire to be celebrities and succeed.

Sinatra always credited the trombonist and band leader Tommy Dorsey, with whom he sang from 1940 to 1942, as the principal element in his musical education. The secret of his style, he said, was his breath control that he perfected after observing Dorsey sneak inhalations through a "pinhole" in the corner of his mouth. In a performance, he became able to sing six and sometimes eight bars without taking a visible or audible breath. "This gave the melody a flowing, unbroken quality and that—if anything—was what made me sound different," he said.

His career exploded with a celebrated long-running engagement at the New York Paramount theater in 1944. The scene at the Paramount, in the heart of Times Square, was the stuff of legend: thousands of bobby-soxers, some of them waiting from the break of dawn, in lines that circled the block—fainting on the sidewalk, smashing store windows, rioting inside the theater, and waving undergarments in the air, all the while shouting "Frank—eee!!"

This was long before the advent of such entertainers as Elvis Presley and the Beatles, who made such behavior familiar; many commentators were baffled and offended by the spectacle. Some editorial writers turned to psychologists for explanations. One popular theory suggested that Sinatra was a surrogate for the soldiers fighting overseas in World War II. Others thought that Sinatra's fragile appearance aroused sublimated maternal instinct. Cynics maintained that the display was engineered by Sinatra's public relations man, one George Evans. Twenty years later, in fact, one of Evans's associates affirmed that some girls had indeed been hired to scream. But nobody paid for the swooning.

There were a few brief periods when Sinatra's star seemed to wane, most notably in the late '40s and early '50s, and again in the counterculture-dominated late '60s and early '70s, during which time he actually retired for two years. ("Nobody's writing any songs for me, and I don't know what to do about it," he explained at the time.)

But he always made a comeback. By the end of his career, his annual income was estimated in the tens of millions—from royalties; record albums;

his (increasingly infrequent) live appearances; real estate ventures; and holdings in several companies, including a missile-parts firm, a private airline, Reprise Records (which he founded), Artanis (Sinatra spelled backward) Productions, and Sinatra Enterprises, a personal corporation. He had his own jet and a rambling house in Palm Springs, California, with a private helicopter pad and a full-time staff of 75. Until his hair transplant operations, he even had one employee whose sole responsibility was said to be the care and transportation of a selection of toupees.

This is not the place to dwell at length on the less attractive aspects of the Sinatra personality. Great geniuses are not always great human beings. Sinatra was exuberant, flamboyant, and vulnerable, quick to feel both deep sadness and profound elation. He was known to fly into fits of rage, in which he might toss an ashtray at an assistant, a pitcher filled with water at a fellow musician, or a fist at a photographer. He particularly detested personality journalism, and some regular targets of his abuse were *The Washington Post*'s Maxine Cheshire and the syndicated columnists Liz Smith and Rex Reed. During a 1974 tour of Australia, his insulting behavior managed to enrage an entire country; indeed, the Australian Transport Union workers refused to refuel his jet, which blocked his departure from the continent, until he proffered a grudging apology.

There was a certain vulgarity about the Sinatra persona, with his misogynist and homophobic onstage comments, his public attacks on people who displeased him, and his ties to the gangland underworld. In the 1980s, comic Joe Piscopo regularly did a fairly good sendup of Sinatra on *Saturday Night Live* that called to mind Lenny Bruce's comment, "There's nothing sadder than an aging hipster." Some Sinatra stories are so wonderfully smarmy as to be irresistible; legend has it that when he sang at the Democratic National Convention in 1956, then–Speaker of the House Sam Rayburn came up and threw an arm around his shoulder. "Hands off the threads, creep," Sinatra is supposed to have snapped.

But he also had a reputation for acts of spontaneous generosity—helping out beginning singers, bestowing extravagant gifts, and bailing out friends who were down on their luck. Sinatra's image, carefully fostered by public relations firms, was that of the cocky, rebellious, but ingenious young man who fought his way out of Hoboken and never stopped fighting.

According to Freedwald's excellent and exhaustive study of the singer's recordings, *Sinatra: The Song Is You*, Sinatra was never a "vocal virtuoso." "But what he has substituted for pure technique in the very good years since his youth has proved far more meaningful," Freedwald continued. "His ability to tell a story has consistently gotten sharper even as the voice grew deeper and the textures surrounding it richer. Generally, rhythm and dynamics are discussed as if they were two distinct qualities, but with Sinatra they're inseparable."

He had an enormously fluid sense of phrasing, with nothing four-square about it. In a word, he swung—teasing along the rhythm of his songs, playing with breath control in a manner that was extraordinarily sophisticated. (Sinatra was revered by most classical singers, who were aware of the difficulties he so smoothly surmounted.) He chose splendid arrangers—Axel Stordahl, Billy May, and Nelson Riddle, among others—and made at least one recording as a conductor. One of his albums—*Close to You*, released in 1956 and considered his masterpiece by some listeners—was accompanied solely by a string quartet. (The ensemble was the splendid Hollywood String Quartet, featuring first violin Felix Slatkin and cellist Eleanor Aller, the parents of National Symphony Orchestra maestro Leonard Slatkin.)

Curiously enough, although Sinatra was a renowned perfectionist in the studio (he worked on *Close to You* for more than six months), he was quite the opposite when working in film. He was notorious for the way his takes would become less and less effective as he repeated them. He was quickly bored by routine. And indeed, once a recording was finished, he had no more interest in it. When he was asked in a 1983 radio interview to name his favorite recordings, he replied, "The ones that stick in my mind are the ones where I think the orchestrator's work and my work came together closely, for instance, *Only the Lonely*, *Wee Small Hours*, and some of the jazz things with Billy May." Then he paused; many who heard the program were convinced he simply couldn't remember the names of any of his other albums.

His fans can remember those titles vividly—*Songs for Swinging Lovers, No One Cares, Come Fly With Me, Nice and Easy, Point of No Return, September of My Years, Strangers in the Night*, and the others, classics all. In many ways Sinatra anticipated the "concept albums" of the late '60s and '70s—he plotted many of these discs not merely as grab bags of recent work but as complete artistic statements.

There is something both antiquated and forever young about Sinatra's artistic vision. He calls up a lost, spurious big-city glamour—a high life fueled by alcohol, tobacco, and willing women—and it is not merely the stern prudery of our own era that has made us mistrust this utopia. No, we will continue to admire and love Sinatra for his ability to capture universal human emotions, in all of their contradictions and complexity, within the straitened limits of a popular song.

The Washington Post
16 May 1998

Michael Tilson Thomas

I had two goals in mind while writing this article. I wanted to salute the phenomenally gifted Thomas on his appointment to the music directorship of the San Francisco Symphony, and it seemed time to present an honest portrait of a decidedly prickly and complicated personality. Thomas's success in San Francisco has been heartening; six years later, the honeymoon goes on.

SAN FRANCISCO

IT'S THE EYES that get you first. They are plastered everywhere, on signboards large and small, staring over the highway or across the subway tracks, gazing out impassively on the Bay Area. Remember T. J. Eckleburg, the billboard oculist brooding atop the ashlands in *The Great Gatsby*? Well, imagine Eckleburg in pastel Pacific colors and then substitute the face of— *gahhh!*—Michael Tilson Thomas, the pouty, petulant, eternal boy wonder of the symphonic world and the newly in-place music director of the San Francisco Symphony.

At the age of 50, Thomas has just landed his first major U.S. orchestra. He might have had such a position almost a quarter-century ago, when he was favored to take the helm of the Boston Symphony, back in the days before Seiji Ozawa and his love beads came to stay and stay. But things *happened*— as they have a way of happening when Thomas is involved. Whether the BSO musicians really threatened to walk out en masse if the appointment went through or management simply decided that this particular 27-year-old was not yet mature enough for such an august (and, for his age, unprecedented) post, there can be little doubt that what was perceived as Thomas's self-absorbed and difficult behavior helped foul him up.

And it only got worse. In 1978 Thomas—then the conductor of the Buffalo Philharmonic, a worthy, venturesome ensemble of the second rank—was busted for cocaine, marijuana, and amphetamine possession while going through customs at Kennedy Airport. (He plea-bargained down to disorderly conduct.) In 1985, before an audience of 9,000, he stormed off the podium in the middle of a Mahler symphony at the Hollywood Bowl after a police helicopter had the temerity to fly over his concert.

Before the nonpareil Kathleen Battle came along to stir up her own virulent blend of collegial animosity, Michael Tilson Thomas was probably the classical musician around whom the nastiest professional "dish," the most unpleasant stories, revolved. Time was when you all but had to stand in line to take a pop at him.

There's more to Thomas than that, of course, or he would have vanished long ago, a footnote in the sad history of musical prodigies. But he is also a brilliant, questing, and visionary artist, arguably the most naturally gifted conductor of his generation. He was exploring obscure corners of the American repertory (notably the angular, granitic masterpieces of Carl Ruggles) before even our most celebrated home-growns—Charles Ives and Aaron Copland, say—had been fully admitted into the international canon. He programmed Steve Reich's *Four Organs*—one magnificent, fathomless chord drawn out for 24 minutes, the minimalist aesthetic at its most rigorous—in the middle of a BSO program of Bartók, C. P. E. Bach, and Liszt in 1973, when it must have seemed nothing short of music from outer space. And in the late 1970s, long before historically informed performances of the baroque and classical repertory became the rage, Thomas was recording graceful, transparent, ineffably musical renditions of Beethoven symphonies with a small chamber orchestra.

In recent years Thomas has spent a lot of his time in England, where his work as principal conductor of the London Symphony Orchestra was much admired. Andrew Porter, music critic for *The New Yorker* from 1972 to 1991, reviewed a 1993 complete Mahler cycle in London for *The Observer*. "Thomas has lived long with these scores; has lost none of a youthful, fresh response to their sheer picturesqueness; knows (and enjoys) their dangers as well as their delights; plumbs the depths and the darkness; exults on the peaks. Emotion and structure were in balance."

Now Thomas is back in his native California, living with his longtime companion and business associate, Joshua Robison, posing for photographers in a leather jacket by the Golden Gate Bridge, and making just about $1 million per season (the San Francisco Symphony refuses to divulge exact figures but does not quarrel with the estimate that columnist Herb Caen provided in the *Chronicle*, and if anybody knows San Francisco . . .). The orchestra is sounding terrific, the programs look exciting, subscriptions are up, and Michael Tilson Thomas would appear to have found his place in life at last.

And he *still* isn't much fun.

"Why do you ask me *that?*" Thomas says with sudden irritation, 20 minutes into a recent interview in his dressing room at Davies Symphony Hall. "Do you really think your readers will *care* about that?" The question was an innocent one—and, it must be admitted, rather arcane, but nothing so offensive as to bring on this huff.

"Maybe to *you* it's interesting, but . . ." And omigod, here we go again. If one were to tally up the proclamations of Thomas's handlers, there would have been almost as many "new Michaels" as there were "new Nixons." But this is definitely the same old guy—those "you-must-be-out-of-your-mind" raised eyebrows that arch higher and higher as a question is posed; the set, self-satisfied smirk alternating with a look that suggests a particularly acrid stink bomb has just gone off beneath the Thomas nostrils.

However, there is one big difference between the 1975 Thomas and the 1995 Thomas: a radically improved ability to set up a rapport with the players in his orchestra, exactly those people who will, after all, be his most knowing and consistent critics.

A rehearsal of the Beethoven Ninth Symphony is revelatory. In the soft, tiptoeing passages of the Scherzo, Thomas orders the strings to be "extremely conspiratorial," and suddenly Davies Hall is awash in mystery when a moment before there had been only cheerful, industrious forward motion. He is full of praise for his players—"Nice!" "Bravo!" "That was just perfect!"—and he has the gift of giving complicated musical instructions in informal phrases. "What I want here is maximum expression with minimum dynamic change," he says before the prayerful Adagio. Exactly. "Distract us!" he shouts to the violins embellishing the cosmic theme—and they do, delightfully.

Working with the orchestra, Thomas calls to mind a prodigious, fascinated child at play, lost to the world. Slim, bright-eyed, and—the word still applies—*boyish*, he weaves and bounces on the podium with balletic grace, his face relaxed into a poetic ecstasy. And yet he knows exactly where he is and what he is doing—in the wrong hands, this Adagio, for all its magnificence, can seem meandering and overlong. "That was just right," he tells the orchestra at the end of the rehearsal. "It was so *clear*. You knew just where it was going, every single note." With a little help from Thomas.

Next on the schedule is Arnold Schoenberg's curious and harrowing composition for narrator, chorus, and orchestra, *A Survivor From Warsaw*. It begins with the lines: "I cannot remember everything. I must have been unconscious much of the time." "I've always wanted to do this piece with Ronald Reagan," Thomas says to the orchestra, and some players hoot and stomp their feet. Thomas laughs with them—one suspects he's used this line before, and maybe it was funnier then—before he launches back into work. "What time is it? Oh, good. Then we just have time to fix the ending."

Thomas grew up in Los Angeles, only a few miles from where *A Survivor From Warsaw* was written. He was born on December 21, 1944, at the Cedars of Lebanon Hospital in Hollywood, the son of two stars of the Yiddish stage, Theodor and Roberta Thomas (originally Thomashefsky). "He was raised on tales of old Russia," Edward Seckerson recounts in *Viva Voce*, a book of conversations with Thomas recently published by Faber & Faber:

> His grandmother would tell of market day in Kiev when it was impossible to talk for the sound of church bells. And she would sing to him—lively, catchy tunes he later recognized as the folk tunes of Stravinsky's *Petrouchka* and *The Firebird* ballets. This was a household where people readily sang: Broadway songs, Yiddish theater songs, Italian opera from the family gramophone. His father wrote and sang songs: Gershwin had taught him the piano. It was an intoxicating environment in which to grow.

Indeed, in the words of Thomas Pynchon, "Los Angeles for a while was probably the center of the musical universe, Stravinsky living just off Sunset, Schoenberg teaching at UCLA, Charlie Parker and Miles Davis playing their historic gigs around South Central, nightclubs booming, radio stations broadcasting from them live." (Leonard Slatkin—the only other American conductor who currently fronts a first-rate American orchestra—was born in Cedars of Lebanon only three months before Thomas and grew up in a similarly eclectic home; his parents worked for the film studios, backed up early recordings by Frank Sinatra, Danny Kaye, and others, while spending their "free time" playing in one of America's great ensembles, the Hollywood String Quartet.) Thomas studied at the University of Southern California, where he played chamber music with violinist Jascha Heifetz and cellist Gregor Piatigorsky and studied composition with Ingolf Dahl. He met Stravinsky and played in local premieres of works by Pierre Boulez, Karlheinz Stockhausen, and William Kraft.

"The avant-garde was my entrance into the music world," Thomas says now. "People needed me around because I was the only pianist on the West Coast who could play the Stockhausen *Kontrapunkte*. I even stopped composing for 20 years because the music I heard in my head was so much more melodic and related to musical theater than the avant-garde compositions of the time. (Thomas, when he began to compose again, completed a setting of *The Diary of Anne Frank*.) I've backed away from playing most avant-garde music now. The best music has something eternally mysterious about it— you can never possess it or even fully know it. But a lot of the music that has been written in this century is more like a puzzle—once you've figured it out, there isn't really a lot of room for interpretation.

"You know, there is a tendency nowadays, particularly among young musicians, to think that there is a right and a wrong way of doing things," he continues. "And maybe that's true if you're talking about technical correctness in terms of playing your instrument. But you can't just follow the score. That's just a skeletal outline of the general area the piece inhabits. Don't play it the way it's written, I always say—play it the way it *goes*."

Thomas graduated from USC in 1967. In 1968 he was accepted as a fellowship student by Leonard Bernstein, with whom he worked at Tanglewood Music Center and who would become his principal mentor. ("He reminds me of me," Bernstein would later explain, which was, for Bernstein, probably the highest compliment he could pay.) In October 1969 Thomas stepped in to replace an ailing William Steinberg in the middle of a BSO concert at Avery Fisher Hall in New York. Steinberg subsequently withdrew from the season, and Thomas led 37 further concerts with the orchestra in the next few months. In 1970 he was appointed associate conductor; he was 25 years old.

Today Thomas avoids discussion of his early years in the limelight. ("I don't think any of us knew what we were doing in those days, do you?" is one of his favorite subject-changers.) But he continues to revere Bernstein, as man and artist, and told Seckerson of their first meeting:

> He said to me, "So what really is your most favorite musical moment? If you could only keep one moment in all of music what would it be?" I went to the piano and played the oscillating minor thirds and then the lonely oboe solo in the last movement of Mahler's *Das Lied von der Erde*. That was a very important moment for both of us. That music was so much the center of what he loved the most. It's so simple and yet the ambiguity is so vast. So much is suggested by just those few notes, because so much is left out. It's like a great poem. There is so much left out, and what you fill in around it is so meaningful.

After the falling-out with Boston (Thomas has led only one program at Symphony Hall since 1976, although he has participated in some Tangle-wood events) and the end of his Buffalo tenure in 1979, Thomas set to work as a busy freelance conductor. In 1988 he was appointed principal conduc-tor of the London Symphony Orchestra; he is also the founder and music di-rector of the New World Symphony, a youth orchestra in Miami Beach that, with the diligence and untested enthusiasm of its players, puts to shame many more "professional" ensembles. And then, in 1993, came word of the San Francisco appointment.

The news was greeted jubilantly by many musicians and critics (some of whom pointed out that Thomas was the first American-born conductor to hold the post since Henry Hadley, the first director, in 1911–15) and by those who were still hoping for a "happy ending" to the story of this enormously talented man. Opening night of Thomas's first fully in-charge season—Wednesday, September 6—would seem to have set him on the right path.

The program was an idiosyncratic and attractive mixture of the old and the new, the traditional and the unusual. There was the world premiere of a beautiful, chiming *Fanfare for MTT* by the West Coast composer Lou Harrison. Soprano Barbara Hendricks sang arias by Mozart and the *Bachiana Brasileira* No. 5 by Heitor Villa-Lobos. Thomas conducted Gershwin's *An American in Paris* and Yo-Yo Ma played a seamless performance of the Saint-Saëns cello concerto.

But the highlight of the evening was a prismatic tour through Benjamin Britten's *Young Person's Guide to the Orchestra*. It is the musical equivalent of a full-body workout. Every section onstage gets a moment or two to show off—now the woodwinds (flutes and piccolo, oboe, clarinet, and bassoon, in that order), now the strings, now the brass, and ultimately a barrage of percussion. It was a masterly demonstration of the orchestra's virtuosity—and of Thomas's organizational skills.

"The new guy has hit town at last," music critic Joshua Kosman wrote in the *Chronicle*. "In his first performance as the San Francisco Symphony's music director, Michael Tilson Thomas last night led the orchestra in one of its most exciting, most joyous season openers in a long, long time."

"That's the good news," Kosman added. "There isn't any bad news."

We may now expect an unusually ardent honeymoon. The orchestra is wealthy, stable, and ripe for growth. Thomas and the San Francisco Symphony have signed a five-year exclusive contract to make a total of 15 recordings with BMG Classics. San Francisco is a quirky, cosmopolitan city that actually merits that frantically overused term "unique," with its active life of the mind, unparalleled scenic beauty, and a charm that, for the susceptible visitor, is almost achingly seductive. (Where else can you find a panhandler so honest as to carry a sign that reads, "Why lie? I need a glass of beer"?) It would seem a city perfectly matched to Thomas, the prodigal Californian, the musical individualist, the maestro/*Wunderkind* from the Southland.

What will happen after the honeymoon is anybody's guess. But those who believe that classical music has not only a glorious past but a future as well, who believe this is an ongoing, ever-renewing art, can only wish Michael Tilson Thomas well. "He has, thank God, finally grown up," says a friend of some 20 years. Well, maybe only part of the way. Still, considering Thomas's talent, vision, and his new and splendid pulpit, it may be enough.

The Washington Post
8 October 1995

Dawn Upshaw

Peter Schumann, director of the Bread and Puppet Theater, has had the curious idea of staging one of Bach's most somber and elevated cantatas, *Christ lag in Todesbanden*, with actors dressed in blankets, pig masks, and wooden rodent heads building to a grand finale with a Sun God that closely resembles a fried egg surrounded by placards of happy Third World peasants.

Oh, well, one more crazy assignment for the junior critic, I think, resolving to have a stern talk with the editor. And then a young soprano engaged for the occasion—Dawn Upshaw, in her mid-20s and fresh out of Manhattan School of Music—begins to sing, and her chaste, loving, graceful performance almost redeems the afternoon.

Upshaw's days of singing with anthropomorphized rats in Brooklyn churches are long past. Here she is performing Mahler's fourth and gentlest symphony—graceful, cheerful, easily approached, constructed with a minimum of grandiloquence—with the Cleveland Orchestra under Christoph von Dohnányi. In the final movement, a soprano is called forth to express in song the composer's otherworldly vision of paradise.

It is an ideal part for Upshaw, whose voice has been variously—and accurately—described as bright, sweet, radiant, and ecstatic. Combining a fresh, childlike awe with seasoned artistry, she offers a performance of tingling, transfigured rapture.

At 32, Upshaw is all over the place these days, singing in concert, making

236

recordings, and, as of last season, essaying leading roles in that holiest of musico-dramatic shrines, the Metropolitan Opera. Her first Susanna in *Le Nozze di Figaro* this year impressed me as all-but-perfect—funny, animated, exquisitely characterized, and beautifully sung.

Yet from the beginning Upshaw has also placed an emphasis on American music, on contemporary works (often by composers from her own generation). And she has declined, politely but firmly, to "specialize." Now, as any manager will tell you, this is not the way a young artist usually builds a career. And yet for Upshaw it seems to be working; her recordings are both critical and popular successes, and she has concert and opera dates lined up through much of the decade.

Moreover, in a business that flourishes on intrigue, where gossip is all-pervasive and character assassination simply part of the landscape, Upshaw is admired and often genuinely *loved* by the people with whom she works. She has been a critic's darling from the start: not only is the singing immaculate, but the musicianship is questing and intelligent. Meanwhile, the person has remained modest and unspoiled. One pays her a compliment for a recording or performance, and she accepts the praise not as a token due a High Priestess of the Art, but with humility and, on occasion, a becoming reddening of the cheeks. A diva who *blushes*—a welcome change from the proverbial arrogant opera star.

After her stint in Cleveland—three concerts and a day of recording sessions to capture this memorable Mahler Fourth for London Records—Upshaw's throat hurt, and she spoke softly. "It's like any other muscle, I guess—you overuse it and you wear it out," she said one recent afternoon in a Manhattan bistro. "I've been to the doctors to see whether there is any swelling, but it really seems to be a case of fatigue. And it's not just from singing. Having a baby in the house can be exhausting, particularly when she's just learning to communicate. She's at an age just now when she's talking a lot and needs a lot of reinforcement, so I want to talk with her constantly."

Upshaw was then in the process of moving with her husband, Michael Nott, a musicologist, and her two-year-old daughter, Sarah (Sadie) Elizabeth, to a suburb of New York after many years on the Upper West Side. "And I'll admit I'm a little nervous about it all," she said.

Everything is so convenient in the city; I'm proud to say that we've been able to take care of the baby by ourselves, with a minimum of help. But when child number two comes along—as I hope it will—I would imagine that it's just not going to be possible to do it all in Manhattan. I've always known that I would want to move out someday. I grew up in the suburbs, and I guess I'm going back to the suburbs.

Specifically, Upshaw grew up outside Chicago, in the town of Park Forest. "I guess it was a lot like any other '60s suburban childhood," she recalled. "Peter, Paul, and Mary on the stereo, the Monkees on television. I liked to sing along with my family—'500 Miles,' that sort of thing, and civil rights stuff. My dad would accompany us on guitar."

Her first serious musical study was learning the oboe, a discipline that demands virtually the opposite technique from singing.

What you do is take in a huge amount of air and then let it out, bit by tiny bit. But I think playing the oboe has helped me a lot with phrasing, and certainly with rhythm and sight-reading. Eventually I came to a point in school when I couldn't schedule both singing and the oboe, and I decided to go with singing. Which was kind of a weird choice, because I was a much better oboe player than singer at the time—that's for sure!

Upshaw attended Illinois Wesleyan University. "In college I sang in some theater pieces and thought I might try my hand in commercial music, maybe jingles or something," she said. "But then I started taking music history courses and spending a lot of time in a choir that performed nothing but classical music. That's when I became serious about making this my life."

With that in mind, Upshaw moved to New York, for graduate classes at the Manhattan School of Music. While there, she established a reputation for unusually sensitive and communicative performances of complicated 20th-century music. "You know, I'd like to be more involved than I am in contemporary music," she says now. "I know I do a lot more of it than some singers, but that still isn't saying very much. I ought to be going to more concerts and hearing the music of today's musicians more often. At Manhattan, I sang *everything*."

The year she graduated from Manhattan, 1984, she was accepted by both the Metropolitan Opera Young Artist Development Program and the Young Concert Artists International Auditions. "They both came through in the same week," she recalled. "I had been wondering what to do with the rest of my life and how I would make a living while taking my voice lessons. And then I got these calls."

Many artists who begin their careers in small roles with gigantic organizations such as the Met find it hard to grow up with the troupe and often have to leave to prove themselves. Not Upshaw. She sang the small role of Barbarina in *Le Nozze di Figaro* and has now moved on to Susanna; perhaps, in a few more years, she will sing the role of the countess. James Levine, the Met's music director, has been one of her strongest supporters, conducting many of her appearances with the troupe and even accompanying her at the piano in solo recital. Meanwhile, she continued to sing elsewhere, giving premieres by composers as disparate as David Diamond and Aaron Jay Kernis. Currently she is booked for about 70 engagements a year—"too many," she says, wistfully. "If I could get it down to 50, I'd be really happy."

Like any artist, she would like to sing in the great European opera houses —La Scala, Covent Garden—if the right part came along. "But I'm really not interested in doing things just for the purpose of getting a better job the next time—you know, climbing up the ladder," she explained. "I want to work on things that *mean* something to me, that *satisfy*. Especially now that I have a family, I get very upset if I feel like my time isn't being used well. Down the line, I'd like to just settle in. I'll perform now and then outside the New York area, but this will definitely be home.

"And I really don't want the grand star treatment," she said. "That sort of stuff embarrasses me. I work hard, I have friends, I have a family, and I love to sing. Things have gotten rather complicated lately—there are people to meet, pieces to listen to, a whole lot of stuff—and I want to simplify my life considerably in the next five or 10 years."

But, for now, it's back to life on the road. This summer, she is in Europe, at the Aix-en-Provence festival. Last winter, in between appearances at the Met, she sang recitals throughout the Midwest, driving to many of the engagements herself, with Michael and Sadie.

"I hate practicing in hotel rooms, because I always worry about the people next door," she said.

I mean, I'd find it irritating if somebody were singing a few feet away on the other side of my wall. But I had no other place to warm up for rehearsal, and so there I was, one day in Ann Arbor, singing away in my room. And this nice lady came to the door and said "I'm awfully sorry, but I'm working with numbers across the hall, and I just can't *think* while you're doing that." And I said, "Oh, I'm terribly sorry, I'll stop right away—no, *really*, it's perfectly fine, please don't worry." And she thanked me and then said, "But I want you to know that I really think you have something there, and I hope you'll stick with it." I guess she thought I was auditioning for the School of Music or something.

One shudders to think how this advice would have been received in some quarters. But Dawn Upshaw threw no tantrum. She smiles at the memory—a warm, enveloping smile, without irony. "Anyway, it was nice to have the encouragement."

Newsday
19 July 1992

Don Van Vliet (Captain Beefheart)

BACK IN the early 1970s, when Captain Beefheart was at the decidedly substratospheric pinnacle of his fame, there was no faster way to clear out a party than to put on one of his records and turn it up.

It was a little like throwing a bomb. The rugged old Garrard turntable (widely favored in those days because it was less than $100 from the college stereo shop) was traditionally stacked with chug-a-lugging paeans to Southern laxity from the Allman Brothers, excruciatingly sensitive analyses of Love Amongst the Famous from Joni Mitchell and Jackson Browne, or—if the crowd happened to be unusually hip—explosive early disco from the Hues Corporation or Shirley & Company.

From the moment the phonograph needle settled into a Beefheart groove, however, everything changed. A crunching dissonance rent the air. Complicated time signatures and opaque poetry upset polite conversation and rattled the Mateus rosé. Beefheart's roar of purest gravel and the untrammeled violence of his rhythms sent resident hippies into bummers; lovers could find no slow dances; young professors would sniff around the turntable, scrutinize the spinning disc, pronounce the music "um . . . interesting," and then move as far away from the loudspeakers as possible. Meanwhile, a small but significant counterforce of Beefheart fans would surround the captured stereo, beaming with anarchic triumph.

More than a quarter-century later, it is still a good bet that slapping on a Beefheart CD in the middle of most parties would raise a few eyebrows. But the gesture might be greeted warmly at other gatherings—especially by those young artists and musicians who have found a wonderfully weird father fig-

241

ure in the good Captain, with his long-ago experiments. Over the years, edgy bands from Pere Ubu through Sonic Youth and songwriters as diverse as Tom Waits and PJ Harvey have all paid their own distinctive homages to Beefheart—and there are undoubtedly more to come.

Fortunately, most of the Beefheart canon is available on CD, so that his influence may continue to spread. Last summer saw the release of two ambitious retrospectives, *The Dust Blows Forward* (two discs, Warner Archives–Rhino) and *Grow Fins* (five discs, distributed by Koch International), complete with rare photographs and unusually extensive and intelligent documentation. Ezra Pound once described a classic as "something that remains news," and whatever else may be said of Captain Beefheart and His Magic Band, this music is not about to fade quietly into the background.

> If you want to be a different fish, jump out of school.
> —Captain Beefheart, 1982

Don Vliet—later Don *Van* Vliet and, still later, Captain Beefheart—was born in Glendale, California, on January 15, 1941. His father was a truck driver; his mother, a part-time Avon Lady and a homemaker. Young Don's eager imagination was apparent from the start; he was drawing and sculpting from earliest childhood, and having grown up near the La Brea tar pits, he reportedly once threw himself into the primordial ooze with the hopes of an encounter with a mastodon or saber-toothed tiger.

In the mid-1950s Vliet's family moved to Lancaster, California, a small city on the edge of the Mojave Desert. There, one legendary day at Lancaster High School, he met a musical soulmate in Frank Zappa, an equally eccentric and free-thinking fellow student. The two became inseparable and spent much of their time listening to wrenching old blues recordings by Sonny Boy Williamson, Howlin' Wolf, and Muddy Waters, as well as shards and squalls from avant-garde jazz musicians like Cecil Taylor and Ornette Coleman.

Zappa and Vliet stayed in touch—they would remain friends until Zappa's death in 1993—and collaborated on several quixotic projects in and around the Los Angeles area during the early 1960s. These included the formation of a band called the Soots and the plotting of an independent film titled *Cap-*

tain Beefheart vs. the Grunt People. It was at this time that Vliet adopted his professional moniker. He later said that it referred to the "beef" (meaning complaint, of course, not meat) that he carried in his heart against the world.

Captain Beefheart and His Magic Band made their first recording in 1966, a catchy bluesy cover version of an old Bo Diddley song, "Diddy Wah Diddy." Beefheart's rendition became a minor hit in California and will likely remind latter-day listeners of the seminal English blues-rock group the Yardbirds. In early 1967 the Magic Band cut its debut LP, *Safe as Milk*, for Buddah, a label that specialized in bubble-gum music—squeaky clean pop singles aimed directly at children and early adolescents.

It was an odd place for the dada Captain to begin, but *Safe as Milk* remains a terrific album—spirited, fanciful, brimming with ideas and intelligence. It is also a relatively *easy* album: the songs are brief, tuneful, and consonant, with irresistible hooks that keep you coming back to play them again. Today *Safe as Milk* sounds predictably dated but still engaging, distinguished by its reflection of a long immersion in rhythm and blues and certain foreshadowings of psychedelia.

Strictly Personal (1968) is a different animal. Among the most controversial of Beefheart's recordings, it began as a series of long, murky, freewheeling, and drum-heavy jam sessions. After the basic tracks had been laid down by the group, producer Bob Krasnow added whooshes, phasing, heartbeats, and other then-fashionable sound effects that, in the opinion of some listeners, all but ruined the record.

I disagree. Although Beefheart would attack Krasnow for the elaborate production on *Strictly Personal* (after the record had been released and had sunk out of sight), there is internal evidence that he not only approved but even encouraged the experimentation. Some of the original, undoctored recordings have been made available on a disc called *Mirror Man*, and they make for stark, hypnotic listening. But *Strictly Personal*—that fractured, elliptical mixture of power chords, bluesy howling, muddy sound, and wildly over-indulgent dial-twiddling—maintains its own fascination. After all, it *was* 1968.

Beefheart's most radical creation was yet to come. *Trout Mask Replica* (1969) must be counted one of the densest, strangest, and most immediately off-putting records ever made; as the composer Charles Wuorinen once said of Schoenberg's *Pierrot Lunaire*, listening to this music, even after decades of experience, is still rather like trying to befriend a porcupine. Spectacularly dissonant, embellished with surrealist lyrics that lend themselves to multiple meanings or none at all, *Trout Mask Replica* remains the apogee of Beefheart's modernism.

Here you will find (among other curiosities) a bizarre gloss on the famous newscast of the Hindenburg explosion as it might have been heard through a fly's ear; long unaccompanied narratives that sound like sea chanteys from an acidhead Ahab; titles like "Neon Meate Dream of a Octafish," "Bill's Corpse," and "Hobo Chang Ba." In the same spirit, Beefheart's musicians were given new names: for example, guitars are credited to "Zoot Horn Rollo" and "Antennae Jimmy Semens" (and, man, do those guys look weird, with hair longer than hair grows and a fashion sense that would have seemed outré in Haight Ashbury). There is laughing-gas silliness aplenty throughout the album, so it is all the more startling and effective when Beefheart bursts into a dead-serious denunciation of human cruelty in a song like "Steal Softly Thru Snow."

By its very design, *Trout Mask Replica* could have no sequel, and Captain Beefheart would never again venture quite so far off into the ether. But his next three albums—*Lick My Decals Off Baby* (1970), *The Spotlight Kid* (1971), and *Clear Spot* (1972)—continued to explore the interface of two aesthetics that had never before been mated: namely, the heartfelt emotionalism of rhythm and blues and the cool cerebration of high surrealism.

These are all vital and exciting discs, much more immediately attractive than *Trout Mask Replica. Decals*, for example, contains three magnificently tangled lute songs for solo guitar, while there are songs on *Spotlight Kid* and *Clear Spot* that really ought to have become hits. (And, indeed, "Click Clack" became a progressive FM staple for a couple of years.) "White Jam" is as pulsing, primal, and sexual as any of the old Victor "race" records, while "Crazy Little Thing" contains the irresistible (and likely irrefutable) lines:

> Crazy little thing has just gone crazy;
> Girl, how'd you get a name like Crazy Little Thing?
> Probably the name that drove you crazy all along.

During this period, Beefheart and the Magic Band toured regularly, offering note-perfect re-creations of the supposed "chaos" to be found on their records. Still, like many avant-garde artists—who seem to win critical plaudits and cult audiences more easily than they do financial security—Beefheart was hungry for some commercial success, and he seems to have re-examined his objectives in the mid-1970s.

Unconditionally Guaranteed, released in the fall of 1973, is generally considered Beefheart's all-time worst album, a judgment with which I shall not quarrel. It is a combination of indifferent pop melodies, timid arrangements, generic lyrics, and a Vegas sort of "star" recording mix that gives the singer infinitely greater prominence than the band. Critic Rhodri Marsden has called the disc "nasty and thoroughly sickly," and there can be no doubt that Beefheart's fans felt betrayed. All told, *Unconditionally Guaranteed* is shocking in its normality, and it is a tepid and uninteresting normality at that.

Those same fans were equally displeased with the album that followed, *Bluejeans and Moonbeams* (1974), which Beefheart cut with a group of session musicians (the Magic Band having all but dissolved after the debacle of *Unconditionally Guaranteed*). But *Bluejeans and Moonbeams* is a much better record, albeit one that has virtually nothing to do with the rest of the Beefheart canon. Here, the Captain's dominant influence seems to have been Frank Sinatra rather than some vanished bluesman: this is a set of slightly oddball love ballads, some of them very beautiful indeed (especially the title track), set to restrained but symbiotic accompaniment. *Bluejeans and Moonbeams* is a "one-off," to be sure, but it is strangely lovable and deserves wider recognition than it has so for received.

It was four long, fallow years before the release of *Shiny Beast (Bat Chain Puller)* (1978), but, from the first note it should have been obvious that, wherever he'd been, Beefheart was now definitely *back*—and at top form. Released at the height of the New Wave movement, *Shiny Beast* fit right in with the taut, herky-jerky sounds of the Talking Heads and Devo. "Tropical Hot Dog Night" is one of the group's best songs ever—a steamy, urgent, and exuberant call to party, complete with raucous trombone slides that would sound just great at Carnaval. (Young children love the continuing reference to a mysterious "monster" that will be coming out of hiding when the sun goes down.) *Shiny Beast* rocked as hard as anything Beefheart had ever recorded, and if it still didn't sell, it nevertheless brought him an excited new audience.

Doc at the Radar Station (1980) and *Ice Cream for Crow* (1982) continued along the same general path as *Shiny Beast*—both albums were filled with strong, quirky songs, tight playing, straight-ahead rhythms, and headlong energy. But Beefheart was growing tired and he refused to undertake a promotional tour for *Ice Cream for Crow*, a tour that might have meant the difference for what should have been an eminently salable record. Shortly thereafter came the announcement that Beefheart was abandoning music altogether and returning to painting and sculpture, his first loves.

Since 1982 there has been only silence. Today Don Van Vliet, the former Captain Beefheart, lives as a near-recluse north of San Francisco, where he firmly refuses any and all efforts to pull him back into making music. His paintings sell for thousands of dollars apiece, and he is said to be financially well off at last. There have been occasional rumors of ill health, rumors Van Vliet denied in a rare interview in 1993. Still, he seems to live a decidedly cloistered life; when asked what he was up to these days, Van Vliet responded: "Just paint. No people. Just painting."

The Washington Post
12 December 1999

Webern after Webernism

The first article I ever published about classical music, for Soho News in 1979, was a study of Anton Webern. Sixteen years later, I expanded on my idiosyncratic take for The New Criterion. *For me, Webern remains one of the 20th century's great composers—I prefer him utterly to Berg or Schoenberg—but the profound influence he cast still seems a decidedly mixed blessing.*

IT IS ALMOST 50 years since Anton Webern was shot and killed in a freakish accident in the aftermath of World War II. From this vantage point, Webern now seems one of those profound and original artists (James Joyce is another) whose work remains not only valuable but, for many of us, positively *essential*, yet whose influence has been baleful and sometimes ruinous to the numerous young artists who have attempted to follow in his steps.

Has any great composer been done so much harm by disciples and admirers? Here is Paul Griffiths, far from the worst of them, writing on Webern's use of serialism in the *New Grove Dictionary of Music and Musicians*:

> Linking serial forms through common terminals is a frequent practice in Webern from Opus 21 onward, but the shared notes are most usually one or two in number; this technique may limit, of course, the range of serial statements that can be chosen to follow a given form.... It should be noted that the three serial forms there shown are in the relation of prime tetrachordal combinatoriality: i.e., a 12-note aggregate is formed by all of the first or second or third tetrachords. How-

ever, Webern did not normally make explicit use of the combinatorial relations in which his symmetrical series are rich.

Sexy stuff—makes you want to run right out and buy all the Webern in the shop, doesn't it? It is not to Griffiths's attempt at explaining a complicated musical procedure that I object; it's rather to the fact that, here as in so much of the other writing on Webern—and certainly in most of the composition that claims to be "post-Webernian"—there is the implication that the curious ordering games he played are the most important thing about his work.

Worse, however, is the ferocious, near-Marxian self-righteousness in the claims of the ardent Webernians, some of whom trotted out the blood-soaked chimera of "historical inevitability." Here, for example, is the young Pierre Boulez: "History is much like the guillotine. If a composer is not moving in the right direction, he will be killed, metaphorically speaking." And on another occasion Boulez referred to 12-tone music as "a music of our time, a language with unlimited possibilities. *No other language was possible.*" (Italics mine.)

Yes, there was certainly a lot of ugly, formula-driven music written, explained, and justified in the name of Anton Webern. His imitators borrowed all his tricks—the spare, elegant orchestration; the long silences; the will-to-order—but captured none of his magic. I suspect that ultimately this composer will be remembered as an inspired, brilliantly talented eccentric—one of those occasional figures in the history of music who, like Berlioz, Busoni, Pfitzner, or the later Richard Strauss, will always stand a step away from whatever passes as the mainstream. Webernism is dead, but Webern lives.

New York had the opportunity to reappraise virtually all of Webern's music when Joel Sachs and the Juilliard School presented a series of evenings called "Focus! The Webern Legacy." I attended the first of these concerts, which was, unfortunately, underrehearsed and not particularly idiomatic (my sources tell me later installments were much better). Still, the program prompted me to take down the two more-or-less complete recordings of Webern's work (set down by Robert Craft in the early '50s and Boulez in the '70s), along with a more recent pairing of orchestral music by Webern and Mozart played by the Cleveland Orchestra under Christoph von Dohnányi. And then, fortified with scores, Sachs's superb program notes, and the vast Webern biography by Hans and Rosaleen Moldenhauer, I played every Webern recording in my collection and discovered, once again, that this is a composer that I not only esteem but love.

Can one "love" Webern in the same manner one "loves" Bach, Mozart, Beethoven, or Chopin, with heart as well as head? I think so. For while it may be helpful for a professional musician to analyze Webern's tone rows, sets, and subsets, the lay listener need not know or care what compositional techniques Webern was using in a given measure any more than it is necessary to understand Bach's complicated and remarkable employment of canonic forms to enjoy his "Goldberg" Variations. What matters is the sounding music—and Webern sounds.

Indeed, it might be argued that there has been no more specific aural creator than Anton Webern. By this I mean that his mature compositions are absolutely mated to the forces for which they are scored: change the orchestration—even slightly—and you change the music. In this way, Webern is the opposite of Bach, whose music survives all sorts of transcription. (I have heard stimulating performances of *The Art of Fugue* on harpsichord, piano, organ, arranged for brass ensemble, saxophone quartet, and full symphony orchestra; Bach himself was quite content to take a violin concerto and transpose it down a step to create a keyboard concerto.)

With Webern, no such tinkering is possible. Among his most famous works is the tiny vignette that makes up the fourth of the *Five Pieces for Orchestra*, Op. 10; it is scored for nine instruments and is only about 20 seconds long. Transcribed for piano, this would be rendered gibberish; played on any other instruments, it would be a different piece. The sound *is* the music: the trumpet has its four notes to play, the solo violin its five, the snare drum gives a rattle, and the piece is over, yet the susceptive listener will recognize that he has undoubtedly *heard* something. Webern called this symbiotic ordering of sound and pitch *Klangfarbenmelodie*—melody of tone colors—and he would develop it to his own pristine, platonic ideal of perfection.

Webern wrote these *Five Pieces* in 1910, at about the same time and in the same place Mahler was finishing up the last of his symphonies. Webern admired Mahler—some of Webern's compositions could have been boiled down from the quieter interludes in the late Mahler symphonies—but his own work represents the antithesis of Mahlerism in Viennese music. The difference is not simply one of length—Mahler's shortest symphony is almost an hour long; Boulez's recording of Webern's only symphony clocks in at nine minutes—but also one of mood and manner.

There is an unintentionally hilarious article by Leonard Bernstein that credits poor Mahler with having foreseen almost every disaster that has hit the 20th century, including "the murder in Dallas, the arrogance of South Africa, the Hiss-Chambers travesty [!], the Trotskyite purges, Black Power, Red Guards, the Arab encirclement of Israel, the plague of McCarthyism, the Tweedledum armaments race." "Only after all this can we finally listen to Mahler's music and understand that it foretold all," Bernstein concluded.

Metaphysical twaddle aside, I think most of us would agree that there is a strong element of *angst* in Mahler's music and in the music of Arnold Schoenberg and Alban Berg, the two other members (with Webern) of the so-called Second Viennese School that, to some extent, grew out of Mahler. But with the exception of a terrifying funeral march he wrote in memory of his mother (one of the *Orchestral Pieces*, Op. 6), there is very little angst in Webern—and certainly no gift of prophecy. Roger Sessions used to say that music was "beyond" emotion. This is not necessarily true of the music of all composers (nor would it be any sort of blessing if it was), but I think it is mostly true of Webern.

Robert Craft's four-record set of Webern's music was a labor of love, recorded in a hurry, and full of technical flaws (Craft himself apologized for the performance of the Concerto, Op. 24, in his liner notes); given the bottom-line mentality that prevails in the record industry, it is unlikely to be reissued on compact disc any time soon. However, for almost a quarter century, this was the only access most listeners had to Webern's musical world (I carried the set around like holy writ all through my 15th and 16th years), and it certainly deserves consideration in any discussion of the composer.

And there are some solid merits in the recording. Marni Nixon (who is probably best known for her work dubbing the film score of *My Fair Lady* for Audrey Hepburn) had a high, bright, dryly attractive soprano voice and she sang her numerous parts with intelligence and musicianship. That eminent Schoenbergian, Leonard Stein of the University of Southern California, brought a sure, idiomatic command to the keyboard music, both solo and ensemble, and many distinguished session players—something of a Who's Who of the mid-'50s L.A. freelancers—joined in the endeavor.

Craft's conducting has come in for some negative comment over the years. There is no doubt that he emphasizes the dissonances and modernist rough edges in Webern's music, gleefully pouncing on the "wrong notes" as if he simply couldn't wait to disturb the complacency of his audience; this composer would never again sound so ferocious. Yet the greatness of Craft's accomplishment cannot be denied. Less than 10 years after Webern's death, with most of the music unknown except to the most specialized of specialists, Craft convinced Columbia Masterworks to take a gamble on a four-record set and then, somehow, pulled it together, creating—from scratch, as it were—his own understanding of Webern, conveying it to his musicians and, by extension, to the world. How many recordings have changed so many lives? It has been said of the American rock group the Velvet Underground that only a few people bought their albums but each and every one of them went out and formed a band; Craft's Webern had a similar galvanizing effect on a generation of young composers.

By 1979 when CBS Masterworks (the heir to Columbia Masterworks and the predecessor to today's Sony Classical) brought out Pierre Boulez's Webern set, everything had changed. Webernism had grown from an esoteric cult into an institutionalized tradition, with manifestations throughout the music world. The Webernian mavericks, grown up and grown sober, were now entrenched in the conservatories and music schools, juggling their charts, balancing their canons, disseminating their theories, blowing the (muted, *pianissimo*) trumpet of Anton Webern, and in more than a few cases fashioning some of the dreariest music ever written, all in the master's name.

And so Boulez's recording came as a different sort of revelation. Boulez, the frosty, hyper-cerebral structuralist—whose pronouncements had done more than anything else to establish meticulously organized Webernism as a secular religion—surprised us with interpretations of a startling and radiant beauty, prismatic in their timbres, sometimes achingly reminiscent of the milieu that had formed Webern's aesthetic. Suddenly it was possible to recognize in Webern's music a man who grew up in a unified and conservative musical environment, a man who adored (indeed, conducted and even transcribed) the work of Johann Strauss—in short, a true son of Vienna.

Curiously, the Boulez set—which remains the essential Webern collection and is now available on compact disc from Sony—helped bury strict, by-the-numbers Webernism, for the performances were so lovely and lyrical that we were presented with a fresh vantage point on Webern. He was a *composer* again, with his own endearing quirks and mannerisms, rather than a mathematical pedant or an all-knowing Cassandra, laying down the law. A younger group of musicians, weaned from any mystical faith in empirical "progress," was less interested in Webern's formulas than in his sound. We listened to Webern, and, by and large, we revered him, but he was no longer the man who had divined the "only possible" musical language for our times; we no longer believed that tonality was necessarily dead; we had no use for codes that would supposedly ensure "correct" compositional procedures; we loved many manifestations of early-20th-century Vienna but no longer thought they had a great deal to teach late-20th-century America.

In the meantime, there had been a revival of interest in the work of such men as Richard Strauss and Jean Sibelius, both written off as hopelessly old-fashioned during the '50s and '60s. Of the three works of circa-1910 modernism that have often (and rightly) been hailed as seminal—*Elektra*, *Rite of Spring*, and *Pierrot Lunaire*—only *Elektra*, created by the derided "reactionary" of the bunch, retained the power to shock an audience speechless in the 1980s. We encountered the Sibelius Fourth Symphony—unknown and untaught to most composition students for many years—and found it as elliptical and enigmatic as anything by Webern, while radically different in its form and expression. We listened to American masters and near-masters, without apology or embarrassment. In short, we discovered that Webern was not the One True Faith his acolytes had proclaimed but, rather, a wonderfully original, exquisitely distilled, and enormously distinctive voice among many—a voice that would always find listeners, even amidst the chaos and raucous diversity of our era. And that is enough.

The "mainstreaming" of Anton Webern continues, at least on disc. Recently the Cleveland Orchestra issued a three-CD set devoted to the last six symphonies of Mozart, with several orchestral pieces by Webern to round things out. It might not be the pairing of a Mozartean's dreams, but conductor Dohnányi's graceful, clear, and acutely nuanced performances, realized with his magnificent orchestra, illuminate textures, subtleties, and continuities in this music that even Boulez sometimes missed. Musicologists used to profess bewilderment at what one writer called Webern's "gnomic, overdelicate puzzle-music"; much of that puzzle now seems to have been in the performances, and as those performances improve, the puzzle would seem much closer to solution.

It should be noted that Craft, Boulez, and Dohnányi have all excluded *Im Sommerwind* from their surveys. This is a student work from 1904, never published during Webern's lifetime, and it proves nothing more than the fact that the composer could write thoroughly conventional, triadic, Austrian "nature music" (chirping birdies in the woodwinds, a dawn-to-dusk programmatic subtext) when he wanted to. Yet, in the past dozen years, I have probably heard *Im Sommerwind* more often in New York concert halls than any other work by Webern (trotted out as if to show that this guy could really *compose* when he wanted to, in the same manner that the seriousness of abstract Picasso used to be "proven" by examples of his early, representational draftsmanship). Clearly, Webern's mature language remains daunting to many audiences—and, more important, to the timid presenters and marketers who increasingly set our artistic agenda.

I hope this will change as dogmatic post-Webernism recedes into memory and as we grow more familiar with the music itself—the symphony, with its lambent sonic auroras and balletic grace; the vocal melodies in the cantatas, with their demands for singers who can leap about the staff with the surety of a mountain goat; the pinpoint clarity of the orchestration, without a wasted gesture. Webern bears no responsibility for the excesses of his cult: he did not say (as did Schoenberg) that he had "ensured the primacy of German music for a hundred years," nor did this modest, retiring man make any claims for having discovered a new world for anybody but himself.

The Moldenhauers' biography is more impressive as a dogged marshaling of facts than as the living portrait of a man, but I've always liked what it has to say about the composer's love for mountaineering: "Webern was not a fanatic about attaining the highest point. His passion was not for conquest; he wished only to immerse himself in the wonders of nature and the stillness of the heights." We should approach Webern's music in the same spirit, with gratitude and affection.

The New Criterion
April 1995

REVIEWS

Paul McCartney's *Liverpool Oratorio*

THERE'S nothing particularly mysterious about writing a piece of "classical music," especially when one commands the power and influence of a Paul McCartney. First, engage a competent arranger to take whatever feeble melodies you have on hand—ditties that would scarcely fill a nursery rhyme—and blow them up to grotesque proportions. (Almost any chord progression sounds impressive when played and sung by a full orchestra and chorus.)

Then, have your composer—pardon, *collaborator*—flesh out the structure with preludes, interludes, and continuity using stock gestures borrowed from other musicians. (Vaughan Williams is quite fashionable just now, and for that special showstopper finale, Mahler did very well with unfettered E-flat chorales for organ, orchestra, soloists, and chorus at full throttle.) Throw in some ersatz Spanish music for spice, a few echoes of Italian opera, and some Latin for *gravitas*. And presto! Faster than you can say "Turn me on, dead man," you have *Liverpool Oratorio*.

A sprawling, mawkish, and excruciatingly embarrassing 90-minute exercise of the ego, *Liverpool Oratorio* (or, as it was billed in the program, *Paul McCartney's Liverpool Oratorio by Paul McCartney and Carl Davis*) received its North American premiere at Carnegie Hall on Monday night. Although the performance—by the Royal Liverpool Philharmonic Orchestra, the Collegiate Chorale, the Boys Choir of Harlem, and soloists Barbara Bonney, Sally Burgess, Jerry Hadley, Willard White, and Jeremy Budd, under Davis's direction—was not technically perfect, enough of the work's spirit came through to confirm one in the sober judgment that Paul McCartney already ranks with Rebekah Harkness, Gordon Getty, and Richard Nanes as one of classical music's wealthiest composers.

It was, however, possible to take some perverse amusement in *Liverpool Oratorio*, for which McCartney has provided his own libretto. The story would seem to be based on the childhood of the 49-year-old, Liverpool-born and -bred McCartney. The introduction to the first movement describes a world at war in 1942, sirens sounding and bombs falling over Liverpool, where couples seek shelter underground. "Amid the blaze and the chaos of an air raid, a child is born. And there is hope." (We are not told whether a star rose in the East.)

One suspects that "Save the Child," the first single from *Liverpool Oratorio*, may be McCartney's oblique apology for missing the "We are the World" sessions. There is a violin solo that can't decide whether it wants to be third-rate Wieniawski or "The Last Rose of Summer." There is a trombone-driven, oom-pah drinking song that Noel Coward might have upchucked after imbibing too much Lehár. By way of feminist consciousness, there is "If you were the same man I married,/You'd know that your woman needs love." Meanwhile the orchestra swoons into sugar shock.

Enough. Suffice it to say that the soloists fulfilled their duties with distinction (particularly the radiant Barbara Bonney and the animated Willard White), that the orchestra sounded ragged at times, that the choruses were vibrant and enthusiastic throughout, and that conductor Davis seems to know the piece (as well he should!). McCartney has written some wonderful melodies over the course of his career (not many of them, it must be admitted, within the past two decades), but nothing of the sort was to be found Monday night. I suspect that, for many, the principal appeal of the evening was the opportunity to gape at a Beatle (and yes, Paul's still "the cute one").

Do I protest too much? Perhaps. After all, the music business is a *business*, and this may prove a bonanza. But with so many better composers at work on music that will remain unheard—without any chance of a recording on EMI or a sold-out show at Carnegie Hall—it is still possible to work up one last froth of righteous indignation for *Liverpool Oratorio*.

Newsday
20 November 1991

Chou Wen-Chung

A T HIS BEST, composer Chou Wen-Chung manages to mix Western modernism with Eastern ambience in a manner that is personal, organic, and altogether beguiling. On Thursday night, three leading contemporary music groups—the New Music Consort, Speculum Musicae, and Boston Musica Viva—presented a 70th birthday tribute to Chou at the Merkin Concert Hall that made a plausible case for him as the musical equivalent of a visionary.

Chou, born in China, studied in the United States with, among others, Edgard Varèse, Bohuslav Martinů, and Otto Luening, and even in the bleakest years of the so-called international style—a period during which composers from Ashtabula to Zanzibar sometimes all seemed to be writing the same grim, dense, dissonant, and meticulously organized piece—Chou had a voice of his own. He never disavowed his heritage, never attempted to extinguish his personality: Even in Chou's most astringent works, there is a curious and appealing mildness behind the mixture of honking, crashing, and squeaking that was the musical idiom of the time.

Yun, for example, a work from 1969, combines brief, shimmering musical modules with unfailing aural sensitivity. The flute pulses and flutters, the trumpet fights against its mute, the pianist alternates between playing the keys and plucking the strings. One loses oneself in a sound world that is both strong and delicate until called to attention by the sudden, violent ejaculation from the percussion that brings *Yun* to an end.

Chou is particularly adept at endings. *Windswept Peaks* (1990), for violin, cello, clarinet, and piano—which sounds a bit like what Anton Webern might have written had he immersed himself in the landscapes of China rather than those of Austria—concludes with the prolonged wail of a clarinet, catching the listener by surprise but then settling in to seem appropriate and even inevitable.

Yu Ko (1965) was probably the most appealing work of the evening, full of potent and engaging crossfertilizations between instruments and idioms. It is always an artistic risk to instruct a pianist to play inside the instrument (all too quickly it becomes a clever gimmick, the equivalent of a magic trick, to which the logical response is "So what?"), and Chou took the risk in three of the pieces played Thursday. Still, in every case, it *worked* for him; he *integrated* the technique rather than sprinkling it on like seasoning. The program closed with a Suite for Harp and Wind Quintet (1951) that might best be classified as juvenilia—too many harp swoops, too pretty-pretty, too self-consciously "exotic"—and a quartet for percussion called *Echoes from the Gorge* (1989). It would be unfair to single out any of the evening's players: suffice it to say some of the finest musicians in the business joined forces to give Chou the tribute he deserves.

The concert, by the way, took place in what was originally called the Hebrew Arts Center but is now the Merkin Concert Hall at the Abraham Goodman House, which shares space with the Lucy Moses School for Music and Dance in the Elaine Kaufman Cultural Center but is in no way to be confused with the Kaufmann Concert Hall at the 92nd Street Y, which is now known as the Kaufmann Concert Hall at the Tisch Center for the Arts of the 92nd Street Y. Got that?

Newsday
5 April 1993

Luciano Pavarotti in Central Park

NEW YORK CITY demands a lot from those of us who live or work here, but every now and then, it gives something back.

Saturday night at eight, after the heat wave had broken and before the rainstorm had moved in, a crowd estimated by police at more than 500,000 came to hear Luciano Pavarotti sing a free concert in Central Park.

It was a wonderful evening in a lot of ways, many—perhaps *most*—of them extramusical. The mood was festive and vibrant, charged with an energy quite removed from everyday Manhattan hyperspeed. Central Park held no terrors (in my experience, people were unfailingly courteous to one another); the NYPD Mobile Arrest Processing Center, a gigantic trailer parked near West 81st Street, had a slow night; the grand old apartment castles of Central Park West stood silent sentinel as the sky turned smoky pink and then darkened. It was possible, for a moment, to imagine oneself in the lost, fabled New York of F. Scott Fitzgerald or Dawn Powell—the center of the universe, a benign, sophisticated Metropolis that knows all, tells nothing, and will see you safely home before sunrise.

There *were* some signs that this was 1993. As far away as Columbus Avenue, big guys with gold chains hawked Pavarotti T-shirts (the prices diminished as one approached the concert area). An enormous amount of youthful flesh was on display, much of it spectacularly toned. ("Hey, we've still got 10 minutes before the concert starts; let's run twice around the park and do 500 pushups!") This being an election year, one had to play "Dodge the Politician" at the Central Park gates—Liz Holtzman with her waxen smile, Mark Green coming on like Robert Redford in *The Candidate*, Alan Hevesi promising "A Strong New Voice for New York City," a lot of flyers accepted and then direct-deposited into the recycling cans. Mayor David Dinkins spoke from the stage, to a lusty mix of cheers and hisses.

And then, a few minutes past eight, after a sloppy and sluggish rendition of Verdi's overture to *Luisa Miller* (which, fortunately, marked the nadir of the evening's orchestral playing, although not by much) Luciano Pavarotti—the man himself, dressed in the requisite tux and carrying his trademark handkerchief—walked out from the wings.

Pandemonium, of course. But a *dignified* pandemonium, rather like an old-time rock concert, back in the love-in days before you were frisked at the door and your view was blocked two minutes into the show by chowderheads standing on their chairs, showing off their prowess with a Zippo.

Where did all these Pavarotti fans come from? After all, we are increasingly a nation of musical illiterates. Many schools have phased out musical training entirely and we no longer have a Leonard Bernstein to pass on his wisdom through television—nor, for that matter, a network that would carry such "elitist" programming. Ticket sales are down throughout the country and many important orchestras and opera companies are in serious trouble. The state of the musical press has never been so bad; within the past five years, *High Fidelity*, *Musical America*, *Opus*, *Keynote*, and *Ovation* have all ceased publication, and much of what *does* see print is bizarre and involuted to the point of solipsism.

Moreover, although there can be no doubt that Pavarotti is a great tenor—reports of his decline are grossly exaggerated—he is not the only one. But would Plácido Domingo or José Carreras have summoned half a million people to Central Park? No. What about Alfredo Kraus? Or, before his retirement, Jon Vickers? No way. Let's go back even further. Franco Corelli? Jussi Björling? Beniamino Gigli? No; indeed, one wonders how many in Saturday's audience would have even recognized these names. Enrico Caruso? Well, maybe—but he's been dead for nearly 72 years.

In no way am I suggesting that Pavarotti is necessarily a "better" tenor than any of the gentlemen listed above. Every artist is unique; all these men had their strengths—and, for that matter, their weaknesses.

Pavarotti, at his best, combines the honeyed sweetness of a lyric tenor with a heft and amplitude all but unprecedented in that range. Yet he can be a lazy interpreter (last year, he actually "lip-synched" a concert—he pretended to sing while a recording was played), and his attempts to move into heavy roles such as Otello and Don Carlo have met with an indifferent press and, on at least one occasion, outright heckling.

So what *is* it about Pavarotti? A cynic might suggest that it is all public relations, and it is true that Herbert Breslin, the tenor's manager, press representative, and all-around guru, has done his best to make him ubiquitous. We've had movies about Pavarotti in China ("Into the land of one billion came one!," the posters panted), televised specials from Las Vegas, spaghetti recipes in glossy magazines, concerts at Madison Square Garden, and so on, ad nauseam. Pavarotti is *out there* before the public, to a degree unmatched by any of his colleagues, and in an era of celebrity journalism, he has been willing to play the game.

Yet the old line about leading a horse to water still applies. Pavarotti appeals to a wide spectrum of people, many of whom have no particular interest in opera, and while the Breslin machine certainly enhanced that appeal, it did not—it *could* not—whip it up from nothing. And, to belabor the obvious, beyond the huggy-bear, "I'm just a happy, regular, overweight Italian guy who loves to sing" persona is a great and serious artist, and if Saturday's concert represented Pavarotti neither at his greatest nor at his most serious, the audience still got a taste of something fine.

The program included arias from two Verdi operas, *Luisa Miller* ("Quando le sere") and *I Vespri Siciliani* ("Lamento di Federico"), a smattering of Neapolitan songs leading up to arias from Puccini's *Tosca*, and as the final encore, the inevitable "Nessun dorma" from *Turandot*. Pavarotti was generally in good voice—a little tight in the strenuous passages, to be sure, and poorly amplified (for technical reasons, I suspect listeners at home probably *heard* a better concert than did the huddled masses in the park), but he sang with the mixture of tonal luster, spontaneous lyricism, and dramatic urgency that has been his domain for a quarter century.

Halfway through the program, the press corps learned that the United States had, once again, bombed Iraq. Last week the FBI said it broke up a ring of conspirators who were planning to blow up tunnels, bridges, senators, and the United Nations, all within a few miles of where we sat. Every morning somebody has smashed in car windows up and down my quiet Upper West Side street. If, for some of us, this city remains the center of the universe, it is now a fierce and frightening universe.

And yet, just when one is tempted to give it all up and investigate the Newfoundland job market, Manhattan plays a hidden card, tries out a new technique of seduction, presents us with one of those "only-in-New-York" experiences that restore, however temporarily, our faith and wonder, our pride in our home. For two hours on Saturday night, there were few places in the world I would rather have been than up in Central Park—and I'll bet there are a couple of hundred thousand people who agree with me.

Newsday
28 June 1993

Georg Solti

My responses to Sir Georg Solti's later performances were mixed. There could be no denying their technical magnificence, but with rare exceptions it was not a magnificence that touched my heart. I have included this little dissent in part as a counterpoint to prevailing public opinion, well knowing that many readers will disagree with my assessment. Still, any critic who is fearful of committing an occasional heresy is in the wrong trade. This review appeared in 1994, some three years before the maestro's death on September 5, 1997, at the age of 84.

S AY THIS for Sir Georg Solti—like him or not, he has his own distinctive sound, which he carries with him wherever he goes. On Monday night at Carnegie Hall, an ad hoc orchestra made up of brilliant young musicians and first-chair players from leading ensembles throughout the land played its first concert. And—surprise!—it sounded very much as the Chicago Symphony Orchestra did during Solti's 22-year tenure at its helm, which, for better or for worse, is more than can be said of the Chicago Symphony these days.

How many other conductors have had such an unmistakable way with an orchestra? Toscanini, Stokowski, maybe Herbert von Karajan, come to mind. (Undeniably great musicians such as Leonard Bernstein and Christoph von Dohnányi never cultivated specific personal *sounds* in the manner of an older generation; they let the music dictate its own terms.) Solti might be described as the Horowitz of conductors; he translates everything he plays into his own language. You know what to expect and if you like it, you probably love it.

And so Wagner's *Die Meistersinger* Overture began with a good solid *mezzo forte* that was already louder than most orchestras at full tilt. It only got louder from there. The strings surged, the brass blared, the strings surged some more, and the brass blared harder. Throughout the evening, one felt rather as if one had fallen into some kind of Olympian musical game of "Can You Top

This?" The results were dazzling, virtuosic, occasionally very exciting indeed, but, to my taste, not very musical.

I suppose it's all in what one wants from a concert. There is a certain Nietzschean ferocity to Solti's interpretations but I find him lacking both tenderness and repose; he understands orgasm but not affection. He sets his goal and he gets there; he does not interpret the music so much as he conquers it. He roared through Beethoven's Symphony No. 5 like a chain saw through a redwood (and, to carry the metaphor a little further, in this case the chips flew everywhere—the performance was too fast and too loud for such a recently formed group to play and much of it was surprisingly sloppy).

Shostakovich's Symphony No. 9 is a slight work, among the composer's most modest and engaging essays in the genre and a vast change from the two wartime symphonies that precede it. Solti's performance was admirable from a technical point of view but he stressed the epical to the point where the symphony was rendered elephantine and charmless.

Still, Solti did his thing, there is no other such thing before the public today, and those who respond enthusiastically to his work are urged to find their way to Carnegie Hall (there is another concert, with different repertory, next Tuesday) before this latest incarnation of his singular musical vision disbands.

Newsday
15 June 1994

The Deep Listening Band

Reactions to the Deep Listening Band, which began a four-night stint at the Kitchen on Wednesday, are bound to be subjective. Some listeners will no doubt find this 90-minute exploration of moans, drones, plinks, swoops, and the inner life of chords frustratingly spare. I thought it one of the loveliest and most restorative concerts I've heard in a long time.

The word "minimalism" has been bandied about in such a promiscuous manner that it doesn't really mean much of anything anymore. (How can something like Philip Glass's *The Voyage*—three substantial acts scored for large orchestra, chorus, and as many solo singers as you might find in Rossini or Verdi, and produced in high style by the Metropolitan Opera—possibly be considered "minimalist"?) Nevertheless, I'm going to use the M word to describe the Deep Listening Band. This is, if you like, "roots" minimalism—a skillful, deliberate reduction to musical essentials that slowly metamorphoses and blossoms in the consciousness of a receptive listener.

Three pieces were performed—two of them, *Pots and Pans* and *The Saucer's Apprentice*, credited to the Deep Listening Band and a central work, *Deep Hockets*, to performer-composer David Gamper. Although I thought I could tell when one piece shifted almost imperceptibly into the next, the evening is best described as a slow, mostly consonant, carefully calibrated journey from silence into sound and then back to silence.

So what "happens" during that journey? Well, depending on one's perspective, not much and a great deal. Pauline Oliveros plays French horn, conch shell, and accordion, and sings; Stuart Dempster sings and plays both trombone and an Australian instrument called the didgeridoo; Gamper plunks occasional riffs on the piano, hammers its strings with delicate precision, plays some other instruments, and sings. All this is augmented by electronics to create a shimmering aural texture, a musical spread.

Throughout, one is acutely aware of the presence and power of silence; every new sound enters as a very specific negation of silence that is also, somehow united with silence in a curious harmony. This may strike readers as mystical mumbo jumbo—isn't *all* music the alternation of sounds and silence? Well, yes. But one is rarely made so conscious of the quiet backdrop on which that music is made, rarely drawn so deeply into the unfolding process of musical narrative.

Those who demand densely packed, empirical "events" from their contemporary music will likely flee the Kitchen within five minutes, panting for some Elliott Carter. The Deep Listening Band's music *is* simple, but it is not simpleminded. Nor is it easy; if you are going to work with only a few sounds for an hour and a half, you'd better choose those sounds carefully. Ultimately, Anna Russell's tart, useful comment applies—this is the sort of thing one likes if one likes this sort of thing. I do.

Newsday
13 January 1995

Andrew Lloyd Webber

A N AWFUL LOT of people out there like Andrew Lloyd Webber. Radio City Music Hall—some 5,800 seats—was all but sold out for a pricey, semi-staged revue of Lloyd Webber's music Friday night and the audience was extraordinarily diverse: senior citizens, harried families with children in tow, spiffy young professionals who walked from work, even a token punker or two. Now that Frank Sinatra has retired, I can think of nobody else who could have attracted such an array of people.

For a critic who, in all good faith, finds practically every note Lloyd Webber has written (including the silences between those notes) four-square, pompous, hackneyed, derivative, and altogether worthless, such popularity is baffling. We excuse the meretricious monotony of, say, Madonna's work with a few plausible reasons for her success—she is "sexy," or "daring," or "a good dancer," and so on. But Lloyd Webber's person would seem to be singularly uncharismatic and he wasn't even in house Friday night (can you imagine a program of Madonna's songs without Madonna's presence?). No, for whatever reason, it is Lloyd Webber's actual music that appeals.

The program was a pretty fair sampling of Lloyd Webber's output over the last quarter-century, with his ex-wife, Sarah Brightman, a genial, somewhat wobbly, and (on this occasion) grotesquely overamplified soprano, as the central attraction. There were selections from *Jesus Christ Superstar, Cats, Evita, Phantom of the Opera, Sunset Boulevard, Aspects of Love*, and an interminable set of variations on a theme by Paganini for cello and rock band that I'm not going to call the worst piece ever written simply because that would be its first and only distinction.

Many of the "hits" were presented—"Memory" (sung in Italian), "Jesus Christ Superstar," "Wishing You Were Somehow Here Again," and others—and there were a few rarities as well, such as a song that suggested that the "female of the species is deadlier than the male" (now *there's* a fresh new idea!). Lloyd Webber's basic trick is to borrow from everybody—Giacomo Puccini, Paul McCartney, Richard Rodgers at his most treacly, the deliberately "arty" European rockers from the early '70s (Jethro Tull, Yes, Focus)—throw it into a blender, then pour the resultant mush into a form.

In *Phantom of the Opera*, that form was gothic horror; in *Evita* it was Carmen Miranda Latin; in *Sunset Boulevard* it was "Come to Sunny California" travelogue (the overture would sound just great during commercial breaks for the Oscars). In a concert setting, all dramatic context is lost, and so, as if to compensate, we were given a new element—"Viva Las Vegas!" (singer Francis Ruivivar looked and sounded rather like a Hispanic Wayne Newton, the carefully coiffed "rock" musicians clapped their hands with evangelical fervor, and a trio of go-go chickies bumped and ground).

Enough. If somebody were to remake *This Is Spinal Tap*, with worse songs, while surgically removing any trace of irony (or, for that matter, any sense of humor at all), it might come off rather like Friday night. When Brightman sang a number from *Sunset Boulevard* entitled "Surrender," it was all one could do to keep from shouting "I will, I will—if only you'll stop *now!*"

Newsday
12 June 1995

Labor Day with the National Symphony Orchestra

Unlike most American newspapers, The Washington Post still prefers to run overnight reviews in the following morning's paper. Because this was my first assignment—and because I had not written for deadline regularly at Newsday or The New York Times—I was more than a little nervous as I walked up Capitol Hill, and I took copious notes through the performance in case I needed them for filler. Still, within an hour of returning to the Post, I had written 2,000 words, many more than I had intended or even thought I could produce. My editor that evening, recognizing mania when he saw it, abridged the story prudently.

SINCE ALL the players in the National Symphony Orchestra are fully paid-up members of the Musicians' Union, it seems only fitting that the group should play its Labor Day concert on Sunday night and then, like most of the rest of us, take today off.

At twilight yesterday, one approached the West Lawn of the Capitol with a certain awe. It was a soft, fragrant evening, and the surrounding trees were filled with mysterious chirping. Frisbees flew, puppies frolicked, children turned cartwheels; one felt far removed from both the tensions of the city and the issues yet to be debated in the Capitol.

A crowd estimated at 25,000—almost 10 times the capacity of the Kennedy Center—turned out to celebrate. After the national anthem (particularly stirring when the listener, hand on heart, is standing between the Capitol and the Washington Monument), Aaron Copland's *Fanfare for the Common Man* opened this program of American music, featuring the two NSO associate conductors, Barry Jekowsky and Elizabeth Schulze.

In the spirit of democracy, Jekowsky led the first half of the program and Schulze took over after intermission. They are both stylish and fluent conductors, at home with the orchestra, if not necessarily with speaking in front of an audience the size of a small city. (Jekowsky, building up to an oratorical climax, announced that "if any composer deserves to have the letters 'U-S-A' in his name, certainly John Philip Sousa *doesn't*!" This was a novel and revisionist thought, and I looked forward to an explication, but Jekowsky immediately corrected himself.)

The Copland *Fanfare* represents the composer at his most austere and proclamatory—timpani, lowing brass, and cosmic drama. An arrangement of the folk song "John Henry" was clangorous but effective. William Grant Still's *Festive Overture* proved a lively and consummately professional work that deserves to be better known.

Frederick Converse's *Flivver Ten Million* is a tribute to the ten-millionth Ford to come off the assembly line. Converse punctuated this tone poem with car horns, sirens, and other extra-orchestral sounds. On paper, it sounds like a prefiguration of the joyful anarchy of Spike Jones or at least the "Powerhouse" of Raymond Scott, that mainstay of cartoon scores. Alas, this is a piece that is much more fun to read about than it is to actually listen to. I did enjoy the conclusion, which sounds rather like a miniature *Rite of Spring* in weird counterpoint with "Hail, Hail, the Gang's All Here."

Within certain circles, any criticism of Charles Ives is considered heresy, rather akin to announcing opposition to Walt Whitman, Norman Rockwell, apple pie, and motherhood. Still, Ives continues to impress me as the Tom Swift of American music—an ingenious tinkerer who only occasionally hit upon a good idea (*The Unanswered Question* and *General William Booth Enters into Heaven* are very good ideas indeed.) The two pieces on last night's program are among Ives's lesser mousetraps—a murky mess called *The Yale-Princeton Football Game* and the Variations on "America," "wrong note" juvenilia for solo organ that was substantially improved by William Schuman's orchestration.

The evening's big composer was Sousa, who was represented by no fewer than six compositions. Nobody would make claims for Sousa as a musical visionary, but he is at least specific. One may enjoy his music or one may not, but, to lapse into archaism for a moment, one always knows where Sousa "is coming from." It is possible to enumerate the qualities of a Sousa march in advance—vigor, conciseness, and some good tunes that will follow you around for days. Indeed, so strong is Sousa's rhythmic profile that one can go to the piano and bang out the contours of *The Washington Post* or *The Stars and Stripes Forever* with one's fists and most listeners will still be able to identify the pieces. (Music critics are a lot of fun at parties.)

While I respect Joan Tower enormously, her *Fanfare for the Uncommon Woman* seems fashioned from Copland's rib. It was probably not a good idea to deliberately set up comparison with an American classic; in any event, Copland certainly meant to honor women as well as men in his own *Fanfare*. Still, there are some stirring moments here, particularly when Tower departs from Coplandia and strikes out with her own riffs, vamps, and trills.

As for the National Symphony itself, this was the first time I've heard the orchestra in some years. Many of us hope (and even dare to expect) that it will soon be transformed into one of America's leading ensembles. It would be unfair to venture anything definitive about the current state of the orchestra on the evidence of one concert, particularly a program such as this.

Outdoor concerts are often wonderful, but much of that wonder is necessarily extramusical, as melodies and balances float off on the breezes. Instead, one appreciated the majesty of the setting, the opportunity to enjoy the cusp between late summer and early fall, to watch the thousands of Washingtonians listening to music with loaves of bread, jugs of wine, and favorite thous. Last night, this was sufficient.

The Washington Post
4 September 1995

The Philadelphia Orchestra Plays Bruckner

T HE PHILADELPHIA Orchestra is widely and correctly perceived as the aristocrat among American orchestras. The Cleveland Orchestra may be more "perfect" (one balanced, synchronized, infinitely adaptable organism from top to bottom) and Chicago may have more muscle (ferocious virtuosity and a brass section that could have done the job at Jericho). But Philadelphia—caloric, sumptuously blended, and refreshingly Old World

—takes the prize for elegance and sheer sonic luster. In a world of lean cuisine, the Philadelphia Orchestra is still pure butterfat.

This group is at its best in leisurely music—not because it cannot play fast and flashy but because so few of its competitors can play slow music convincingly. And a work like the Bruckner Symphony No. 8, of which the Philadelphia Orchestra offered a magnificent performance last night at the Kennedy Center under the direction of Wolfgang Sawallisch, demands not just slow but *slow*.

In fact, the symphony really demands that the listener suspend time. This is a long work—-just about 90 minutes—and it is quite the opposite of suspenseful. To wait for sudden, startling *events* is to miss the point of Bruckner. Rather, one immerses oneself in his symphonies as in an absorbing landscape, in which change happens inevitably over an expanse of time.

The Philadelphia Orchestra's unusually good program notes referred to the "luxuriant leisure" by which Bruckner's symphonies reach their formal climaxes and goals. "With Bruckner firm in his religious faith," Deryck Cooke wrote, "the music has no need to go anywhere, no need to find a point of arrival, because it is already there."

It is not music that appeals to the tastes of all listeners. For some, Bruckner makes for a long evening in the concert hall; his symphonies seem informed by a sort of elephantine mysticism—earnest, humble, undoubtedly deeply felt, but somewhat ungainly. For others—particularly in the Symphony No. 8 and the unfinished Symphony No. 9—he offers nothing less than spiritual transport. Rarely does one see so many people in the audience who obviously know every single note of such a mammoth work (some of them conducting along at their seats, smiling beatifically at especially lovely moments). And rarely does one see such an immediate, full-hearted standing ovation as Sawallisch and his players received at the end of the score.

Sawallisch was tender with the music but never sentimental. He kept things moving, even in those passages (rather less common in the Symphony No. 8 than in earlier works) when Bruckner can seem to be running in place. The Scherzo was terrific—joyful, unfettered, cosmic, as if the Alps themselves had come to life and started to dance—while the great Adagio had that sort of heavy, am-I-losing-my-mind? languor that we associate with the ever slower, ever more grandly exhausted, late recordings of Herbert von Karajan and Leonard Bernstein.

With the exception of some occasional weird tuning from the lower brass, the orchestra playing was little short of spectacular (is there a better string section in the world?). Sawallisch, conducting without score, proved that he knows every subtlety, every silence in this long and complicated work. From the beginning, the symphony seemed one unbroken trajectory. And yet there was plenty of room to meander, to ruminate—essential in any performance of this composer. Despite Cooke's assertion, many of us find Bruckner's questions as interesting as his answers.

In short, it was a splendid night to have been at the Kennedy Center. This is ideal repertoire for Sawallisch; he gave us a performance informed by Austro-Germanic tradition, a respect for musical architecture, a delight in the capacities of his orchestra, and an abiding and glowing love for Anton Bruckner.

The Washington Post
6 February 1996

A Vietnam Oratorio

ELLIOT GOLDENTHAL'S *Fire Water Paper: A Vietnam Oratorio* is everything one might expect from a massive and ambitious piece by a young composer who does most of his work in Hollywood studios. It is slick, it is sometimes overblown, it is deeply derivative, it takes on a bigger subject than it can possibly address.

It is also, despite all, a pretty effective work on its own terms—particularly in so spectacular a performance as the one Seiji Ozawa conducted Saturday afternoon at the Kennedy Center Concert Hall, when the Boston Symphony Orchestra gave *Fire Water Paper* its Washington premiere.

The piece had its genesis when the gifted young California-based conductor Carl St. Clair read an article by Art Buchwald suggesting that the Vietnam Veterans Memorial was "crying out for music." Shortly thereafter, St. Clair commissioned Goldenthal to write an oratorio for the Pacific Symphony Orchestra in Orange County, California, which is now home to the largest

Vietnamese population outside Vietnam. (It is St. Clair who leads the recording of *Fire Water Paper* on Sony Classical.)

Goldenthal responded with an hour-long piece for large orchestra and chorus, children's choir, solo soprano, and baritone. He built his text from a variety of sources: ancient Vietnamese poetry, Virgil, Tacitus, Cicero, Horace, a suicide letter from one of the several monks who immolated themselves to protest the war, nursery rhymes, code names for American military operations—all over the bedrock of the Requiem Mass of the Roman Catholic Church, sung in Latin. The world premiere took place on April 26, 1995, on the 20th anniversary of the official conclusion of the Vietnam War.

 Fire Water Paper is expertly made; as one music professional in attendance Saturday afternoon put it, Goldenthal "knows his stuff." The vocal writing is assured and responsive to the words (in Latin, French, Vietnamese, and English). The music falls easily on the ear and makes a stirring first impression; nothing is much more visceral and exciting than a great orchestra and chorus in full thrall and Goldenthal gives both of them a lot to do.

The score's derivations are obvious: Benjamin Britten's *War Requiem* for the overall form; Bartók or Kodály for the cello cadenzas; Stravinsky, Orff, Mahler, and *Satyagraha*-era Philip Glass in passing. But genuine innovators are few and far between; better, perhaps, in a piece of this sort, for a composer to take time-tested gestures and, through feeling and technical expertise, make them his own, rather than sailing off into yet another narrow avant-garde rivulet.

Fire Water Paper flows. It is linear. It has a beginning, a middle, and an end. It never gets mired down in its allusions. It holds the listener's attention for an hour. These are not small accomplishments.

Still, there is a central problem: *Fire Water Paper* ultimately seems grossly insufficient to its purpose. Indeed, I'm not sure what that purpose was intended to be, other than to encourage some spurious "healing" process. I was never convinced that Goldenthal had any real ideas about the Vietnam War, save that it was tragic and that it is over. I was often reminded of one of those newsweekly articles on controversial subjects that strive so mightily to offend neither left nor right that they end up sweeping all their readers into a weird, quasi-lobotomized DMZ. I learned nothing new about Vietnam from Goldenthal's piece; much more to the point, I *felt* nothing new about Vietnam.

One couldn't have asked for a finer performance, however, and that helped carry the afternoon. This is the sort of thing Ozawa does best—the huge orchestra-chorus-soloists showpieces (other examples include the Mahler Symphony No. 8, Schoenberg's *Gurre Lieder*, and Richard Strauss's *Elektra*). Ozawa is usually a middling interpreter, but he is a wonderful sonic engineer: the choruses came in where they were supposed to, the balances were carefully calibrated, the climaxes were just so.

Jayne West has a high, pure, strong, and affecting soprano voice; I should call it "angelic" if it were not so filled with worldly emotion. James Maddalena sang his part with dignity and musicianship, although his voice is probably a size too small for this score. Jules Eskin did a masterly job with the strenuous and intricate cello cadenzas. The Tanglewood Festival Chorus and the New York Concert Singers' Project Youth Chorus made their own valuable contributions.

Two last thoughts on *Fire Water Paper*: the incorporation of the Latin Mass seemed rather too easy a solution to some vexing artistic problems. In no way am I questioning Goldenthal's religious convictions, nor am I suggesting there is no room for further settings of these great words. But in this particular case, I occasionally had the sense that the composer, in search of some extra *gravitas*, had simply grabbed out for something that all but defines high seriousness and then appropriated its solemnity for his own.

Finally, I'm not at all convinced that the Vietnam Veterans Memorial is "crying out for music," by Goldenthal or anybody else. On the contrary, it should be approached silently, humbly, in a grave and dignified confusion. It has its own music, made up of time, wind, and old sorrow.

The Washington Post
15 April 1996

John Cage's *Europera 5*

CHARLESTON, South Carolina

THE EXPATRIATE American author Gertrude Stein reportedly once sent some of her unusual prose to an editor, who returned it promptly with a rejection letter written in Stein-ese: "I do not understand your story. I do not understand. I have only one life. Only one. One life. Only one life."

A similarly spirited review of John Cage's *Europera 5*, which was presented Wednesday night by the Spoleto Festival USA, might read something like this: Fourscore and. Wednesday night Spoleto. This. When in the course of. Presented. Stately, plump. Europera. Whrrr. Across the sky. John Cage. Corn syrup, lecithin. Call 1-800. Buzzzzzzzz. One hour. Tweet.

Okay, in English now, here's what happened. A few minutes after eight, three people—pianist Judith Gordon, electronic music supervisor Charles Wood, and director John Kennedy—walked onto the stage of the Dock Street Theater. Over the course of the next hour, Gordon played an impressive transcription of Wagner's *Liebestod* and some of a Liszt transcription of themes from Verdi's *Rigoletto*, at times letting her hands dance across the keyboard, only occasionally alighting on a note.

Wood sat impassively next to some sort of electronic instrument, twiddling a dial or two. Every now and then Kennedy picked out an ancient opera recording (I think I recognized the voices of Giovanni Zenatello and Ezio Pinza, among others), wound up an old Victrola, and played the scratchy disc. A radio blared in the background; a television set clicked on and off.

Every few minutes, two professional singers, tenor Enrico di Giuseppe and mezzo-soprano Korby Myrick—both of them excellent, by the way—would wander onstage and, unaccompanied, sing a familiar aria ("Amor ti vieta" from Giordano's *Fedora*, the "Habanera" from *Carmen*, selections by Mozart and Strauss). Now and then, somebody in an animal mask would come out and prepare to begin an aria but never quite commence. After about an hour, the television was turned off, the pianism ceased, the singers sang no more, and the event was over.

What did it all mean? Nothing at all, of course. Was that the point? No. There was no point; never underestimate the simple-mindedness of Cage's later aesthetic. To say that *Europera 5* is thoroughly uninteresting is to give it a power it does not possess; it's not even *interestingly* uninteresting. For this spectator, the only remotely stimulating question of the evening was whether the authors of "Rescue Me" and the old Troggs hit "Love Is All Around"—both played in their entirety on the radio during the show—might have the right to sue the Cage estate for their complete incorporation into a work that was supposedly "by" John Cage.

Cage (1912–1992) was one of several 20th-century composers who realized that noise could be music—that we were not limited to voice and traditional instruments alone to create an aural statement. So far, so good; unfortunately, he took this valid and radical observation one step further and decided that *all* noise was music, a different proposition altogether. Any sound was just as good as another. Cage's late works were so "indeterminate" as to be virtually random.

Not to belabor the obvious, but no valuable work of art is ever random, unless the random artist gets very lucky (like the proverbial monkeys at their typewriters that will, statisticians insist, eventually type *War and Peace*). Composition is the art of choosing and arranging pitches, rhythms, and sounds into a musical unity. If a composer evades this responsibility, it must be made up for by other people: usually by performers and sometimes by credulous listeners.

Virtually any qualities this production of *Europera 5* may have had must be credited to people other than John Cage—to the composers of whatever borrowed music that was sung, played, or broadcast; to Kennedy, for several cute directorial touches (including the animal masks); to the vocalists and pianist, who chose the pieces they would sing and play. Aside from that, it was time wasted—probably more time than Cage took to "compose" the piece.

In retrospect, it is apparent that something terrible happened to Cage about 1952; he began to believe he was a Thinker. And so we had the spectacle of somebody who had been one of our most vigorous and playful composers—the creator of marvelous early pieces for prepared piano, a haunting string quartet, and the ballet *The Seasons*—relinquishing his craft to follow and echo dubious philosophers, ranging from Thoreau to Mao. Like Andy Warhol after his near-murder by Valerie Solanas, Cage turned into a media personality—Mr. Avant-Garde, a benign, grinning visage, always good for the elliptical quote, a sphinx without a secret.

It has become a truism to suggest that Cage's ideas were more important than his music. The famous *4'33"*, judged as music and music alone, is a long silence and nothing more. But it was a phenomenal declaration of independence.

Cage was doing a lot of things with that piece: suggesting that a work of music can be anything at all, even nothing; making an oblique comment on the highly ordered music that was then fashionable in Europe; giving silence its due place in the musical hierarchy (there have certainly been pieces of music without rests, so why not a piece of rests without music?). And all the while, he was exercising his own puckish humor. But the actual musical demands of *4'33"* were, to put it mildly, nothing very special.

If Cage ever wrote another important piece after 1952, the year of *4'33"*, I have not heard it. His musical universe grew obsessively inclusive and he spoke often and eloquently, in his gentle manner, about the danger of making any qualitative evaluations whatsoever.

And yet Cage was a passionate mycologist—a connoisseur of mushrooms. When some basic contradictions in his "everything goes" philosophy were pointed out to him—when, for instance, he was reminded that one type of mushroom would feed him while another might kill him—he would sometimes grow quite testy. *Europera 5* will neither kill nor feed, but it's pretty much of a flat-liner so far as intrinsic interest goes.

Oh, well. Cage's early works will survive. So will Spoleto. Indeed, *Europera 5* probably made for some good chat at the post-performance party. And it *was* nice to hear "Love Is All Around" again.

The Washington Post
2 June 1996

The Klezmer Revival

THE FIRST transcendent moment of the Klezmer Conservatory Band's concert at the Kennedy Center came when vocalist Judy Bressler urged the thousand or so members of the audience to get up and dance in the aisles. "Dancing in the aisles isn't terribly ordinary at the Kennedy Center," she acknowledged, "but this ought to be a great place for it."

And so several hundred people—young and old, gay and straight, black and white, people who have known and loved klezmer music since childhood, and people for whom it is still a mysterious novelty—joined hands, stepping, weaving, and sometimes writhing ecstatically through the auditorium, carried by the wild whirl of melody. For a few minutes, self-conscious, workaholic Washington seemed far away. To paraphrase the poet Delmore Schwartz, the world was a wedding.

This concert represented multiculturalism in the best sense of the word: spontaneous, appreciative, without coercion, informed by a central tradition but—like one of those cartoon snowballs rolling downhill—picking up additional matter all along the way.

Indeed, a central reason for the renewed interest in klezmer music (particularly this sort of "neo-klezmer") is its inclusiveness. Over the course of the evening, I heard passages that reminded me of Dixieland jazz, nightclub blues, European torch song, flamenco music (a long and intricate passage for unadorned mandolin), Sicilian funeral bands, Chopin, '60s rock (a drum solo Cream's Ginger Baker might have been proud of), gypsy melodies, and much more. You can tune into klezmer from almost any perspective and find your own path into its heart.

And yet klezmer music retains its own identity through all of this variety—the distinct, modal interplay of Jewish dance tunes, folk songs, and liturgical melodies, in a manner that is simultaneously exuberant and deeply melancholy. There is an emphasis on hard-blown reed instruments, mainly saxophone and clarinet, that exude a near-vocal wail that is part smirk, part sob. (Gershwin's *Rhapsody in Blue,* so often called the first classical adaptation of jazz, owes at least as much to klezmer music, as any audition of the original Paul Whiteman recording will quickly reveal.)

Hankus Netsky, the chairman of jazz studies at the New England Conservatory of Music, is the director of the Klezmer Conservatory Band and plays saxophone, accordion, and piano. Yet this is very much a collective effort and each musician in the 11-member group was given an opportunity to demonstrate his or her virtuosity. Singling people out is decidedly unfair under such circumstances so here's the roster: Ilene Stahl on clarinet, Miriam Rabson on violin, Grant Smith on drums, James Guttman on bass, Javier Perez-Saco on piano, Mark Hamilton on trombone and Gary Bohan on cornet (a lively, New Orleansy duet), Robin Miller on flute and piccolo (almost fifelike in its brilliant brightness), and Jeff Warschauer on banjo, mandolin, and guitar.

Vocalist Bressler deserves her own paragraph. She has a warm, bounteous soprano voice and an unerring sense of pitch, which allows her to play all sorts of inventive games with the melodic line. The sheer sweetness of her sound suggests that she would do well with the operettas of Emmerich Kalman and Franz Lehár, but she brings an emotional intensity to the music that would be unusual in such fairytale scores.

The music ranged from originals by members of the group to anonymous, plaintive tunes from Eastern Europe, created by some sad small-town genius lost to history. Still—from festive songs to lullabies to a number titled "My Dear In-Laws"—this was pulsating, primal stuff, filled with joy and sorrow, an eager affirmation of life that was, like the best of such affirmations, infused with the awareness of death.

The Washington Post
9 June 1996

David Helfgott

As one who admired the movie Shine—*even after its supposed factuality
had been convincingly debunked by Richard Dyer in* The Boston Globe—
*I had some hopes for the American debut recital of David Helfgott, the film's
ostensible hero. Many readers were angry about this review. But at a time
when thousands of pianists were struggling to make any kind of career,
I was unhappy with the idea that Helfgott, with no credentials except a sad
story, should have become the year's great classical "hit." It was the beginning of a ghastly trend—Andrea Bocelli would be next.*

BOSTON

DAVID HELFGOTT'S North American debut recital—which took place
here at Symphony Hall on Tuesday night—proved a painful and disturbing experience.

Helfgott was the inspiration for the movie *Shine*, a surprise hit that has
already earned more than $27 million worldwide and is a candidate for seven
Academy Awards. *Shine* tells the story of a gifted young Australian pianist,
brutalized by his father and tormented by mental illness, who is eventually
redeemed and rehabilitated by the love of his second wife, a professional
astrologer named Gillian Murray Helfgott.

The weakest part of the film was that ending, which comes across as both
pat and Pollyannaish. And now it also seems misleading. For Helfgott, who
began a tour of 10 cities in the United States and Canada with the Boston
program, is still obviously unwell. Moreover, he is hardly the frustrated titan
of the keyboard portrayed in *Shine*; at this point, he is hardly a pianist at all.

None of this is to take away from the pathos and courage inherent in Helfgott's struggle; to go from a state of near-catatonia to playing a sold-out international tour is a moving human victory. Still, it is necessary to draw a line
between Helfgott the man and Helfgott the pianist. And throughout his program of Mendelssohn, Chopin, Liszt, and Beethoven plus encores, Helfgott's

pianism was foggy, arbitrary, anti-linear, and almost entirely lacking in technical finesse.

The whole day had a surreal quality. At 11 A.M., Gillian Helfgott, Scott Hicks (the director of *Shine*), and seven other people (mostly businessmen with a financial interest in the film, the tour, or one of two best-selling records now available of Helfgott's playing) met the press in a conference room at the Four Seasons Hotel. The pianist himself was notably absent; it was explained that he was upstairs, "doing push-ups, singing, and gazing out over Boston Common."

Responding to music critics who found Helfgott's recording of the Rachmaninoff Third Piano Concerto disappointing, a bristling Gillian Helfgott responded by reading an adoring letter her husband had received from a cancer patient who thought it inspirational.

The weirdest item in the press kit was a photocopied letter from one Peter Feuchtwanger (identified as the vice president of the European Piano Teachers Association of the United Kingdom) that compared Helfgott to (among others) Artur Schnabel, Alfred Cortot, Clara Haskil, and Sergei Rachmaninoff. In his letter, Feuchtwanger proclaimed, "David Helfgott in top form . . . can measure himself against the greatest pianists of any time." As it happens, Feuchtwanger himself is part of what has been dubbed "The Shine Tour" (he is credited as "specialist piano coach") and he ducked questions about whether Helfgott's recording represented him in "top form."

Art used to be defined as an imitation of life, but "The Shine Tour" is a case of life trying to devise a sequel to art. The thinking seems to have gone something like this: because *Shine* was such a terrific movie and because it told such an inspiring story, wouldn't it be grand if the real David Helfgott turned out to be a marvelous pianist, received some belated world acclaim, and (let's be frank) made fistfuls of money for his promoters and handlers?

In fact, it *would* have been grand. But, except for the money part, it simply didn't happen that way. A few minutes past eight, Helfgott bounded from the wings, an endearing grin on his face. Then he planted himself at center stage and gave some tautly elastic bows.

Within the first three measures of Mendelssohn's *Rondo Capriccioso*, Helfgott had hit his first clinkers. Far worse was to come in some incoherent performances of Chopin's Etude in E (Op. 10, No. 3), the great Ballade No. 4 in F Minor (interrupted on one occasion by some premature applause—from which, to his credit, the pianist quickly recovered), Liszt's *Un Sospiro* and Hungarian Rhapsody No. 2, and Beethoven's Sonata in C, Op. 53 ("Waldstein"). Throughout, Helfgott's dynamic range was severely limited (most *forte* passages sounded like blunt and desperate stabs); he repeated some sections and forgot others altogether; and he generally seemed to be operating on a purely measure-to-measure basis, without memory or anticipation.

It would be presumptuous to judge Helfgott's emotional state during the performance; for all I know he may have been enjoying himself enormously. But the whole evening seemed profoundly exploitative and Helfgott was excruciating to watch. He talked to himself incessantly (for much of the evening, one had the sense he was lecturing an invisible little man at the top of the keyboard), repeatedly gave great, haunted-house groans, and made superfluous, pseudo-romantic hand gestures.

We have reached the point where a disturbed man who can barely play the piano is suddenly the hottest person in classical music, duly hailed for bringing in a "new audience"; it's a little like Peter Sellers's film *Being There* come to life. *Shine* auteur Hicks has been criticized for some narrative distortions in the purely biographical sections of his film. This seems to me unfair; *Shine* was never intended as pure biography (one might as well complain that Thomas Mann's *Dr. Faustus* fails to trace the career of Arnold Schoenberg, whose thought pervades the book). No, *Shine* is a powerful mixture of fable and fantasia, complete with a reassuring ending. Unfortunately, life promises no such uncomplicated outcomes.

The Washington Post
6 March 1997

Alfred Brendel

LFRED BRENDEL played a fine, strange, thoughtful piano recital at DAR
Constitution Hall on Sunday afternoon.

Brendel is rightly regarded as a musician's musician—one of those
artists whom other artists may (and should) study with profit. And yet it is
probably safe to say that only Brendel himself could have pulled off the distinctly unusual program he brought to Washington this time around.

There were no warhorses, no pyrotechnical showpieces, no concessions to
popular taste. The first half of the program was entirely given to brief, dense,
contemplative compositions by Ferruccio Busoni and Franz Liszt, here
arranged into murky, fascinating little suites so that it would have been difficult for listeners unfamiliar with the music to tell when one piece ended and
another began. The second half was even more surprising—Schumann's great
Fantasy in C, Op. 17, one of the most searching utterances of the romantic
age, followed, improbably, by the playful Haydn Sonata in G, Hob. XVI/40.

The Busoni/Liszt portion of the program called to mind a long meditation. Brendel's tendency to go immediately from one piece to the next (there
were only two breaks in the first nine compositions) made for a sort of hyper-
intellectual answer to so-called New Age radio broadcasting. The emphasis
was on setting a sustained mood and Brendel pulled it off brilliantly. The
pieces themselves—two Busoni elegies, several late Liszt pieces (*Nuages Gris*
and *Aux Cyprès de la Villa d'Este I: Threnodie*), and some of this composer's
earlier works as well—have the eerie gray quality of daguerreotypes: they are
definitely antiquated, a little blurry, perhaps, but still recognizably of our
world, harbingers of modernism.

Schumann's Fantasy in C is among the most tender and radiantly beautiful of love songs (complete with quotations from Beethoven's *To the Distant
Beloved*), and so intimate that it should properly be played only person to
person. Listening to it in a large hall is rather like hearing one of your diaries
read aloud. And yet the Fantasy, for all its unmatched directness of expression, is terribly difficult to play through, with a staggeringly virtuosic second

movement that keeps it from the repertory of all but the world's most finished pianists.

And so, by necessity, we listen to the Fantasy mainly on record, and on those rare occasions when a worthy pianist dares add it to a program. Brendel had the usual struggle with the finale of the middle movement (which is all but unplayable anyway) but, for the most part, gave us a rapt, loving, and steady performance, straight from the heart. I do wish the hall had been able to provide more acoustical support to the simple, naked chordal proclamations in the finale, which sounded and died away too quickly to make their full effect.

When a musician so intelligent as Brendel places a charming but fundamentally light piece such as the Haydn Sonata in G immediately after the cosmic Fantasy, you know he must have had a reason for it. The ability to take risks is a test of a great artist; still, despite the grace and humor of his performance, I confess to finding the presence of the sonata superfluous and a little disruptive after what had come before. Perhaps Brendel wanted to allow us to emerge from the Fantasy's depths slowly, over time, to avoid the musical equivalent of the bends.

The Washington Post
22 April 1997

Hans Pfitzner's *Palestrina*

AFTER 80 YEARS, Hans Pfitzner's grave, stately, radiant, and beautiful opera *Palestrina* (1917) finally came to America last week, when the Lincoln Center Festival 97 presented three performances here at the Metropolitan Opera House.

Palestrina is apparently not for everybody; the Met had hundreds of empty seats during the short run, and the reviews in New York have been mostly negative or befuddled. But those of us who take to *Palestrina* take to it wholeheartedly. As one who has loved this music since Deutsche Grammophon released an excellent complete recording in 1973, I watched Saturday night's performance with the rapt gratitude of one for whom a dream had been realized.

If you insist upon lubricious tunes, elemental passions, or a fast-moving drama to accompany your evening out, *Palestrina* is certain to disappoint. This five-hour work (there were two intermissions) is closer in spirit to a Renaissance mystery play than to traditional opera; Pfitzner himself called it a "musical legend." Nothing much really "happens" in the score or the stage action, so far as such matters can be quantified. And yet a susceptible member of the audience will depart the theater with the recognition of having been immersed in and guided through an uncommonly deep and fulfilling meditation. (Comparisons have been drawn to Wagner's *Parsifal* and, more recently, to Philip Glass's similarly static *Satyagraha*—and they are apt.)

Palestrina is, in fact, the supreme ivory tower opera, complete with a subscript from Schopenhauer that is printed at the beginning of the published score: "Alongside world history there goes, guiltless and unstained by blood, the history of philosophy, science, and the arts." The events of the 20th century have made us mistrust these words—and, indeed, Pfitzner himself lived to write some particularly noxious works glorifying the Third Reich. Still, Schopenhauer's dualism provides an appropriate introduction to the rarefied world of *Palestrina*.

The story is based very loosely on the life of the 16th-century Italian composer Giovanni Pierluigi da Palestrina. The Catholic Church, shocked by the perceived ugliness of some recent compositions, is on the verge of banning all music except for pure monophonic chant. A Catholic cardinal (and nominal "friend"), Borromeo begs Palestrina to "save" the art by writing a Mass that will prove to all parties that complexity, innovation, and religious devotion can coexist. But Palestrina—aging, recently widowed and spiritually exhausted—feels he no longer has the strength for such a task and declines the invitation. However, the misty spirits of the great musical masters of the past appear before his eyes and insist that his tasks on earth are not yet completed, that it is his duty to preserve and continue their work. Thus inspired, Palestrina creates a new Mass in one night; it is sung, the pope is persuaded, and the course of music is permitted to continue unfettered.

Still, as Pfitzner presents it, popular acclaim—even papal acclaim, on which Palestrina depends for both his livelihood and his physical freedom— ultimately means little to the composer. He is above the battle, abstracted and lost to the petty concerns of the world—a servant of music and, by extension, a vessel for all of what the late Russell Kirk used to call the "permanent things."

As it happens, Pfitzner (1869–1949) was a cranky and fiercely ambitious man, and he had a definite agenda in mind when he wrote *Palestrina*. The opera may—indeed, *should*—be read in part as an allegorical attack on musical modernism. Pfitzner detested the radicalism of such composers as Stravinsky, Sibelius, Schoenberg, and Richard Strauss, whom he thought little more than nihilists who were heedlessly destroying the precious continuum of Western music. He therefore considered it his duty to cherish past traditions, amend them gently, and carry them reverently into the 20th century. One can't escape the sense that Pfitzner believed that he, too, like the historical Palestrina, would be recognized someday as the savior of music.

It didn't work out that way, of course, and Pfitzner is now a footnote in musical history, remembered, if at all, only for this magnificent and reactionary testament of faith. But what a moving testament it is! The great medieval work on mysticism speaks of the "cloud of unknowing" that surrounds a worthy pilgrim; once accustomed to the breadth and gravity of *Palestrina*, a sympathetic listener experiences something similar—a lumina of heightened awareness, a summons from the ether. Spare, leisurely, linear, and consonant, the first and third acts of *Palestrina* have scarcely a vulgar or unconsidered note.

Admittedly, Act II is a problem—a noisy, clattering depiction of the Council of Trent, where Palestrina's work is judged by some decidedly unsympathetic counts, bishops, cardinals, and other authorities. This act was intended as the most extreme possible contrast between the two acts that surround it, opposing the chaos of the world (including the squabbling hierarchies that purport to speak for religion) to Palestrina's retreat, where everything is pure spirit. Intentionally brash, Act II lasts more than an hour; it is marred by the absence of female voices (which necessitates a certain timbral monotony) and it succeeds in conveying ugly emptiness rather too well for the health of the complete work. But Acts I and III carry the show.

The production, directed by Nikolaus Lehnhoff with sets by Tobias Hoheisel, is a simple, handsome, modular creation in dark and light that was first presented at the Royal Opera House, Covent Garden, earlier this year and is highly suited to the opera. There is only one grievous misstep: Palestrina is actually *shown* writing his Mass in one night (about two minutes as it is presented onstage), moving his hands along with the heedless haste of a bored speedreader, dropping pages of finished manuscript on the floor like leaves from a deciduous tree, and generally behaving as if he had been placed under a "speed-up spell" on the old television show *Bewitched*. Such a profound epiphany, so ecstatically illumined in the music, might have been better left to our visual imagination.

Christian Thielemann, probably the most searching and exciting figure among the younger generation of German conductors, led the Royal Opera House orchestra with love, attention to detail, and meticulous control. Thomas Moser, in the role of Palestrina, proved rather a cumbersome stage actor, but he sang with such intelligence and sensitivity in such an expressive, clarion tenor voice that we were quickly won over. Soprano Ruth Ziesak, as Palestrina's son Ighino, was simply splendid: she has the rare ability to convey deep emotions without either devolving into histrionics or compromising her vocal purity; her scene with the equally fine Randi Stene (as Silla, Palestrina's wavering disciple) was characterized by a near Straussian rapture. Alan Held brought a fierce intensity and some strong, sustained singing to the role of Cardinal Borromeo. The huge—and startlingly distinguished—cast also included such artists as Robert Tear, Sergei Leiferkus, Anthony Rolfe-Johnson, Thomas Allen, and Kim Begley.

One need not accept all of Pfitzner's aesthetic strictures to believe in his *Palestrina*. It is a noble and elevated opera that will always find its audience, however limited. Those of us who were moved at all by the Lincoln Center 97 performance will probably never forget it.

The Washington Post
28 July 1997

La Rondine at the Washington Opera

GIACOMO PUCCINI'S *La Rondine*, which was revived by the Washington Opera at the Kennedy Center Saturday night, is a work that invites tender affection rather than wholehearted admiration.

Nobody has ever argued that *La Rondine* (1917) was one of Puccini's masterpieces. Instead, it was the composer's ambitious attempt to write a sophisticated, bittersweet comedy of manners, set in Paris toward the end of the 19th century.

Magda, the heroine, is the pampered mistress of a wealthy banker but has never really fallen in love with him. Along comes Ruggero, a young man from the provinces. The two are immediately attracted to one another and Magda sneaks out to a nightclub, theoretically disguised (although everybody who knows her—including her banker—sees through this immediately). Magda and Ruggero run away to a villa on the Cote d'Azur but an anonymous letter arrives, revealing Magda's scandalous past, whereupon Ruggero denounces and abandons her. What happens to Magda thereafter is a matter of opinion —or so it seems to director Marta Domingo.

Puccini deliberately left Magda's fate ambiguous. I've always thought that he created his character in the mold of the worldly Marschallin in *Der Rosenkavalier*. Ruggero was not Magda's first lover, nor will he be her last; she was unhappy about his departure but life would go on. Domingo, however, believes that the usual performing edition of *La Rondine* and its "dramatically weak ending" leaves the audience unmoved and has therefore had Magda drown herself just as the curtain goes down. As the Washington Opera announced, this is a "considerable departure from the standard version—moving it from a classification of bittersweet comedy to that of tragedy."

All of which sounds like a dangerous parlor game: "Change that Fate!" Maybe we will live to see a feel-good production of *La Traviata*, in which the heroine spontaneously recovers and bounces off into the wings on a pogo stick. How about a *Falstaff* in which all the characters will drink poison before the final octet and then drop dead, one after one, during their famous declaration that life is all a joke?

In fact, Domingo's amendment is easily—and wisely—ignored. There are no sudden floods on the Kennedy Center Opera House stage, no gurgles and glub-glub-glubs coming from the sound system. Instead, Magda merely walks into a watery mist, sinking slowly as the opera ends. Think "metaphor" and you'll be all right.

As it happens, the production is one of the Washington Opera's most winning. Domingo's direction is fairly assured (certainly, there are no great gaffes) and the scenery and costumes, by Michael Scott, are appropriate and attractive. I could, however, have lived without the worn, hazy scrim blocking our vision throughout Act III—was this a hangover from Domingo's original production in Bonn with the dread Giancarlo del Monaco?

The casting was unusually even, particularly for this company. Ainhoa Arteta, who sang Magda, sounded most comfortable in lyrical passages for the middle range, but also negotiated some of the highest and most strenuous writing for soprano that Puccini ever wrote. As a singing actress, she is a little on the cool side but her presence is both regal and captivating.

Had I not known otherwise, I would have identified tenor Marcus Haddock (Ruggero) as a baritone. His voice is especially deep, with a certain hard intensity more commonly identified with the lower register. He sang the role with a mixture of ardor and clarity, straining only on occasion. One only wished Puccini had written more interesting music for this character.

Lyric tenor Richard Troxell and soprano Inva Mula were sparkling and funny as Prunier and Lisette, the jolly young couple. Their voices complemented one another nicely, as if they shared a soulmate sweetness. William Parcher was properly gruff and authoritative as the banker Ramboldo, yet he brought unexpected tenderness to his final appearance.

Finally, Emmanuel Villaume, who conducted the Kennedy Center Opera House Orchestra and Washington Opera Chorus, was top-drawer. The orchestra sounded bright and alert and Villaume gave full due to the score's sweet sentiment. The only truly memorable music is the ensemble for quartet and nightclub toward the end of Act II. But there are small delights throughout and a good many spectators will enjoy this curious *Rondine*.

The Washington Post
2 March 1998

Paul Dresher

Paul Dresher, who presented an exhaustive and exciting concert at Coolidge Auditorium Friday night, is a remarkable musician and thinker.

He first came to attention about 20 years ago as a second-generation minimalist, one among many young composers whose musical ideas—and lives —had been changed by the pioneering, fiercely reiterative early works of Terry Riley, Steve Reich, and Philip Glass. Dresher's music from that period combined formal rigor with a refreshing personal style. It was smart but never didactic, directly expressive yet highly subtle, and such pieces as *This Same Temple* (1978) for two pianos continue to hold up very well.

Even then, he had formed his own Paul Dresher Ensemble, and he now also fronts the Electro-Acoustic Band, which presents music by other composers working in similar veins. On Friday, we were privileged to hear not only both of these groups but also the Abel-Steinberg Duo—violinist David Abel and pianist Julie Steinberg—in the only piece for acoustic instruments on the program: Dresher's own *Elapsed Time*, a tidy, sonata-like composition in three interrelated movements.

All the other instruments were electronically enhanced, attached to computers, digital samplers, and the like. As a result, one never knew exactly what sounds would be heard when percussionists Amy Knoles or Gene Reffkin lowered their mallets, and when bassoonist Paul Hanson played his own *Inner Openings for Bassoon and Electronics*, it sometimes evoked the entire wind section of a symphony orchestra. There were usually only seven players onstage, but with one tap on a pedal or one switch of a dial, the auditorium would fill with pulsing, ethereal sonic textures. A brave new world, indeed!

And yet there are precedents. Dresher is based in the Bay Area, and I was startled by how often his concert put me in mind of the more experimental San Francisco rock music of the 1960s—especially the soaring, digressive live performances by Quicksilver Messenger Service, Country Joe and the Fish, Jefferson Airplane, and even the Grateful Dead. Dresher is far more technically sophisticated, of course (one tiny computer from a local electronics store will be more versatile and effective than anything that was available 30 years ago), and the decibel level was mercifully low. But these two ensembles maintain some of the strange, spirited "from-scratch" qualities of a communal musical quest that made the best of that long-ago music so compelling.

It was Dresher's own Concerto for Violin and Electro-Acoustic Band that started the program. Much of the violin writing in the first movement was pizzicato—soloist Abel's plucking sometimes sounded like a shower of Ping-Pong balls—while the second movement was a long, impassioned legato melody infused with a near-Sibelian intensity. This is a serious and ambitious contribution to the concerto repertory; one hopes that other violinists will pick it up.

Jay Cloidt's bright, energetic *Life Is Good . . . And People Are Basically Decent* (1996) concluded with a marvelous etude, spooky and exhilarating, constructed over a tape loop of a speeding car. Cindy Cox, whose *Cathedral Spires* the National Symphony Orchestra took along on its recent European tour, was represented by *Into the Wild*, a dark, fertile musical fantasy with some haunting and desolate chords.

Eve Beglarian's *Creating the World* seemed overlong and only fitfully inspired, with passages of poetry recited, Monty Python–style, on a recording by Roger Rees; snippets of Puccini's "Vissi d'arte" and longer quotations from Vivaldi's *Gloria*; and a ponderous explanation of what all the piece "meant." Still, the catchy, exuberantly rhythmic finale was highly attractive.

David Lang's *Follow* is in keeping with much of this composer's other work—it is brash, boxy, unrelentingly aggressive, filled with dramatic gestures that most often impress this listener as spasmodic and theatrical. But *Follow* is also, in its own way, expertly made. One has the sense that Lang knows what he wants to do and then goes ahead and does it. More power to him—even if the point continues to elude me.

Whatever one thought of any given piece, the concert as a whole was deeply stimulating. It is presumptuous to refer to any one "music of the future." There will be thousands of such musics; the concept of a single, unified avant-garde is thoroughly discredited. But it is certainly good to know that Dresher's music will be there for us—and that he is out there serving as both lightning rod and seismograph for his colleagues.

The Washington Post
6 April 1998

Ned Rorem's Masterpiece

NED ROREM'S new song cycle, *Evidence of Things Not Seen*, which received its Washington premiere Saturday night at the Library of Congress's Coolidge Auditorium, is probably the composer's finest musical creation—epic in its ambitions, encyclopedic in its range, immaculately shaped for the human voice.

"Music is song and inside all composers lurks a singer striving to get out," Rorem wrote in his lucid and provocative program notes; he estimates that he had written 400 songs by the time he turned 40. Now, at the age of 75, he must have passed the 500 mark.

Most of *Evidence of Things Not Seen* was written last year, in response to a commission from the New York Festival of Song and the Library of Congress. Rorem selected 36 disparate texts, mostly poems but also fragments from sermons, journals, and autobiographies. Then he set them to music for soprano, mezzo-soprano, tenor, baritone, and piano, solo numbers interspersed with ensembles of all kinds. The result is a massive composition that lasts some 100 minutes without intermission. It is, therefore, one of the longest song cycles ever written—a physical and emotional workout for both performers and listeners.

From the beginning, Rorem was drawn to what is commonly called the "art song." (Although Rorem himself detests the term, it will serve to distinguish his genre from other, more folkish, more reiterative, and, if you like, more "hummable" songs, which have their own traditions.) His songs are written for classically trained vocalists and usually include an elaborate part for piano that is less accompaniment than it is complement.

The characteristics of a typical Rorem song are easy to describe. Above all, one admires his understanding of just what the voice can and cannot do. His melodies, although strenuous at times, are inevitably linear, and the words usually come out in a natural, unforced rhythm, almost as enhanced speech. His songs are subtle and concentrated, and they rarely outstay their welcome. His harmonies are often moderately dissonant, but serious listeners, however conservative their tastes, should have no difficulty following his emotional argument.

In some of Rorem's earlier pieces, I have felt that his undeniable craft overshadowed his artistry—rather as if I were listening to a master workman doing his perfectly accomplished thing rather than to a human being trying to tell me something. It is not quite fair to say that *Evidence of Things Not Seen* is more direct than some of Rorem's other work—he has always addressed his audience straightforwardly. But I do believe his work has taken on a new intensity of expression. It is not merely because he has addressed the Big Issues in this cycle—love, death, youth, infirmity, infinity. Rather, even the smaller, subtle themes and passages ring with conviction.

One paradox: a few of the strongest poems were just the ones that seemed most resistant to Rorem's settings. I am thinking particularly of "Faith," by Mark Doty, a bleak, harrowing narrative that is far stronger on the page than on the stage. But who can tell what makes a good lyric? Walt Whitman—to this taste, a garrulous, clattering egotist—has inspired more great music than any other American writer; Rorem has done him proud yet again. And the Auden settings seem to me just about perfect.

Mezzo-soprano Delores Ziegler stood out among the soloists for the power, glow, and opulence of her singing. Baritone Kurt Ollmann sang elegantly, lyrically, all but caressing the words. Rufus Muller has a high, clarion tenor voice that he uses with skill; I'd be interested to hear what he might do with an Elgar oratorio. Soprano Monique McDonald had some pitch problems and displayed an occasional tendency toward hooting, but the empathic quality of her voice at its best and the warmth of her delivery were affecting. Michael Barrett and Steven Blier, the co–artistic directors of the New York Festival of Song, traded off duties at the piano with enthusiasm and aplomb.

All in all, it was a memorable evening, and the prolonged standing ovation at the end of the program was merited. *Evidence of Things Not Seen* was recorded for broadcast and eventual release on New World Records. A good idea, for this is an important work, imbued as it is with the distinguished and terrible sense of a summing up.

The Washington Post
20 April 1998

Andrea Bocelli

Andrea Bocelli, a much-advertised Italian tenor who made his American debut at the Kennedy Center Spring Gala on Sunday night, does one thing spectacularly well.

Rarely have I heard such clear, calibrated, and ravishingly beautiful soft high notes. They are simply stunning, and Bocelli made sure the program was filled with opportunities to show them off. The effect upon the audience was phenomenal, and it begins to explain why Bocelli has sold millions of records.

But that is about all that can be said in Bocelli's favor. His tone is occasionally sweet but more often thin and pallid, the musical equivalent of violet-flavored candy. His phrasing is unreflected and uninteresting, and he doesn't seem to have had more than a smidgen of training. Moreover, he is a lazy interpreter: he barely approximated the turns and flourishes in Verdi's "Libiamo" from *La Traviata* and never varied his rhythmic emphases in succeeding verses of "La donna è mobile" from *Rigoletto*. Even four hearty Neapolitan songs by Tosti were lifeless. In short, Bocelli is a rank amateur, albeit one gifted with a few—very few—wonderful sounds.

Bocelli has been completely blind since the age of 12 and it is, of course, remarkable that he has been able to build such a career for himself against the odds. He might be considered as this year's answer to David Helfgott, the disturbed Australian pianist who inspired the film *Shine*—like Helfgott, Bocelli is a man with a story that engages our sympathy. But noble human victories do not lead automatically to great art.

The rest of the program was somewhat more attractive. Leonard Slatkin led the National Symphony Orchestra through effusive, enthusiastic, and often very exciting performances of Bernstein's *Candide* Overture, Verdi's overture to *La Forza del Destino*, and—with the Choral Arts Society of Washington—Borodin's "Polovtsian Dances" from *Prince Igor*. I was particularly pleased with the Intermezzo from Mascagni's *Cavalleria Rusticana*, which was played very slowly and took on a luscious and stately grandeur. If the orchestral playing was rather less polished than it usually is these days, it remained spirited throughout.

Soprano Hei-Kyung Hong, who was so recently a fresh, fetching Zerlina in the Washington Opera's production of *Don Giovanni*, sang an appropriately sentimental "Vilia" from Lehár's *Merry Widow* and a radiant "O mio babbino caro" from Puccini's *Gianni Schicchi*. Her duets with Bocelli were naturally problematic, simply because her voice is so much larger than his—that is to say, of normal size. Some subtle amplification gave Bocelli a boost and the worst was avoided.

The Kennedy Center is the premier arts complex in our nation's capital, and it could serve as a beacon for the most elevated creative aspirations throughout the world. But we must acknowledge the fact that the high-ticket concert event of early 1998—not only presented but actually sponsored by the Kennedy Center—proved a hype-driven and artistically dispiriting affair.

The Washington Post
21 April 1998

Evgeny Kissin

THERE ARE musicians and then there are phenomena. Evgeny Kissin, who played a spectacular piano recital at the Kennedy Center Concert Hall last night, belongs in the latter category.

Born in Moscow 27 years ago, Kissin has been famous in musical circles since he was in his early teens. Fortunately, he shows no signs of burning out, as do so many prodigies as they venture ever deeper into adulthood. On the contrary, he is playing better than ever, and he is already a very great pianist indeed.

Kissin is sometimes compared to Vladimir Horowitz, and, indeed, he shares some qualities with the older man—Herculean power, tonal brilliance, magnificent octaves, and a somewhat nervous interpretive manner. But Kissin is a much smarter musician; in his ability to shape, shade, and control a musical composition—every note, every run—from start to finish, he recalls Maurizio Pollini at his best. There were moments in last night's program that I expect to remember all my life.

Never before have I heard the piano sound so much like a bowed string instrument—a viola, say, or a soaring cello—as it did during some left-hand legato passages in Beethoven's Sonata No. 28 in A, Op. 101. It seemed both natural and miraculous. Throughout the night, one was taken aback by some hitherto unimagined sonic resource in this most familiar of instruments.

Kissin burst onto the stage a little after 8:30, acknowledging the applause and moving quickly toward the piano with an awkward and almost fawnlike skittering. Once he sat down, however, a palpable and expectant silence filled the hall. And then the Beethoven began—that amazing first movement (with as much concentrated chromaticism as you'll find in any music before Arnold Schoenberg set up shop) leading ultimately to a magnificent, cathedral-like fugue. This is a strange, abstracted, and profoundly beautiful score, and Kissin made the most of its mystery.

The music of Brahms is both formal and full of feeling. As any pianist will tell you, the keyboard works are also enormously difficult—densely packed with inner voices that render even the composer's slower, less obviously virtuosic works a challenge. Kissin met that challenge in the four piano pieces that make up Brahms's Op. 119: three intermezzos and a rhapsody. I can understand listeners who may have found the performances rather agitated (particularly some of us who came to know these pieces through Glenn Gould's brooding, achingly nostalgic recording from the early 1960s), but they were always plausible and, to my taste, original and effective.

Indeed, even when we disagree with Kissin about one point or another, it is impossible to doubt his motives or authority. There is never anything cavalier about his playing; it is always grounded, contemplated carefully, and then executed immaculately. We never sense he is doing anything for the mere sake of show. Still, there was no shortage of excitement: The Brahms Rhapsody gonged out with such majesty and power that one could almost believe every church bell in Washington had joined in.

I confess a marked distaste for most of Franz Liszt's music and would happily have forgone the 35-minute Sonata in B Minor that concluded the formal program. Still, if Liszt we must have, let it be played like this—as one long trajectory from the terse, staccato opening notes through the elaborate modulations and that simple, stepping, recurrent melody that is intended to sound so noble and usually sounds so facile.

But some pieces depend upon a terrific interpreter. Longtime *Chicago Tribune* music critic Claudia Cassidy used to say that the so-called "Rach Three"—the Rachmaninoff Piano Concerto No. 3—was "cheap unless it was magnificent." Certainly much of the Liszt sonata sounded magnificent last night. I particularly enjoyed the fugue, which had a hyper-caffeinated, jazzy jitter.

In short, it was a grand evening, exhilarating on any number of levels. Many thanks to the Washington Performing Arts Society, the organization that has brought Kissin to town for all three of his Kennedy Center recitals. May he return soon and often.

The Washington Post
30 April 1998

A Streetcar Named Desire

SAN FRANCISCO

THERE IS SUCH an abundance of talent in the San Francisco Opera's production of André Previn's *A Streetcar Named Desire*, which received its world premiere here on Saturday night, that one only wishes the opera were more persuasive than it is.

Over the course of the long evening—on opening night, *Streetcar* lasted four hours, including two intermissions—we heard a great deal of adept, opulent, and sometimes shimmeringly beautiful writing for voice and orchestra; looked on as librettist Philip Littell's elegant and faithful condensation of the Tennessee Williams play ran its gloomy course; and admired the unfailingly high quality of the San Francisco Opera production (created by Colin Graham), which included everything from a virtuoso orchestra to lacy evocations of New Orleans streets and balconies. Moreover, the star performances ranged from the worthy (Rodney Gilfry as Stanley Kowalski, Anthony Dean Griffey as Harold Mitch) to the memorable (Elizabeth Futral as Stella and—especially—Renée Fleming as Blanche DuBois).

A Streetcar Named Desire is an opera in the grand tradition. It is filled with arias and ensembles that are carefully crafted for the human voice (a few numbers might make attractive pendants to the concert repertory). Previn's score is essentially conservative, a mixture of Bergian expressionism and raucous, bluesy, orchestral jazz, usually allotted to the brass—"Slaughter on Bourbon Street," if you will—and contains some of the composer-conductor's most eloquent music.

Much thought has gone into the creation of Littell's libretto. Blessedly, he decided against setting Stanley's feral howls of "Stell-*lahhhhh!*" to music, instead letting the character shout it out, as he does in the play. Since this may be the most parodied scene in all of American drama, any musical translation would have been at least disrupting and more likely uproarious (imagine that cry, set to any music you choose, coming from the mouth of Luciano Pavarotti, and prepare to giggle). There were similar touches and amendments throughout the evening; from first to last, the opera's aspirations are elevated and of the utmost seriousness.

Still there can be no doubt that *Streetcar* simply doesn't *work* as it now stands. Indeed, I'm not convinced that the thoughtful, urbane Previn really had much affinity for all the sordid goings-on in the play; whatever the case, the opera is marked by a curious paucity of animal spirits. It is as if Richard Strauss were to have set *Cavalleria Rusticana* and drowned the libidinous ferocity of the drama in purest butterfat.

One example will suffice: toward the climax of the story, Stanley brutally rapes the disheveled and increasingly disconnected Blanche. The orchestra lets out a roar, the percussion pounds, and the wailing reaches fever pitch. And yet it all seems expertly wrought fustian—there is nothing primal about this interlude, nothing especially tragic or gripping, no catharsis. Rather, the music merely seems generically loud and unpleasant, and we squint to read our watches in the dark.

As it happens, Previn gave the role of Stanley to a baritone. Rodney Gilfry sang with distinction and force, yet his presence never magnetized the action as a fully effective characterization of Stanley must. Tenor Anthony Dean Griffey sang Mitch's music with empathy and some soft, ringing high notes. Mezzo-soprano Judith Forst was a savvy, worldly wise Eunice, while Jeffrey Lentz made a youthful appropriately awkward Young Collector.

Elizabeth Futral sang the role of Stella with a radiant sweetness; how splendid and uncommon to find, a first-class coloratura soprano with such spirit and intelligence. But the evening belonged to Renée Fleming, who essayed the long and taxing central role of Blanche. I found Fleming less convincing in the opera's heavy drama than she might have been (some of this reaction may have been due to the fact that the material is pretty unconvincing in itself). But the lyricism, vocal luster, and patrician style she brought to Previn's quieter and more reflective passages were impeccable and sometimes wrenching.

There was worthy support from Matthew Lord, Luis Oropeza, Josepha Gayer, Ray Reinhardt, and Lynne Soffer. Previn himself led the premiere, with a loving hand that was both sweeping and detailed.

There will be seven more performances before October 11, and a national telecast is promised. I do not predict a long performance history for this *Streetcar*, but a pruned suite or song cycle may prove valuable and moving. Make no mistake, there is some rich music here, amid the mire, but it doesn't have much to do with Tennessee Williams. Ultimately, an opera based on *Streetcar* should have been made nasty, brutish, and short—or not at all.

The Washington Post
21 September 1998

George Gershwin at 100

SATURDAY marked the 100th anniversary of the birth of George Gershwin, and the San Francisco Symphony, under the direction of Michael Tilson Thomas, was in Washington to celebrate the occasion in style.

The Kennedy Center Concert Hall was sold out to an exuberant audience that cheered and rose to its feet after three of the four selections in the program devoted entirely to Gershwin's music. Rarely have I been surrounded by such palpable, deliriously appreciative collective energy. It was a terrific first fall offering from the Washington Performing Arts Society, which began its 1998–99 season with this presentation.

San Francisco has had an admirable orchestra for some years, but the appointment of Tilson Thomas as music director in 1995 seems to have recharged the ensemble, which now produces a gorgeous sound, all velvet and electricity. The musicians are seamlessly blended, section by section, and they respond reflexively to Tilson Thomas's choreographic but efficient leadership—the brass swinging the blues with a raspy growl, the strings soaring and ecstatic. Acting concertmaster Nadya Tichman, in particular, plays with a honeyed tone so sweetly fluid that it startles.

The program began with the bright, jaunty overture to *Of Thee I Sing*. Thereafter, soprano Audra McDonald and baritone Brian Stokes Mitchell took the stage to collaborate in a performance of *Catfish Row*, Gershwin's own adaptation of highlights from *Porgy and Bess*. McDonald has a beautiful voice—fresh, strong, versatile, and brimming with feeling. She has spent most of her career in music theater; it would be interesting to learn what she might do in opera. Mitchell sang and acted with high spirits, sure inflection, and the proverbial "way with a song." Gershwin's suite unaccountably leaves out "It Ain't Necessarily So," an omission Tilson Thomas handily repaired by leading an impromptu sing-along as a mid-concert encore.

The Second Rhapsody for Piano and Orchestra (sometimes presented, in a different edition, as the *Rhapsody in Rivets*) will never rival the earlier *Rhapsody in Blue* for the public's affection. Truth to tell, it's not a very good piece—patchy, ponderous, poorly organized, and curiously lacking in melodic distinction. I was reminded of one of those ersatz piano concertos Bugs Bunny used to play in old Warner Bros. cartoons—Raymond Scott meets Rachmaninoff. Still, Tilson Thomas's performance of the solo piano part, alternately brash and meditative, could not have been much bettered. The afternoon closed with the evergreen *American in Paris*.

Just after intermission, Tilson Thomas delivered an odd speech in praise of "George," asserting, among other things, that Gershwin could and should be ranked with Monteverdi and Schubert "and all the other great composers." We've heard a lot of such talk this year—feelings run high during centennial celebrations. Still, with all due respect, such evaluations seem to me absolutely over the top, informed by the same unnecessary American boosterism that used to place Longfellow, Whitman, and Lowell on a level with Milton, Keats, and Tennyson a century ago.

There can be no doubt that Gershwin was an extraordinarily fertile songwriter. He made ripe, luscious melodies as an apple tree makes apples—melodies that sound equally at home in a jazz club and a concert hall, melodies characterized by driving energy, near-magical immediacy, and a seemingly inevitable vector—and his early death (in 1937, from a brain tumor) was an artistic calamity.

But why can't we appreciate Gershwin for what he was—a masterly, tragically short-lived American songwriter of the top class—and leave it at that? We do his memory no favor by suggesting that *Porgy and Bess* is a fully satisfying opera, that the Concerto in F deserves consideration among the significant works for piano and orchestra, that the composer ever began to grasp the fundamentals of large musical form. In each case, direct experience will quickly convince us otherwise. Gershwin's concert and operatic works are best understood as inspired medleys—one juicy tune after another, in the manner of Gilbert and Sullivan overtures, yet infused with a vitalizing strain of the American vernacular. Without exception, his longer pieces are better moment by moment than they are in sum.

Never mind. Gershwin's melodies persist—and they aren't making any more of them. Of "George" I sing.

The Washington Post
28 September 1998

Yo-Yo Ma in Contemporary Music

ONLY AN ARTIST with the charm, charisma, and celebrity of Yo-Yo Ma could have sold out the Kennedy Center Concert Hall—down to the last stage seat—for a program so defiantly uncompromising as the one the cellist played there late Saturday afternoon. Yet Ma, who is also a musician of the most profound and serious order, was not only able to keep his audience members in their seats throughout the whole challenging concert (with virtually no attrition after intermission) but left them cheering at the end.

Concerts for solo stringed instruments (the piano, of course, excluded) are never easy, for either performer or listener. By necessity, even the most extraordinary violinist, violist, or cellist has to contend with the intrinsic difficulties of the chosen instrument—not only the natural limitation of harmonic and contrapuntal possibilities but also a certain timbral sameness. Even the greatest works for solo strings—the sonatas and partitas for violin and the suites for solo cello by Johann Sebastian Bach—do not make for easy listening; we must immerse ourselves in their majesty if we are to take anything home with us.

On Saturday, Ma had the splendid audacity to play only works by 20th-century composers, three of them still living. The program began with a work by the country music fiddler Mark O'Connor, *Appalachia Waltz*, a plaintive, quietly suggestive melody that might have emanated from a Walker Evans photograph. Ma played this haunting miniature in a plush half-voice that only made it the more affecting.

Bright Sheng's *Seven Tunes Heard in China* followed immediately. One might quibble with the inclusion of a "Tibetan Dance" in such a collection—if Tibetan music is indeed "heard in China," that may be due in part to an occupation of unspeakable brutality. Yet Sheng has himself written works protesting the excesses of the Chinese government: *H'UN (Lacerations): In Memoriam 1966–76* is a much-admired musical response to the Cultural Revolution.

In any event, the *Seven Tunes* proved a mixture of folk melody, meditation, and musical experimentation. The fourth in the series, "The Drunken Fisherman," called for Ma to pluck and strum his strings repeatedly; in an amusing spoken introduction, the cellist explained the method in which he discovered that the computerized plastic strips that many hotels now offer in lieu of traditional room keys made the perfect pick. Although the *Seven Tunes* were not consistently compelling, the best of them were lively indeed and the "Tibetan Dance" called for Ma to rap his knuckles upon his instrument on several occasions, endowing the music with a percussive, tabla-like beat.

David Wilde's *The Cellist of Sarajevo*, described as "a lament in rondo form for solo cello," proved a searching, eloquent work built in a long arch—from silence it came and to silence it returned, after a brief, desperately impassioned reverie.

But the unquestioned highlight of the concert was Ma's magnificent reading of the great Sonata for Solo Cello (Op. 8) by the late Hungarian composer Zoltán Kodály. Wrenching, exhaustive, exhilarating, this 35-minute work must be counted among the most jagged and precipitous Himalayas in the cello repertory. In Ma's hands, the sonata unfolded with the direct inevitability of an ancient epic, its considerable knots and dissonances only part of an endlessly absorbing narrative.

Before the program, Douglas H. Wheeler, the president of the Washington Performing Arts Society, which produced this event, mentioned that Ma had played four concerts for the organization within the past 14 months; moreover, the cellist spent much of Friday working with local youngsters. How rare it is to find an authentic superstar who continues to care so much about the future of music that he will teach children in their schools—and their parents in the concert hall.

The Washington Post
25 January 1999

POSTSCRIPTS

Radical Music That Will Remain That Way

THROUGHOUT much of the 1980s I was the host of a radio program on New York's WNYC-FM. My emphasis was on contemporary music; however, one afternoon I devoted an entire show to works by the 12th-century composer Perotin—spare, ethereal, yet startlingly intense vocal compositions based on the sound (still fairly rare in Western music) of stark parallel fourths. The record played for a while, then the studio phone rang and I was confronted with a furious gentleman who claimed I'd ruined his drive home (and, one might have surmised, his life as well). He swore that he would never again contribute to public radio until we stopped playing what he called "all that *damned* new music"!

Obviously, 800 years on, Perotin is still not exactly an "easy listen." In fact, almost any musical language with which we are unfamiliar will seem "new" to us at first. But let's face it: for many well-disposed music lovers, this has been an especially tough century. Indeed, so far as the absorption and appreciation of 20th-century concert music and opera go, a lot of people out there pretty much missed it.

Exactly why and how this happened can and will be debated for many years to come (some possible reasons—the collapse of music education in many countries, including the United States; the split between the "high arts" and popular culture; the decline of the concert and the increased importance of mass media; and the perceived impenetrability and/or ugliness of much 20th-century creation). In any event, rightly or wrongly, many listeners never came to terms with the main classical music trends of this century.

This will not be one of those "Here are some nice, not-too-frightening, recent works to pull you into your own time" articles. I approve of such ventures entirely (my own "getting started" list might include music by Olivier Messiaen, Allan Pettersson, Henryk Mikolaj Górecki, Einojuhani Rautavaara, Arvo Pärt, Steve Reich, and Philip Glass).

Instead, let's break out the hard stuff. For once, let's give frank radicalism its due, without apology and without sugarcoating. The following is a list of substantial 20th-century pieces that make no special effort to be liked. Indeed, if I may anthropomorphize for a moment, these pieces really couldn't care less whether you like them or not. They are works that were bold, original, and in some cases downright horrifying to their audiences when they were first performed, and even today a first encounter with them can inspire anything from intrigue to befuddlement to inchoate fury.

I have made no attempt to be comprehensive, nor have I attempted to present only "the best" 20th-century pieces. (Great works of art are not necessarily radical; Richard Strauss's nostalgic, deeply reflective, and immaculately conservative *Four Last Songs* speak just as profoundly to us as his manic, off-the-wall *Elektra*.)

Moreover, the shock has worn off of some once-notorious pieces. In 1927 George Antheil's *Ballet Mécanique* appalled traditionalists with its use of sirens, car horns, and multiple pianos; today, in the era of computer sampling, this seems little more than a collection of gimmicks and barely holds our interest.

A much greater piece, Igor Stravinsky's *Rite of Spring*, was so influential in its time that listeners, hearing it co-opted and recycled by composers of every stripe, have become accustomed to its language. While we admire *Rite* today, it no longer shocks us silly (indeed, Walt Disney incorporated it into *Fantasia* almost 60 years ago—and how disconcerting can a Disney soundtrack be?). And the once-recalcitrant works of Pierre Boulez—*Pli Selon Pli, Le Marteau Sans Maître*—now sound positively *pretty*, and very much in the tradition of Debussy and Ravel.

Still, here are 10 important 20th-century pieces, in chronological order, that have never quite been tamed. Indeed, the subversive in me hopes they will inspire perplexed listeners and angry calls for at least 800 years.

Charles Ives: *The Unanswered Question* (1906). There is still some debate about whether Ives was a genuinely visionary musical thinker or merely a primitive dabbler who occasionally hit upon a good idea. In general, I lean toward the dabbler theory; such works as the "Concord" Sonata seem arbitrary and incoherent—one dissonance as good as another—and his endless quotation of hymn tunes and Civil War songs seems little more than a cheap, ready-made, cosmetic Americana. But there are a few Ives pieces that are undoubtedly works of art and *The Unanswered Question* is among the best of them.

Scored for orchestra and solo trumpet, it begins with a slow, seraphic, barely audible chorale played by the strings. A quizzical, angular phrase for trumpet poses the musical "question" which is "answered" by a gaggle of wind instruments. This is repeated, with greater intensity, and the piece eventually devolves into a controlled cacophony, after which it regains its gravity, repeating the question again before dying out into cosmic stillness.

This is great music in a number of ways. It is both consonant (the soft bedding of the string chorale) and abrasively dissonant (the "questions" and "answers" are naked and awkward). It is a work that creates its own form, perfects it, then breaks the mold. There was nothing like *The Unanswered Question* before it was written and, by its very nature, it can never have a legitimate sequel. Finally, it conveys, in a manner unlike any other piece I know, the vastness of infinity, at once mystical and humbling, all-inclusive and achingly lonely. (Recommended recording: Leonard Bernstein, New York Philharmonic, Sony Classical.)

Richard Strauss: *Elektra* **(1908).** This is an utterly horrible piece; it is also magnificent. Strauss and librettist Hugo von Hofmannsthal took Sophocles's tragedy *Elektra*, set it to music that combines graphic violence with convulsive (and wildly inappropriate) sexual ecstasy, and, in so doing, created the most disturbing opera in the repertory. From the slashing outline of the D minor triad that opens the opera (rather as a punch in the face might be said to open a dialogue) through the triumphant, frazzled, obsessively reiterated C major chord that concludes the slaughter 80 psychotic minutes later, *Elektra* is a study in overkill so bloodthirsty that it is not surprising Strauss completely changed course once he had this venom out of his system (his next opera was *Der Rosenkavalier*, that gentle, graceful Viennese comedy of manners).

A good *Elektra* should leave an audience speechless. This is the most unhealthy of masterpieces; it incites us, with huge orchestra, chorus, and a cast of iron-voiced soloists, to cheer on Elektra's revenge, a brutal matricide, all set to music that is both enormously sophisticated and primal as hell. (Recommended recording: Birgit Nilsson in the title role, with the Vienna Philharmonic Orchestra under Sir Georg Solti, Decca/London.)

Jean Sibelius: Symphony No. 4 (1911). Another one-of-a-kind. Sibelius had earned a world reputation with the romantic, somewhat Tchaikovskian grandeur of such works as *Finlandia* and the Symphony No. 2. In 1911 this dour, austere, and weirdly beautiful score came as a complete surprise to Sibelius's listeners and critics (many of whom were vociferous in their denunciations) and it remains unsettling and enigmatic to this day.

The first movement in particular is built block by sonic block, with an absolute minimum of padding; rarely has a composer said so much so tersely. The second movement always seems to be about to break into a Tchaikovsky waltz, but it never quite gets there and ends abruptly, with dark, disturbing, birdy tritones and a peremptory roll from the timpani. The third movement is another study in delay—in this case, we wait some seven minutes for the full exposition of a long, sweeping melody that climbs mournfully for two and a half octaves and then dies away. And what can all those bells in the finale be about?

The entire symphony is very strange. "There is nothing, absolutely nothing of the circus to it," Sibelius once said. To be sure, and it is as mystifying to a general audience today as it was when it was written. (Recommended recording: Herbert von Karajan, Berlin Philharmonic, EMI Classics.)

Arnold Schoenberg: *Pierrot Lunaire* (1912). Even Schoenberg's most passionate admirers admit that *Pierrot* is difficult. The composer Charles Wuorinen once compared the experience of listening to it to that of befriending a porcupine. Another composer, George Perle, acknowledged that *Pierrot Lunaire* is "not a work that one ever gets used to." So why, almost 85 years later, with Schoenberg-ism largely abandoned as a musical movement, do we still care about *Pierrot Lunaire*?

Because it is *there*, that's why. This bizarre, arty, expressionist song cycle may not be Schoenberg's most appealing piece but it is undoubtedly his most radical—indeed, it is the culmination of a certain strain of Viennese decadence. Here, the composer truly breathes "the air of other planets" that he alluded to in his String Quartet No. 2; this is cabaret music for Martians.

Schoenberg set 21 poems (by Albert Giraud) in what he called *Sprechstimme* —a form of speech-song where the vowels in each word momentarily touch on the indicated pitch, then fall away from it for a sort of creepy-crawly, haunted-house effect that works well in the right material. This is the right material. (Recommended recording: Jan DeGaetani, with Arthur Weisberg and the Contemporary Chamber Ensemble, Nonesuch Records.)

Virgil Thomson/Gertrude Stein: Four Saints in Three Acts (1928–34). To begin with, the opera is in *four* acts (with only one intermission, if any) and has more than 30 saints in it. Stein's words come across as genial, cracked logorrhea ("To be asked how much of it is finished. To be asked Saint Teresa Saint Teresa to be asked how much of it is finished. To be asked Saint Teresa to be asked Saint Teresa to be asked ask Saint Teresa how much of it is finished.") Thomson's music is straightforward, deceptively uncomplicated, chock full of C major. The opening cast was an all-black one (a tradition that has been preserved in many later productions), the sets were cellophane, and nothing really "happens" in the sense of a recognizable plot. All the standard rules of musical theater were at least ignored, and sometimes gleefully broken.

"Do not try to understand the words of this opera literally nor seek in the music of it undue references to modern Spain," Thomson wrote. "If, through the poet's liberties with logic and the composer's constant use of the plainest musical language, something is evoked of the inner gaiety and the strength of lives consecrated to a nonmaterial end, the authors will consider their labors rewarded." Today, *Four Saints* seems a great-great-grandparent of both minimalism and performance art, and maintains a freshness, clarity, and contemporaneity that is absolutely up to the moment. (Recommended recording: The 1947 abridged performance on RCA Gold Seal, conducted by Thomson, is the most idiomatic, but only Joel Thome, with the Orchestra of Our Time, on Nonesuch, gives us the whole score.)

Aaron Copland: Piano Variations (1930). Forget such gentle, homespun scores as *Appalachian Spring* and *Quiet City*. When Copland was in the mood, he could be as ferocious and uncompromising a modernist as America has produced. The Piano Variations—all cold steel and tactile fury—was once described by Leonard Bernstein as a "synonym for modern music, so prophetic, harsh and wonderful and so full of modern feeling and thinking."

Copland starts off what he called his "10-minute monster" with a gonging four-note cell that sounds a little like the familiar "Westminster Carillon" turned on its head. On this, he constructs 20 succinct variations that build to a conclusion that is little short of cataclysmic. And yet there is an overriding structural clarity to this music: "As I listen to the Piano Variations," the author (and sometime composer) Paul Bowles once said, "I'm aware of its construction; its beams and struts are beautifully visible, unmarred by any ornamentation." (Recommended recording: Gilbert Kalish, Nonesuch Records.)

John Cage: Sonatas and Interludes for Prepared Piano (1946–48). It sounds like one of the dada stunts for which (unfortunately) John Cage would later be known—take an ordinary piano, then insert screws, erasers, nuts, bolts, and pieces of plastic among the strings, then sit down and try to play it. In fact, Cage had found a "whole new gamut of sounds, which was just what I needed," he wrote. "The piano had become, in effect, a percussion orchestra under the control of a single player."

Those who dismiss Cage's later work out of hand owe it to themselves to listen to the music he wrote in the '30s, '40s, and early '50s, for it is charming, dynamic, attractive, and unfailingly original. (What wonderful pieces he might have given us had he not fallen into his curious obsession with perpetual novelty!) The 16 sonatas and 4 interludes he created here make up his longest and most ambitious piece from this era. They were written at a time when Cage was just becoming interested in Zen philosophy: "I decided to attempt the expression in music of the permanent emotions of Indian traditions: the heroic, the erotic, the wondrous, the mirthful, sorrow, fear, anger, the odious, and their common tendency toward tranquility." Strange and glorious noisemaking, this hour-long exploration can stand as Cage's testament—"The Well-Prepared Piano." (Recommended recording: Maro Ajemian, Composers Recordings Incorporated.)

Alvin Lucier: *I Am Sitting in a Room* (1970). Describing this piece, however eloquently, will not do it justice and may actually frighten off some listeners. Still, because I love this music and believe many readers will love it, too, I'm willing to take the risk. Alvin Lucier, the most austere and intellectually rigorous of musical minimalists, sat in his Connecticut living room one day, read a speech into one tape recorder, then played the recording of that speech back into another tape recorder, then played that dub back into yet another tape recorder, and continued the process until natural overtones completely obscured the words and created a sort of distilled shadow music.

What may initially seem intolerably arch and arty (not to mention dull) metamorphosizes into a listening experience that is, in fact, deeply engrossing and, ultimately, eerily and arrestingly beautiful. Words become music, sound becomes shimmer, and a natural process of acoustics is demonstrated in the most elegant manner. There is nothing like *I Am Sitting in a Room* and Lucier's own recording is a definitive version of a modern masterpiece. Definitive, that is, unless you make your own performance—which is, of course, quite possible, and would likely be welcomed by Lucier. (Recommended and only commercial recording: Lucier on Lovely Music.)

Steve Reich: *Four Organs* **(1970).** If you respond to musical minimalism, you likely find it both hypnotic and invigorating; if you don't, you probably find it more boring than *Forrest Gump,* white guilt, and the collected works of Enver Hoxha put together. Either way, you can't get much more "minimalist" than *Four Organs.*

Reich once described this work succinctly: "short chord made long." From a technical standpoint, that pretty much sums it up—four organs, kept in time by steadily shaken maracas, repeat a single chord again and again, emphasizing different voices in the chord, held for different lengths of time, until we have examined the structure from what seems every possible vantage point. But this cannot convey the score's pristine formal perfection, the suspense it builds in a susceptive listener, the ecstasy one feels as the organists dive slowly, deeply, inexorably into Reich's wonderful chord and then come up renewed. I'm mad for *Four Organs*; however, it is fair to warn the reader that those who *aren't* mad for *Four Organs* usually despise it and that performances have provoked near-riots. (Recommended recording: Steve Reich and Musicians—including the young Philip Glass! Mantra Records.)

Meredith Monk: *Tablet* **(1977).** *Tablet* begins with four women furiously shrieking out a cappella syllables as loudly as possible. The effect is both bracing and unsettling (and has scared at least one five-year-old out of the room and under his covers). Thereafter, however, this is a rich, warm, variegated, and startlingly evocative composition and, for me, Monk's most consistently satisfying musical work. But its strangenesses are genuine and manifold: *Tablet* is scored for recorder, three pianists (who share one piano), and four specially trained voices singing, parrying, and babbling made-up words and nonsense syllables. How to explain the extraordinary, other-worldly effectiveness of this piece?

Monk is a true original. She follows no leaders, leads no followers. In addition to her work as a composer, she is a respected choreographer, playwright, and filmmaker, all of which endeavors she pursues with the same single-minded sense of purpose she brings to her music. You may love her work or you may detest it but you certainly haven't heard it before. Nor will it soon fade into the background. (Recommended recording: *Songs from the Hill/ Tablet*, Meredith Monk, Wergo Records.)

Obviously, there are many works that could be added to this list—the String Quartet No. 3 and the Brass Quintet by Elliott Carter; *Stimmung, Song of the Youths*, and *Hymnen* (among others) by Karlheinz Stockhausen; and—to test one's endurance, if nothing else—one of the very long chamber pieces by Morton Feldman (*For Philip Guston*, perhaps, or the six-hour String Quartet No. 2), to name only a few. But the 10 compositions above represent a good crash-course in the best sort of avant-garde 20th-century music—radical music that has remained radical, created with the utmost integrity and understanding.

The Washington Post
7 January 1996

The End of the Classical Dinosaurs

I wish this article hadn't proven so prophetic. The causes of the crisis were clear to me even before they began to manifest themselves; indeed, this is an expansion of a similar article I had written for Newsday *as far back as 1988. Things have only worsened over time.*

O N SOME LEVELS this would seem the best of times for the classical record business. *The Three Tenors,* that initial musical collaboration among Luciano Pavarotti, Plácido Domingo, and José Carreras, continues to sell at an amazing rate—more than 10 million units now, making it far and away the best-selling classical recording of all time.

Discs by a few young vocalists (especially soprano Dawn Upshaw, mezzo-soprano Cecilia Bartoli, and tenor Roberto Alagna, no matter what they are singing) are sure to climb the *Billboard* charts. And there has been an explosion of interest in some contemporary music (Henryk Mikolaj Górecki's Symphony No. 3, works by Steve Reich, Philip Glass, and John Adams), and material from the Renaissance and baroque (discs by Anonymous 4, the Hilliard Ensemble, Roger Norrington, and John Eliot Gardiner).

Still, the fact remains that this is a nightmarish time to be in the business of making new classical recordings. Indeed, the industry, as we have known it, might just be coming to an end.

Consider. Philips is in the middle of finishing up its obligations to the Boston Symphony Orchestra and Seiji Ozawa. Deutsche Grammophon is winding down one arrangement with the Metropolitan Opera Orchestra and another one with the Dresden Staatskapelle. The Philadelphia Orchestra is nearing the end of its contract with EMI Classics, and although the talks go on, there are no current plans for renewal, according to sources within EMI. Sony Classical has downgraded its exclusive contract with the Berlin Philharmonic into an every-now-and-then arrangement. The agreement between the magnificent Cleveland Orchestra and Decca/London has been drastically cut back: a long-planned Mahler Symphony No. 2 has been canceled and the completion of a half-finished recording of Wagner's *Ring* cycle, conducted by music director Christoph von Dohnányi, has been indefinitely postponed until after the turn of the century.

A few orchestras have been spared the scythe. BMG Classics—the successor to RCA Victor—plans to issue its first disc with Leonard Slatkin and the National Symphony Orchestra this fall and has spent a fortune establishing (and publicizing) a new deal with the San Francisco Symphony and Michael Tilson Thomas. But BMG itself is in some disarray, with a near-complete turnover of upper-level personnel within the past two years; sources close to the SFS and Thomas have complained that they don't know to whom they are to report.

Meanwhile, according to the London *Daily Telegraph*, EMI Classics has reduced its international recording schedule from 85 albums per year to 47. And within the past five years, BMG has already cut its schedule from a high of nearly 100 releases down to about 45; by the end of 1997, that number may be reduced to 30—fewer than three new releases a month. The *Telegraph* quoted an unnamed senior vice president at BMG as saying, "We are reducing capacity but not shedding artists." This isn't quite the case: last year, over the course of a single meeting, BMG Classics summarily dropped most of its "baby acts"—such developing artists as pianist Barry Douglas (a winner of the Tchaikovsky Competition) and the violinist Kyoko Takezawa.

Why is this happening? There's an easy answer: outside of a few flashy hits, the vast majority of new classical recordings simply aren't selling very well. It is now almost impossible to come close to breaking even on a major orchestral recording, traditionally the meat and potatoes of the business. After union costs for the musicians, stage labor, and the recording engineers, a new Beethoven, Brahms, or Sibelius recording with a major American orchestra can cost up to $200,000. Something really long and complicated like the Mahler Symphony No. 8 might easily run to half a million.

Keep those figures in mind, and then ponder the following: new CDs generally sell for between $10 and $15, a sum that must be split with distributors and record stores. First-year sales for a classical CD are considered respectable—maybe even pretty good—if they exceed a mere 5,000 units in the United States (add a few thousand more for the rest of the world) and many recordings never even approach that. Do your math. The numbers are bleak.

Nobody in the upper echelons of the record industry would speak for attribution in this article (as one executive put it: "How would it look for the CEO of a multimillion-dollar business to admit the game is over?"). But a glance at the current list of best-selling recordings for the Tower Records chain is instructive.

Of the top 10 orchestral discs, fully six of them are reissues (all from Deutsche Grammophon's acclaimed *Originals* series, most of them featuring Herbert von Karajan, who died in 1989). Of the remaining four, two are directly associated with motion pictures (*Always and Forever: Movies Greatest*, conducted by John Mauceri, and the soundtrack for *Mr. Holland's Opus*); one is a sort of special case (*Paper Music*, well-known material conducted and sung by the successful and phenomenally gifted pop vocalist Bobby McFerrin); and only one—the album *African Portraits* featuring the Chicago Symphony Orchestra under Daniel Barenboim—can possibly be considered a "music-driven" new classical recording.

"It's no secret to anyone in the music business that the recording industry is undergoing some very significant changes," Thomas W. Morris, the executive director of the Cleveland Orchestra, says. "It's been a dozen or so years since the last major technological innovation—the CD—and there's an absolute glut of material on the market, at many different prices. It's confusing to the buyer—it's confusing to us—and sales are down worldwide."

The back catalogue of a record company has always been an important asset, but nowadays this seems a case of the proverbial tail wagging the dog. For example, it is thrilling to have the complete recordings of violinist Jascha Heifetz available in one huge collection, sounding better than ever (BMG brought this out last year). But our ability to infuse the work of past masters with vivid new life also means that today's performers have to compete not only with their contemporaries but also with the ghosts of geniuses past. It

sometimes seems that, through technology, we are establishing a permanent pantheon of great artists—many of them long dead—and that no new-
comers need apply.

In the past, everything needed to be rerecorded every few years to keep up
with advancing technology. Remember the early 78s, those fabled Caruso
discs that seem to occupy space in everyone's attic? We heard the artist
through a sizzling hiss that sounded as if somebody were frying an egg just
inside the loudspeaker. And because the 78 had only a four-minute playing
time, it was constantly necessary to get up and change the disc—not exactly
the ideal format for a five-hour Wagner opera! Moreover, 78s were notori-
ously impermanent: if you dropped them once, they were gone.

The advent of the LP in the late 1940s changed everything. You could now
get pretty close to an unbroken half-hour of music on one side and the discs,
while scratchable, were not easy to break. Much of what was best on 78 was
ultimately transferred over to LP; new recording activity increased exponentially. By the late '50s, we had countless Beethoven Fifths from which to
choose (we now have well over 300, in and out of print). In the mid-'60s, there
was only one complete cycle of the Mahler symphonies (by Leonard Bernstein) and one complete recording of Wagner's 16-hour *Ring* (by Georg Solti).
By the mid-'80s, there were a dozen unified versions of each of them.

Enter digital technology and the compact disc. Now it became possible
to transfer recordings of the past to a new format with hitherto unimagined
force, vividness, and—given tender care of the CD—a certain permanence.
Recordings from 30, 40 years ago no longer sounded antiquated; indeed, in
some cases, they could have been made yesterday. No music lover can regret
this—it is cause for jubilation. But not without certain premonitions, especially the fear that we may be in the process of recording ourselves out.

When I count up my favorite "new" releases at the end of each year, I am
always startled by how many of them are reissues—many, perhaps most, of
which would cost a buyer less than would a new recording. Reissues are particularly profitable for record companies, after all. There are no studio costs
to pay, only some residuals to the artist (or artist's estate), and, in the case of
orchestral music, a possible fee to the Musicians' Union. There can be no
doubt that it is less expensive to reissue an existing recording than to create

a new one, and in the case of, say, Glenn Gould or Vladimir Horowitz, the artist may arrive with a ready-made legend and the disc will all but sell itself.

Now assume you're a typical classical FM listener—not a musician, nor a fanatic collector, just somebody with a certain fondness for classical music, somebody who buys maybe 10 to 20 compact discs every year. One day WETA plays a beautiful Chopin prelude on the air and you decide you have to have it. So you walk into a store, browse through the Chopin section, and notice that you can buy a set of the preludes played by Joe Recent-Juilliard-Graduate for $15.99 or take home an older (but decent-sounding) performance by the legendary Arthur Rubinstein for $9.99. Again, on the assumption that you are not one of those collectors who want every set of the preludes ever made, which recording are you likely to buy?

Right now there are more than 40 versions of the Chopin preludes in the catalogue. It's extraordinary music, no doubt about it. But is there really an audience for these discs? What about 100 recordings of Vivaldi's *Four Seasons*? Twenty-five recordings of Mahler's Sixth Symphony? If you were a stockholder in Deutsche Grammophon, would you really want your CEO to order up another multimillion-dollar Beethoven symphony cycle, especially when the label already has complete sets recorded by Claudio Abbado, Leonard Bernstein, and Herbert von Karajan (three different versions), as well as distinguished performances of individual symphonies by Karl Böhm, Ferenc Fricsay, Wilhelm Furtwängler, Carlos Kleiber, and a dozen others, dating all the way back to 1913 and Arthur Nikisch's very first recording of the Beethoven Fifth?

Don't misunderstand me. In no way am I suggesting that the classics of the past are "played out" or that they have revealed all of their secrets. The Beethoven "Eroica" will surprise us every time we hear it; it is a supreme masterpiece, by any standards. So is Shakespeare's *Hamlet*. But imagine a world in which Columbia Pictures would make a film of *Hamlet* one year, and then Disney, just to keep up, would make its version the following year, and then Tri-Star would weigh in with a *Hamlet* right after that—and so on, ad infinitum. Now take matters one step further, and imagine that all of the film studios bringing out these multiple *Hamlet*s already have dozens of other versions in their vaults.

From a purely aesthetic point of view, it's kind of a lovely idea. But it would be crazy business practice—sheer, barking lunacy—and all involved would lose their shirts. Still, something similar actually goes on in the classical record industry. Last time I checked, BMG had no fewer than three versions of the German conductor Günter Wand leading Anton Bruckner's Symphony No. 9. Nothing against either Wand or Bruckner, mind you, but was this really necessary?

As a passionate adherent of that much derided canon of Western Art Music, I believe that most classical music is more substantial, and more likely to endure, than most popular music. But the pop world has one characteristic the classical world does not: it changes constantly, renewing itself every generation or two.

But the classical music business has been hidebound for a long time—more so than it needed to be—and is now paying the price. After all, we simply haven't generated much new repertory in the past half-century and that is only partially the fault of our composers (there are some fine creators out there, if our orchestras, opera companies, and presenting organizations would only let us hear them). What was the last major work to really enter the repertory big time—*Carmina Burana* (1937)? *Appalachian Spring* (1944)?

And so the industry mavens were completely taken aback when an obscure Polish composer named Henryk Mikolaj Górecki's Symphony No. 3 became a smash international hit in 1993, actually rising not only to the top of the classical charts but, for a time, to the top of the British popular charts as well. But why shouldn't the Górecki have become a hit? It was stately, consonant, from the heart, unfamiliar but both accessible and attractive; it spoke for our time, a few prescient radio hosts put it on the air, it was used in a couple of movies, and the record sold and sold. This was a healthy sign; Górecki proved there was an audience out there and that it was hungry. Perhaps new repertory—and the occasional fresh take on the standard repertory—might just save the classical record industry.

If it can be saved, that is. I have my doubts. For the immediate future, at least, we can expect increased reliance on reissues of back catalogue, the occasional corporation- or foundation-subsidized new recording, some solo and chamber music discs (easier and cheaper to record than orchestras), a couple of stars for whom the general rules do not apply, an occasional fool-proof circus item like *The Three Tenors*—and a continuing diminution of releases across the board.

Much of what is brought out will likely be marketing department–driven novelties, such as the recent *Opera's Loudest Hits* (the "Anvil Chorus," the "Ride of the Valkyries," and so on), *Out Classics* (famous works by composers who, according to the publicity, "just happen to be gay"), and the forthcoming *Exile on Classic Street* from Decca/London, which will feature the favorite classical works of some celebrated pop stars. (For the benefit of inquiring minds: Elton John likes three of the "Enigma" Variations, Brian Wilson is a fan of the *Rhapsody in Blue*, while Elvis Costello reveals himself as a closet Vivaldi freak.) And—surprise!—Decca/London just happens to have some old recordings of all these pieces in its vaults. Think about the business appeal of this project: no studio costs whatsoever, no additional payment to artists, just a cute idea, a few long-distance phone calls, and a lot of money coming into the coffers.

It wouldn't surprise me if the classical divisions of multinational record companies were ultimately folded into their pop divisions. After all, pop has helped pay for classical at least since the 1950s, when the late producer and executive Goddard Lieberson of Columbia Records used the funds from bestsellers such as *My Fair Lady* to bankroll his great, visionary—and defiantly unprofitable—Modern American Music Series. But there is no Goddard Lieberson within our major companies today, and many—if not most—of the folks who make decisions about what classical music we will hear have little or no musical training.

There are exceptions, of course, notably over at the nonpareil Nonesuch, under the direction of Robert Hurwitz, which continues to explore unfamiliar and rewarding corners of the repertory. But Nonesuch very deliberately breaks the rules; it has never given us a complete set of Beethoven symphonies, nor does it seem likely it ever will. (This does not represent any subversive prejudice against Beethoven, merely a recognition that the other companies have covered him pretty thoroughly.) Instead, Nonesuch gives us the Kronos Quartet playing African music, song recitals by Dawn Upshaw, the collected works of Adams, Reich, and Glass, recordings for tape loops and electric guitar. Nonesuch is a smart company—it is often a visionary company—but, by its own design, it cannot be judged by the same standards as BMG/RCA, Sony Classical, EMI, Deutsche Grammophon, Decca/London, and the other traditional major labels.

Meanwhile, there are some lively "boutique" companies, usually run by one or two people, that continue to bring out interesting discs (notable among these are ECM, Mode, Conifer, HatArt, Ondine, CRI, New World, New Albion, Albany, Bridge, Eagle, and several others). And recently, on other small labels, some orchestral discs have begun to emerge from Eastern Europe, where costs are a fraction of what they would be here (one hears it said that Chinese orchestras will be next). Still, with all due respect, the impoverished ensembles from Bratislava or Shanghai cannot yet rival the standards set by orchestras in Berlin or Cleveland.

When the late Glenn Gould renounced live performance in favor of recordings in 1964, he stated unequivocally that the concert was "finished." On one level he was right: records, radio, and other media have long provided us with most of the music we listen to, and concerts—however we may love them and however many we may attend—are now a supplement to our musical understanding, rather than its core. Yet for the first time in many years, the future of the classical concert begins to look brighter than the future of the classical record.

The Washington Post
12 May 1996

Pittsburgh's Dumbing Down

THE ORCHESTRA INDUSTRY is in a panic.

Not only have most major ensembles lost whatever exclusive recording contracts they once had, but in many cities, subscription audiences are aging and diminishing at an alarming rate. And so, increasingly, there is a panic to reach the young and (presumably) hip, to lure those fabled under-40s into the concert hall and dose them with Beethoven and Tchaikovsky before they can escape. For many orchestras, marketing directors have become almost as important as maestros, and classical music is one more thing to be *sold*, like soft drinks and hair spray.

Nobody can doubt that some audience-building would be beneficial. But is it really necessary to debase a timeless musical inheritance with an onslaught of references to pop culture and trendy ephemera?

I have before me a flier announcing the upcoming season of the Pittsburgh Symphony Orchestra, a worthy, wealthy ensemble in a sophisticated city with strong musical traditions. All in all, it looks like a pretty good season. The flier, however, is an amazing document—shamelessly vulgar but also, in its macabre way, hilarious.

Open the booklet and you will see a group of attractive young instrumentalists from the orchestra, sporting blue jeans and spiffy haircuts, posing as if they were the cast of some yet-to-be-aired situation comedy. "Get to know YOUR Pittsburgh Symphony Orchestra," the copy reads. "Hang out with old friends and make some new ones!" Okay, it's a little dumb, but firmly in the tradition of folksy American populism which, one fears, will eventually cover the Earth.

Much worse is to come. "Introduce yourself to your favorite music!" the brochure reads. "The songs you hum and the tunes you tap your toes to—from your favorite movies and TV shows—are among classical's 'Greatest Hits.' You might not know the names, but you *do* know the melodies. We're playing them all season long."

There follows a list of pieces, matched with some supposedly familiar associations that the Pittsburgh Symphony clearly hopes will result in a box office stampede. Ravel's *Bolero*? "Caused a sensation in the movie *10*." The *William Tell* Overture? "Heigh-ho, Silver!" Rossini's *Thieving Magpie*? "Used in the commercial for Q-tips." Most grotesquely of all, Mozart's overture to *The Marriage of Figaro* is described as the "theme to the 'pork' commercial"!

Moreover, Pittsburgh doesn't have its facts straight. Rachmaninoff's Piano Concerto No. 2 is listed as having "inspired the Top-40 hit, 'Never Gonna Fall in Love Again.'" Wrong. It was Rachmaninoff's Second Symphony that inspired Eric Carmen's lubricious ditty; the Second Piano Concerto engendered the marginally less glutinous "Full Moon and Empty Arms," by Buddy Kaye and Ted Mossman.

Turning to the mini-biographies of visiting artists, Sir Neville Marriner is identified as the "music director for the soundtrack to *Amadeus*." Violinist Pinchas Zukerman has "earned 21 Grammy nominations and 2 Grammy awards!" And Sarah Chang, the young violinist, will make her "long awaited return appearance." (Please celebrate in moderation.)

Poor Gil Shaham gets the worst of it, however. The violinist is described as "offbeat"—not exactly an ideal compliment for a musician who must, after all, pay close attention to rhythm. Then we are informed that this young wag has "Tweety and Sylvester cartoon characters lining his tailcoat." Wow—order your tickets *today*!

Meanwhile, there's some rilly groovy programming, too. In May 1997 Pittsburgh will present a concert called "Symphony for the Devil": "Goethe's classic tale of the ultimate temptation has inspired music from centuries of composers. See how 'the devil made them do it' when Roger Norrington makes his PSO debut leading the powerful Faust interpretations of Liszt, Schumann, Wagner, and Berlioz." Just love that Flip Wilson reference; who says postmodernism hasn't reached the heartland?

Then we have "Music of *Fantasia*," all taken from the Disney classic of

1940: "James Conlon leads a magical program that will set cherubs and uni-corns dancing in your head (Beethoven's sweeping 'Pastoral' Symphony) and dinosaurs roaming in your mind (Stravinsky's idyllic *The Rite of Spring*)." Now, nobody can resist the prospect of a dinosaur roaming through his mind, but since when has the ferocious *Rite of Spring* been in any way "idyllic"?

To be fair, this sort of marketing is not unique to Pittsburgh. A few years ago, the musical press was informed that the reason Anne-Sophie Mutter's violin tone sounded so rich and full was that she always played in strapless gowns; the meeting of wood and flesh was said to create a unique acoustic symbiosis. Most of us suspected that the real reason for Mutter's costuming was the opportunity to show off some shapely arms and shoulders—and in-deed, a spy at one of her recording sessions later confirmed that she made at least one disc wearing a sweat shirt. But imagine what might have happened if the wood-flesh theory had proved true. Poor Isaac Stern!

And there were similar efforts to make the classics "relevant" as far back as the early 1970s. When Herbert von Karajan's second recording of Wagner's *Die Meistersinger* was released in 1971, Angel Records put up a huge billboard above the Sunset Strip. "Into German opera?" it asked. "Karajan's *Meister-singer*—a very heavy set." (And so it was—five LPs, an elaborate booklet, and a weighty cardboard container.)

Even Deutsche Grammophon, established in 1898 and traditionally one of the more conservative and respectful record companies, made the hippie scene in 1971 with a legendary advertisement that ran in several magazines: "We'd like to turn you on to what we consider some of our best albums. We have a full color catalogue that's outta sight. . . . Just walk into your local record store and say 'Hey, how about laying that new Deutsche Grammo-phon catalogue on me?'"

Far out, man! Lay it on me—and can I dig on that Pittsburgh Symphony mailer while I'm at it?

Will this sort of lowest-common-denominator hard sell infect all of the arts? Maybe Jim Carrey will end up as a pitchman for the Louvre. ("Check out the *Venus de Milo*; the face isn't much, but what a bod!") How about playing up the sex aspect to sell teenagers on Shakespeare? ("Romeo and Juliet: they did it, too!") The *Iliad*? "More blood—and brains—than *Pulp Fiction*!" And we can explain Gilbert and Sullivan patter songs as one origin of rap music.

To this we've come; in a world where the overture to *The Marriage of Figaro* can be described in an official mailing from a major orchestra as the "theme to the 'pork' commercial," anything is possible.

The Washington Post
23 June 1996

The Pops Perplex

THE NOTION of crossover music is hardly a new one. Mozart heard his arias played by organ grinders in the streets of Prague. Enrico Caruso and John McCormack recorded popular songs of their native lands as well as operatic classics. And the tradition of orchestral "pops" concerts dates back at least to the 19th century, in Paris, London, Vienna, and other musical capitals. Anybody inclined to flare elevated nostrils at the thought of cross-fertilization between musical genres could stand a history lesson.

And yet it is increasingly difficult to define what, exactly, an orchestral pops concert should be. I once suggested that jazz and classical music needed each other as a discotheque needs whaling songs. And many, if not most, of the classical pops concerts I've heard in the past few years have epitomized a sort of weird potpourri—a little of this, a little of that, and nothing very specific at all.

These ruminations are inspired by the first six programs promised from Marvin Hamlisch, the new National Symphony Orchestra Pops conductor. The opening concert, in October, will feature Hamlisch in a program of Broadway favorites by Richard Rodgers, Jerome Kern, Leonard Bernstein, and others, with Barbara Cook as the guest artist. The November program is titled "Prom Night" and will feature teen favorites (all very grown up now) from '30s swing through the '50s hits of the Platters. There will be a Christmas show in December, an evening of dance music ("from tap to tango") in January; Linda Eder, generally acknowledged as one of the better things about the musical *Jekyll & Hyde,* will be the guest artist in February; and the season will close with Hamlisch, the NSO, and the U.S. Army Band Jazz Ambassadors

327

playing works by Count Basie, Louis Armstrong, and Duke Ellington, among others.

Okay. There's going to be some good music here, no doubt, as well as some Andrew Lloyd Webber to provide proper context. But does it add up to a genre? Each of these concerts seems to me a "one-off," an event with a very specific audience in mind, an audience that may or may not return when the next program comes around. The same thing happens with standard classical series, too—a Mozart enthusiast may not be able to bear Bruckner—but it is likely that there will be some sense of unified tradition in the overall presentation, something that is lacking in the NSO's pops concerts. In no way am I picking on the NSO; virtually every other contemporary series along these lines has many of the same characteristics. It seems there is no longer a common language.

It was different 50 years ago. Back then, when you purchased a ticket to hear Arthur Fiedler and the Boston Pops (the most celebrated and successful of these ensembles) you could have a pretty good idea what would be on the program. Chances were you'd hear some wonderful light music—Emanuel Chabrier's *España*, for example, Jacques Offenbach's *Gaîté Parisienne*, a Rossini overture, a waltz by one or another of the Strauss family. A winsome soprano might warble something from *The Merry Widow* or one of Noel Coward's less acerbic works; perhaps a pianist would hammer through *Rhapsody in Blue*. And then there might be a few tidily arranged popular songs, to carry the audience safely back to its own time and place.

This was an attractive formula, but it could not work forever. Some of the music fell out of fashion completely (who today knows such one-time pop standards as Anton Rubinstein's "Melody in F," Albert Ketelbey's "In a Chinese Temple Garden," Jules Massenet's "Last Dream of the Virgin," or Karl Goldmark's "Rustic Wedding Symphony"?). Other pieces have long since graduated to the standard symphonic repertory. And rightly so—after all, unless one equates passionate intensity with profundity, the fact that a work of music is deemed "light" should not be taken as any reflection on its quality. (I'll trade you most of the Mahler symphonies for a single, perfect Rossini overture, and feel that I had the better deal.)

Finally, the advent of rock changed everything—and I don't mean that as any sort of "Decline of the West" hand-wringing. At least in part, it was the very specificity of rock recordings—the fused, symbiotic relationship between artist and song—that made it impossible to incorporate most of this music within the boundaries of a classical concert. Traditional standards such as "Misty," "Stormy Weather," and "As Time Goes By" were designed to be played in a wide variety of arrangements, by vastly divergent artists. But when we wanted to hear "I Want to Hold Your Hand," we wanted to hear it done by the Beatles, not by Arthur Fiedler. This was music that simply didn't need—in fact, was usually sapped by—the lush sounds of an orchestra.

Some of the softer Beatles songs—"Michelle," "Yesterday," "Eleanor Rigby" —could still be adapted for pops programs. And George Martin's orchestrations were a proud adornment to such recordings as "Penny Lane" and "A Day in the Life." In general, however, the teaming of orchestra and rock band has been fruitless. Even the most classically schooled band of the '60s and '70s, the high-minded and still underrated Procol Harum, sounded absurdly over-marinated when it made an album with a Canadian orchestra in 1972. And the idea of something like the Velvet Underground with strings was simply ludicrous (although Lou Reed tried his best with "Berlin").

A brief fad, seven or eight years back, for orchestral augmentations of songs by popular bands, proved a flatulent disaster. Poor Jerry Hadley, an impressive American tenor, was called upon to croon "Sympathy for the Devil" on something called *Symphonic Rolling Stones*, inspiring beer-through-the-nose giggles and new respect for Mick Jagger throughout the music world. Symphonic "transformations" of songs by the Moody Blues, Yes, and other ensembles were equally rancid.

One had the sense that these releases were aimed at the uncomfortably middle-aged who were somehow embarrassed by their early fondness for this music and so needed to hear it "classicized." It was rather akin to slapping a leather binding on an old copy of *The Hobbit*.

Meanwhile, show music has changed, too. Stephen Sondheim, far and away the most distinguished of today's "Broadway" composers, does not write melodies that are easily yoked into little suites or medleys. (This is not a complaint, simply a fact of Sondheim's art.) As for the music of his supposed rivals, why would anybody employ a full symphony orchestra to run through scores originally intended to serve distinctly subservient roles to the whirl of a helicopter or the crash of a chandelier?

Pops concerts continue to sell out in Washington and throughout the country, and their atmosphere remains less formal than the one found at most symphonic programs. But nobody pretends anymore that these events are an effort to seduce young, susceptible people into the world of classical music, as they used to be justified. Savvy young folk know they can usually find better renditions of traditional songs, better show music, better jazz, better rock, and (although it is hardly over-represented in the 2000–2001 NSO Pops season) better classical music in other venues.

In any event, according to NSO officials, the average subscriber to its pops series is now slightly older than the average subscriber to a traditional symphonic series. There's nothing wrong with this, of course, but it does represent a change, and yet another paradox for Hamlisch to consider as he prepares to take on his Washington assignment.

Clearly, pops concerts should remain a part of American musical life— too many people enjoy them to suggest otherwise, and the revenue is essential to keeping their parent orchestras alive. But is there some way to make a full pops season both unified and intellectually interesting? Unlikely—but, then again, that's really not what this genre is about. We'll probably have to pick and choose our concerts carefully until the day when there is a consensus about what a contemporary pops program should represent. And I don't see that happening any time soon.

A pessimist might suggest that pops concerts are becoming a mixture of Vegas glitz and an updated edition of the legendary, Geritol-sponsored Lawrence Welk television show, which presented a gently generic succession of known-by-heart songs in easy-to-swallow arrangements for some two decades. Or perhaps we are merely replacing the sentimental favorites of our parents' and grandparents' era with sentimental favorites from more recent years. They swung and swayed to Tommy Dorsey and "I'll Never Smile Again"; we sweated and suffered through Chicago and "Colour My World." Either way, it's a long way down from "España," which now seems to exist only on radio.

But "España" won't fill the house anymore. That whole genre of light music no longer has the ticket-buying audience it once did, sad to say. And so we are left with a motley of different music, some of which might work in a symphonic context, some of which probably won't. My own paltry advice for a pops programmer today would be to concentrate on artists who can play popular material that would not seem ridiculously overdressed in a concert hall—James Galway, maybe, or Evelyn Glennie, or some particularly specialized rock, jazz, and gospel performers. (I'd go hear Aretha Franklin or Van Morrison with anybody.) But no "White Rabbit" for strings, please—and let's not try to blow modest virtues up into pompous ones. We are all the worse for it.

Who knows what the pops series of the future will be? Maybe the genre has completely overrun its bounds and will remain the catch-all it seems to be today. That might not be all bad; the world is full of a number of things. Hamlisch's first program here (as a guest conductor in March 1999, shortly after his appointment was announced) contained a few minutes of absolute wizardry. On that night, Larry Adler, in his 80s and still the world's supreme master of the harmonica, played desolate and lyrical renditions of Debussy's "Claire de Lune," Gershwin's *Rhapsody in Blue,* and Hamlisch's own "The Way We Were" to a rapt and grateful audience. It was perfect, it was poetry, and it was pure Pops. In the classical sense of the word.

The Washington Post
9 July 2000

National Anthems I Have Known

WHAT IS the most famous melody in the United States? A good guess might be John Stafford Smith's "To Anacreon in Heaven," a popular drinking song from the early 19th century.

Never heard of it? That's because it is best known under another title—"The Star-Spangled Banner."

We've been listening to a lot of national anthems lately, what with the incessant media coverage of the Olympics. (Has Washington declared any of its bars "Olympics-free"?) A brief, informal survey of the anthems is probably in order and we may as well start with our own.

Francis Scott Key, a Georgetown lawyer and poet, was inspired to fit new words to John Stafford Smith's tune in the course of his detainment by the British on the Patapsco River near Baltimore during the War of 1812. When the sun rose on September 14, 1814, over Baltimore's Fort McHenry after a bitter, 1,500-shell bombardment, "our flag was still there" and Key began scribbling a poem.

Lyricists and librettists always complain that their contributions go unnoticed. Key is the exception. Ask a thousand people who wrote "The Star-Spangled Banner" and the chances are better than even that every single person who "knows" the answer will credit Francis Scott Key. Poor John Stafford Smith never made the history books.

Not that everybody is crazy about "The Star-Spangled Banner." Far from it. The song has been called confusing, overly militaristic, and impossible to sing. It has been pointed out that the lyrics are merely a long question ("O say, does that Star-Spangled Banner yet wave . . . ?") rather than any sort of affirmation. It hasn't even been our national anthem for very long (it was adopted in 1931) and a lot of people would like to see it replaced with "America, the Beautiful," "God Bless America," or "My Country, 'Tis of Thee."

Still, it's likely that "The Star-Spangled Banner" is here to stay and that it will open baseball games, opera seasons, and other official and would-be-official events for the foreseeable future. It is firmly entrenched, and most people don't welcome changes of this particular sort. After all, with the possible exception of a few hymns, there is no more music that has greater symbolic value to more citizens in any given country than their national anthem.

The *New Grove Dictionary of Music and Musicians* reminds us a national anthem is "the equivalent in music of a country's motto, crest or flag."

"It is now as much a matter of course for every country to have its own anthem as to have its own flag." Most anthems, it seems, are based on hymns, folk songs, marches, or—especially in South and Central America—musical forms that are clearly derived from Italian opera. (According to *Grove*, the anthem from El Salvador "would not be out of place in one of Verdi's middle-period operas.")

Anthems from two winners in the current Olympics deserve our attention. Russia's grand, formal "Czar's Hymn"—dating from 1833 and familiar to us from its use in Tchaikovsky's *1812* Overture—is once again in place, after an unfortunate three-quarters-of-a-century hiatus. China sports a drab little horehound of an anthem with the first line "March on, brave people of our nation," composed by Nie Erh in 1933. Marxists around the world will rejoice to learn that its present lyrics were written *collectively*.

It is difficult to judge a national anthem the same way we might judge another piece of music. Too many additional considerations enter into the equation. Sometimes beautiful music has been put to ignoble ends. One remembers Franz Joseph Haydn's happiness when one of his melodies was adopted as the Austrian anthem in 1797; how horrified he would have been to have heard it transformed into "Deutschland über Alles" in the 20th century. (Haydn's blameless hymn now serves a reunified Germany, but the lyrics have been changed and are no longer aggressive or pernicious.)

How about "La Marseillaise," which has been the national anthem of France on and off since 1795? A glorious tune, no doubt about it, but hard to dissociate from the French Revolution, that hideous forerunner of the modern totalitarian state, for which it was written. And talk about bloody-minded!

Anybody tempted to complain about the lyrics for "The Star-Spangled Banner" should take a look at the words Claude-Joseph Rouget de Lisle fashioned for his great melody.

> The dogs of war, let loose, are howling,
> And lo! our fields and cities blaze . . .
> The vile, insatiate despots dare,
> Their thirst of power and gold unbounded,
> Lo meet and vend the light and air.

Even earlier than "La Marseillaise" is Great Britain's "God Save the King/ Queen," an anonymous melody that dates from about 1745 and was apparently the first official national anthem. Several composers have been credited with the piece (including Thomas Arne, who wrote the magnificently stirring but politically unfashionable "Rule, Britannia!"). "God Save the Queen," as it has been known since the ascension of Queen Elizabeth II in 1952, is fundamentally a serene and all-embracing statement of affection and pride; a rather irritable second verse ("Confound their politics/Frustrate their knavish tricks") is usually omitted nowadays. Within the United Kingdom, both Wales and the Isle of Man have national anthems, too.

Indeed, you may be surprised by the number of countries that have national anthems. Albania, that ferocious little Chihuahua of a place, bares its teeth appropriately in "Hymni i flamurit" ("The flag that unites us in battle"). Andorra has a national anthem, as do Bhutan, Brunei, Burundi, Chad ("People of Chad, arise and get to work"), Liechtenstein, Mauritius, Qatar, San Marino, the Seychelles, and Western Samoa. A number of national anthems have no words, including those from Bahrain, Iraq, Kuwait, Mauritania, Morocco, and Spain.

I have a fondness for Greenland's anthem, "Nagminek Erinalik," which begins with the line: "Our immemorial land under the beacon of gleaming ice." A hardy lot, those Greenlanders; one recalls with pleasure Schopenhauer's story of their mass refusal to accept Christian conversion when they were informed there would be no seals in Heaven.

It is often thought that the central hymn from Jean Sibelius's *Finlandia* is the national anthem of Finland. While this music (which has been set to several texts) is very dear to Finns, the actual anthem is titled "Maamme" and was written by Frederick Pacius (1809–1891), a distinguished composer of his time. (Finland's extraordinary musical activity is still too little known outside its borders; several of the finest composers in the world are in the Helsinki area, and there are said to be more functional opera houses per capita in Finland than in any other country.)

In this country, it should not be forgotten that most of our states have their own songs, too. These include not only such prosaic titles as "Arizona," "Arkansas," and "Illinois" but "Where the Columbines Grow" (Colorado), "The Old North State" (North Carolina), and "On the Banks of the Wabash" (Indiana), composed by Paul Dresser, the brother of novelist Theodore Dreiser. (Guess which of the two brothers is honored with his own memorial in Terre Haute, where both grew up?)

Some of these choices are a little peculiar—it is difficult to understand why the "Tennessee Waltz," a melancholy story of lost love, should be the official song of Tennessee. And what are we to make of the concerted effort, a few years back, by some New Jersey residents to turn local-boy-made-good Bruce Springsteen's "Born to Run" into the state song? Had anybody actually listened to the lyrics? ("Baby, this town rips the bones from your back/It's a death trap, it's a suicide rap/We gotta get out while we're young.")

Moreover, it is dangerous to assume that simply because a state is prominently mentioned in a song it would make an appropriate anthem, as was proved in a famous incident at a political convention some years ago.

When, amid applause and confetti, a state delegation is announced from the podium, it is customary for the band to break into a song closely associated with home turf. For example, New York might be represented by "Sidewalks of New York," California by "California, Here I Come!" But a problem arose on this particular occasion when the Georgia delegation was recognized and a hapless band leader, confused by the title, struck up "Marching Through Georgia." As it happens, this is no cheery advertisement but rather a Yankee Civil War song about General William Tecumseh Sherman's scorched-earth assault on the South. The visiting Georgians were decidedly less than pleased.

In any event, the world is marching, sprinting, and shot-putting through Georgia just now. Already, the United States has won some competitions, and we have been rewarded with "To Anacreon in Heaven."

The Washington Post
28 July 1996

When Good Art
Happens to Bad People

I T'S HARD to interest a youngster in opera, and so one recent evening, when a favorite nine-year-old wandered away from his computer game and began listening intently to the final duet from Claudio Monteverdi's *The Coronation of Poppea*, we encouraged him happily.

"What are they singing?" he asked, after a time.

Uh-oh. "Well, it's sort of a love song," I explained. "These two people love each other very much, and sometimes, well, they just have to sing about it."

A moment's silence. "And who are they?"

Trapped. The question deserves a response, but what do you say? "Well, Willy, this is the Roman emperor Nero singing to his new empress, Poppea, see, and they're celebrating their victory after murdering his elderly teacher and any and all potential enemies, and that's why Monteverdi wrote such beautiful music, because they've consolidated all their power!"

In fact, we gave a much simpler answer ("They're *singers*, Willy!") but this encounter started off a long meditation on what Lionel Trilling used to call "the bloody crossroads"—that intersection where art and morality meet. Don't expect any cosmic maxims here: how we come to that crossroads and whatever lessons we may take away from it are both much too personal to dictate and much too complicated to sum up with a universal rule.

And even if a work of art is blameless, sometimes our opinion of the artist will interfere with our appreciation. Try this dialectic on for size.

You're out one night at the local Tower store, feeling your age, browsing through the oldies. You spot Cat Stevens's *Tea for the Tillerman* album and you remember that you kind of liked his song "Wild World" back in 1971. Yes, you think, I'll play this sometime, and you pick up the disc and start toward the register.

Suddenly you recall that Cat Stevens is now known as Yusuf Islam, that he has been a Muslim fundamentalist since the 1970s, and that he publicly endorsed Ayatollah Khomeini's death sentence, still in effect, handed down to Salman Rushdie after the 1989 publication of *The Satanic Verses*. No, this sort of literary criticism you don't want to encourage—and so the CD goes back into the bin.

Wait a second. *Tea for the Tillerman* was a happy, gentle, harmless album. Back then, Stevens was just one more hippie songwriter, and some of his songs were pretty good; "Wild World" wasn't even the best cut on the record. Your mind drifts back to misty afternoons, driving through the countryside with temporary friends, teenage reveries syncopated by the lost *ca-chunk* of the eight-track player. You pick up the disc again.

But hold on now. The former Cat Stevens has now turned most of his publishing rights and much of his not-inconsiderable fortune over to various religious organizations, some of which support the Rushdie death sentence. That means the money you're shelling out for some cheap '70s nostalgia could conceivably go toward the support of an expensive '90s hit man.

Can't have that. You put the disc back.

It's possible to draw this out for quite a while. For example, would it be all right to buy *Tea for the Tillerman* at a yard sale, where no money would find its way back to Stevens? How about if somebody picked it out for you as a gift —would you be able to enjoy the present in good conscience?

A trickier question: what if this were an album you really couldn't do without—something like Van Morrison's *Astral Weeks* or the third Velvet Underground record? Would your scruples then go out the window? After all, life without *Tea for the Tillerman* is one thing; life without *Pet Sounds* would be something else again.

These dilemmas are not limited to the art of music. For example, there are at least three classic films that regularly inspire a sort of aesthetic-political agony among those who cannot help admiring them on some levels while despising them on others. The first is D. W. Griffith's *The Birth of a Nation* (1915)—which, more than any other single film, virtually invented the modern cinema as we know it. And yet it seems distinctly racist to contemporary sensibilities (indeed, it seemed racist to some viewers when it was made), and so whatever merits it has must be balanced against this enormous demerit.

Still, at least *The Birth of a Nation* tells a story, gives us fully realized characters, and contains long sections that are as morally unobjectionable as they are beautifully wrought. It's much harder to defend Sergei Eisenstein's *Battleship Potemkin* or Leni Riefenstahl's *Triumph of the Will* on any but exclusively aesthetic grounds, and even that feels hollow: the former glorifies the onset of the Russian Revolution; the latter is a beatification of Adolf Hitler. There is no character development and little plot in these films, and the final outcome is pure propaganda for some evil causes. Dazzlingly crafted propaganda, to be sure—but any real enjoyment or enrichment for most spectators is out of the question; indeed, if we get caught up in it, we feel somewhat ashamed of ourselves.

It is possible to end up with a purism that excludes artists who were also, in their "spare time," unpleasant human beings. A college friend refused to listen to the music of Richard Wagner, on the principle that since Wagner was a horrible man, he must therefore write horrible music. To be sure, Wagner was a self-obsessed, abusive monster, but with the exception of a few pieces (the final chorus in *Die Meistersinger* with its paean to maintaining the "purity" of holy German art, perhaps), his musical creations were pretty much apolitical. Or, if the reader is among that subset for whom nothing is apolitical, let's put it another way: one would not be able to surmise Wagner's anti-Semitism and personal viciousness from a cursory listen to *The Flying Dutchman* or *Tristan and Isolde*.

What about Vanessa Redgrave's 1980 appearance in *Playing for Time*, the CBS TV movie about Fania Fenelon, a musician who survived her internment in Auschwitz by playing in the concentration camp's all-female orchestra? The Anti-Defamation League of B'nai Brith, the American Jewish Congress, and even Fenelon herself made strenuous public objection to Redgrave's casting in the role; Redgrave was an outspoken supporter of the Palestine Liberation Organization and critical of Israel. Still, Redgrave won wide acclaim for her performance.

As even a quick scan of the reference books will reveal, once you start judging works of art by the biographies of the artists who made them, you're asking for trouble. What about Don Carlo Gesualdo, that extraordinary 16th-century composer whose innovations prefigure the harmonies of Stravinsky? Wife murderer. What about Romain Rolland, whose massive novel *Jean-Christophe*, first published in 1908, has awakened a yearning romanticism and a sense of individual conscience in generations of young readers? Stalinist toady. Can you imagine anybody much more arrogant, violent, and self-aggrandizing than the Renaissance Italian metalsmith, sculptor, and author Benvenuto Cellini, as he reveals himself in his autobiography? Can we read Philip Larkin's poetry with the same enthusiasm after digging through his sour, nasty, petty letters? How can we continue to esteem John Cheever as a stoic and master moralist after reading his self-absorbed, whiny diaries?

Then there is the reverse dilemma: What do we do when "good" politics translates into lousy art? When John Corigliano's Symphony No. 1 received its first performance several years ago, it was denounced in some circles because it very specifically addressed the issue of AIDS. One critic called it "musical journalism"; another dismissed it as "victim art." I happen to admire the piece—but what if I hadn't? Some critics who disliked the symphony and thought it manipulative promptly found themselves labeled "homophobes" in the gay press, with no justification whatsoever, aside from their failure to respond to a single work of art.

Last year the dance critic Arlene Croce wrote a much discussed article about the HIV-positive choreographer Bill T. Jones and his piece *Still/Here* for *The New Yorker* magazine. "In this piece . . . Jones presents people (as he has in the past) who are terminally ill and talk about it," she wrote. "I understand that there is dancing going on during the talking but of course no one goes to *Still/Here* for the dancing." She went on to call Jones a "director-choreographer who has crossed the line between theater and reality—who thinks that victimhood in and of itself is sufficient to the creation of an art spectacle."

Fair enough—if you are a victim, you are not necessarily an artist. (Croce fatally compromised her argument by announcing that she hadn't actually seen *Still/Here*.)

But what if you create something valuable out of your suffering? It *has* happened before, after all. Would it be possible to discuss *The Diary of Anne Frank* without taking the circumstances under which it was written into account? Would such an appraisal be appropriate—or even moral? Probably not; this is, first and foremost, a tender and poignant human document, written by a child whose sheer guilelessness is one of the most attractive things about her. We cannot judge her as we would a Virginia Woolf—as a seasoned pro, with leisure, financial comfort, and "a room of one's own" at her command. Anne Frank was a scared teenager without even an attic that belonged entirely to her.

Other works command respect for what they say rather than the way they say it. Has anybody ever really finished all three volumes of *The Gulag Archipelago*? We know Alexander Solzhenitsyn was an important moral figure— fought the bad guys against all odds, suffered for his people, lived to see an oppressive system fall, in part through his own efforts. Still, as Samuel Johnson once said of a contemporary playwright, most of us would rather praise Solzhenitsyn than read him.

There really is no bottom line on issues such as these. Great art has been created by some rotten people, while some splendid, thoroughly deserving human beings will toil diligently throughout their lives without their solid craftsmanship ever taking off into the realm of art. Everything would be so much simpler if our best artists were also our best human beings.

And so, do you buy the Cat Stevens disc or do you browse elsewhere— maybe in the bin of some comparable rock star who wants to save the rain forest rather than shoot the author? The answer is up to you; we can only pose a few questions. But ooh, baby, baby, it's a wild world.

The Washington Post
19 November 1995

A Plea for the Solitary Cheer

L AST WEEK I watched *Providence* again, for what must have been the 14th or 15th time. This film, directed by Alain Resnais and starring John Gielgud, Ellen Burstyn, Dirk Bogarde, and David Warner, utterly mystified me when it was released in 1977; still, something had to have caught my attention because I returned to the theater the following week and saw it again.

After that it became a habit. I now believe *Providence* is a great film—at once as complicated and densely plotted as the fathomless *Chinatown*, as clipped and witty as an early Noel Coward play, as searching a study of the agonies of the creative artist as the recent *Crumb*, as beautifully crafted and rich in moral and religious significance as all but the very best of Ingmar Bergman.

Problem is, I seem to be about the only person in the world who feels this way.

Rarely has a film with such a pedigree (Sir John Gielgud, no less) received such wretched press. Back in 1977 *The Washington Post* called *Providence* "your basic insufferable literary film." *The New York Times* called it "a disastrously ill-chosen comedy" and "a lot of fuss and fake feathers about nothing." To be sure, some critics were willing to acknowledge Gielgud's performance and, less often, Miklós Rózsa's lush film score or some directorial "touches" by Resnais. Otherwise, the reviews were grim and often hostile. To make matters worse, most of my friends agreed with these dismissals; eventually, I stopped dragging them along to screenings.

It's a lonely experience to love and esteem something the rest of the world finds noxious. On occasion, we are ultimately vindicated. I remember ruining a hippie party back in the '60s by shutting off whatever coy ode to pot or living off the land was on the turntable and insisting that we hear some magnificent noise by a group called the Velvet Underground.

And many of us know the privileged, insider pleasure of having found a great little restaurant before anybody else did, telling our friends about it, then watching smugly as the place becomes an enormous success. That's a cozy feeling: Trendsetter for a Day. Efforts to proselytize for *Providence* have turned out differently, however—rather as if you'd told your friends about this terrific place, they went and hated it, and then a restaurant critic pronounced the food septic.

Still, my affection persists—and this has nothing to do with sentiment. Some works automatically call up a nostalgic fuzziness, whether we want them to or not. We like them because we like them or because we remember them or because we remember liking them. Youngish, middle-class people of my generation invariably slow-danced to a song called "Colour My World" by a group called Chicago. I have my share of smoky, pimply, and not unpleasant sentimental-biological associations with "Colour My World," but the song itself, judged only on its merits, makes me want to spit blood.

Nor are we talking about one of those quirky affections triggered by some purely personal association ("I like *King of Hearts* because it was the only film that ever played in Boston for five years," say, or "I like *The Avengers* because Emma Peel is so much like my mother"). And, finally, this isn't the campy fondness some of us feel for the truly grotesque—films such as *Glen or Glenda?* or *Mommie Dearest*—where sheer awfulness is part of the giggle.

No, there are certain works of art that, for whatever reason, move some of us to our depths and leave others stone cold. Questions of right and wrong don't really enter into the matter. For the critics who hated *Providence*—and for a lot of the general public as well—their view was right and mine was wrong. But not for me.

Curiously enough, those of us who develop passions for elusive works of art do sometimes find soulmates. In 1990 *Newsday Magazine* ran an article about an underground network of aficionados devoted to a Christopher Reeve film called *Somewhere in Time*. Turns out there is (or was, in 1990) a newsletter called INSITE—International Network of *Somewhere in Time* Enthusiasts—that served as a clearinghouse for these novitiates. Far be it for a *Providence* obsessive to dismiss anyone who loves another obscure and derided film.

Lately, particularly on university campuses, there has been much talk about reappraising what has come to be dubbed "the Canon"—that selected list of Great Masterpieces (music, literature, art, film, and other disciplines) that are supposed to represent the highest standards of civilization. I don't much approve of nominating new works for inclusion *strictly* on criteria of race, gender, or ethnic background (that whole mind-set smacks of the joke that got James Watt fired), but the concept of a periodic reevaluation strikes me as an entirely healthy thing.

There is a delightfully infuriating book by Brigid Brophy, Michael Levey, and Charles Osborne called *Fifty Works of English Literature We Could Do Without*, published in 1967. The targets include such touch-me-nots as *Beowulf* ("Boring and unattractive as a story, pointlessly bloodthirsty"), *Pilgrim's Progress* ("No book, not even one with such pious claims to greatness, has the right to be as dull as this"), and *Leaves of Grass* ("What is one to say of this garrulous old bore? For all his loudly proclaimed earthiness, his language continually shies away from the realities of feeling").

Feel your blood pressure rising? Good. It is not that we should necessarily agree with these condemnations, or that such eccentric opinions should now be institutionalized in place of the rote rapture that has traditionally greeted these subjects. But periodic reexamination—blunt, personal, unfettered, unsentimental—is essential to artistic awareness. If the negativity of *Fifty Works of English Literature We Could Do Without* bothers you, go out and make your own list: "Fifty Books You Need to Read Right Now" or "Great Movies Everybody Missed."

The only danger comes when artistic judgments—good or bad—are automatically deemed permanent. Some classics likely are permanent, of course—certainly Greek tragedy, after 2,000 years, shows no sign of losing its urgency—but it never hurts to question the matter and prove it to ourselves once more. Meanwhile, let's take a fresh look at what may have been passed over.

This is neither the time nor the place to mount an elaborate defense of *Providence*, a movie that is rarely revived and is deucedly hard to find on home video. And a summary of the plot probably won't help win new fans. On the most fundamental level, the story is a simple one: a dying, besotted author incorporates members of his family into a bizarre novel he is writing as he passes in and out of consciousness. But this is like saying *Gravity's Rainbow* is the story of a rocket that goes up and then comes down, or that *Moby Dick* is about a crazed hunt for an albino whale. These are true statements, so far as they go, but they are also completely inadequate to describe the nuances, the subplots and contradictions, the brooding, convulsive beauties of these works.

Ezra Pound once defined a classic as "something that remains news." But what happens if we miss the scoop the first time out? Savor those works of art that speak directly to you and defend them proudly. They may be tomorrow's classics, tomorrow's news.

The Washington Post
4 February 1996

Boom Boxes in Willimantic

"Music is feeling, then, not sound." So said Wallace Stevens in his early poem "Peter Quince at the Clavier," written while he was living on Farmington Avenue in Hartford, Connecticut. It is only appropriate that the two final pieces in this collection, which describe feelings occasioned by neither concerts nor any sort of traditional performance, should be set in Stevens's New England. This is my home country as well—I grew up 10 minutes from Willimantic and about an hour from Northampton—and I knew my turf.

WILLIMANTIC, Connecticut

IN SOME WAYS, it was similar to many other Independence Day celebrations that took place throughout the country today.

Flags flew proudly up and down the length of an old-fashioned Main Street. Several hundred people participated in a big parade—old, young, on foot, in cars, or waving from homemade floats—while a thousand or more spectators came to watch and cheer. And stirring march music, composed by John Philip Sousa and other practitioners of the trade, provided a rhythmic and melodic impetus for the whole shebang.

And yet the 2000 Boombox Parade, which ran its course in this gritty, charismatic mill city this morning at 11:00, is unlike any such gathering in the country. Its most immediately apparent distinction is the lack of a marching band—or for that matter, of any live music whatsoever. Instead, participants and spectators bring their own radios and tune them in to WILI-AM, which then provides a sort of soundtrack to the day's activities. The two-thirds-of-a-mile procession thus takes place to the accompaniment of dozens, maybe hundreds, of radios all playing the same tune.

Kathy Clark, a Section 8 subsidy coordinator for the Willimantic Housing Authority, came up with the idea for the Boombox Parade in 1986. Funding for the arts had been cut throughout the United States and Willimantic was no longer able to support a high school marching band.

"I was drinking with some friends at the Victorian Lady," she said, referring to a popular restaurant in the middle of town, "and we came up with this crazy idea. We agreed to get our friends involved, and then we took the idea to the radio station. And I think they may have thought the idea was pretty weird, but they went with us. We had only a few floats the first year, and not too many people. But we kept coming back."

As it happened, the event was widely reported and greeted with some initial shock. John Glasel, then the president of the Associated Musicians of Greater New York, issued a Jovian statement calling the parade "grotesque."

"The Orwellian year of 1984 has come and gone and the predictions of 'Brave New World' are coming true," he wrote.

If so, on today's evidence, it's a fun new world.

Many would agree that the diminishment of arts funding is no good for anybody, let alone in a place like blue-collar Willimantic. And yet the Boombox Parade is now more popular—and unquestionably more interesting—than many a "live" celebration.

Lynn Castelli, director of Arts in Action, an educational and presenting organization in Willimantic, applauds what she calls "a very artistic parade": "There is no sign-up, no structure. Anybody can be in the parade. There's no accreditation, no set message. It's merely a reflection of the community."

For Wayne Norman, the WILI radio host who has been associated with the event from the beginning, the parade "captures the true spirit of Independence Day. No matter who you are, you're welcome in our parade. There's a mixture of historic pride, local politics, and a certain tongue-in-cheek quality that makes it all a little wild."

Westward along Main Street traveled representatives from the Light on the Hill Christian Fellowship, the Moose Lodge, the 4-H Club, the Green, Democratic, and Republican parties, and the Wild Women of Willimantic. Several floats called for the preservation of Hosmer Mountain, an 82-acre enclave of open space reportedly being considered for development.

Residents of the dilapidated Hotel Hooker (a name that has inspired giggles for years) came out to look over the festivities. Doug Fraser proudly paraded by in his 1956 fire engine, which was towing a plastic buffalo and an even older firetruck—a Model T from 1926. At the encouragement of the crowd, he turned on his old siren and the crowd heard a moment that might have come from a 1950s movie.

A poodle, fancily shaved and decked out in wildly clashing pastels, was a favorite of some children. Candy and beads were thrown from the floats, as if this were a little northern Mardi Gras. You could have your picture taken with W. C. Fields, Albert Einstein, or Bozo the Clown. A woman in front of a Baptist church offered free lemonade, while a young boy made an Indianapolis-size roar with his go-cart. It was a hot day and one gentle soul wandered around with a watering can, drenching the bare feet of kids sitting on the curb.

Willimantic, a city of 15,000 located seven miles south of the University of Connecticut at Storrs, has been through some rough times. In 1974 it was the first city to go bankrupt since the Great Depression. (It is now officially incorporated as part of Windham County.) The following year, a mall opened just over the border in Mansfield, and many of the businesses on Main Street moved to the newer site shortly thereafter. Suddenly the city took on an eerie postwar quality.

In 1984 it was announced that the American Thread Company was moving south to Georgia, and the largest industry in Willimantic closed up its vast and wonderful Victorian factory within two years. Many people feared this was a mortal blow to the city.

And yet, somehow, Willimantic has persevered. Gigantic gingerbread homes on Prospect Street have been lovingly restored, and the old post office is now a thriving bar and restaurant. There are ambitious plans for the old factory building. The city seems battered but absolutely unbowed.

"Willimantic is turning around," affirms selectman Tom DaVivo. "There's a lot of positive mental energy here these days."

As the floats went by, Catherine Crossgrove, a 10-year-old who will begin classes at Mansfield Middle School in the fall, collected sack after sack of what used to be called penny candy. "I'd like to build a float that said 'Happy

Fourth of July!' on it and then I'd throw Tootsie Rolls over the side. I'd bring along some streamers and some farm animals, too—a chicken and a rooster."

"Everybody cheers and nobody boos," said her aunt Camilla Crossgrove. "The parade is diverse and friendly. People put aside their differences."

Poet Gray Jacobik, a professor of literature at Eastern Connecticut State University, celebrated the parade in a recent opus titled "Under the Sign of Walt Whitman":

> . . . Church groups, clubs, proponents
> of this-or-that, businesses, bureaus, kids on bikes
> and skateboards, dogs, politicians, and librarians
> all convey themselves down Main Street, so
> American you could cry and of course you do
> for the wonder of it, for the glory of the human pageant
> and its gift for self-expression. . . .
>
> . . . In this wild discombobulated
> American-style hubbub, we celebrated community
> and the blessing of liberty, we celebrate ourselves.

Kathy Clark is certain that there will be another Boombox Parade next year. Despite the success of her endeavor, there are no plans to "move up" to live music.

"A band wouldn't really work with what the parade has become," she said. "As a matter of fact, we had a group of musicians in from Venezuela and they wanted to play in the parade. We talked it over with them and they understood. In the end, they carried radios. And they had a very good time."

The Washington Post
5 July 2000

Singing Walls

NORTHAMPTON State Hospital, a vast Victorian brick structure that is in equal parts imposing, dreary, frightening, and magnificent, has stood on a hill high above Smith College for more than 140 years. One of the oldest of American mental institutions, the hospital, which eventually grew into many buildings, reached a peak population of about 2,500 in the 1950s. Since 1992 it has been deserted altogether, a genuinely haunted house, and it is now slated for demolition.

On Saturday afternoon, the hospital was the site of an extraordinary commemoration. At the close of a two-day symposium at Smith titled "Beyond Asylum: Transforming Mental Health Care," former patients and employees of Northampton State, along with at least 1,000 other observers, were invited to take the steep climb to the hospital once more. There, from deep within the bedrooms, lounges, offices, and service areas of the main building, 102 state-of-the-art loudspeakers played conductor Philippe Herreweghe's Harmonia Mundi recording of J. S. Bach's celestial *Magnificat* to the winter day. It was artist Anna Schuleit's final tribute to the hospital and the thousands of men and women who passed through its doors.

> I propose an unusual and unprecedented way of honoring
> this hospital, of triggering our remembrance on one single
> day before its removal. . . . I WANT TO MAKE THE BUILDING SING.
> —Anna Schuleit, proposal to the Massachusetts Cultural
> Council and the Commonwealth of Massachusetts (1999)

It began with a walk Schuleit took in 1991, when she was still an aspiring art student at the nearby Northfield Mount Hermon School. "I wandered through the hospital and marveled at the architecture," Schuleit, now 26, reflected last week. "It was created with such care, such amazing attention down to the smallest detail. It was obvious to me that the people who built the hospital were idealists, that they thought it was going to be a great place—a real contribution to human happiness and fulfillment. And it all went bad so quickly."

Indeed, on the day the cornerstone was laid—July 4, 1856—Edward Jarvis, one of the most influential psychologists of his time, spoke of the hospital with evangelical fervor:

> You of this town and the counties can and will do much for the prosperity and the comfort of this new Institution. You can cheer, support and strengthen it, you can pour the oil of joy on its machinery and give the power of confidence to its operations and, we doubt not, you will do so, and then this Hospital will ever have reason to rejoice that it is placed in the midst of an enlightened and a generous community.

Drenched as it is in cockeyed Emersonian optimism, Jarvis's speech now comes across as both naive and authoritarian. And, of course, the "oil of joy" was always in short supply at Northampton. By definition, such hospitals are not happy places, and much past treatment of the mentally ill seems downright barbaric today. (As late as the 1950s—a full century after the cornerstone was laid in Northampton—one Washington psychiatrist used to provide his patients with ice-pick lobotomies in an office just west of Dupont Circle.) Moreover, the state of Massachusetts never had enough money to keep the hospital properly maintained; by the time it closed, the building was in such wretched condition that it was condemned outright.

In 1997, years after the last patient had left the premises, Schuleit revisited Northampton. "What struck me then was the incredible silence," she said. "It reminded me of an indrawn breath. Here was this place where people had lived and worked, had struggled and suffered and sometimes gotten better for more than 100 years. Now it felt like the end of the world."

And so Schuleit became obsessed with what she calls the "hospital's call for tribute." "I couldn't find a way to express my thoughts about Northampton in my paintings, drawings, or photographs," she said. "Something quite different was needed. And so I returned to the idea of taking a walk—and inviting as many people as possible to take it with me." She joined forces with J. Michael Moore, a local historian, and set to work.

The resulting project, "Habeas Corpus," was, in Schuleit's words, "a call for remembrance before returning to our modern homes and gardens, our cities and towns and a new century. A call for celebrating human existence, for creating a ceremony for the uncounted anonymous who lived and died in this and many more such institutions. A ceremony for mistakes and impossible efforts to correct our inherited share of 'insanity' and 'madness.'"

Since Northampton State Hospital is owned by the state, cutting through bureaucracy was not easy. Schuleit was backed with letters from the Massachusetts Historical Commission, the University of Massachusetts Medical School, the Massachusetts Cultural Council, and even former governor Michael Dukakis. When permission was finally granted, she was told that spectators would not be allowed within the building itself. "I signed a 13-, 14-page document promising that only 30 people could go inside," she apologized to one of many who wanted to venture past the weather-beaten doors on Saturday.

Still, it was more than sufficient to stand outside, as the building exploded into glorious sound, as enveloping as headphones, and continued ringing for the full 28-minute duration of the *Magnificat*. It echoed from the walls, it came from the sky, it seemed to emanate from everywhere and nowhere. Those in attendance, including a goodly number of children and dogs, were invited to wander around outside the labyrinthine building, and many did. An elderly, immaculately dressed woman stood off to one side and wept quietly throughout, tears cracking through her makeup. Meanwhile, a young man, as skilled and articulate as many a radio correspondent, read eager reports into his cassette recorder, describing "Habeas Corpus" as the "event of a lifetime."

And so it may have been. The faces in the crowd wore an infinity of expressions—ranging from the blissful and philosophical to the curious and, occasionally, the frankly bored. This was a mass event that was also intimately personal; it seemed appropriate to greet your neighbor but not to watch too closely for any reactions. Far better to swim your own course through the sound and spirits.

When one spends more than two years planning for an outdoor event that, by its very design, can never happen again, it is helpful if nature cooperates. And for these particular purposes, the weather on Saturday couldn't have been more ideal. All was cold and clear under iron-gray skies, with tattered curtains flapping in open windows, the ground carpeted with brown leaves with a few red and orange stragglers still clinging to the trees. Purest November. There was some gentle hail, the first of the season, early in the *Magnificat*, and when the sun burst through in the chorus "Fecit potentiam," the effect was so perfect that it might have been dismissed as a Hollywood touch if it hadn't been so wonderfully, palpably real.

Schuleit considers "Habeas Corpus" an opportunity to "honor the rituals of care and treatment, and to excuse the mistakes before a new century and millennium sweep over them." She knows full well the nightmares that took place within the walls of such places as Northampton but wants to acknowledge the hospital's "peculiar dignity as a building with a good cause at its core."

"There was one woman I met who worked at Northampton and wanted to quit every day because it was so horrible," Schuleit said. "Instead, she stayed 35 years. She was devoted, and determined to do good, and this was her life. My piece isn't one of those so-called permanent memorials for a building—you know, those little plaques they put up that are quickly overgrown with grass and weeds. This is something different. But I hope it will linger in the memory."

The Washington Post
20 November 2000

Index